The Lyric in the Age of the Brain

The Lyric in the Age of the Brain

Nikki Skillman

Harvard University Press

Cambridge, Massachusetts & London, England / 2016

First printing

Library of Congress Cataloging-in-Publication Data

Names: Skillman, Nikki, 1982– author.
Title: The lyric in the age of the brain / Nikki Skillman.
Description: Cambridge, Massachusetts : Harvard University Press, 2016. | Includes
bibliographical references and index.
Identifiers: LCCN 2015041148 | ISBN 9780674545120 (hardcover : alk. paper)
Subjects: LCSH: American poetry—Explication. | Experimental poetry, American. |
Creative ability. | Art and science.
Classification: LCC PS305 .S54 2016 | DDC 811.009—dc23
LC record available at http://lccn.loc.gov/2015041148

For my parents

Contents

The Lyric in the Age of the Brain

Introduction

The Lyric in the Age of the Brain

I N HIS POEM "Mechanism" (1957), A. R. Ammons describes an extraordinary encounter with an ordinary bird.¹ As he watches a goldfinch alighting on a branch and flashing its plumage in a wild cherry bush,
the poet realizes that what he knows about the goldfinch supervenes upon
his perception of the bird and transforms his experience of it. What he
knows—about the orchestra of its body parts and their harmonious co-
operation, about the animal's nuanced role in a vast ecological system,
about the serendipitous course of its evolution toward such distinctive
beauty—leads him to identify the finch's singular splendor with the
splendor of all kinds of "working order[s]," both natural and artificial.
Ammons begins his poem by asking us to revere the bird as a system, a
mechanism not unlike the adaptable armature of a moral code or the dynamic scheme of labor and profit within a commercial enterprise:

> Honor a going thing, goldfinch, corporation, tree,
> morality: any working order,
> animate or inanimate

It proves to be not just "any working order," in fact, but the biological
order of the sentient goldfinch that particularly interests Ammons in the
poem. As he comes to imagine the creature as a marvelous working

fulfillment of the chemical prescriptions of its DNA, his encounter evolves into a meditation on the emergence of consciousness from the interaction of inanimate parts—on the origins of mind in matter.

As the poem proceeds, Ammons associates the array of physical processes that make up the goldfinch—"enzymic intricacies," "gastric transformations," "physical chemistries"—with the intangible textures of experience that characterize conscious life—"control," "knowledge," "instinct," and, most capaciously, "mind":

> honor the chemistries, platelets, hemoglobin kinetics,
>   the light-sensitive iris, the enzymic intricacies
> of control,
>
> the gastric transformations, seed
>   dissolved to acrid liquors, synthesized into
> chirp, vitreous humor, knowledge,
>
> blood compulsion, instinct: honor the
>   unique genes,
> molecules that reproduce themselves, divide into
>
> sets, the nucleic grain transmitted
>   in slow change through ages of rising and falling form,
> some cells set aside for the special work, mind
>
> or perception rising into orders of courtship,
>   territorial rights, mind rising
> from the physical chemistries
>
> to guarantee that genes will be exchanged, male
>   and female met, the satisfactions cloaking a deeper
> racial satisfaction:

A hybrid of a lyric blazon and a CT scan, "Mechanism" displays specialized knowledge of "hemoglobin kinetics" and the self-replicating "nucleic grain." But even as Ammons luxuriates in the argots of biological, chemical, even evolutionary science, the poem expresses what seems to be common knowledge in the age of the brain. It assumes that the connection between the physical and the mental is close and direct ("mind ris[es] / from the physical chemistries"), even if the character of that connection remains deeply mysterious. Indeed, as Ammons contemplates the nature of human and animal minds through the imagined physiology of the goldfinch, his fundamental premises prove to be ones that have overwhelmingly dominated scientific, philosophical, and popular conceptions of mental life since the mid-twentieth century: he takes for granted that the mind has its origin in tacit, autonomic interactions of nonintentional matter; he assumes that mental experience, subject to somatic necessity, is shaped constitutively by genetic and evolutionary forces; and he situates all dimensions of mental experience, from perception to reason, within a finite economy of physical resources.

Ammons goes on to ask how such close identification between chemical and experiential aspects of being affects the translation of experience into poetry. The goldfinch synthesizes the seed it consumes not only into "control" (agency), "vitreous humor" (the substance of its eye, a metonym for perception), "knowledge," and "instinct," but also into the bird's "chirp"—its mating call and individual song. Ammons reminds us that while the goldfinch is a representative of an actual avian species, it is also an emblem of the poet—Yeats's own mechanistic, golden bird, perhaps, brought back into nature. The self-deprecating parenthesis of the poem's final lines, in which the poet observes that the goldfinch is "not a / great songster," confirms that Ammons has in mind the biological operations that shape his own subjectivity and his own singing. As the poem concludes, the "isolated, contained reactions" that regulate the bird's temperature proceed unrecognized,

while the

> goldfinch, unconscious of the billion operations
>   that stay its form, flashes, chirping (not a
> great songster) in the bay cherry bushes wild of leaf.

Ammons surmises that the physiological mechanisms that generate and shape experience also shape our attempts to make sense of experience, from the moralities we construct to the texts we compose. He thus poses the question that centrally occupies this study of contemporary American poetry: What happens to the poem when the poet becomes so vividly conscious of the billions of operations that stay his or her forms of thought, perception, memory, and imagination?

Recent American poetry—belletristic and radical, virtuosic and defiantly "unoriginal," canonical and experimental alike—reveals that what we know, or think we know, about the mind has transformed our experience of it. Though poets writing since the "cognitive revolution" have greeted our increasingly physiological conception of the mind (and the soul, and the spirit) with ambivalent deference and resistance to scientific authority, they have also exhibited a common faith in mechanistic interpretations of mind that threaten to dissolve the ideal unity of the expressive, lyric "I." With this philosophical consensus, poets have ruptured the continuum of transcendental representations of human mentality that extends from Romanticism through the twilight of high modernism, even as they have found exhilarating aesthetic possibilities in contemplating the constraints embodiment imposes on invisible processes of feeling and intention. Accustomed to giving consciousness a material body in language—to embracing the productive, self-imposed limitations of poetic form—recent poets discern in their era's zealous biologization of subjectivity fresh demands to reconsider their own practices of incarnating thought and feeling in verse. Through both concentrated bursts of focus on inner life and exacting interrogation of the boundaries of "interiority" per se, they exercise their genre's special aptitude for registering the powers and limits of human consciousness in the age of the brain.

At once deferential witnesses to the explanatory power of science and embattled defenders of human mystery, the poets here reveal the intricate, inconsistent outcomes of their era's precipitous solidification of mind into matter. The energy with which poetry has responded to this transformation, however, presents an opportunity to do more than acknowledge the commanding presence of "mind science" and other materialist influences within popular consciousness. It offers an occasion to revise our understanding of many of the most influential poetic oeuvres of the late twentieth century, and to reconsider, within an era of contextually oriented criticism, the special kinds of reading that poetry demands as a distinctly literary genre. Tracing the emotional, stylistic, and conceptual meanings of embodied mentality in poetry written since the mid-twentieth century requires a style of criticism that interprets signs of historical change within verbal artifacts, but that also reveals these signs' contribution to the wholeness—uniqueness, coherence, beauty—of individual works of art. Such a criticism must not only draw on the valuable capacity of poetry to disclose historical and philosophical contexts, but also treat individual poems as irreducible objects—as "working orders" that become more comprehensible, and more marvelous, when their environments illuminate their form.

The Embodied Mind in Popular and Poetic Consciousness

Poets such as Ammons, who came of age as artists in the 1950s or later and bore witness to the proliferation of empirical discourses that addressed themselves with increasing optimism to investigation of the "mind," have become more vividly conscious of the biological systems that mediate inner life than the poets of any other era.[2] Over the past sixty years, the empirical study of the brain has touched nearly every discourse concerned with the actions we ascribe to minds, from learning language to suffering grief. The poets in this study thus place scientific insight where most of us, as uninitiated observers outside the scientific establishment, encounter it: on the periphery of our experience, as a conceptual backdrop against which everyday life plays out. This backdrop comes into focus on particular, if crucial and frequent, occasions: when illness or intoxication alters consciousness; when we ask what becomes of the spirit when the body dies; when addiction pits conscious will against corporeal will; when we consider the less accessible subjectivities of nonhuman animals; when computers seem to think; when inconceivable propositions lead us to confront the limits of the imagination; and so on. Disinclined to adopt narrowly neurological perspectives on inner life, these poets tend not to isolate materialist terms but to absorb them into a din of overheard discourses—a din that coalesces at times into syncretic music and devolves at others into menacing, meaningless noise.

This book, then, does not trace the history of developments in mind science but instead considers what biological descriptions of inner life have meant to lay observers—what human possibilities scientific reconceptions of selfhood and subjectivity have seemed to open, to foreclose, and to bring back into focus. The mind sciences' conceptual diffusions within American poetics undoubtedly emanate from many of the most conspicuous developments of human knowledge since the mid-twentieth century, including the invention of neural imaging in the 1960s, the engineering of sapient machines (named "artificial intelligence" in 1956), and the prodigious expansion of the pharmaceutical industry from the century's central decades to the present. But the growth of these technologies, fields of inquiry, and industries is too vast in scope to be surveyed meaningfully in these pages, and its manifestations may be too plain and pervasive to require account. So widely has the cognitive revolution disseminated the materialism of the mind sciences, so efficiently has it channeled into vernacular discourse its terms for describing what happens when we sense, think, and feel, that we have come to identify subjective experience intuitively with objective, biological fact. We know that love is both an experience and a chemical phenomenon, that attention and mood are dimensions of interiority and also processes that can be regulated by drugs, that memories are both representations of lived experience and dynamic networks of activation in the brain. As devoted to love, mood, and memory as they have ever been, poets have innovated to accommodate this synoptic view, and have made escalating use of biological terms to frame their accounts of mental experience—from James Merrill's "polypeptides / on the dimmest shore of consciousness, / in primeval thrall," to Jorie Graham's image of perceptual data that ascend like salmon leaping "upstream" from the retina to the brain.[3]

Such physiological descriptions of will and perception reflect the mind sciences' expanding explanatory ambitions over the past several decades. In the second decade of the twenty-first century, it is clear enough that empirical disciplines have for some time now been appropriating questions that traditionally belonged to humanists—questions about agency, the meanings of "mind" and "body," the origins of knowledge, the sources and ontology of the self—but the circumstances that have given rise to this crucial context for contemporary poetry bear rehearsing. Within the philosophy of mind, physicalists—who unite in proposing, despite nuanced internal contention, that all phenomena in the universe are of a single substance, and that minds are ultimately like everything else in nature— have drawn extensive support from the insights of accelerating neuroscientific discovery. Jerry Fodor updates Hilary Putnam's early computational functionalism using the concept of neurological modularity; Daniel Dennett adapts Gilbert Ryle's classic critique of "the ghost in the machine" in explicitly evolutionary terms; Paul and Patricia Churchland radically extend Wilfrid Sellars's empiricist epistemology, espousing an extreme form of eliminative materialism; John Searle proposes a "biological naturalism" in which physical causes yield subjective effects; and so on.[4] Physicalist perspectives are so pervasive and widely accepted that the most visible accounts of consciousness in recent decades have been presented by scientists—Steven Pinker and Antonio Damasio most notably, perhaps—who interpret the significance of neuroscientific findings to our understanding of emotion, reason, and "human nature," and who speculate about consciousness in popular books and essays that circumvent the rigid disciplinary dogmas (and disciplinary standards) of strictly academic genres.[5] The authority of physicalism has contributed to the impression that science has ruled out the existence of an immaterial spirit, that "soul" is a superannuated folk-psychological term, and that the tendency to dissociate psyche from soma is a vestige of centuries of ingrained religious superstition.[6]

This philosophical shift is but one convulsion within a much vaster, seismic surge of secular feeling, and but one indication of the ascent of scientific thought to a position of corroborative power over humanistic inquiry in an age of skepticism. Though materialist conceptions of mental life have traditionally been circumscribed by religious belief, they have waxed and waned in popular consciousness for millennia; as the more historically minded poets in this book remind us, our materialist moment is a cyclical repetition—an "upstart rephrasing," in John Ashbery's words—of a perennial and sporadically dominant philosophy of mind.[7] The conceptual foundation of our still-evolving version of embodied consciousness (distinct in expression, if not in essence, from the embodied minds of Democritus, Lucretius, and Hobbes) was surely laid by Darwin, who believed that thought would eventually be proven to be a biological function—"as much [a] function of organ," in fact, "as bile of liver."[8] Unable to produce an evolutionary account of how the body came to "secrete" consciousness, however, Darwin characterized the question of exactly how "the mental powers were first developed in the lowest organisms" as a "hopeless" problem "for the distant future."[9] When Hensleigh Wedgwood, his cousin, dismissed Darwin's growing faith in the biological origin of consciousness—to say "brain thinks per se is nonsense," Wedgwood proclaimed—Darwin attributed Wedgwood's widely held opinion to vanity and superstition: "Man in his arrogance thinks himself a great work worthy the interposition of a Deity. More humble and I believe truer to consider him created from animals."[10] Six years after Darwin's death, the evolutionary biologist George John Romanes would expound on the revelation of the natural origins of human consciousness in *Mental Evolution in Man* (1888), observing that man "has begun to perceive a strong probability, if not an actual certainty . . . that even the most amazing side of his own nature—nay, the most amazing of all things within the reach of his knowledge—the human mind itself, is but the topmost inflorescence of the one mighty growth, whose roots and stem and many branches are sunk in the abyss of planetary time."[11]

The emergence of our twentieth- and twenty-first-century embodied mind has thus been, like the ascent or descent of most cultural features, hazy and incremental. According to Raymond Williams's epochal taxonomy of "emergent," "dominant," and "residual" cultural states, materialist interpretations of mind were certainly emergent during the late nineteenth and early twentieth centuries. Fluid and diverse, models of mind rooted in nature were fleshed out alongside, and in conversation with, diverse secular theories of metaphysical dualism and the obsolescing theory of divine "interposition." This eclecticism of materialist and spiritual perspectives was firmly in place in the first decade of the twentieth century: in 1902, Pavlov began his study of the physiological psychology of conditioned reflexes; in 1903, Frederic Myers's vast *Human Personality and Its Survival of Bodily Death* appeared; in 1906, Camillo Golgi and Santiago Ramon y Cajal were awarded the Nobel Prize in Medicine and Physiology for their discoveries in neuronal structure; in 1907, Henri Bergson published *Creative Evolution* (*L'Évolution créatrice*), positing the animation of matter with the numinous force of élan vital. During the first decade of the twentieth century, evidence that the nervous system is made up of discrete cells (the "neuron doctrine") appeared within a highly open and experimental European-American cultural milieu accustomed to treating mental states and biological processes as ambiguously and reciprocally related. By the early years of the century, the explosive, intertwined emergence of disciplinary neurology, psychiatry, and psychology had resulted in the enthusiastic application of empirical procedures to the investigation of psychological and spiritual phenomena; treatment practices for mental illness were being structured upon both physical theories and psychosomatic ones; the (verifiable) concept of "unconscious cerebration" and the (spurious) concept of genetically inherited memory were in wide circulation; and scientific methods were being rigorously applied to the experimental study of localized brain function, aphasia, hysteria, personality, automatism, hypnotism, clairvoyance, and religious experience alike.[12]

In the second quarter of the twentieth century, however, the sciences began rapidly elaborating their description of physiological mechanisms that correlate to mental experiences. Hans Berger recorded the first human electroencephalogram, popularizing the concept of the brain wave, the mechanisms of chemical transmission between nerve cells were detailed, the genetic bases of various psychiatric disorders were discovered, and the first human patients were treated with electroconvulsive therapy (ECT) and the frontal lobotomy (leukotomy). By the 1950s, nuanced correlations between chemical activity in the brain and psychological phenomena had seemed to confirm the mind's status as a function or epiphenomenon of physical processes. The ambiguous directionality of the mind-brain relationship was eclipsed by a glut of evidence suggesting that cognition proceeded directionally from physical causes to phenomenological effects. Rising faith in this new dogma of directional emergence, visible in the widespread prescription of psychoactive drugs and the extensive practice of ECT and leukotomy at mid-century, occurred as "the gods," in Wallace Stevens's words, "dispelled in mid-air and dissolve[d] like clouds"—as "religious meanings and values" were becoming, according to Raymond Williams's scheme, firmly residual forces in organizing experience.[13] By the 1960s, the supernatural determination of mental life had become as embarrassing a proposition among the educated Anglo-American laity as the natural determination of mental life had been to Hensleigh Wedgwood in the 1840s, and cognitive materialism had assumed a firmly dominant position within philosophical, scientific, and popular consciousness.

Materialism, however, has a long-standing reputation as a facile and promiscuous concept; among the most accessible of philosophical positions, materialism tends to seem more full of explanatory, demystifying power than it actually is. As Simon Jarvis has put it, "Only matter, and material needs, are real, it seems to say; any claims to know anything beyond them are 'metaphysical' or 'idealist' or 'ideological.' Materialism's job is imagined as a relatively straightforward one: to break those idols and leave us undeluded."[14] In practice, materialism tends to negate, depend on, and veer stubbornly back toward its metaphysical opposite, and to replace one central mystery with a rash of small ones. Indeed, despite the dominance of mechanistic perspectives in framing our accounts of mental life, in recent decades a minority of dualist philosophers has articulately stressed the "explanatory gaps" in physicalist accounts of consciousness. Thomas Nagel defines the empirically elusive feeling of what it is like to be sentient—to have will, to be a *self*—as the characteristic of mind that sets it apart from other aspects of reality.[15] Raymond Tallis claims that "aboutness"—an essential aspect of the experience of mind—"has no place in the material world . . . since no material object is *about* any other material object." A thought can be about a chair, but a chair cannot be about an apple; thus, the mind cannot be like everything else in nature.[16]

Most helpfully, David Chalmers proposes that there are "easy" and "hard" problems of consciousness; easy problems of consciousness, he explains, are ones that "seem directly susceptible to the standard methods of cognitive science"—they are problems that can be answered by describing a phenomenon in terms of computational or neural mechanisms. How we focus our attention, how exactly we discriminate and react to external stimuli, how wakefulness differs from sleep—these are "easy" problems in that "there is no real issue about whether [they] can be explained scientifically," even if "getting the details right will probably take a century or two of difficult empirical work." The hard problem of consciousness, on the other hand, is the problem of how it is that matter possesses consciousness at all, how organisms become subjects of experience, how and why a set of automatic processes should give rise to the feeling that there is something it is like to be a self with a coherent inner life. "It is widely agreed that experience arises from a physical basis," Chalmers concedes, "but we have no good explanation of why and how it so arises"; twenty-first-century science and philosophy of mind, then, are no closer to resolving this hard problem than Plato or Descartes were, despite the fascinating insights the brain sciences have offered in recent decades.[17]

What distinguishes our age is a tendency to project the sense of possibility that has accompanied rapid, demonstrable progress in resolving "easy" problems of consciousness onto the hard problem, a tendency to see all questions about mental life as physiological questions that are subject to inevitable, empirical demystification. Whether this is astonishing hubris or good sense—since problems that now seem easy were once hopelessly beyond our reach—remains to be seen, but as poets diagnose this predicament, they inevitably become tangled up in it as well. From their positions as observers outside scientific institutions and discourses, the poets here have a strong interest in investigating the human implications of the findings of cognitive science, and in keeping with the scientific and philosophical consensus of their time, they tend to view the mind as something essentially physical—of one substance with all other visible and invisible forms of creation. But even as they set out to demonstrate the capacity of poetry to assimilate the "news" of twentieth- and twenty-first-century brain science, they continue to attest to structures of feeling that have rendered the dichotomy of body and soul intuitive and culturally pervasive. As they reckon with the ubiquitous neuroscientism of their age, they insist that the vocabulary of cognitive materialism is both seductive and intuitively reductive, that traditional, transcendental metaphors of mind are obsolescent and yet also, somehow, true to subjective experience and therefore necessary as well.

This widespread, if ambivalent, acknowledgment of the mind's basis in concrete, physiological states and processes has changed not only the terms but also the forms poets use to describe consciousness. As poets come to conceive of the mind as an embodied machine, the linguistic reflection of the mind—the machine of the poem—inevitably transforms as well. In its description of "mind rising / from the physical chemistries," Ammons's "Mechanism" exemplifies recent poetry's ubiquitous absorption of empirical terminology within its descriptions of consciousness, but we might return briefly to the poem to illustrate the latter dimension of response—the poem's answer, in its formal shape, to an embodied conception of the mind. Its forty-eight lines are divided in turn into jagged, isomorphic tercets, and constitute a single sentence punctuated by commas and colons. Ammons initiated his widespread use of colons instead of periods in *Expressions of Sea Level* (1964), the volume that contains "Mechanism"; the appearance of the colon coincides with the pervasive appearance of the kind of clamorously scientific diction that appears in the poem. Here again, for reference, are the lines quoted above:

> honor the chemistries, platelets, hemoglobin kinetics,
>   the light-sensitive iris, the enzymic intricacies
>   of control,
>
> the gastric transformations, seed
>   dissolved to acrid liquors, synthesized into
>   chirp, vitreous humor, knowledge,
>
> blood compulsion, instinct: honor the
>   unique genes,
>   molecules that reproduce themselves, divide into
>
> sets, the nucleic grain transmitted
>   in slow change through ages of rising and falling form,
>   some cells set aside for the special work, mind
>
> or perception rising into orders of courtship,
>   territorial rights, mind rising
>   from the physical chemistries
>
> to guarantee that genes will be exchanged, male
>   and female met, the satisfactions cloaking a deeper
>   racial satisfaction:

From Ammons's perspective, the definitive gaps marked by periods would rupture the unified substance of the poem—what he calls its "tissue"— which is itself a representation of the unified texture, the seamless process, of inner life.[18] In another poem, he writes that "mind . . . flows and stalls, holds and gives way," identifying the motions of the mind with the punctuated flow of impulses through cells, with the peristaltic and pulsating operations of his organs, with bodily processes that are defined not by closure but by continuity.[19] As Ammons himself observed, the colons equalize the poem's syntactic parts by obviating initial capitals, transforming the poem into a reticulated network of equivalent, dynamically interconnected clauses. The verbal object thus becomes a rhizomatic structure that is itself an image of the complex biological activity—the billions of operations—whence it emerges. In his *ars poetica* "Corsons Inlet," Ammons uses open, improvised, organic forms to evoke mental flow, but in keeping with the interest of "Mechanism" in the genetic mechanisms through which evolutionary processes "redeem," as he puts it, "random, reproducible" actions from chance, the poem's identical replications of its idiosyncratic stanza form resemble the integral ur-activity of life, the autonomous action of genetic "molecules that reproduce themselves."[20] Having juxtaposed the intangible system of a "morality" to the animate system of a goldfinch, Ammons also evokes with his orderly textual silhouette the emergence of elegant, abstract orders—the coherent orders of rational consciousness—out of apparently chaotic and nonintentional natural events.

"Mechanism," then, expresses Ammons's biological materialism in the substance of its formal structure; its third-person account of the goldfinch defamiliarizes human consciousness and attempts to picture its objective dynamics through both its content and its form. And yet while thematic and formal descriptions of consciousness as a physiological phenomenon are among recent poetry's most patent responses to our embodied conception of mind, there exists an even more fundamental aspect of response, for the body's role in shaping interiority touches not only how poets describe the mind but also how they experience it. Unlike their modernist precursors, poets writing since the mid-twentieth century tend to associate embodied being not with experiential amplitude but with constraint, determination, passivity, and mortality—concepts that permeate what it feels like to perceive and attend and think and remember. As a result, poetic accounts of these processes widely attest to the feeling—the almost *physical* sensation—of running up against the boundaries of apprehension. The signs of mortal imperfection that riddle conscious experience become for poets invitations to reevaluate the conception of the poetic subject as keenly perceptive, mnemonically reliable, and fundamentally empowered by imagination; these signs also occasion lavish engagement with the concept of material constraint itself, an idea that bears special significance both for the lyric—the most corseted and self-consciously minimal genre of literary art—and for the avant-garde anti-lyric—the most self-consciously materialist strain of contemporary literature. (I will return to the contested poetic category of "lyric" shortly.) More indirect than Ammons's poem in their manner of registering our ascendant, physiological conception of consciousness, such representations of mental failures and constraints register pervasive, tacit effects of the biologization of subjectivity upon our appraisal of the possibilities and parameters of conscious life.

To illustrate these imaginative consequences of the embodied mind for poetic representations of subjectivity, we might turn from "Mechanism" to a very different kind of poem. While Jorie Graham's "To a Friend Going Blind" draws no descriptive terms from science, it explores what it feels like to run up against the limits of embodied perception—limits that close in with distressing urgency on Sara, Graham's friend, as she loses her power of sight.[21] Two interwoven vignettes unfold within the walls of an Italian town, each an allegory of the process of reckoning with the "built-in / limits" of the perceiving body. In one, Graham, a disoriented visitor to the town, traces its "inner / perimeter" in a circuit along its medieval ramparts; in the other, Bruna, a well-adapted native of the city, balances practical and aesthetic concerns as she selects material to sew a dress:

> Today, because I couldn't find the shortcut through,
> I had to walk this town's entire inner
> perimeter to find
> where the medieval walls break open
> in an eighteenth century
> arch. The yellow valley flickered on and off
> through cracks and the gaps
> for guns. Bruna is teaching me
> to cut a pattern.
> Saturdays we buy the cloth.
> She takes it in her hands
> like a good idea, feeling
> for texture, grain, the built-in
> limits. It's only as an afterthought she asks
> *and do you think it's beautiful?*
> Her measuring tapes hang down, corn-blond and endless,
> from her neck.
> When I look at her
> I think *Rapunzel,*
> how one could climb that measuring,
> that love.
> But I was saying,
> I wandered all along the street that hugs the walls,

a needle floating
on its cloth. Once
I shut my eyes and felt my way
along the stone. Outside
is the cashcrop, sunflowers, as far as one can see. Listen,
the wind rattles in them,
a loose worship
seeking an object,
an interruption. Sara,
the walls are beautiful. They block the view.
And it feels rich to be
inside their grasp.
When Bruna finishes her dress
it is the shape of what has come
to rescue her. She puts it on.

Cultivating our empathy for Sara, Graham stresses that the extreme privation that awaits her friend as she goes blind differs only in degree from the prohibitions the body imposes on all human sensation. Both vignettes center, appropriately, on moments of touch. Relinquishing sight altogether as she feels her way along the stone, Graham imagines sunflowers "as far as one can see"—a view that clearly transcends the real, impoverished view she pieces together from her glimpses of the blurred "yellow valley" that flickers through the "cracks and the gaps / for guns." The deteriorating wall is an inexorable physical limit that is also, its cracks reveal, vulnerable to time; the wall is a figure for the boundary of the corporeal senses that conduct the given, imperfectly, to "inner" life. There is no "shortcut through" to a fuller picture of reality; all looking is "a loose worship / seeking an object"—a humble, hopeful endeavor to touch the actual through approximation, to feel out knowledge through a vast, concrete array of embodied constraints.

　Just as Sara, offstage, forcibly confronts the limits her body imposes on her vision, Graham, the disoriented visitor, runs up against the surrounding ramparts, searching unsuccessfully for someplace they might "break open." The "texture, grain, the built-in / limits" of Bruna's cloth remind Graham of the experiential texture of an "idea," for thought, she reminds us, *feels* material; even a "good idea," in its almost tangible presence, has constraints recognizable to both the senses and the intellect—constraints Graham identifies with the constraints of material substance. The question, then, is what to make of those limits, how to reckon with the confinements of the material without reference to anything beyond the material. This recuperative act of making, of course, is precisely what the artificer Bruna accomplishes; aware of the city's walls but unconcerned by them, sensitive to the possibilities of the finite cloth, she is preoccupied with generating a workable, inhabitable, beautiful form out of the resistance of physical substance. It is not because she subordinates aesthetic concerns to practical ones that she asks, as an afterthought, *"and do you think it's beautiful?"* The question is an afterthought because Bruna is equipped, however modest the material, to make it so. She not only accepts limits but masters and wields them: the measuring tapes she uses to shape the dress drape over her shoulders like Rapunzel's braids, the archetypal image of escape through beauty. When Bruna puts on the dress, it is "the shape of what has come / to rescue her"; the consolatory reckoning with limits that accompanies any act of creation (particularly the act of creating poetry, which is both confined and liberated by its own forms of measure) is the model Graham proposes for redeeming the exigent limitations of the perceiving body.

Contemporary American poets are always walking the perimeter of interiority, feeling its limits. They attribute to the built-in constraints of a physiological mind our intuition that human experience misses, mistakes, and distorts the given in countless knowable and unknowable ways. Breakdowns and failures—from forgetting a word to going blind—highlight these omissions and distortions, rendering the body's invisible determinations of conscious life suddenly obvious; like lightning in a dim landscape, crises of perception, memory, and attention violently illuminate a correlation between the scope of human mental power and the frailty of the mortal body. By isolating and investigating such crises, recent poems have become, like the proliferating technologies that scientists have developed to investigate mentality over the past several decades, refined instruments for tracing the scope of cognitive potential in disenchanted terms. As they ascribe the limits of consciousness to universal conditions of physical reality, these poems deconstruct boundaries that have traditionally framed our self-understanding: boundaries between

self and world, between inside and outside, between human will and the
furtive biological operations out of which that will ostensibly arises.

The pervasive perception among poets that the mind is not metaphysical but naturally constrained has thus meant that putative oppositions
within the expressive manifold of contemporary verse—between the
theory-conscious self-effacements of Language poetry and the strident voices of confession and social protest, between the Janus face of
tradition-conscious formalism and the headlong formal heterodoxy
of conceptual poetry—have, for all their meaningful distinctions,
emerged upon shared ground. They have articulated in diverse modes a
common set of suppositions about our aptitudes as observers and inter-
preters, and consequently framed a skeptical, embodied theory of knowledge through a host of significatory practices that envision the subject
and its textual reflection—the poem itself—as emergent expressions of
natural form. Indeed, the shifting premises underpinning our concept
of mind have placed special pressure on lyric poetry—"the dialogue of
the mind with itself," in Matthew Arnold's words—to recognize our era's
reimagining of consciousness as more truly substance than spirit.[22] Recent
theorists remind us that the capacious, vernacular meaning of "lyric"
that twentieth-century poets and their readers inherited from Romantic
sources—its ultimately Hegelian definition as the genre of relatively
short, nonnarrative poetry that "takes as its sole form and final aim the
self-expression of subjective life"—has historically implied a transcendental (and thus, now, obsolescent) understanding of the self manifested
in the metaphor of a speaking voice (the personal "I" associated with
lyric presence).[23] As eager as the poets of any age to make subjectivity
conscious of itself in language, but finding a narrowly expressive model
of lyric as "the complete utterance of the inner spirit" inconsistent with
their attitudes and ambitions, the poets in these pages force the genre to
evolve under the equal and opposite pressures to evoke the feeling of inner
life and to dismantle the objective unity of the subject—to give sensuous
form to the fluid, phenomenological content of self-experience while challenging the very category of the self, which appears to them ever less
distinct from the physical forms and forces of the "exterior" world beyond it.

Close scrutiny of the philosophies of inner life implicit in recent poetry thus refutes the commonplace among poets and critics alike that contemporary poetry of personal feeling continues to entertain a naïve confidence in the ideal unity of the expressive subject, while experimental poetry, including recent manifestations of "anti-lyric" conceptualism, relinquishes that ideal unreservedly, eschewing the concepts of poetic presence and voice. Among poets perceived to represent the belletristic, literary center, there abides deep skepticism toward the unstable, biologically manufactured congeries of the self, while vanguard poets often exhibit persistent attachment to poetry's sources in imaginative quarters that resist disintegration into "mere" somatic or verbal matter.[24] Thus, in addition to proceeding in a loose chronology that examines a range of lyric oeuvres from the mid-twentieth century to the present, the chapters of this book are arranged to stress the common ground upon which borders of affiliation in post-45 poetics have been too superficially drawn. Placing critically valued poets of the "mainstream" canon (Robert Lowell, James Merrill, and Jorie Graham) in alternation with critically valued poets of the "experimental" canon (Robert Creeley, John Ashbery, and the poets of the conclusion) reveals continuities that make it difficult to accept the enduring premise that countervailing attitudes toward "the stability and sovereignty of the individual," as one critic has put it, distinguish these traditions.[25] Indeed, Tan Lin, Juliana Spahr and David Buuck, Harryette Mullen, and Christian Bök, whose complex relations to the category of lyric I consider at the end of this book, may be only the most explicit in posing the question of where the most ancient ambitions of poetry and the burgeoning ambitions of brain science converge. What is the nature of the self, they ask, and where are its boundaries?

The gentle arc of the book's chronology reveals some important phenomena, to be sure: the increasingly circumspect attitude poets adopt toward the mind sciences' claims to transformative revelation; the expanding diversity of poets who perceive questions of embodied subjectivity to be vitally relevant to their identities and oeuvres; and a burgeoning ethical incentive, among the most recent generations of poets, to explore the moral and political challenges that biological conceptions of feeling and action present in the midst of ecological and humanitarian crisis. The poets here finally occupy the same epochal horizon, however, and ultimately represent not so much a historical progression as a parallax view. Each major oeuvre offers special insight into the effects of cutural neurologism within a different domain of mental life, as it is both experienced and represented: emotion and personality in the case of Robert Lowell, conscious thought in Robert Creeley and A. R. Ammons, memory in James Merrill, attention in John Ashbery, and perception in Jorie Graham. The trajectory of the chapters begins and ends with poets who are especially conscious of their own renderings of mind in terms of matter, while the chapters on Merrill and Ashbery venture out toward poetic engagements with biological materialism that may appear to be more attenuated or oblique. Thus, in shifting proportions, the science of mind operates as a thematic presence (revealing the conscious, specific uses to which poets have put the embodied mind to individuate their works of art) and as a context through which to interpret poems that subliminally or implicitly transmute this cultural given (revealing the value of cognitive materialism as an interpretive frame of reference).

Examined through these shifting perspectives, the poets in this book represent the imaginative ramifications of widely evident technological, historical, and philosophical transformations. But like all artists, they are most interesting when they are least representative—when they see in the matter of written language distinctive, unforeseeable opportunities to render and interpret the signatures of time and substance upon conscious experience. The unique provocations to artistic invention each poet finds in the "built-in limits" of mind thus form the central subjects of the chapters that follow. Lowell, whose mental illness acquainted him with the brain's chemical tyranny over personality, invents in *Notebook 1967–1968* an epic form that collapses and enacts the determinisms of biology and history. Creeley's experiments with mescaline and LSD encouraged him to fashion minimalist forms that emphasize the temporal and spatial impositions of embodiment upon the "motion" of thinking. Ammons, after much searching, arrives at the biological membrane as a central metaphor of mind (and of language and of the poem), and thereby unifies and clarifies his philosophies of mind and language in his undervalued late work. The distortions and perforations of embodied memory offer Merrill a model for poetry's distorted translation of life into art, encouraging him to reimagine the literary monument in the image of his own deteriorating body. Luxuriating in the representational possibilities of mindlessness as a structural and thematic principle, Ashbery uses the limits of embodied concentration to mark the dissolution of the transcendental spirit. Graham identifies the anatomical limits of the visual system with our limits of empathetic perspective, constructing her poems as prosthetics that can enhance our feeble power to imagine other minds, while her contemporaries Lin, Spahr, Mullen, and Bök find in convergences of embodied and technological media occasions to reinstate spurned immaterialities associated with the lyric—creativity, originality, presence, emotion, voice—even in poetries that openly militate "against expression."

Evolving Incarnations of Mind: Embodied Imagining before the Age of the Brain

In claiming that the embodied mind has transformed how American poets conceive of the self that underpins the lyric "I," this study diverges from the many recent interpretations of the literary history of twentieth-century poetry that have emphasized continuities between modernist and postmodernist poetics. Such histories rightly question the picture of mid-century aesthetics poets offered at the time; much as modernists distanced themselves from their Romantic and Victorian parentage by "break[ing] the pentameter," postwar poets framed a narrative of decisive "breakthrough" to carve out distinct identities for themselves.[26] Robert Lowell described the confessional poetry of *Life Studies* as a "breakthrough back into life" from the "metaphysical" intricacy, totalizing ambitions, and professed impersonality of high modernism; "breakthrough" applies just as well, however, to the *ethoi* that Allen Ginsberg and Frank O'Hara conferred upon beat and personist brands of apparently spontaneous poetics, that Charles Olson and Robert Creeley conferred upon projective verse, that Adrienne Rich and Amiri Baraka conferred upon their poetries of radical politics.[27] Like the many critics who have intervened to revise and complicate the narrative of modernism's disavowal of nineteenth-century sentiment and rhetoric, James Longenbach, Marjorie Perloff, Jennifer Ashton, and Christopher Ricks have recently made a trend of rejecting postwar narratives of parricidal breakthrough, demonstrating how close ties of personal and literary influence have channeled the voices of iconic literary modernists into contemporary oeuvres. Longenbach, for example, points out that the " 'breakthrough' narrative offers a narrow and inadequate reading even of Lowell's career," and persuasively demonstrates that postmodernist poets from Elizabeth Bishop to Jorie Graham have written "within an Eliotic inheritance that poets found more varied and accommodating than most readers recognized"; Perloff, who also focuses on T. S. Eliot's legacy, counts the Language poetry of Lyn Hejinian, Steve McCaffery, Charles Bernstein, and Susan Howe within a "second wave of modernism."[28]

The revelation of intricate continuities between modern and contemporary poetry amplifies our comprehension of poets' distinctive sensibilities and reminds us that the writers of every generation discern a broader array of aesthetic possibilities in the works of their predecessors than they and their earliest readers are generally prepared to admit. Emphasizing the inevitable affinities between successive literary movements, however, allows intergenerational lines of imaginative influence to eclipse epochal, ideological influences that foster poetic manifestations of historical change. It may therefore be more illuminating—from a cultural perspective and from a literary-historical perspective attuned to innovation rather than inheritance—to observe how the conceptual ramifications of materialist consensus have contributed to a fundamental rupture between modernist poetry and the poetry that has succeeded it.

Charles Altieri has suggested that a mid-century shift from humanism to antihumanism in American poetry coincided with and transcended the local breakthroughs declared by various factions in the 1950s and 1960s, a shift in which the model of the self as an agent who informs his or her reality gives way to a model of the self who is passively informed by the conditions of specific social, cultural, and biological environments.[29] The body's ambiguous status as both an essential aspect of selfhood and a context of selfhood, however, has surely contributed to the dearth of critical interest in the biological "environments" to which contemporary poets are so solicitously attuned.[30] Jack Spicer, for example, describes the shift in American poetry from sovereign agency to constructed passivity as a dispersal of the poet's aura from the "Outside": "Instead of the poet being a beautiful machine which manufactured the current for itself, did everything for itself—almost a perpetual motion machine of emotion . . . instead there was something from the Outside coming in."[31] This encroachment of extrinsic circumstance upon the immanent, autonomous force of the expressive subject has been widely observed in the literature of the late twentieth century, but an equivalent disruption at the corporeal core of the self has intensified this phenomenon, undermining the autonomy and integrity of the "beautiful machine" from within. This convergence of destabilizing forces has meant that recent poets are, in fact, notably *disinclined* to pit nature against the conditioning environments of language and society. Inheritors of Nietzsche's skepticism of language, Marx's skepticism of ideology, and Freud's skepticism of the transparency of consciousness to itself, these poets are disposed to interpret the embodied mind as yet another system that invisibly mediates the production of knowledge and that therefore conceals as much as it reveals. In emphasizing the extent to which scientists' and philosophers' sharpened yet incoherent picture of biologically determined selfhood has contributed to the poetic transference of agency from subjects to environments, this book aims to redress the indisputable precedence linguistic and social contexts have taken over biological ones in critical discussions of American poetry over recent decades.

Sharpening our own picture of this transference of agency from transcendental to physiological causes requires a longer view and a fuller account of the relationship between the imagination and the body in the poetry of the nineteenth and early twentieth centuries. Distinctively adapting the Romantics' exalted vision of human consciousness to accommodate increasingly embodied interpretations of mental life, Walt Whitman, Emily Dickinson, Gertrude Stein, and T. S. Eliot demonstrate American poetry's evolving rhetorical postures in relation to life science—and its tenacious retention of a fundamentally transcendental vision of the mind well into the twentieth century.[32] Whitman's and Dickinson's spiritualized conceptions of nature, their common will to contravene Christian dogma, and their tendency to associate science with infinite human improvement fostered their self-assured equation of the body with boundless creativity. Increasingly alarmed by the sciences' ever-expanding explanatory ambitions, however, Stein and Eliot sought to consolidate mental power against the threat of mechanistic reduction, cultivating an idealist rhetoric of the poetic imagination that would prove unsustainable for their mid-century successors.

The revolution in philosophy of mind and aesthetics that defined Romantic poetics is analogous in scale to the transformation I observe here in American poetry since the mid-twentieth century. Scholars have demonstrated how Romantic poets anticipated philosophical developments of the counter-Enlightenment as they formed and promoted their boldly humanist vision of mental power, revising neoclassical portrayals of the mind as a passive, imitative reflector of the world outside the self.[33] The aesthetic philosophies underpinning this poetry empowered the poet not only to discern evidence of divine order in nature through intuitive perception but to "half-create" reality through experience—from Blake's occult sense of his own mind as eternal and visionary, to Wordsworth's conception of the mind as an "auxiliar light" that shapes as it illuminates, to Shelley's vision of Mont Blanc as the sublime image of the creative intellect, to Coleridge's definition of the imagination as "a repetition in the finite mind of the eternal act of creation."[34] American transcendentalism likewise derived human consciousness from supernatural consciousness, interpreting the body as an aspect of nature in which divinity is immanent. Emerson writes in 1836 that "the Supreme Being . . . does not build up nature around us, but puts it forth through us. . . . As a plant upon the earth, so a man rests upon the bosom of God; he is nourished by unfailing fountains, and draws, at his need, inexhaustible power." Distilling this vision of divine reinforcement to a single question, Emerson wonders, "Who can set bounds to the possibilities of man?"[35]

By the mid-nineteenth century, Walt Whitman's and Emily Dickinson's forms of spiritual materialism had begun to adapt this idealist vision of consciousness by harmonizing the infinite human possibility of the Romantic zeitgeist with Anglo-America's deepening imaginative investment in the specifically embodied realization of consciousness. Identity, continuity, and correspondence between body and soul alternately define Whitman's fluid, sensual mysticism; "And if the body were not the soul," he asks in "I Sing the Body Electric," "what is the soul?" This indeterminate relationship also animates the practical phrenology Whitman enthusiastically proclaimed, in 1846, to have "gained a position, and a firm one, among the sciences."[36]

Leaves of Grass frequently invokes phrenology's distinctive taxonomy of faculties—"alimentiveness" (appetite for food and drink), for example, "amativeness" (sexual and romantic love), and especially "adhesiveness" (friendship, the force of social cohesion)—faculties whose relative states of development were said to be expressed in the corresponding morphologies of the brain and skull. In 1849, Whitman had his bumps read by Lorenzo Fowler, cofounder of the Fowler and Wells Phrenological Cabinet in New York, under whose imprint the *American Phrenological Journal* appeared; following Whitman's self-publication of the first, 1855 edition of *Leaves of Grass,* Fowler and Wells published the second edition in 1856. Whitman included his cherished (and embellished) phrenological chart in the first three editions of *Leaves of Grass* "to credential himself," Nathaniel Mackey explains, for "it was, according to phrenological opinion on the subject, a poet's chart." By demonstrating that his was a poet's head—"large and rounded in every direction"—Whitman sought to persuade his readers that he was physiologically suited to fulfill Emerson's vision of the American poet, "the man without impediment, who sees and handles that which others dream of, traverses the whole scale of experience, and is representative of man."[37] This representative poet's "brain is the ultimate brain," Whitman explains in his 1855 preface, and the beauty of the poem, like "all beauty[,] comes from beautiful blood and a beautiful brain"; he even names the phrenologist among the "lawgivers of poets": "they are the lawgivers of poets and their construction underlies the structure of every perfect poem."[38]

Despite the deterministic interpretations that led to infamous uses of phrenology to attempt to "prove" the racial superiority of white Americans, the animating premise of phrenology's entrepreneurial practitioners was "that the mysteries of the soul could be best studied and unraveled through the medium of its mortal instrument"—an instrument that did not fundamentally determine mental life but merely expressed it.[39] The principle that invisible transformations of character yielded legible physical effects (that is, that one might change one's bumps) allowed phrenologists to market the power of their diagnostic "science" to facilitate not only individual but social perfection; as the Fowlers put it, "Our present desire is this—to PHRENOLOGIZE OUR NATION, for thereby it will

REFORM THE WORLD."[40] Whitman's faith in the moral possibility and synthetic power of the pliable, spiritually determined brain was deep enough for him to consider the possibility that it might eventually obviate its own creative works—including "poems, churches, art":

> Brain of the New World, what a task is thine,
> To formulate the Modern—out of the peerless grandeur of the modern,
> Out of thyself, comprising science, to recast poems, churches, art,
> (Recast, may-be discard them, end them—may-be their work is done, who
>   knows?)[41]

Like the perfect union America brought to the New World—"The United States themselves are essentially the greatest poem," the poet declaims—human faculties are for Whitman always greater than the sum of their parts.[42] Phrenology, with its aura of empirical authority, could describe the brain without circumscribing its powers, and even offered to chart a path to the mind's limitless improvement; it thus confirmed Whitman's vision of the inclusive "Brain of the New World" as an organ at once material and ideal, a worldly incarnation of infinite possibility.

Like Whitman's, Dickinson's optimistic vision of the human mind continuous with, but not determined by, the physical universe denaturalizes our tendency to associate embodiment with the unyielding parameters of consciousness. Drawn to depicting unities through balance rather than synthesis, Dickinson describes herself as a daunted, "unsuspecting Heir" upon whom God has entailed the "Double Estate" of soul and body; she is obligated to steward this "Profound—precarious Property" both materially and morally.[43] For all her schematic recourse to Christian antinomies, Dickinson stubbornly resists her New England Calvinism's hierarchal insistence on the subordination of natural orders to supernatural ones. She envisions corporeal and spiritual aspects of experience to be as equal and contiguous—as "double" and yet unitary—as continuous land divided into adjacent "estates." Dickinson's pervasive use of physical and often anatomical terms to describe the feeling of consciousness reveals her objection to scripture's epistemological assaults upon the truths of the body—the more urgent and abstract the metaphysical crisis, the more physiologically concrete her description of it. "I felt a cleaving in my mind / As if my brain had split," she begins one poem of psychological displacement; in "After great pain a formal feeling comes—," she proclaims that "The nerves sit ceremonious like tombs"; in the poem that begins "I've dropped my Brain—My Soul is numb—," she describes her helpless withdrawal from emotional life as a kind of marmoreal paralysis ("My nerve in Marble lies—"); as the floor of her soul "creaks" and finally gives way under the leaden steps of processing mourners in "I felt a Funeral, in my Brain," Dickinson recalls despair so catastrophic that "it seemed / That Sense was breaking through," rupturing the boundary between emotional and physical pain.[44]

This continuity between the physical and the experiential that Dickinson reveals through psychological rupture undermines the Calvinist dissociation of spiritual knowledge from sensual knowledge and denies the priority of the former over the latter. Even more blasphemous, however, is Dickinson's presumptuous estimation of the composite power of her "Double Estate" relative to the monadic power of the divine mind. Her oceanic experience of consciousness—she describes it as absorbent, infinitely capacious, free—leads her to identify the miracle of the mind to be one that rivals, rather than reflects, divinity:

> The Brain—is wider than the Sky—
> For—put them side by side—
> The one the other will contain
> With ease—and You—beside—
>
> The Brain is deeper than the sea—
> For—hold them—Blue to Blue—
> The one the other will absorb—
> As Sponges—Buckets—do—
>
> The Brain is just the weight of God—
> For—Heft them—Pound for Pound—
> And they will differ—if they do—
> As Syllable from Sound—

The poem's many forms of balance—its symmetries of diction and syntax, its obedient alternating tetrameters and trimeters, its perfect ballad rhyme—foreground the irreverent argument Dickinson constructs through imbalance.[45] The cumulative presence of "The Brain," reiterated at the beginning of each stanza, overwhelms the shifting, natural and divine forces against which Dickinson invites us to "heft" its mortal power, tipping the balance toward the left margin of the poem rather than the right. The two sublime manifestations of the natural ("Sky" and "sea") that are easily subsumed by the brain accentuate the climactic, single manifestation of its supernatural rival, God himself. And, most consequentially, the imbalance between "Syllable" (the syllables of human language, which issue from the brain of the poet) and "Sound" (the sounds of nature, which issue from God) reveals the extent to which cognitive power and divine power do indeed "differ" in Dickinson's estimation. The syllables of the poet, so carefully ordered in this metronomic poem, arrange and order meaningless sound into intelligibility; they redeem the inscrutability of pure sensation just as Dickinson, in her searching iconoclasm, impatiently longs to see the inscrutability of the divine logos clarified, justified, and redeemed. In her comparison of human creativity to divine creativity, Dickinson favors the clarity of the verbal brain over the obscurity of an unintelligible God.

Whitman and Dickinson thus critique idealist and doctrinal epistemological biases toward metaphysical revelation without in any way divesting the brain of its transcendental possibility. Their ecumenical and inchoate philosophies of mind enable them to admit the terms of the physiological within the realm of the mental unreservedly, and allow them to question the absolute authority of the spirit over the actions of the body without extending the implications of that doubt to its extreme consequences within the domains of causation and agency. The rapid divergence and institutional consolidation of scientific and humanistic disciplines, however—and the sciences' surging credit for the "vast multiplication of the commodities and conveniences of existence," as T. H. Huxley put it—placed Whitman's and Dickinson's twentieth-century literary successors in an increasingly defensive position as practitioners of what Wordsworth had called the "science of feeling."[46] Modernist thinkers lost faith that any intrinsic relationship linked scientific and social progress, or that "modern ethical, political, and aesthetic ideals," John Brenkman writes, "were destined to fuse with scientific, technological, and economic advances and lift humanity into a new life."[47] This disillusionment rendered the enduring mystery of human consciousness—condensed in the intentional magic of the imagination and in the lavishly theorized, libidinal welter of the "unconscious"—all the more crucial as a reservoir of transformative potential that lay beyond the reach of scientific, technological, and economic formations.

Contrast, for example, Whitman's and Dickinson's exuberant references to the physical underpinnings of human creativity to D. H. Lawrence's description of the positivist offenses of "the scientist" in 1925:

> As for the scientist, he has absolutely no use for me so long as I am man alive. To the scientist, I am dead. He puts under the microscope a bit of dead me, and calls it me. He takes me to pieces, and says first one piece, and then another piece, is me. My heart, my liver, my stomach have all been scientifically me, according to the scientist; and nowadays I am either a brain, or nerves, or glands, or something more up-to-date in the tissue line.
>
> Now I absolutely flatly deny that I am a soul, or a body, or a mind, or an intelligence, or a brain, or a nervous system, or a bunch of glands, or any of the rest of these bits of me. The whole is greater than the part.[48]

As James Joyce puts it, "the modern spirit is vivisective."[49] This scientific picture of the exsanguinated, anatomically dismantled human led modernist poets not to withdraw but to redouble their investment in mental possibility—to fortify the mind against empirical assaults by making extravagant claims for its irreducible power. Much as the "accurate" photographic and filmic descriptions of the visible world fostered the inward turn of the psychological novel (which offered a faithful realism of inner life that none but an expressive, literary "technology," such as stream-of-consciousness narration, could claim), the lyric, accustomed to training its eye on the inward flow of impressions, responded to the evermore "up-to-date" parsing of the visible person into quantifiable "bits" by intensifying its focus on invisible structures of experience. Pervasive revulsion from the "spilt religion" of Romanticism rendered the concept of the soul less and less serviceable, but the sublunary faculties of the mind—poised to conjure supreme fictions, to shore fragments against ruin, to make the chaos of history cohere in epic forms—readily ascended to assume its renovating energies.[50] Modernist poetry's fetishization of style threw authority back upon the stylist as form giver—as the framer of aesthetic coherence in a world where meaning could no longer be found, only made—while the New Criticism incorporated the scientific values of rigor and impersonality to develop an intricate scholastic language for exalting the virtuosity of the poet and flaunting the discernment of the critic. "What makes poets not just modern but Modernist," Albert Gelpi writes, is "the conviction that the imagination, even without the Romantic props furnished by 'the Nineteenth Century mind,' was capacious enough, resilient enough, energetic enough to contend with its situation, maybe even to transform or transcend it."[51]

This idealist resistance to the pressure of reality cuts across belletristic and experimental extremes of high modernism, involving poets with and without obvious interest in the insights that the rising mind sciences had begun to promise theories of art. Those poets who were especially receptive to such insights, however, project the most nuanced picture of modernist poetry's consolidation of mental power against the methodological and interpretive strategies of empirical disciplines. Gertrude Stein and T. S. Eliot contributed directly to the inextricably enmeshed physiological, philosophical, and psychological discourses of mind at the turn of the twentieth century, and their contributions in turn shaped their enormously influential definitions of poetry and its practice. Trained in scientific psychology, Stein would seek in poetic experimentation an alternative to the passive, descriptive forms of scientific experimentation that her teachers espoused; trained as a philosopher, Eliot read widely and deeply in the physiological psychology of mystical experience, and would assimilate the findings of neurologists into his fundamentally idealist conception of reality.

As Steven Meyer has meticulously demonstrated, Stein's intellectual apprenticeship as a descriptive physiologist of the brain formatively affected her subsequent artistic development.[52] Stein worked closely with William James and Hugo Münsterberg from 1893 to 1897 as a student at the Harvard Psychological Laboratory before attending Johns Hopkins Medical School until 1902. "Practical medicine did not particularly interest her," she wrote of herself in *The Autobiography of Alice B. Toklas*, "and soon she specialized in the anatomy of the brain in the direction of brain tracts."[53] During her undergraduate years, Stein conducted experiments in automatic writing under James's supervision and witnessed his prominent participation in the ongoing debate delineating the disciplinary boundaries of psychology. This debate focalized the perplexing question of how much the study of the soul ought to address itself to the ancient discourse of metaphysics and the burgeoning discourse of neurology.

Over the course of his career, James expressed a wide range of dispositions toward the problem of consciousness. In *The Principles of Psychology,* first published in 1890, he veers from materialist reduction to dualist epiphenomenalism to neutral monism—the indefinite continuity between thought and reality upon which he would finally settle at the end of his career. Importantly for Stein, however, James is especially consistent in his manner of reconciling psychology's knotty problem of applying an empirical method to a fundamentally subjective phenomenon. For him, the scientific aspect of psychology consists in the practices of observation and description—of "looking into our own minds and reporting what we there discover"—for "*Introspective Observation is what we have to rely on first and foremost and always.*"[54] Stein would go on at Johns Hopkins to study under the anatomist Franklin Mall and his assistant, Lewellys Barker, who would cite Stein's morphological description of an enigmatic cluster of nerve cells known as the nucleus of Darkschewitsch in his textbook *The Nervous System and Its Constituent Neurones* (1899); in his autobiography, Barker recalls having "often wondered whether my attempts to teach her the intricacies of the medulla oblongata had anything to do with the development of the strange literary forms with which she was later to perplex the world."[55]

Crucial among the things physiological psychology "had to do" with the development of Stein's anomalous literary forms was a range of implicit and explicit repudiations of the sciences' mechanistic interpretations of language and mental life. Stein would flatly deny, for example, the legitimacy of the phenomenon of automatic writing, which divested the writer of the glory, authority, and responsibility of conscious intention.[56] She would likewise recover her vital faith in the intellectual imagination, recalling in *Everybody's Autobiography* how James's sterile, tautological ideal of the scientific "observation of things observed" had suppressed her own conception of science as a creative practice of speculation and interpretation:

> I began when evolution was still exciting very exciting. . . . Science meant everything and any one who had an active mind could complete mechanics and evolution, philosophy was not interesting, it like religion was satisfaction in a solution but science meant that a solution was a way to a problem. . . . That was what science was every solution was an opening to another problem and then William James came that is I came to him and he said science is not a solution and not a problem it is a statement of the observation of things observed and therefore not interesting perhaps therefore only abjectly true.[57]

As Meyer observes, Stein's ambition to describe "every possible kind of human being" in her early, thousand-page novel *The Making of Americans* applies James's scientific method within a distinctly verbal form of experimentation.[58] For the mature Stein of *Everybody's Autobiography,* however, description as an end in itself had become a compound heresy. James's description of phenomena dismisses mystery and difficulty as meaningful ends of experimentation, fundamentally opposing the guiding aesthetic principle Stein posits in her famous question, "If it can be done, why do it."[59] Description, furthermore, subordinates the status of the observing subject to the status of the observed object, dissipating the intentional force that drives Stein's cubist practice of imaginatively de-creating a thing in order to "recreate that thing" in poetry.[60] Most crucially, however, empirical description tends to make a naïve instrument of language, denying its opacity, its physicality, and the intricacies of its subliminal force by treating words and sentences as transparent vehicles of meaning. "Language *as a real thing* is not imitation either of sounds or colors or emotions it is an intellectual recreation," Stein writes; words in all their volume and heft correspond to "the physical something that a writer is while he is writing."[61]

While Stein turns to poetic language to supplement the "abject truth" of science, Eliot turns to science to fortify his metaphysics. Eliot's graduate papers and his doctoral thesis on the idealist philosophy of F. H. Bradley reveal his misgivings about psychology's pretensions to the status of a natural science, even as these early works demonstrate his drive to adapt Bradley's idealism to account for the correspondences between inner life and physiological events that psychologists were beginning to describe with increasing precision.[62] Both religious and skeptical by nature, Eliot was particularly fascinated by the studies of mystical experience Pierre Janet and Théodule Ribot, immediate predecessors of Freud and Jung, had conducted; they proposed that physiological and psychological states caused the kinds of mental phenomena commonly associated with religious experience—ecstasy, obsessive thoughts, and especially auditory, visual, and tactile hallucinations. Indeed, in *Knowledge and Experience in the Philosophy of F. H. Bradley,* Eliot would use hallucination as a test case in his argument for the partial, but not total, reducibility of ideas to "neural process."[63] In one sense, he claims, a hallucination is real because its neurological aspects are (conceivably) verifiable, but in another sense, a hallucination is not real because its subjective aspect cannot be verified empirically. Such "half-objects," as Eliot calls them—hallucination, will, attention, ideas, and finally, he concludes, the soul itself—are special entities that exhibit a duality of aspect that defies human comprehension:

> The point of view from which each soul is a world in itself must not be confused with the point of view from which each soul is only the function of a physical organism, a unity perhaps only partial, capable of alteration, development, having a history and a structure, a beginning and apparently an end. And yet these two souls are the same. And if the two points of view are irreconcilable, yet on the other hand neither would exist without the other, and they melt into each other by a process which we cannot grasp.[64]

That materialist and idealist perspectives upon the soul cannot be reconciled ultimately strikes Eliot as something more like a solution than a problem. "The more accurately and scientifically one pursues the traces of mentality in the 'mind' of the individual, the less one finds," he concludes, while "the more closely one scrutinizes the 'external world,' and the more eagerly and positively one plucks it, the less there is to see and touch."[65] Eliot interprets this elusiveness as evidence that apparently discrete facets of being are in fact somehow identical—that the soul is an absolute unity that finds expression in physical and phenomenological manifestations.[66]

Posterity has judged "The Love Song of J. Alfred Prufrock" to be the first of Eliot's poems to embody his utterly distinctive sensibility in language, and for all its ironic misdirections, the poem dramatizes the struggle to assume an authentic poetic voice—a voice that incarnates the absolute unity of the soul within the fallen medium of debased, modern language. As Prufrock feels himself judged and dismissed by the women who indifferently come and go from his company—and as he articulates the poet's struggle to unfetter himself from the confinements of inherited language—Eliot pictures Prufrock in the desperate position of a specimen "pinned and wriggling on the wall":

> And I have known the eyes already, known them all—
> The eyes that fix you in a formulated phrase,
> And when I am formulated, sprawling on a pin,
> When I am pinned and wriggling on the wall,
> Then how should I begin
> To spit out all the butt-ends of my days and ways?
> And how should I presume?

Prufrock finds himself fixed and formed by language—by the "formulated phrases" of ritualized courtship and idle social judgment, and by the "formulated phrases" of received poetic conventions inadequate to a vision of inner life whittled down to "the butt-ends of my days and ways." At the climax of the poem, as Prufrock finally "presumes" to imagine what it would be like to articulate his crisis of voice, Eliot rewrites the image of Prufrock "pinned and wriggling on the wall" as a fantastic image of consummate self-expression, of "the substantial unity of the soul" translated intact:[67]

> And would it have been worth it, after all,
> Would it have been worth while,
> After the sunsets and the dooryards and the sprinkled streets,
> After the novels, after the teacups, after the skirts that trail along the
>   floor—
> And this, and so much more?—
> It is impossible to say just what I mean!
> But as if a magic lantern threw the nerves in patterns on a screen:
> Would it have been worth while

If one, settling a pillow or throwing off a shawl,
And turning toward the window, should say:
    "That is not it at all,
    That is not what I meant, at all."

No! I am not Prince Hamlet, nor was meant to be.[68]

Eliot's image of the soul made visible—of the Platonic ideal of a poem, of the princely soliloquy, of saying just what he means—is the lucid projection of the nerves themselves in stanzaic "patterns" on a page-like screen. In his fantasy, Eliot enchants not the mind but the medium—the lantern, the language—for he identifies the obstacles to his soul's expression within the mechanisms of translation, not the mechanisms of consciousness itself. For Eliot, the motions of mind stand only to be distorted by "the natural sin of language," and style precedes its incarnation in the poem; it is therefore not enough, he writes in "The Metaphysical Poets," "to 'look into our hearts and write.' . . . One must look into the cerebral cortex, the nervous system, and the digestive tracts."[69] Eliot's distinctly physiological conception of the soul facilitated his well-known incorporation of comparative mythology and structural anthropology into his vision of poetry and its functions, laying the foundation for his later, theological modernism. From his postulate that "hard-wired" mythic structures organize collective consciousness, Eliot derived an aesthetic theory in which poetry, drama, and religious ritual could tap into a primitive, unifying resource at once genetic and transcendental, evolved and absolute.[70] Since, he believed, poetry and drama originated in primitive impulses to express embodied rhythms, "civilized" art should aspire to touch the reader *physically*, through rhythm and sensation. Such art, "like a religious service," he writes, "should be a stimulant to make life more tolerable and augment our ability to live; it should stimulate partly by the action of vocal rhythms on what, in our ignorance, we call the nervous system."[71]

The cases of Stein and Eliot are benchmarks against which we can measure a marked shift in the discursive and disciplinary positions of mind science and poetry over the course of the twentieth century. Stein framed her avant-garde poetic experimentation as an empowered, humanistic alternative to descriptive science. In the genres of the philosophical treatise, the literary critical essay, and his poetry itself, Eliot weighed in on the hard problem of consciousness that the advent of physiological psychology had reinvigorated. Unlike these artists, however, the poets in the chapters that follow write in an age of rigid disciplinarity, heightened specialization, and intensified scientific authority, and thus tend to see themselves as peripheral observers, illiterate immigrants, even poachers when they advance toward the problem of consciousness that has become so densely circumscribed by empirical terms. Stein's unapologetic preference for poetry as a method of investigating objective reality—much like William Carlos Williams's observation that he could detect only "a subtle loss of dignity in saying a man is a poet instead of a scientist"—underscores the drastic redistribution of artistic and scientific discourses' cultural authority over the course of the twentieth century.[72]

Stein's and Eliot's ultimate subordination of empirical epistemologies to intuitive ones illustrates modernism's overwhelmingly idealist responses to the materialism of the rising mind sciences. W. H. Auden, however, a figure who embodies so many of twentieth-century poetry's transformations of practice and attitude, may summarize this literary-historical transition best. At the time of Freud's death, Auden honored him in a masterful, ambivalent elegy that pictures Freud not as the scientist of mind he controversially imagined himself to be but as a dauntless humanist whose desperate, consolatory belief in a "talking cure" he shared with the poet commemorating him. The poem describes Freud as a "climate of opinion // under whom we conduct our differing lives," a force that guides with compassion and without judgment, that empowers the psychologically wounded through therapeutic renovation, and that countervails oppression by demystifying the will to power.[73] "In Memory of Sigmund Freud," written in 1939, is in fact a portrait of the modernist mind itself: the mind that is an abstract, transcendental receptacle for a capacious personal past, that is malleably subject to intentional transformation, and that exerts its metaphysical crises and improvements, top down, upon its somatic, familial, and civilizational environments. Three decades later, Auden would dedicate his poem "Talking to Myself" (1971) to his friend Oliver Sacks, presenting a version of the mind that reflects an utterly transformed climate. In "Talking to Myself," the "self" Auden addresses is in fact his body: the "mortal manor, the carnal territory," that he manages like a tenant overwhelmed by the wanton growth of autonomous, natural terrain. This body proves to be an authority that de-termines the entire scope of his mental life; in the poet's pointed terms, it is a tutor "but for whose neural instructions I could never / acknowledge what is or imagine what is not."[74]

As twentieth-century poetry's perspectives on the mind begin to ar-range themselves, in hindsight, into one clear view, we can now see that the Romantic conception of the mind as an infinite reservoir of possibility enabled modernism, in its despairing apostasy, to project its residual forms of faith upon the power of the imagination to unify experience in aesthetic objects. W. B. Yeats, the spiritualist, pictures the mind as an in-strument of supernatural manifestation immaterially tapped into *spir-itus mundi,* while Langston Hughes defines poetry as "the human soul entire, squeezed like a lemon or a lime, drop by drop, into atomic words."[75] Wallace Stevens's very titles—*Harmonium, Ideas of Order,* "Notes Toward a Supreme Fiction," "The Planet on the Table"—unabashedly credit the *mundo* of the imagination, "pressing back against the pressure of reality," to arrange, deepen, and enchant experience.[76] The jagged as-semblage of the *Cantos* audaciously illustrates Pound's vision of the mind as a magnet commanding iron filings into the shape of a rose, and in the preface to *Spring and All* (1923), Williams proclaims that "only the imag-ination is undeceived"; "To refine, to clarify, to intensify that eternal moment in which we alone live there is but a single force—the imagina-tion."[77] Marianne Moore, for all her naturalistic precision, proclaims that the mind is an enchanting and enchanted thing; "It tears off the veil; tears / the temptation, the mist the heart wears, / from its eyes."[78] Pound, Wil-liams, and Moore (and their successors Louis Zukofsky, George Oppen, and Lorine Niedecker) exhibit in their imagist propensities piercing forms of observational clarity that rarely admit the physiological faults or em-bodied constraints poets pervasively identify with perception after late modernism; the "direct treatment of the 'thing,' whether subjective or ob-jective," the first, animating premise of imagism, presupposes an infallible introspective and perceptual intensity unimaginable in poetry after 1960.

It remains for the rest of this book to demonstrate that our vision of the embodied mind not only substantively departs from the ideal minds of Romanticism and modernism but also underpins the vision of the in-creasingly soluble lyric subject to which late twentieth-century American poetry gives such diverse expression. The selection of poets in these pages thus represents a number of demographic preferences—for poets who are preoccupied with the nature of consciousness but also ambitious enough to represent more than a niche interest in cognitive science or "the mind / body problem"; for poets (excepting the mid-career poets in the conclusion) who have been prolific enough to manifest significant philosophical and aesthetic change over time; and for poets who represent a range of stylistic modes, registering the period's philosophical upheaval by exercising a wide array of poetry's resources as an art form. Writing in 2002, one reader described Eliot's image of the magic lantern in "Prufrock"—a vision, we have seen, of a poetics that might assimilate and project a distinctively modern way of imagining consciousness in relation to the body—as a "formulation that is still a challenge thrown down to the poets of this century."[79] Eliot might have had, in 1920, an inkling of how urgent that challenge would become, but he could hardly have imagined how ingeniously poets of his own century, and of this one, would greet it.

Toward a Methodological Dualism

By now it may be evident that my critical method embodies a dialectic between contextual materialism and aesthetic idealism—a dialectic that is analogous to the physical and metaphysical ambivalence I identify in contemporary poetry. I propose, on one hand, that mind science has exerted discursive power within the cultural imaginary and has thus widely determined literary translations of subjective experience, uniting them below the horizon of poets' intentional differences. Demonstrating that such translations draw upon a popular "science" of mind that absorbs and often distorts scientific principles, I situate poetic representations of the embodied mind in relation to a lineage of mass cultural interpretations of scientific meaning for which commercial phrenology and Freudian pseudoscience are crucial antecedents. And yet I also take it for granted that poets can produce original interpretations of cultural information that are not overdetermined, and that the differentiated results of such originality are of greater interest to readers of literature than homogeneous markers of tacit cultural consensus. I maintain that focusing closely on individual authors profitably illustrates the grappling of unique minds with collective données, and that isolating poetry from other kinds of literary texts profitably illustrates the genre's distinctive capacities for expressing and reflecting upon a broad array of epistemic conditions. These countervailing sets of suppositions—which configure the artist as a passive conduit of cultural meaning and as an autonomous maker of original meaning—are underwritten by the limited vision of consciousness that cultural materialism favors and by the empowered vision of consciousness that literary criticism in the New Critical tradition has espoused. Needless to say, dancing this dance amid the pitfalls of excessive skepticism and apparent naïveté requires a cautious, hopeful choreography.

Through a succession of necessary liberations, culturally and contextually oriented reading practices have transformed and enriched the study of poetry in recent decades. The concept of the "material" or "social" text—the text that inscribes historical events, circulates as a commodity, conducts transactions within interpretive communities, and is enmeshed and reciprocally constituted within a range of discursive environments—has released the poem from confining assumptions about the nature of artistic production. It has dispelled the illusion of monolithic, expressive "meaning" and erected paradigms of value through which to credit artists for disrupting and exposing the determinations of normative interpretive codes. It has embedded the acts of writing, reading, and performing within institutional and disciplinary systems, revealing the inextricability of historical and literary phenomena; in doing so, it has liberated readers from undue deference to authorial intention, fostered a reckoning with the baleful sociological effects of the concept of literary genius, and recovered authors excluded from the canon. These important recognitions have led us to incorporate political self-awareness into critical practice and to revise our claims to authority—to acknowledge, that is, that all acts of description and interpretation are acts of power. Transcending the complacent exaltation of aesthetic closure and dissipating the aura surrounding the enduring verbal icon, the material text has come to represent a vital, dynamic process of decentralized signification.

The broad swath of materialist impulses and practices responsible for these developments has by now begun to resolve into distinct configurations in the practice of poetry criticism. The dominant syncretism of cultural studies and poetry criticism has been devoted to the recognition of ideological positions in poems and to their interpretation through the lenses of various social formations—gender, class, ethnicity, national and transnational origin, sexuality, and political and religious cultures. In their introduction to *Poetry and Cultural Studies: A Reader,* Maria Damon and Ira Livingston summarize the distinct hierarchy of historical and aesthetic concerns that has tended to characterize such approaches:

> Cultural studies rewrites the category of the aesthetic to place it in active engagement with political, social and economic realms, displacing aesthetic judgment as the centerpiece of analyses of expressive culture. This revision does not necessarily dismiss aesthetics but makes aesthetic judgments and the category of the aesthetic itself (along with multiple attendant political and social implications) important objects for analysis rather than givens. Accordingly, cultural studies tends to defer the project of aesthetic judgment generally as an impediment to studying the use-value of cultural productions. By deferring the question of how good a poem is, one can begin to ascertain what it is good for, and how and for whom.

As they pit historical value against literary value, Damon and Livingston suggest that the crucial project of denaturalizing aesthetic judgment may legitimately (though not necessarily) entail the wholesale dismissal of the formal and sensual aspects that make poems, in all but very few cases, recognizable as poems. They propose that the question of "what [a poem] is good for" is less crude than the question of "how good a poem is," and that the congeries of propositions that surround each question have little to do with one another.[80]

Context-driven approaches to poetry have thus exhibited a tendency to flatten distinctions between literary genres and to instrumentalize poems in the process of educing historical and cultural knowledge. Diagnosing the limitations of such reading methods, Michael Davidson and Barrett Watten each refer to the use of the term "cultural poetics" in the context of New Historicism, where it describes the interpenetration of text and context and frames a method of "reading" diverse forms of cultural production without specific reference to poetry per se.[81] Davidson observes that while "the New Historicist use of the phrase 'cultural poetics' breaks down the barrier between high art and mass culture, it does leave the issue of poetry's particularity as a specific kind of discourse somewhat in the lurch."[82] Watten proposes that "what is often missing from these [New Historical and cultural studies methodologies] is a specific consideration of literary form."[83] Rachel Blau DuPlessis, voicing her unease with contextual reading strategies by which poems are opportunistically mined for symptoms of culture, argues that "scanting the aesthetic, generic, and conventional aspects of poetry limits criticism to an extractive reading strategy that reduces a text to a message." She goes on to chart a course for "a more inclusive kind of cultural studies practice," arguing that "readings evoking cultural studies methods need to assimilate formalist readings dialectically, making sure that a poem gets treated as an art object saturated with aesthetic choices (even banal ones)."[84]

A small subset of materialist critics, including Watten, Davidson, DuPlessis, and Christopher Nealon, have thus sought to place greater emphasis on form within a revised practice of cultural poetics. Expunging the concept of the lyric voice as a sign of authorial presence and emphasizing, in Gertrude Stein's dichotomy, "entity" over "identity," they highlight the concrete materiality of texts and often focus on artists inclined to see words in their most thingly aspect—as primarily real, concrete objects rather than as referential or symbolic ones. From this perspective, social and linguistic materialities are not distinct but integral and mutually constitutive—they exist on a continuum within which subversions of linguistic convention amount to subversions of social convention, and socioeconomic crisis announces itself in crises of form.[85] These practitioners of cultural poetics have begun the daunting task of addressing how we ought to assimilate the crucial lessons of cultural and historical criticism within the analysis of poetry as a specific kind of literary discourse. Thus far, they have valuably focused on situating material constructions of poetic form within paradigms of historical contingency, but they have also chosen to retain cultural studies' hierarchal priority of context over text by stressing the indexical aspects of formal expression (in registering, for example, socioeconomic crisis), by concentrating on oppositional literary movements that conceive of form as a mechanism of cultural critique, and by addressing themselves to the cultural functions that style performs (coercion and subversion, social identity formation and consolidation).[86] Locating value in formal articulations and destabilizations of ideology, such paradigms of reading exhibit a bias that differs in degree but not in kind from the bias that subtends Damon and Livingston's instrumental focus on the ethical use-value of the poem in the social world and on the epistemological use-value of interpreting poetry for what it can tell us about the social world. A question that remains, however, is whether this hierarchy of value is a requisite dimension of any contextually sensitive critical practice, or whether it is possible to envision a cultural poetics that asks not what kind of cultural work texts perform but rather what kind of work cultural contexts can perform in interpreting the unique imaginative enterprises of specific works of art. It seems appropriate for literary criticism to ask (and strive, in its practice, to answer) a fundamentally literary question: What is the *aesthetic* use-value of placing a poem in context?

The value of contextualizing any work of literature historically is self-evident from an exegetical standpoint—the meanings of texts are always amplified, clarified, multiplied by awareness of their contexts. Aesthetic criticism, however, addresses a different set of concerns. As Helen Vendler defines it, "the aim of a properly aesthetic criticism . . . is not primarily to reveal the *meaning* of an art work or disclose (or argue for or against) the ideological *values* of an art work. The aim of an aesthetic criticism is to *describe* the art work in such a way that it cannot be confused with any other art work (not an easy task), and to *infer* from its elements the aesthetic that might generate this unique configuration."[87] It seems to me that a poem's intricacy of conscious or unconscious engagement with any aspect of "extrinsic" circumstance—socioeconomic, philosophical, "high" cultural, "low" cultural, discursive or objective—is as much an aspect of its aesthetic texture as any purely formal quality. Inscriptions of ideology attest to the cultural determination of all human artifacts, whether they are intentionally expressive (like poems) or unintentionally expressive (like reality television). Within literary artifacts, however, such inscriptions also function as constitutive components of meaning making and literary experience—as elements of style. Like metaphor or rhythm or avant-garde agitations against mainstream practice, the citational and allusive marks of putatively external discursive spheres may function in virtuosic or banal ways, enrich literary experience or diminish it, operate intentionally or unintentionally, chime in accord or screech in meaningful discord with other aspects of a poem's construction. The traces of wider cultural influence naturally facilitate fresh returns to the extratextual world, but they also require some kind of synthetic account within the artificial context of the poem itself. As dimensions of how poems work (not just what they say or what they indicate about social reality), these traces represent occasions to reorient critical attention on the poem, the volume, the oeuvre, and the diachronic arcs and synchronic landscapes of specifically literary history. Within this paradigm, the unity of the work of art is not organic or autotelic, but it is not entirely soluble, either; the poem does not disintegrate into its cultural elements but assembles and transmutes cultural elements in a process "saturated with aesthetic choices."

A vital benefit of a new aesthetic criticism of this kind—less postformalist cultural analysis than postcultural formal analysis—is its acknowledgment of aspects of literary art that tend to fall in the blind spots of materialist criticism. Predictably, materialist approaches largely exclude subjective and phenomenological aspects of literary significance in their concentrated focus on signatures of historical transformation. The small cohort of practitioners of cultural poetics have emphasized the most concrete, morphological features of poetic form (collage, typographic experimentation, rhyme, and so on) that cultural critics have overwhelmingly ignored, but by addressing themselves to poets who make arguments primarily through form (and who conceive of poems as places to make arguments in the first place), these critics have circumvented the sensuous uses to which formal elements are most often put. Charles Altieri addresses materialist approaches' enduring omission of literary qualia in a sympathetic critique of traditional cultural studies, cultural poetics, and historical ontology, attributing their common disinclination to acknowledge poetry's sensuous aspects to their tendency to impose "problematic distinctions between means and ends that make it very difficult to correlate the sensuous and the reflective":

> This [tendency] is most evident in the glee with which materialist critics dispense charges of "aestheticism." Apparently "aestheticism" is attributed to all emphases on formal or internal relations within a text, then that emphasis is presumed to be the end shaping the endeavor rather than an aspect of a more inclusive project. Of course some authors do make the medium the matter. But it is much more

common to consider this internal density as the means to build imaginative engagements with how characters and lyric speakers think and suffer and find satisfaction. The text's sense of the world interprets and puts to work its exploration of the powers of the medium.[88]

The premise that a "sense of the world" puts form to intentional purposes underlies most readings by materialist critics, however summarily they may dismiss the idea of a unified subject on theoretical grounds and attribute that "sense of the world" to an ideological Weltanschauung. The confusion of means and ends Altieri describes likewise underlies indictments of aesthetic criticism—or in Altieri's terms, idealist criticism—as intrinsically complacent or conservative in political disposition.[89] Reducing social value to political value, such indictments propose that the kinds of requests that internally referential, self-consciously "literary" texts make of readers—injunctions to identify imaginatively with lyric speakers, to attend to and expect nuance in expressive objects, to abide contradiction—are more corruptible and less charged with socially transformative possibility than the processes of identifying refractions and condensations of power that materialist analysis rightfully asks of us as well. To be sure, there is the danger of intensifying the authority of economically privileged culture producers through innocent reverence for literary genius; however, there is also the danger of ensconcing individual consciousness in matrices of determination so binding that political empowerment, ethical accountability, and personal agency terminally disperse. The fallacy that a criticism whose practices diffuse individuality is more subversive than a criticism whose practices consolidate individuality has emerged out of zealous remonstration against American New Criticism on political grounds—and, consequently, out of a too-narrow conception of materialist practice as the exact obverse of New Critical practice. Materialists' (waning) suspicion of close reading as a critical instrument is another outcome of this ardent reaction. Practitioners of cultural poetics have proven that the meanings of formal operations—in poetry and surely, too, in criticism—are not essential but contingent; thus, as Susan Wolfson observes (and DuPlessis reiterates), " 'close reading' as a practice of attention need not be complicit with the methods and agenda of the New Criticism in which its skills were first exercised and refined."[90]

Inverting the hierarchy of context over text in the practice of cultural poetics thus has the advantage of acknowledging the claims poems make on us as emotional beings who not only have ideas but also have feelings about them. It also acknowledges that most poems aspire to elicit in readers some kind(s) of pleasure—of recognition, of conceptual novelty, of political solidarity, of linguistic beauty, of ethical galvanism, of de-familiarization, of analytical rigor, of consolation. It treats these aspirations, in fact, as fundamental dimensions of literary experience rather than decorative ones, and focuses on poems' requisitioning of cultural materials to amplify literary pleasure. Solicitous attunement to the emotional depths beneath conceptual surfaces tends to undermine the supposition that empirical truths are truer than phenomenological ones, and that getting down to material causes is a sufficient aim for literary criticism. Marjorie Perloff lamented precisely this tendency in literary scholarship when she observed in her 2006 presidential address to the MLA that "it would be more accurate to call the predominant activity of contemporary literary scholars other-disciplinary rather than interdisciplinary," arguing that when we treat literary works primarily as "windows through which we see the world beyond the text," we are importing historical and anthropological terms of value in self-negating articulations of discipline envy. "Thus," she adds, "the classical and medieval rhetorical triad—*docere, delectare, movere* (to teach, to delight, to move)—a triad operative for centuries—has been reduced to a single one: the teaching function."[91] Vendler makes a similar point about disciplinary ends in her declaration of the aims of aesthetic criticism: "The critic may well begin, 'Look at it this way for a change,' but the sentence must continue, 'and now don't you see it as more intelligibly beautiful and moving?'—That is, if the interpretation does not reveal some hitherto occluded aspect of the aesthetic power of the art work, it is useless as art criticism (though it may be useful as cultural history or sociology or psychology or religion)."[92]

My method here recognizes that the impossibility of defending the "literary" in absolute terms is matched by the impossibility of denying the kinds of experiences the term seeks to describe. I have therefore sought to mitigate the offenses of "extractive" reading by striving to clarify the kinds of affective engagement to which particular poems and poets aspire, balancing the top-down process of identifying cultural symptoms with the more satisfying burden of accounting for their arrangement in a way that enhances literary experience.[93] In one sense, then, my chapter on Jorie Graham sets out to demonstrate her representative assimilation of the language of cognitive science that pervaded the discourse of consciousness in the 1990s (designated "the decade of the brain" by George H. W. Bush).[94] The more demanding aim of the chapter, however, is to demonstrate how her initial captivation with the concept of the embodied mind evolves into an increasingly frantic ethical critique of empiricist perspectives' dehumanizing, "virtual" picture of the self—a critique that she asserts stylistically in her incremental reassertion of a strident, unified lyric voice. I likewise come to Robert Lowell with an interest in the successive religious, psychoanalytic, and scientific understandings of character to which his poems, letters, autobiographical writings, and interviews attest. My argument, however, centers on the radical (and much maligned) long poem *Notebook 1967–1968,* written just as the transformative chemical treatment of Lowell's bipolar disorder seemed to reveal to him the somatic determination of his character; I propose that in *Notebook* he devised a poetic form that was a desperate, despairing picture of flesh itself, atomized and embedded in arbitrary arrangements of nature and history. In some cases, demonstrating the refraction of Lowell's concept of self through a succession of ideological paradigms requires the extraction of specific examples for their conceptual relevance only. But in my readings I set out to treat Lowell's poems, as much as possible, as wholes—and to render vividly the potent consequences of his embodied concept of mind within the realm of feeling.

I therefore balance here the deductive analytical style of cultural approaches to poetry and the inductive analytical style of aesthetic approaches to poetry. Like Theodor Adorno's claim that the lyric critiques the social world by withdrawing from it appeared to be to Fredric Jameson, my methodological hybridity might appear to some to be "betting on both sides at once."[95] As materialist critics, however, have continued to pit themselves divisively against aesthetic critics in ardently politicized and extravagantly theorized declarations of method, and as aesthetic critics have dismissively declined to justify their assumptions within a transformed critical climate, both perspectives have sacrificed persuasiveness for purity.[96] My use of terms that have become distinctly polarized—my references to both the cultural "imaginary" and the individual "imagination," for example, and to poems both as "texts," in the tradition of materialist criticism, and "lyrics," in the tradition of aesthetic criticism—demonstrates the practical utility of both perspectives to my line of argument. The specifically textual, formal aspects of poems require sustained consideration as I trace how poets use the concrete materiality of written language to interpret the matter of embodied consciousness. I favor the term "lyric," however, both because it complements my mode of reading in the idealist tradition and because it signals the balance of incarnation and inspiration embedded in poetry's self-conception as a genre.[97] As poets explore the implications of the conceptual identity of mind and brain through concrete transformations of poetic form, they are playfully, solicitously, often ingeniously conscious of the timeless analogies between the verbal, sensual aspects of the poem and the human body, between the irreducible, inspirited "meaning" of the poem and the immaterial soul.

That this methodological hybridity provokes and acknowledges intractable questions of intention and literary value may be its greatest strength. While idealist criticism, preoccupied by its own enchantments, tends to fixate on the glories of aesthetic mastery, materialist criticism, with its own axes to grind, so thoroughly mistrusts intention that it often disregards glaring signatures of artistic will. The tendency among aesthetic critics to interpret personal and institutional preferences as immutable conditions of literary value invites charges of elitism, while the tendency among cultural critics to dismiss literary value altogether denies the unusual imaginative and persuasive hold that works of verbal art can claim on readers. Within such a critical climate, a contextual practice less embarrassed by pleasure and more willing to "rely on each particular poem to show you the way in which it is trying to be good," as William Empson put it, might remind us that every act of criticism must negotiate fundamental questions of meaning and value that are, or ought to be, as open as ever.[98] The greatest challenge of reading in a way that balances what we want to learn from poems with what they want to teach us, however, is to isolate those cultural discourses that stimulate poetry as a specifically literary form—that recast the commerce of self and circumstance, possibility and limitation, subject and object, mind and matter.

CHAPTER 1

Robert Lowell and the Chemistry of Character

For Robert Lowell, the most urgent philosophical questions about the nature of mind issued from emotional imbalance—from the torment biological circumstance relentlessly wrought upon him over the course of his adult life. Lowell suffered his first manic episode and subsequent depressive collapse at thirty-two, and would be hospitalized fourteen times during his remaining twenty-eight years as a result of debilitating breakdowns. The severity of these breakdowns is difficult to overstate; gripped by hallucinations, monomania, delusions, disfiguring transformations of personality, and the emergence of identities other than his own, Lowell described witnessing his "mystical experiences and explosions" in a pathological ecstasy, his "fascinated spirit watching the holocaust of irrationality."[1] This dissociative quality of Lowell's psychosis meant that clear memories remained after his mania subsided; he would describe the aftermath of his breakdowns—the "purgatorial feelings" (*L* 458) of humiliation and regret—as "the worst part."[2] In the rounds of apologies that followed his bouts of madness, Lowell's attempts to accept accountability for "imbecilic, inhuman, dangerous, embarrassing" (*L* 239) behavior forced the question of how he could claim responsibility for his actions when he could not claim continuous will or, in any meaningful sense, continuous selfhood; in the wake of his manic episodes, he would pit physical and spiritual interpretations of his mental condition against one another, ever alert to the philosophical challenges posed by a mind that seemed to be, somehow, *physically* ill. Apologizing to T. S. Eliot, Lowell proposed that his "true" self was mysteriously dispersed across his well and ill temperaments, for "fragments of the true man, such as he is, are in both phases" (*L* 444); in a perplexed letter to another friend, Lowell describes his convalescence from his first manic crisis to have been "like recovering from some physical injury, such as a broken leg or jaundice, yet there's no disclaiming these outbursts—they are part of my character" (*L* 239).

The aura of the deranged, suicidal artistic genius certainly contributed to Lowell's popular image during his lifetime—in his fictional portrait of the poet in *Armies of the Night* (1968), Norman Mailer speculates that "Lowell's brain at its most painful must have been equal to an overdose of LSD on Halloween"—but Lowell himself was for the most part without illusions about his illness, perceiving it to be an impediment to his creativity.[3] "To make the poems possible," he once explained, "a huge amount of health has to go into the misery."[4] Along with his treatments, Lowell's understanding of his "manic seizures" became increasingly medical over time, and the more closely he came to identify his experience of mind with the intractable determinations of his body, the more intellectually significant to him his condition became. Indeed, the metaphysical quandary his surges of "high blood" occasioned, and the intellectual reckoning with the problem of mind and body he undertook in light of them, formed a climate within which he restlessly revised his style.

Lowell's dynastic New England Calvinism and rebellious conversion to Catholicism have framed our relatively limited picture of him as a philosophical thinker, and lyrics such as "Beyond the Alps"—the inaugural poem of *Life Studies*—have encouraged us to identify his watershed stylistic transition from symbolic density to conversational intimacy with his descent from spiritual rarefaction to the "terra firma" of an ostensibly Freudian humanism.[5] But while this familiar account of Lowell's most famous formal transition rightly implies a close correspondence between his interpretation of the nature of subjective experience and his patterning of mental life in poetic language, significant facets of that correspondence and its fate over the remaining decades of Lowell's career remain to be explored. The controversial and widely influential formal ruptures that continued to punctuate Lowell's poetics of the 1960s and 1970s reflect fitful transformations in his philosophy of mind that were inextricably bound up with his experiences of illness and somatic treatment—transformations that reveal him to have been not only captive to but captivated by the natural forces that govern the articulation of character, emotion, and selfhood.[6] As he lived through a paradigm shift in the diagnosis and treatment of mental disorders, Lowell witnessed, shared, and finally rejected the hysterical enthusiasm for chemical treatment fostered by the commercial juggernauts of the pharmaceutical industry in the 1960s. His illness, in other words, tapped him directly into the era's transforming conceptions of mind just as the institutional scientism of today's mental health landscape was emerging. David Healy, writing in 2008, observed that "In recent years drugs like Prozac, Valium, Viagra, and chloropromazine . . . have changed how we view ourselves, and these changes now occur within years or sometimes within months of each other."[7] Lowell's philosophical and aesthetic trajectories, indebted in unacknowledged ways to his evolving, experimental treatments, illustrate the emotional consequences of this historical phenomenon, demonstrating the effects of its shifting premises and promises within one ravaged life.

In an elegant summary of recent critical biases against Lowell, Dan Chiasson gives pride of place to "facticity": to Lowell's vision of the self as an accumulation of autobiographical facts and to his faith in the transparent epistemological value of recording "what happened"; by his own account, Lowell was a poet not of "the imagined," but of "the recalled" (*CP* 838).[8] Lowell's commitment to fact, Chiasson notes, has seemed naïve to readers after the linguistic turn, who emphasize the specifically semiotic distortions that confound self-knowledge; this facticity has also seemed politically suspect to readers who observe, as Elizabeth Bishop once did, that Lowell's confidence in the inherent significance of his life's facts draws unearned force from his exceptional privilege as a member of the Lowell clan.[9] And yet, Chiasson concludes, "Robert Lowell cannot be read satisfyingly without an interest, on his reader's part, in autobiography—an interest, that is, in the way the self is constituted in the social world, by means of autobiographical fact: the names and dates that plot us on the various grids that constitute familial, social, and political life. (If you think that such data have no place in lyric poetry, you won't enjoy reading Lowell)."[10] Chiasson's assessment acknowledges the integral role of circumstantial "data" in Lowell's conception of the self, even as it reflects endemic assumptions about the kinds of facts that matter to Lowell as he makes and remakes himself in language. An unusually sensitive reader of Lowell, Chiasson nonetheless takes it for granted that "Lowell's facts are not scientific but historical."[11]

In fact, embedded in the history of Lowell's mature poetics is a history of attempts to make sense of his riven emotional life as a function of biological process; as his faith in spiritual and libidinal schemes of psychic determination waned, the notion of a curable, chemical self presented Lowell with a new dogma—a source of zealous hope, an object of necessary skepticism, and a structure of thought demanding a new form. In the years following his earliest breakdowns, Lowell's physiological descriptions of mental life implicitly question the epistemological premises of confession as an aesthetic mode that privileges introspection and expression as reliable sources of knowledge. It is only in the polarizing experiments *Notebook 1967–1968* (1969) and *Notebook* (1970), however, that Lowell invents an experimental form shaped by the extreme biological determinism he entertained upon discovering, in a crucial turning point in his life and art, an apparent cure for his ruptured selfhood in a pill—in the lithium carbonate that seemed to justify, while its success lasted, a fundamentally materialist interpretation of the self as a chemical effect. The disarticulation and reconstitution of *Notebook* in the subsequent volumes *History* (1973) and *For Lizzie and Harriet* (1973) reflect Lowell's withdrawal from the materialist extremity of that initial experiment, a withdrawal that anticipates his disillusioned reinstatement of dualist logic in *The Dolphin* and his "heartbreaking" poetics of philosophical exhaustion in his final volume, *Day by Day*.

Though it would be in the late 1960s that Lowell would devise a form that depicts the chaos of inner life as an expression of chemical accident, the volumes that precede *Notebook* chart the descent of these mental phenomena—emotion, temperament, consciousness itself—ever deeper into the body. Suffused with the homespun materialism Lowell extrapolated from the phenomenology of his "ill-spirit" and from the electroshock and early chemical treatments that supplemented his psychotherapy, many poems of the late 1950s and 1960s trace psychic pain to its perceived sources and symptoms in the body. Written when his manic episodes and hospitalizations had become yearly occurrences, *For the Union Dead* (1964) contains many poems depicting the surreal terrors of his mania and the exhaustion of recovery; interspersed among these are portraits of loved ones and historical figures in whom Lowell saw his own distinctly physical experience of mental illness reflected.[12] Other poems ask unreservedly what the insentient blood and bone of the poet have to do with the sources and surfaces of poetry itself. Lowell's long habit of using the problem of mind to frame the puzzling relationship between life and art is evident in these poems that confront the mysteries of (monstrous) behavior by contemplating the physical operations of a wayward brain. In "The Neo-Classical Urn," for example—a diptych self-portrait of the poet in childhood and middle age—Lowell envisions verse not as an inspirited vehicle of the immaterial soul but as a hollow counterpart to the inanimate parts that somehow anchor human wholes.

"The Neo-Classical Urn" associates an inhuman act Lowell committed as a child with the nonhuman machinery that inexplicably generates "cerebration" and "free will," and with the mercenary tendency of writing itself to transform experience into artistic "material." The poem's central vignette—Lowell's memory of charging from an ornamental garden into a swampy wilderness, stopping to "snatch / the painted turtles on dead logs"—is bracketed by a pair of images of the poet's skull; "The Neo-Classical Urn" begins with a surreal fusion of Lowell's remembering head with the object of his memory ("a turtle shell") and an image of memory itself as a roil of electrical charges and fermenting juices—a hydraulic mechanism powered by decay:

> I rub my head and find a turtle shell
> stuck on a pole,
> each hair electrical
> with charges, and the juice alive
> with ferment. Bubbles drive
> the motor, always purposeful . . .
> Poor head!
> How its skinny shell once hummed,

as I sprinted down the colonnade
of bleaching pines, cylindrical
clipped trunks without a twig between them. Rest!
I could not rest. At full run on the curve,
I left the cast stone statue of a nymph,
her soaring armpits and her one bare breast,
gray from the rain and graying in the shade,
as on, on, in sun, the pathway now a dyke,
I swerved between two water bogs,
two seines of moss, and stopped to snatch
the painted turtles on dead logs.
In that season of joy,
my turtle catch
was thirty-three,
dropped splashing in our garden urn,
like money in the bank,
the plop and splash
of turtle on turtle,
fed raw gobs of hash . . . [13]

The image of the poet's "poor head" as both a fermenting mire and a "motor," a "purposeful" machine and a painfully electrified lump "stuck on a pole," contrasts with the benignly but ominously "humming" head of the rapturous child "at full run on the curve." Looking back upon the boy as he hurtles from the domesticated garden through the liminally artificial "colonnade / of bleaching pines" and into the wild, eroticized swamp, the aging poet distinguishes the inert, sepulchral realm of art (the bare-breasted nymph is "gray from the rain and graying in the shade") from the teeming realm of nature; the impervious child, however, tramples heedlessly through both, eager to amass and preserve his "turtle catch."

Much as Lowell imagines the action of the mind emerging from a flow of electrical charges and fluids, in the mossy bog the child finds life perched vulnerably upon lifelessness; the "painted turtles on dead logs" recall the poet's "turtle shell / stuck on a pole." While the brutal "plop and splash" of the animals dropping "like money in the bank" anticipates the child's catastrophic confusion of animate and inanimate forms of being, in the second part of the poem the speaker acknowledges and repeats this confusion, pitting his hesitation to impute sentience to the turtles against his withering remorse for martyring (or so the number suggests) "thirty-three" of them. Lowell implicates the objet d'art—the prison of the urn, the vessel of the poem—in perpetuating this confusion, in aestheticizing and commemorating life to death; the boy, we learn, cashed in his objectified "catch," exchanging pity for artistic purchase as he "strummed / their elegy":

> Oh neo-classical white urn, Oh nymph,
> Oh lute! The boy was pitiless who strummed
> their elegy,
> for as the month wore on,
> the turtles rose,
> and popped up dead on the stale scummed
> surface—limp wrinkled heads and legs withdrawn
> in pain. What pain? A turtle's nothing. No
> grace, no cerebration, less free will
> than the mosquito I must kill—
> nothings! Turtles! I rub my skull,
> that turtle shell,
> and breathe their dying smell,
> still watch their crippled last survivors pass,
> and hobble humpbacked through the grizzled grass. (*CP* 358–359)

Echoing the "scummed / surface" of the urn in the "strummed" poem clanging with intensifying chimes, Lowell acknowledges his repetition of the "pitiless" boy's artistic opportunism in the verbal performance of "The Neo-Classical Urn" itself. The final lines of the adult poet's elegy, however, are less concerned with artistic complicity than with the nature of mind itself. Rubbing his "skull, / that turtle shell," Lowell both scents the mortal "ferment" of his own head in the rotting turtles' "dying smell" and puzzles over the question of how the inner lives of the mosquito, the turtle, and the human meaningfully differ. Inferring phenomenological differences from physiological ones, Lowell distances himself from the animals, first by feebly reasoning away their pain and then by disclaiming, in a rising scale, their capacities for "grace," "cerebration," and "free will." Nevertheless, by the end of the poem the poet and the turtles have become nearly indistinguishable; the proposition that "a turtle's nothing" has been eclipsed by the tragic parade of the recognizably human "crippled last survivors" and by the poet's recognition of his own "poor" head's pain in his fellow sufferers' "limp wrinkled heads." Even the pitiful hobbling of the final line ambiguously describes the "humpbacked" survivors and the lumbering poet who rubs his skull in remorseful sympathy and confusion. Despite his protestations to the contrary, the speaker of "The Neo-Classical Urn" suggests that there is nothing spiritually exceptional about his mental life: once formed, it is, like everything else, in the process of decay. Mosquito, turtle, and man alike prove to be kindred "gobs of hash" whose mortal form and frailty define their experiences of mind.

"Caligula," the refracted self-portrait that follows "The Neo-Classical Urn" in *For the Union Dead*, likewise attributes psychic pain to physical conditions as it describes the poet's demented namesake (Lowell's brutal adolescent tyranny over his school friends earned him the enduring nickname "Cal"). The poem, comprised of fifty-one lines, is a nearly perfect succession of rhyming couplets thrown into misalignment by a single tercet. That tercet, fused by the end-rhymes *pain / brain / pain*, isolates the despotic imbalance "Cal" and Caligula share; its embraced *rime riche* positions the agonies of the soul as proliferating emanations of the body. In the "mean, thin, agonized" face engraved on a rusted Roman coin, Lowell sees his likeness and his "lowest depths of possibility" reflected:

> What can be salvaged from your life? A pain
> That gently darkens over heart and brain,
> a fairy's touch, a cobweb's weight of pain,
> now makes me tremble at your right to live. (*CP* 360)

The position of the first line break initially posits "pain" as an answer to Lowell's desperate question, suggesting that suffering (and the art that issues from it) might be inherently redeeming. The line's swift enjambment summarily dismisses this possibility, however, for while Lowell sympathizes with Caligula's helpless subjection to the tyranny of the brain, he also recognizes in himself the tyrant's tendency not to be dignified by torment but to be disfigured by it—to be corrupted to the point of compromising his human value, his "right to live."

What might be salvaged from a tormented life and what salvation might redeem the frailty of human character were questions Lowell had been asking himself for some time when "The Neoclassical Urn" and "Caligula" appeared in the mid-1960s, his manic episodes and hospitalizations having become by then menacingly cyclical occurrences. In the early 1940s, years before his first breakdown and soon after his conversion to Catholicism, Lowell had read and recommended Rudolf Allers's *The Psychology of Character* (1931), a synthesis of Catholic and psychoanalytic conceptions of personality that aspired, in Allers's words, to "overcome Catholic indifference and hostility to modern applied psychology."[14] It aimed to do so by asserting, against increasingly medicalized notions of personality, that the self is fundamentally insubstantial and that character, irreducible to physical and environmental determinants, can be educated. For Allers, the "person himself, the possessor of character, the mainspring of all action and behavior," is a transcendental essence; it therefore, he insisted against the consensus of his time, *"cannot be affected by destructive cerebral lesions"* (19; Allers's italics).[15] Allers's already anachronistic vision of the disembodied psyche is consistent with the ambiguously Calvinist and Catholic spirituality of *Lord Weary's Castle* (1946), in which Lowell's uses of "soul" and "spirit" are dissociated from the physical and appear not to be ontologically conflicted. By 1949, however, Lowell's firsthand experience of psychic disunity had brought the notion of a transcendental "mainspring of all action and behavior" precipitously into question, forcing an urgent reckoning with the contingency of the self upon conditions of physical being. In a letter of that year, Lowell implies a meaningful correlation between the "narcotic" experience of his first manic break and the crisis of faith that would lead to a permanent breach with the Catholic Church:

> I am still far from having digested it all, but I realize that my experiences were like those that might have resulted from a narcotic—terrific lifts, insights, pourings in of new energy, but no work on my part, only more and more self-indulgence, lack of objectivity; and so, into literal madness. . . . Coming-to, after the shock treatments, was proportionately dismal.
>
> I'm not in the Church now—nor do I know, except gropingly, what I believe. (*L* 144)

It is evident even from Lowell's most mundane descriptions of his psychotic experiences that the notably physical aspects of his madness and the unevenly successful somatic treatments used to stabilize his emotions and behavior during this period had begun to dislocate his conceptions of self and spirit. Of the antipsychotic drug Sparine, Lowell wrote to Elizabeth Bishop that "one's thoughts are not directly changed and healed, but the terrible, over-riding restlessness of one's system is halted so that the mind can again see life as it is" (*L* 282); describing the painful effects of Thorazine, another antipsychotic medication, Lowell imaginatively fuses the drug's biological operations and its spiritual effects: "Waking, I suspected that my whole soul and its thousands of spiritual fibers, immaterial ganglia, apprehensive antennae, psychic radar, and so on, had been bruised by a rubber hose."[16]

That the "system" of the self might be restless, that thoughts might be directly or indirectly "changed and healed," that neuronal "ganglia" might have "immaterial" aspects, were all implicit premises of Lowell's medical treatments that ran counter to the premises of his psychotherapeutic ones.[17] The surfaces of *Life Studies* ripple with these philosophical countercurrents. Like so many of the lasting poems from that volume, the libidinal family drama of "My Father's Bedroom," the freighted returns to childhood in "91 Revere Street," and the parricidal family portrait of "Commander Lowell" all situate the sources of Lowell's emotional turbulence in the depths of private, personal history. But the world of *Life Studies* is also a world where the "lights of science" (*CP* 113) have irradiated Christian myth, where libidinal aggression is "tamed by Miltown" (*CP* 189), and where the private and public crises of "the tranquillized *Fifties*" (*CP* 187; Lowell's italics) are muted by drugs. Having climbed "the hill's skull" to watch for young lovers, the demented speaker of "Skunk Hour" famously proclaims, "I feel my ill-spirit sob in each blood cell"; he not only identifies his madness with the exertions of nature upon his mental life but also *feels* his mental affliction as a state of the body.[18]

As everyone has noticed, *Life Studies* pits the "external" determinations of public history against the autonomous, expressive force of private consciousness. But an analogous friction between opposing etiologies of mental suffering—between physiology and psychology, somatic surface and experiential depth—also jeopardizes the unity and autonomy of the subject. Binding the lyric self in a second matrix of determination that issues from the opposite (biological rather than historical) end of the materialist continuum, *Life Studies* launches assaults on the sovereignty of the creative mind from outside and inside; by highlighting these impersonal extremes of circumstance, Lowell undermines the psychoanalytic (and "confessional") premise that through introspection and expression consciousness can heal itself from within.[19]

"Memories of West Street and Lepke," for example, compares networks of socioeconomic and political contingency to the friable networks of the nervous system, stressing the embeddedness of consciousness in both.[20] The poem begins where the enervated song of recovery "Home after Three Months Away" leaves off. In the earlier poem Lowell, just released from the hospital, frets over his electroshocked memory as he reunites with his infant daughter: "Our noses rub, / each of us pats a stringy lock of hair— / they tell me nothing's gone" (*CP* 185). Though he is free from the hospital, Lowell's exhaustion has confined him afresh in his mortality—stretching below his window is a "coffin's length of soil," where a row of felled tulips reminds him of himself: "Cured," he writes, "I am frizzled, stale and small." In "Memories of West Street and Lepke," Lowell remains ineffectually confined in his home, but here he is also confined in the political and cultural conformity of postwar Boston and in a dispassionate emotional equilibrium unrecognizably remote from his earlier "manic" states—the states of the "ill" self, confined in a hospital just months before, and of the spiritually and politically impassioned self, who was a "fire-breathing Catholic C.O.," righteously raving in his "seedtime." Lowell's allusion to the religious mania of his young adulthood marks a starting point in the poem's descent from metaphysical to materialist epistemologies—a descent evident in the shifting reflections Lowell discovers, with the clarity of hindsight, in his memories of the West Street jail. Receiving a spiritual education from an unnamed Jehovah's Witness, "yammer[ing] metaphysics with Abramowitz," the young Lowell appears to the Lowell of the present to have been "out of things"—disconnected, in the colloquial sense, from his situation and surroundings, but also impervious to the pressure of physical reality, occupying a realm of ideals. It is therefore in the figure of Lepke—carnal, "sheepishly" animal, faced with imminent death—that the middle-aged, mentally infirm speaker of the poem truly recognizes himself in the present; like the recovering poet sequestered in indolent privilege on Marlborough Street, the once violently potent Lepke "dawdl[es] off to his little segregated cell full / of things forbidden the common man." The men's many likenesses culminate in the final image of the poem, which depicts a material and phenomenological resemblance between their minds; drawing on the experience, vocabulary, and physiological aspects of his own electroshock therapy—a reflection and rehearsal of Lepke's impending electrocution by the state—Lowell pictures the inside of Lepke's "lobotomized" head:

> Flabby, bald, lobotomized,
> he drifted in a sheepish calm,
> where no agonizing reappraisal
> jarred his concentration on the electric chair—
> hanging like an oasis in his air
> of lost connections. . . . (*CP* 188; Lowell's ellipses)

The prospect of death itself, embodied in the electric chair that looms in Lepke's mind, offers a respite from the "agonizing reappraisal" Lowell identifies with the compulsions and frustrations of intellectual synthesis; the certain, unassimilable fact of death emerges as an "oasis" within the desolation of mental life. Typical of this poem in which all egos echo alter egos, all parts counterparts, Lowell's reification of mental disorder in the disintegrated network of lost neuronal connections mirrors the social disorder he evokes in the sinewy, "sooty clothesline entanglements" strewn between the tenements that surround the West Street jail. The "lost connections" of the disintegrated brain also model the poem's method of making meaning through the use of such reflections—its practice of drawing suggestive resemblances that associate objects and circumstances without ever definitively or rationally "connecting" them. Revealing itself to be an "air" (a song, a lyric) of lost connections, "Memories of West Street and Lepke" dissolves into oblivion just as it discloses this principle of organization; by modeling his poem's internal structure on the damaged physiological circuitry that makes imperfect sense of the given, Lowell places consciousness and its reflection, the poem itself, *in things* rather than out of them—in a line of descent from physical, rather than mystical, first causes.

An earlier draft of "Memories of West Street and Lepke" concludes with a decisive couplet rather than ellipses, and pictures Lepke from the outside rather than within: "His cell door hung open like a loose grin. / Usually, nobody bothered to lock him in."[21] While the published ending emphasizes the experience of mental disintegration, in form and content the draft ending emphasizes the forces that confine the self even as they maintain the illusion of freedom—the "loose grin" of the open cell door reminds us that the prison of Lepke's "flabby, bald, lobotomized" body renders his cell altogether redundant. Such uses of somatic language to frame the concept of human freedom only intensify in Lowell's poetry after *Life Studies* (1959), as the gentle contraction of the volume's free verse into the more intricately patterned forms of *For the Union Dead* (1964) finally clenches into what Vereen Bell has called "retrograde classical formality" in *Near the Ocean* (1967).[22] The opening stanzas of *Near the Ocean* voice Lowell's restless searching in the mid-1960s for a new style that could release him from his confining oscillation between the license of confession and the limits of classicism ("O to break loose" is the book's opening phrase); the memorable early stanzas of "Waking Early Sunday Morning" reach extraordinary heights of lyricism in evoking the extremes of emotional and intellectual perspective that confounded Lowell as his manic episodes escalated in frequency to the point of agonizing, annual inevitability over the course of the early 1960s. Lowell's fantasy of "breaking loose" thus conflates doxological exhaustion with stylistic fatigue, and implies an expressive impasse consistent with *Near the Ocean*'s craning glances back to Horace and Juvenal and Dante for fresh draughts of sound and sentiment. Indeed, the specters of the Holy Ghost and of the "stiff" quatrains "shoveled" like earth from a grave haunt the poem's most memorable image of expressive freedom: Lowell's fantasy of himself "elated as the President" on Sunday morning, "swimming nude, unbuttoned, sick / of his ghost-written rhetoric!" (*CP* 385).

Three converging forms of longing, then, distinguish Lowell's frame of mind at the time "Waking Early Sunday Morning" first appeared in print in 1965: longing for relief from the strain of cyclical insanity, longing for some positive evidence of the ontology of the self, and longing for a poetic language not superstitiously "ghost-written" but credible and vitally embodied. Beginning in the poems of *Life Studies,* the characteristics of "physical injury" Lowell recognized in his emotional breakdowns and the medical treatments prescribed to treat his "ill- spirit" had conspired to produce a vivid impression of the tranquilized, electroshocked, lobotomized "immaterial ganglia" of the soul; this somatic conception of consciousness became robust enough in Lowell's poems of the period to counter the psychoanalytic paradigm of metaphysical damage and repair, and to disrupt any straightforwardly directional, top-down flow of influence from spiritual causes to physiological effects. Unlike the abstract, infinitely pliable Freudian psyche, the unyielding influence of the body upon the expression of emotion and selfhood offered Lowell fresh metaphors for describing the labors and sorrows of "nosing up to the impossible" (*CP* 383). And by depicting the imminent exertions of physical conditions upon the realm of feeling, Lowell balanced the fundamentally introspective epistemology of confession with an empirical epistemology alert to the confinements of biological circumstance. Accelerating in flight from Christian dogma and doctrinal psychoanalysis, however, Lowell found no clear path opening before him; the resistance of his breakdowns to an array of somatic treatments only seemed to confirm the explanatory limits of physiological accounts of mental life. The poet had thus found himself hastening toward a junction of stylistic and philosophical dead ends when he undertook a new course of treatment early in 1967, writing to Elizabeth Bishop that there "seems to be the real hope that my manic seizures can be handled by a new drug, Lithium, and that all my giddy reelings come from a kind of periodic salt deficiency in some lower part of the brain" (*L* 483).[23] A few months later he would begin, after a year and a half "drained of anything to write" (*L* 486), the torrential experimental sequence of poems he believed might be his most lasting contribution to American poetry.

Robert Giroux, Lowell's friend of thirty-six years, recalls that "of all our conversations, I remember most vividly Cal's words about the new drug, lithium carbonate, which had such good results and gave him reason to believe he was cured: 'It's terrible . . . to think,' [said Lowell], 'that all I've suffered, and all the suffering I've caused, might have arisen from the lack of a little salt in my brain.'"[24] At the time the drug was prescribed to him, its use for the treatment of mania was still experimental (lithium would not be approved by the FDA until 1970), and Lowell was only cautiously optimistic, after the failure of so many medical treatments, about the promise of a chemical cure. Once the drug had averted a major annual breakdown that winter, however, he began to offer his friends the new explanation of a chemical imbalance in terms that echoed his initial observation, nearly twenty years earlier, that his breakdowns and recoveries resembled a "broken leg or jaundice." "All the psychiatry and therapy I've had," he wrote to Bishop, "almost 19 years, was as irrelevant as it would have been for a broken leg. Well, some of it was interesting, tho most was jargon" (*L* 494).[25]

Lowell's readiness to accept a chemical explanation for his "ill-spirit" reflects the excitement that psychoactive drugs had come to inspire among researchers and psychiatrists in the late 1960s, as well as Lowell's own long-standing intuition that the emotional forces that governed his character moved in an independent, natural rhythm that preceded and transcended conscious will.[26] Lithium salts offered an elegantly minimal, and even chemically simple, solution for what had seemed to be an impossible spiritual and psychological quandary. Lowell saw in the success of lithium experiential proof of a chain of cause and effect tying the most apparently disembodied aspects of conscious life to nature. While he was elated, in one sense, to be free of his mania ("even my well life is much changed," he explained, "as tho I'd once been in danger of falling with every step I took" [*L* 494]), he inferred from the happy occasion of a viable treatment the disturbing conclusion that tacit, natural determinations of character were more extensive and arbitrary than he had ever imagined. Not only did Lowell find it terrible to think, as Giroux recalls, that the suffering he had caused might have hinged on a remediable circumstance, he also found it terrible to think that the texture of inner life could be so contingent on meaningless accident, that character could be so reducible to senseless arrangements of matter, that fate was real. The grace of a medical intervention that could alter his own chemical destiny was an exception that only proved the rule—and its annunciation coincided, like his earlier philosophical transition from Christian idealism to secular humanism, with a drastic transformation of poetic form.

As the drug's effects took hold, Lowell conceived and enthusiastically began to compose the verse that would be collected in *Notebook 1967–68.* Deliverance from his relentless cycles of madness freed the poet, whose familial blood embedded him so visibly in the course of his nation's public history, to reenter the flow of historical time—to participate in the political activism that his depression and exhaustion had foreclosed. The raving, "fire-breathing" mania of his days as a conscientious objector was gone, and in its stead there emerged the humility and confusion of a rational man witnessing the irrational emotional extremes of a politically chaotic public sphere. In "The March," Lowell balks at "the remorseless, ampli-fied harangues for peace" that spur on his fellow antiwar protesters; their affective extremity, eclipsing their righteous logic, distorts and falsifies the scene "Under the too white marmoreal Lincoln Memorial, / the too tall marmoreal Washington Obelisk."[27] *Notebook 1967–68* traces the intersections of day-to-day interiority with the events that commandeered shared, public consciousness in that decisive year: the presidential cam-paigns, the Vietnam War, the Third Arab-Israeli War, the execution of Che Guevara and assassinations of Martin Luther King and Robert Kennedy, race riots in Newark, and the French students' and workers' uprisings. In the tradition of Wordsworth and Milton, Lowell adopts a minute form to explore the prodigious historical transformations he wit-nessed unfolding around him: "I fear I have failed to avoid the themes and gigantism of the sonnet" (*N* 160), he apologizes in his epilogue to the book's first edition.

And yet while *Notebook 1967–68* appears to be a chronicle of blank-verse sonnets, Lowell himself, influenced by John Berryman's book-length sequence of isomorphic *Dream Songs,* imagined the volume as "a long poem . . . in 14 line sections" (*L* 501). Exemplifying a modular structure that would render the poem easily expandable and retractable, *Notebook 1967–68* was built and published to exhibit its own extraordi-nary mutability. Lowell published *Notebook 1967–68* twice in 1969, issuing an expanded reprint of the first edition in the same year; he then pub-lished a much enlarged version, titled *Notebook,* in 1970 before disman-tling the book a final time, separating out the sections by theme and dividing them into *History* (1973) and *For Lizzie and Harriet* (1973). Publishing and republishing the volume in successive phases of revision over five years, the unconventional publication process Lowell adopts in *Notebook*—an experiment unlike any other in his career—complements his stylistic ambition not to present "stills as in *Life Studies*" but rather "the instant, sometimes changing to the lost."[28] In the 1970 edition of *Notebook,* Lowell explains that "more than ninety new poems have been added. These have not been placed as a single section or epilogue. They were scattered where they caught, intended to fulflesh my poem, not sprawl into chronicle."[29] Resisting the artifactual, historical order of the chronicle in favor of an evolving, diaristic, improvised record of life, Lowell stipulates that the poem swallows and digests experience. His zealous descriptions of the first iterations of *Notebook* nearly always make reference to its distinct formal shape—to his conception of the work not as a sonnet sequence but as a single textual body made up, in turn, of subsidiary, cellular wholes. Writing in May 1968, Lowell's optimism about his medical treatment and his enthusiasm for his experimental poem's freshness of form suffuse his recollection of the year's major events:

> A lot has happened to me this year. These pills for my manic seizures seem to have made a cure, tho I will take them to my dying. This has changed my life, not only no attacks, no hospitals, but even, and perhaps most, health itself is different, freer and out of the shadow. The other is a long poem, Notebook of a Year, in 14 line sections, now about 1500 lines and close to done. I follow the seasons loosely, but the real structure is personal happenings, moods, brushes with the great events etc. Accident gave it such a form as it has, yet a true one I hope, and I hope too it's the best thing I've done, one to end on if nature should wish. (*L* 501–502)

The letter hints at the close relationship between nature and chance in Lowell's notebook project, a relationship he acknowledges explicitly in his "Afterthought" to *Notebook 1967–68:* "Accident threw up subjects," he writes, "and the plot swallowed them—famished for human chances" (*N* 159). Just as the rhythm of the seasons obscures a "real structure" governed by accidental "happenings, moods," and unexpected personal "brushes" with public history, nature's appearances of design, Lowell suggests, obscure a deeper disorder. He identifies the "truth" of the poem's form with its integration of accident into its very substance, his text a tissue of internal and external "happenings" spatialized as form.

If the rhizomatic structure of *Notebook* subliminally replicates the assemblage of minute, equivalent parts that underpin somatic wholes, the book's most innovative stylistic quality—its incorporation of Lowell's process of revision into the work itself—contributes to the "living" dynamism of the book as well. Having published *Notebook 1967–68* in a putatively spontaneous form (as the title suggests), Lowell added many poems to the 1970 edition, subtracted a few, and occasionally altered but seemed not to aspire to perfect those he had included in the earlier edition. In its style and publication practice, then, *Notebook* not only prioritizes a poetics of ongoing process over the inert, monumental stasis of the well-wrought poem, but also incorporates the instability and mutability—the simultaneous processes of growth and decay—that characterize a living being. That he considered the poem "the best thing [he'd] done" suggests his imaginative attachment not only to its organic architecture and publication process, but also to the jagged, chatty, unprocessed verbal texture that so complemented it; by publishing the "14 line sections" in provisional, imperfect, and ever-changing forms, Lowell repeats his poem's accidental, orderless design in its "raw" surfaces of language, a style "less concerned with line by line excellence," as Ian Hamilton puts it, than with capturing the immediacy of a provisional, embodied present.[30]

Lowell emulates a living system in the form and publication style of *Notebook*, but the poem also expresses his obsession with the defamiliarizing effect of viewing oneself as biological matter: "You could say you stood in the cold light of science," he writes in one poem, "seeing as you are seen, espoused to fact" (*CP* 470). Imagining oneself as an assemblage of inanimate parts, he realizes, approximates imagining oneself as a dead body. "Reading Myself" performs precisely this self-estrangement; in the poem, Lowell compares *Notebook* to a honeycomb and himself to a bee "adding circle to circle, cell to cell," praying

> that the perishable work live long
> enough for the sweet-tooth bear to desecrate—
> this open book . . . my open coffin. (*N* 128)

Because it is a living work, *Notebook* is also perishable, presented to us alternately as a living and lifeless body, the self estranged from itself; as Lowell puts it in the book's final poem, "Obit": "I'm for and with myself in my otherness" (*N* 156). Vereen Bell, observing the role of what he calls "the pressure of history" in Lowell's work, writes that "in Lowell's poetry, as a rule, the inner life cannot displace the external, and the external in fact introjects so deeply that it infects the very language that might be used to displace it."[31] Bell has in mind "external" forces of national and autobiographical history, but in *Notebook,* the pressure of history is balanced by the equal and opposite pressure of nature itself, the pressure of the "external" emanating from within.

Originally titled "Do You Believe in God?," "Harriet," the first sonnet-like segment of *Notebook,* is a philosophical poem that looks to the ground of material being in the halfhearted hope of finding a cosmological "key." The poem forswears the designs of history and myth and acknowledges the volume's allegiance to a "true" form consistent with Lowell's interpretation of inner life itself as an accident of nature. "Harriet" begins with Lowell's daughter counting her advancing age in half birthdays and striving to comprehend the concept of divinity by approximation to things known or at least imagined: an exotic sea slug, a fabled queen. The rational instruments of counting and naming, however, prove to be crude, even violent, tools for parsing reality—instruments that disfigure the given in an attempt to "square" it. If Harriet's precocious mind is just such a powerful, unwieldy instrument (a "chainsaw bit," in Lowell's metaphor), his own obsessive philosophical mind is its more tragic, grown-up counterpart; "slic[ing] through fog" that only closes behind him, he is doomed to an endless, futile search:

> Half a year, then a year and a half, then
> ten and a half—the pathos of a child's fractions, turn-
> ing up each summer. God is a seaslug, God a queen
> with forty servants, God . . . she gave up—things whirl
> in the chainsaw bit of whatever squares
> the universe by name and number. For
> the hundredth time, I slice through fog, and round
> the village with my headlights on the ground,
> as if I were the first philosopher,

as if I were trying to pick up a car
key . . . It can't be here, and so it must be there
behind the next crook in the road or growth
of fog—there blinded by our feeble beams,
a face, clock-white, still friendly to the earth. (*N* 3)

The tormented driver circling the village recalls the speaker of "Skunk Hour" stalking lovers in his Tudor Ford, but the torment "Harriet" describes is epistemological rather than pathological or satanic. While the earlier speaker proclaimed "My mind's not right" and groaned "I myself am hell," here the speaker is lucid but hopelessly fogged in, not blind but blinded; obscurity and absence are conditions not of perspective but of fact. In a pathos of shrinking fractions, divinity diminishes to the point of oblivion in "Harriet"; the poem begins with the vanishing trail of the child's "declining conceptions of God" (*N* 159), in Lowell's paraphrase, and ends with a benevolent countenance that proves to be not divine but vulnerably animal, a "blinded" comrade embedded, "clock-white," in time.

Like "Beyond the Alps," another counterpart to "Harriet," this inaugural segment of *Notebook* announces a stylistic reorientation that coincides with a philosophical one. If "Beyond the Alps," in which a "mountain-climbing train . . . come[s] to earth," announces the transition of *Life Studies* from a vertical, theological frame of reference to a horizontal, human one—from the spiritual history of man to personal and psychological history—"Harriet" marks yet another increment of descent. By comparing himself to "the first philosopher," Lowell suggests that his search for coherence is a solitary one, the groping pursuit each soul must undertake from scratch. He also alludes, however, to the pre-Socratic philosopher Thales, whom Aristotle identified as the founder of natural philosophy, who dreamed up the scientific method, and who rejected, in a crucial turning point in the history of Western thought, mythological explanations of natural phenomena.[32] In draft versions of the poem and in the revised version collected in *For Lizzie and Harriet,* Lowell identifies Thales explicitly, citing his theory that water is the most basic unit of substance that unifies everything. Lowell alludes not only to Thales's monism but also to the story of his death, in which the natural philoso-

pher's absorbed concentration on the night sky—the physical universe—
leads to his demise.[33] In the republished version of "Harriet," the speaker
describes driving, "headlights on the ground, / like the first philosopher
Thales who thought all things water, / and fell in a well" (*CP* 607). The
subtextual question "Do You Believe in God?" thus finds a subtextual
answer in Lowell's sympathy with Thales, who rejected supernatural explanations in favor of natural ones—who, when he defined reality, bound
it to an element and not a god.

   In another intertextual clue to *Notebook*'s philosophical premises,
"Harriet" echoes lines that appear in Lowell's adaptation of *Prometheus
Bound,* composed only a few months earlier, in which he casts himself in
the role of the archetypal ur-scientist at odds with divinity in his pursuit
of truth.[34] Fettered by "the laws of Nature," as Lowell puts it in a note appended to the play, Prometheus is a figure "justly fighting against necessity, or . . . *un*justly fighting, because he is fighting necessity, what is."[35]
Though bound by *physis,* Prometheus vows to persist in his search for the
elusive "key" that reappears, or once again fails to appear, in "Harriet":

> Around some bend, under some moving stone, behind some thought,
> if it were ever the right thought, I will find my key. No, not just
> another of Nature's million petty clues, but a key, *my* key, *the* key, the
> one that must be there, because it can't be there—a face still friendly
> to chaos.

That Lowell exchanged "chaos" for "earth" in the final line of "Harriet"
is consistent with this picture of nature as a puzzle without a key (in a
fitting paradox, it "must be there, because it can't be there"), a puzzle that
will lend its shape to the structure of the volume as a whole. The wild,
wanton form of *Notebook* conforms to a prescription Lowell also utters in
Prometheus's voice: "I should have been more loyal to the idiocy of things,
or bolder, or more careless."[36]

   With the ominous images he conjures in "Harriet"—of a blinded animal positioned where a divine countenance might have revealed itself, of a
natural philosopher tumbling down a well, of "feeble beams" illuminating
only the ground before him—Lowell announces the materialist perspective from which he will navigate experience in his living poem

even as he acknowledges its dangers. In *Notebook,* Lowell's physical treatment of his sickness of the soul inspires gnomic, philosophical optimism—"In sickness," he writes, "the mind and body make a marriage" (*N* 29)—but just as often his wonder is tempered by despair as he lowers his gaze earthward, discerning in arbitrary natural processes a meaningless point of origin for his suffering.[37] In "High Blood," Lowell watches as his blood, tested monthly to monitor its lithium level, is drawn into "crystal pipes"—vials whose shape, color, and chemically volatile contents suggest to him a pack of firecrackers. Though his blood has been treated (and tempered—"it's lukewarm"), it remains irremediable, "lousy stuff." The diction is offhand and the circumstance is mundane, but the source of the poem is a revelation of the highest order—that this inanimate substance has governed his view of himself and of the universe all along:

> I watch my blood pumped into crystal pipes,
> red sticks like lady crackers for a child—
> nine-tenths of me, and yet it's lousy stuff.
> Touched, it stains, slips, drips, sticks; and it's lukewarm.
> All else—the brains, the bones, the stones, the soul—
> Is peripheral flotsam on this live flow.
> On my great days of sickness, I was God;
> And now I might be. I catpad on my blood,
> and the universe moves beneath me when I move. (*N* 134)

As the blood assumes possession—"nine-tenths" of the law—over the disputed property of the self, Lowell imagines himself to be a "peripheral" epiphenomenon of the diseased substance: "All else—the brains, the bones, the stones, the soul— / Is peripheral flotsam on this live flow." Inverting the hierarchy of fathomless spirit and corporeal shallows, here the soul is just another surface that shifts upon the depths of the blood, a surface with the valueless, wrecked buoyancy of inert debris. Lowell's madness had made him feel, during his violent attacks of megalomania, like he was God, but now his blood discloses the related, rational "truth" that his own movements are unified with the live flow of the universe, on a continuum of material being that effaces distinctions between God, man, animal, and finally machine. Once again rendering himself in animal form, Lowell "catpad[s]" on his blood; the image ingeniously anticipates a metaphor that concludes the poem, in which the music of the self is depicted as an animal sound that emerges from a (malfunctioning) mechanical device—as the static of a record "purring" on a turntable "as if the sapphire in the cat were stuck" (*N* 134). Indeed, by writing in rhymelessly "blank" verse, by arranging undifferentiated, isometric stanzas in a shifting field, and by assuming a stabilized, sometimes droning voice that avoids transcendental flights of lyricism, Lowell generates a flattened, ambient kind of verbal noise in *Notebook*—a style equivalent to the acoustic static of a monist, "monotonous sublime" (*CP* 386).

Like "High Blood," "Sound Mind, Sound Body" despairs at the identity between soul and substance that Lowell's treatment seemed to him to disclose. In the latter poem, however, Lowell is unusually explicit in contemplating how this revelation affects the texture of his verse. As Lowell celebrates his freedom "from twenty years of the annual mania," he wonders if he has exchanged a healthy body for a healthy mind and whether, under chemical treatment, he can claim to be altered in substance as he is in spirit:

> *Mens sana?* O at last; from twenty years
> of the annual mania, thirty of adolescence:
> this crown. And I am still *in corpore sano?*
> Some mornings now my studies wane by eleven,
> afternoons by three. The print, its brain,
> clouds in mid-chapter, just as I will go—
> two score and ten . . . less than common expectation?
> All the new years turned in for old? (*N* 130)

In the version of the poem revised for publication in *History,* the rhetorical question of the third line is rendered as a statement: "*mens sana in corpore insano*" (*CP* 597). Lowell thus answers his earlier draft's question by altering Juvenal's "*mens sana in corpore sano*" to assert that his body will always be insane—never cured, only treated.[38] By disclosing an unsound, aging body and a brain that would require chemical readjustment "until [his] dying," Lowell's sanity revealed to him mortality. Mirroring the strained unity of mind and body in "Sound Mind, Sound Body" is a similarly troubled continuity between the embodied mind and "print" itself. With a transferred epithet that associates the imperfection of his mortal brain with the nature of the texts he consumes and produces, Lowell's distracted, medicated mind finds a counterpart in the "brain" of the very text he reads, which "clouds in mid-chapter." Lowell expected to die, like his own father, in middle age, so to have recovered his sanity and identified the physical cause of his agonies just in time for his body to deteriorate and die seemed to him a tragic exchange of one kind of embodied torment for another, of illness for decay. The partially read text thus reminds the poet of his partially lived life, to be abandoned halfway through, in "mid-chapter."

In "Sound Mind, Sound Body," and in *Notebook* as a whole, Lowell attests to the awakening into time and mortality that being *"mens sana in corpore insano"* fostered in him, complicating and compounding the experience of physical decline that years of breakdowns, recoveries, violent physical treatments, and alcoholic self-medication had obviously accelerated. In his sequence "Mexico," Lowell introduces eros into this constellation of mortalizing forces, exploring the baffling experience of falling in love while in a medicated state of putative sanity. The result is Lowell's clearest articulation of the reciprocal philosophies of mind and poetic style he forges, however ephemerally, in *Notebook*. The sequence alludes to an affair that took place in the winter of 1967–1968, when Lowell spent ten days at Ivan Illich's Center for Intercultural Documentation in Cuernavaca, Mexico, and fell briefly but passionately in love with a young Irish woman named Mary Keelan, who worked there. Lowell's affairs with younger women frequently coincided with his manic phases, and in the aftermath of his breakdowns his infidelities often appeared to have been symptoms not only of the destructive, egotistical tempests of his "enthusiasm" but of his terrified hope, as the chaos of his mania took hold, for the curative potential of a fresh domestic start. The wounds these affairs inflicted on Elizabeth Hardwick, Lowell's second wife, were only rendered more harrowing by the painful ambiguities of will and accountability that his illness generated. In 1959, after Lowell's fifth breakdown, Hardwick had written to Allen Tate, "I do not know the answer to the moral problems posed by a deranged person, but the dreadful fact is that in purely personal terms this deranged person does a lot of harm."[39] Lowell's periods of mental health generally suspended these "moral problems," but in "Mexico," the correlation Lowell discerns between the ecstasy of his former "derangement" and the ecstasy of sexual passion animates quandaries of the will familiar from his bouts of insanity. In the poem, he frames the entire spectrum of passions and feelings associated with love to the coercions of the body, identifying normative and pathological ranges of emotion to exist on a continuum that runs on blood. From the correlation he draws between insanity and desire—a correlation grounded in the condition of *helplessness*—Lowell infers a (convenient) rationale for succumbing to his passion: "drawn on by . . . unlimited desire," he is "like a bull with a ring in its nose and a chain in the ring" (*N* 60). In "Mexico," Lowell contrasts his spiritual, moral, and emotional predicament to that of his young lover, stressing that unlike her, he is used to being buffeted by the arbitrary forces of biological reflex and by the historical and circumstantial "ways of the world" that disenthrall him from accountability: "I have lived without / sense so long the loss no longer hurts," he writes; "reflex and the ways of the world will float me free— / you, God help you, must will each breath you take" (*N* 58).

Within the sequence's overlaid contexts—of the poet's life-changing chemical treatment, of the central scenario of his intergenerational romance, and of Illich's monastery, populated by many varieties of searching, credulous disciples—the poems' erotic and emotional intimacies burgeon constantly into metaphysical significance. Lowell proclaims in the opening sentence of the sequence that "The difficulties, the impossibilities, / stand out"; the statement is at once a regretful summary assessment of the love relationship and a description of Lowell himself as a hopeless predicament, a once grand and potent force shriveled to a human scale. (As Ian Hamilton observes of *Notebook*, "there is every so often a flicker of nostalgia for the majestic lunacies of his pre-lithium winters.")[40] Carrying "dead laurel" on his back, he is withered physically and humbled by success—by the dubious alchemies of literary creation and fame that gild the "garbage" of a misspent life:

> The difficulties, the impossibilities,
> stand out: I, fifty, humbled with the years' gold garbage,
> dead laurel grizzling my back like spines of hay;
> you, some sweet, uncertain age, say twenty-seven,
> unballasted by honor or deception.

> What help then? Not the sun, the scarlet blossom,
> and the high fever of this seventh day,
> the wayfarer's predestined diarrhea, nausea,
> the multiple mosquito spots, round as pesos.
> Hope not in God here, nor the Aztec gods;
> we sun-people know the sun, the source of life,
> will die, unless we feed it human blood—
> we two are clocks, and only count in time;
> the hand's knife-edge is pressed against the future. (*N* 58)

The "high fever" of Lowell's desire emerges as part of a larger pattern of physical affliction that besets and mortifies him, from nausea to mosquito bites; this speaker, for whom diarrhea is "predestined" and spirituality is sustained by "human blood," describes his travelers' maladies with the notably sacrilegious vocabulary of materialist apostasy. Here, Lowell draws on the generic conventions of the carpe diem poem to remind his lover that we "only count in time" and ought, therefore, to make the most of it. The poem's original principle of energy demands a blood sacrifice—the couple's hedonism, their death-denying abandon—while the sacrificial knife of the clock's hand menaces them in a godless, spiritless terrain, where the sun is the only "source of life" and they are its acolytes ("sun-people").

It is consistent, then, that Lowell mocks the ideologues who occupy the intellectual commune and monastery at Cuernavaca, devoting themselves to systems of belief that appear to him, in light of his materialist revelation, to be disposable and naïve. The insatiable, "immovable nuns, out of habit, too fat to leave the dormitory," founder in their asceticism, attesting to the limits of purely spiritual nourishment by living on "cookies bought and brought from Boston." "The soul," Lowell sneers, "groans and laughs at its lack of stature" (*N* 62). He pictures the commune, in fact, as a haven for comically pitiful votaries of psychoanalytic and Marxist dogmas that have filled the vacuum of religion:

> lay-neurotics peeped out at you like deer,
> barbwired in spotless whitewashed cabins, named
> *Sigmund* and *Karl*. . . . They live the life of monks,
> One revelation healing the ravage of the other. (*N* 59)

The barbwired and whitewashed cabins suggest the sterility and institutional confinement of Lowell's hospital stays, and for all the facetiousness of the image, it is in the desperate, psychically fragile longing of the "lay-neurotics" for a new dispensation that he recognizes his own experience. (These alienated intellectuals are among the nonclergy in residence at the monastery, but they also appear to be a "laity" of amateur neurotics to Lowell, whose years of madness, he imagines, consecrated him.) At Cuernavaca, Lowell encounters a community whose forms of faith remind him of his own succession of tentative devotions leading up to the winter of 1967–1968—forms of faith that now appear to him ridiculously misguided. The teleological trajectory that he implies in "Mexico"—from Christian self-denial to psychoanalytic self-disclosure to scientific demystification of the self—squares with an account he would later offer in hindsight:

> When I was at Iowa—'50 or later in '52[—] I read 2/3 of Freud, like reading Tolstoy. In that sense (memory randomly renewed) *Life Studies* is full of him; a replacement to the Christian Church, more intimate but without boundaries or credo, or philosophy. I have never taken him as gospel, been psychoanalysed, suffered an emotional or intellectual transference in therapy—my own decisive trouble was, as with all manics, a *salt* deficiency. (*L* 632)

Imagining Freudian and chemical interpretations of mental illness as "replacements" for Christian ones—as occasions for reinterpreting the kinds of metaphysical premises that "fill" his poems—Lowell offers his reader an emotionally neutral description of what he characterizes in "Mexico" as the violent spiritual process of "one revelation healing the *ravage* of the other" (italics mine). In the sequence's extravagant surfeit of salt, a substance that laces the landscape and marks the continuity of his medicated body with everything he touches, Lowell implies that he had arrived, with the explanation of a "salt deficiency," at a final, "decisive" revelation. In terrain lush with "salt grasses," coursing with streams "where the water turns red, as if it were dyed," the lovers wander in an aura of replenished, predestined arrival:

> We've waited, I think, a lifetime for this walk,
> and the white powder beneath our feet slides out

> like the sterile white salt of purity; even
> your puffed lace blouse is salt. (*N* 60)

In the climactic poem of the sequence, Lowell compares the peaks of this eroticized, saline landscape to heights of passion—"altitudes" that resemble not only the "shivering, ache and burning" of bodily illness but also the extravagant flights of "measured cunning" with which poets are wont to project erotic feelings into the realm of the ideal. Lowell mistrusts these dubious ascents of physical passion and literary language alike ("Not an artist," Mary's simple language "go[es] beyond" his own [*N* 62]), but from their fraudulence, he stresses, we fall back into fresh recognitions of the real:

> This is not the greatest thing, though great; the hours
> of shivering, ache and burning, when we'd charged
> so far beyond our courage—altitudes,
> then the falling . . . falling back on honest speech:
> infirmity, a food the flesh must swallow,
> feeding our minds . . . the mind which is also flesh. (*N* 62; Lowell's
>   ellipses)

Heights of feeling and rhetoric are "great," but greater still are "honest speech" and the unity of mind and body that our descents—from the manias of illness and love—force us to acknowledge. The mind, Lowell now concludes, *is* flesh, and he links this matter-of-fact monism with the stylistic immediacy to which *Notebook* as a whole aspires, identifying the putative authenticity of physical first causes with the putative authenticity of improvised, conversational speech. As he "fulfleshed" his poem, Lowell tinkered restlessly with its existing parts while expanding the whole, but in the sequential iterations of *Notebook* he assiduously preserves the coarse, unpremeditated finish he associated with "honesty"—and that laid the book open to notoriously harsh criticism.

Describing Lowell's "logorrhea" during the era that produced *Notebook 1967–68, Notebook, For Lizzie and Harriet,* and *History,* Joseph Epstein writes, "Reading the poems produced by Lowell's new aesthetic of immediacy, one finds oneself freshly impressed by the paean of W. H. Auden to careful prosody: 'Blessed be all the metrical rules that forbid automatic responses, force us to have second thoughts, free us from the fetters of the Self.'"[41] Intended to deprecate *Notebook,* Epstein's invocation of Auden's tribute to closed form highlights precisely the iconoclastic ambitions of Lowell's experiment, particularly his commitment to materialist episte-mology over literary beauty—to exposing how the facts of blood, biography, and history shape life as we know it. *Notebook* credits the special power of verbal "automatic responses" to disclose historical and biological "fetters of the Self," fetters that seemed more significant to Lowell at the time than the licenses of imaginative self-creation. And by publishing the poem in suc-cessive stages of revision, by advertising his "second thoughts" rather than concealing them, he reimagines revision not as a teleological, artificial process of incremental perfection but as a concrete and ongoing pro-cess of "natural" cognitive mutation, grounded in cycles of growth and decay.

Critical distaste for the sequential iterations of *Notebook,* however, has to do not only with the "seedy grandiloquence" and willfully grotesque immediacy of Lowell's language ("I want words meat-hooked from the living steer," he writes [*N* 127]), but with the elusive logic of the poem's structure.[42] David Bromwich acknowledges that *Notebook* marks a radical stylistic departure that is "just as significant as [Lowell's] earlier shift in *Life Studies,*" but Bromwich stipulates a crucial difference: "*Notebook* is not likely to affect the mainstream of poetry, because the style it invents is bad." Deeper than his objection to the poem's "bad" style is Bromwich's frustration that its ordering principles seem to be at once grandiose and irksomely obscure: "Resorting to various coded privacies, *Notebook* lies partly submerged, like an iceberg, and . . . proceeds by a law of asso-ciation unknown and unknowable to the reader."[43] Bromwich reads Lowell's haphazardness as hermeticism, but he identifies precisely the effect Lowell sought to achieve by allowing forces beyond his intentional control (the cycles of the seasons, accidental personal and historical "happenings," unforeseeable political contingencies, and "the vagaries of thought" [*L* 492]) to govern his poem's structure. In *Notebook,* Lowell militates against idealist paradigms of reading that empower the author to submit the chaos of experience to intentional design, and declines to reassure us that any known or knowable force governs the poem's order, mood, or meaning.[44]

Free of transcendental delusions, stoically bereft of spiritual consolations, armed with a "meat-hook" for rupturing inherited language and dismantling the self into smaller, ostensibly truer, physical bits, the speaker of *Notebook* resembles the nihilist Lowell describes in one of the book's famous stanzas, the heroic skeptic who "has to live in the world as is, gazing the impossible summit to rubble."[45] The successive editions of *Notebook* represent Lowell's only attempt to invent a form in the shape of that churning rubble—the rubble of events from which we abstract "history" and the rubble of inorganic parts out of which we hallucinate "the impossible summit" of the self. The years during which Lowell produced his versions of *Notebook* would prove to be philosophically, aesthetically, and biographically anomalous, however. Never again, after 1970, would material contexts appear to him so patently determinative, mind and body so legibly unified, and the self so divested of mystery; never again would he use procedures of publication to expose the process of revision, or conceive of a book as an organic, mutating whole, or hold the reassurances of intentional design so insistently at bay; never again, after his madness resurfaced the summer of that year, would he cherish a credible vision of a normal life or exhibit headlong faith in the science of the mind to resolve the intractable enigma of his ill spirit.

In early 1972, Lowell began to undo the formal innovations of *Notebook,* dismantling its accidental structure with the resolve he had previously applied to maintaining its calculated disorder through successive revisions. Shunting *Notebook*'s stanzas addressed to family into *For Lizzie and Harriet* and arranging the remaining ones in chronological order from Genesis to the present in *History,* Lowell finally published the two volumes separately the following year.[46] In the prefatory note to *History,* his metaphors recast what had been living and chaotic (the "jungle" of his experiment) as something more dignified, ordered, and lifeless: "All the poems have been changed," he explains, "some heavily. I have plotted. My old title, Notebook, was more accurate than I wished, i.e., the composition was jumbled. I hope this jumble or jungle is cleared—that I have cut the waste marble from the figure" (*CP* 1074). As he distanced himself from the "jumble" of his process poem, using his final round of revisions to divert its unified flow of "rivers, linguini, / beercans, mussels, bloodstreams" (*CP* 600) into two shapelier, classical entities, he was also composing the poems he would collect as *The Dolphin*, a book haunted by proliferating forms of doubleness. The volume tracks the exhausted devastations of the breakdown that would so dramatically redirect the course of Lowell's life and art in his few remaining years. After arriving in England to begin a fellowship at Oxford, he exhibited signs of a rising attack and soon began the impetuous affair with Caroline Blackwood that would lead, after their son's birth, to Lowell's divorce from Elizabeth Hardwick and his permanent expatriation to England. Within a few months, he was confined, with a sense of ultimate doom, to a hospital in London—"My twentieth in twenty years" (*CP* 649), he would write. Though he tried to emulate his doctors' "unruffled trust in lithium," his own trust in the drug, or in any prophylactic chemical therapy that might function as a cure, was permanently shaken.[47]

"Pulled apart and thinning into mist" (*CP* 550), Lowell now found himself divided by the claims of two women, by prospective lives in America and England, and by the sundering of the "one flesh" he had assumed in marriage—"I have felt as if a governing part of my organism were gone" (*CP* 551), he wrote to Hardwick. He had also been severed yet again into well and sick selves marked by their phenomenological correlates: "reality" and "unreality."[48] Twos appear on every page of *The Dolphin*, it seems: in Hardwick's reproduced pleas for his return ("You left two houses and two thousand books, / a workbarn by the ocean, and two slaves / to kneel and wait upon you hand and foot" [*CP* 653]); in the symbolic landscape of the hospital ("I see two dirty white, punctured tennisshoes, / empty and planted on the one-man path" [*CP* 650]); in the despair of "No Messiah," where Lowell laments that "Even the license of my mind rebels, / and can find no lodging for my two lives" (*CP* 704); in "Sick," where "two elephants are hauling at my head" (*CP* 698). Anything but sharp or Cartesian, however, the perplexed dualisms of *The Dolphin* collapse into each other, confusing rather than ordering Lowell's experience. In the agonized poem "Double-Vision," chemical sedation seems to sunder reality itself, troubling the distinction between things and people in a hospital room filled with "double-shadows":

> I tie a second necktie over the first;
> no one is always waiting at the door,

> and fills the window . . . sometimes a Burmese cat,
> or maybe my Daughter on the shell of my glasses.
> I turn and see persons, my pajama top
> loose-knotted on the long thin neck of a chair—
> *make yourself at home.* The cat walks out—
> or does it? The room has filled with double-shadows,
> sedation doubles everything I see. . . .
> You can't be here, and yet we try to talk;
> somebody else is farcing in your face,
> we haggle at cross-purposes an hour.
> While we are talking, I am asking you,
> "Where is Caroline?" And you *are* Caroline. (*CP* 652; Lowell's italics)

Persons real or imagined (we cannot know) bid Lowell to "*make yourself at home*"; in the sanitarium—a nightmarish echo of a true home—he is charged with the overwhelming task of "making" himself once more. The indistinguishability of authentic and hallucinated forms and the detachment of selves from their appearances make this process impossible, however; the opening lines of the poem present the alternatives of being fragmented into multiple selves, superimposed but never unified, and being "no one" at all. Here, Lowell cannot distinguish Caroline from the stranger "farcing in [her] face," but in another poem of the same sequence, Lowell cannot distinguish himself from her, and even invents a compound pronoun, "you-I" (*CP* 651), to describe their ambiguous double being. Extending Lowell's retreat from the monism of *Notebook*, *The Dolphin* is suffused with the confusion and despair that descended upon him as he became certain that the fog of metaphysical quandaries surrounding his illness would outlast him.

The book's divisions run to ontological depths, where Lowell "squirm[s] from small incisions in the self" (*CP* 658), but they also splinter the very substance of his language. *The Dolphin* is possessed by repetition—"Climbing from chair to chair to chair to chair," he reports in one ghastly portrait of his paranoia, "I cannot look the stairwell in the eye" (*CP* 651)—and its unrhymed sonnets, the last he would ever write, relinquish the associations with organic unity he had so eccentrically imputed to them in *Notebook*. The book's confused and tormented dissolution of unities finds its fullest verbal expression, however, in Lowell's infamous method of reproducing and adjusting extracts from Elizabeth Hardwick's letters. Where *Notebook* had been diaristic and univocal, *The Dolphin* is epistolary and dialogic, often representing both sides of Lowell's transatlantic conversations with his abandoned wife. While *Notebook* quotes directly from historical figures and poets and friends, *The Dolphin* presents an indistinguishable amalgam of original and re-worked language from Hardwick's letters, creating yet another dualism of indistinguishable parts. Lowell's apparently sloppy boundaries of poetic voice, in fact, meticulously enmesh the "authentic" Hardwick of the poems' source texts and the imagined version of her that the ill poet educes from them.[49]

When Lowell sent Elizabeth Bishop an early version of *The Dolphin,* she famously insisted that the collection should not be published as it stood. "There is a 'mixture of fact & fiction,'" she objected, "and you have *changed* her letters. That is 'infinite mischief,' I think. . . . It's not being 'gentle' to use personal, tragic, anguished letters that way—it's cruel."[50] Lowell would make superficial adjustments to mitigate the book's offenses, but his "mischief" was aesthetically consistent with the nebulous divisions that suffuse and distinguish the book, undermining any clear, directional flow of cause and effect that might issue, as it had in *Notebook,* from historical and biological sources. *The Dolphin*—hurtful in ways Lowell believed to be unavoidable from its "donnée," as he put it—asserts but obscures the boundary between "fact & fiction," refusing to respect the authority of Hardwick's original texts in their role as final, determining sources of their meaning.[51] In *Notebook,* Lowell had identified objective fact—the array of verifiable events available to the senses and thus to historical and biographical memory—with "honest speech," but "mostly I'm not very very forthright" (*CP* 548), he admitted to Bishop of *The Dolphin.* True to the subjective distortions his illness exaggerated, the honesty of his method in the latter book lies precisely in its falsification of fact—in its rendering, that is, of Hardwick's voice as a version of his own made remote, an expression of his own thought untethered to immediate textual or embodied origins.

The authority of fact that had presided so assuredly over *Notebook* had thus begun to subside in *The Dolphin* as new lyric opportunities emerged from germs of ontological doubt. Acknowledging and insisting upon the book's injurious forms of "half-fiction," in the defiant, penitent closing line of the book—"my eyes have seen what my hands did" (*CP* 708)—Lowell dissevers himself yet again, affiliating his controversial method of splicing together the real and the imagined with the perplexing philosophical and phenomenological divisions that underpinned the book from its inception. ("When I was troubled in mind," he writes, ambiguously addressing Caroline Blackwood and *The Dolphin* itself, "you made for my body" [*CP* 708]). Each of the pensive final poems of Lowell's last two volumes pit objective and subjective, veridical and imaginative forms of knowledge against one another, not to adjudicate their relative value or to posit final explanations but to reveal and revel in the "grand obscurity" of the questions they pose. "Epilogue," the final poem of *Day by Day*, has appeared to many readers to present an ultimate defense of the factual premises that anchor Lowell's autobiographical art—"Yet why not say what happened?" (*CP* 838), he half asserts, half wonders. But the poem draws its affective power from calling such integral premises into question, from admitting that the desire "to make / something imagined, not recalled," has cast his life's work into doubt:

> Those blessèd structures, plot and rhyme—
> why are they no help to me now
> I want to make
> something imagined, not recalled?
> I hear the noise of my own voice:
> *The painter's vision is not a lens,*
> *It trembles to caress the light.*
> But sometimes everything I write
> with the threadbare art of my eye
> seems a snapshot,
> lurid, rapid, garish, grouped,
> heightened from life,
> yet paralyzed by fact. (*CP* 838; Lowell's italics)

It is the "threadbare art" of the eye—an art that equates the visible with the true, and credits the empirical disclosures of the "*lens*" above the tremulous revelations of intuition and feeling—that Lowell questions in "Epilogue." To be "paralyzed by fact," we presume, is to be constrained by the kinds of biographical circumstances an artless "snapshot" confesses, but the "fact" underlying all others proves to be the condition of embodiment itself: "We are poor passing facts," the poem concludes, "warned by that to give / each figure in the photograph / his living name" (*CP* 838). The acts of questioning, praying, and warning structure the poem, not anything so conclusive as a committed defense of a style; the inexorable fact of the body, both "paralyzing" and productive for its mortal, aesthetic, and explanatory limits, is one that breeds questions instead of answering them.

Such exceptional facts, which seem not to produce knowledge but to heighten our emotional and imaginative investment in the things of the world, are the ones that matter to Lowell in his last books, particularly *Day by Day*. The certainty of death is one such fact, inspiring wonder and fear as it defies comprehension. Another proves to be Lowell's incurability, which he took to be certain after two more hospitalizations and an overdose of lithium in a failed attempt to avert a manic episode. " 'Remarkable breakdown, remarkable recovery,' " his doctors chime in the despondent poem "Home," "—but the breakage," Lowell insists, "can go on repeating / once too often" (*CP* 824). Throughout his last collection, he reiterates his painfully definite conclusion that the spiritual puzzle of his mental illness had proven, finally, to be insoluble. In "Seesaw," he bemoans "The encroachments of our bodies we occupy but cannot cure" (*CP* 818), and in "Ants," he sees "the lost case of the mind" (*CP* 778) reflected in the baffling complexity of an ant colony's enmeshed natural and social orders; contemplating the "causes of [his] misadventure" in yet another poem, he recalls Carl Jung's prescient warning to his mother: "If your son is as you have described him, / he is an incurable schizophrenic" (*CP* 832). Yet the helplessness and abject confusion the poems express also prove to be the material from which Lowell forges new forms of poetic dignity, and even new structures of logic, in *Day by Day*. Situated beyond any hope of rational interpretation, Lowell's mental illness is transformed in his final book into a representative instance of life's inescapable, inexplicable miseries, into an affliction that is not exceptional and isolating but familiar and shared. This philosophically exhausted, impassioned solidarity in turn inspires an almost sacerdotal sensitivity to the infirmities of others, a responsiveness that is evident in the book's

many elegiac portraits. In "Endings," for example, the restless philosophical tumult his own recurring illness has occasioned pervades Lowell's
empathetic depiction of his cousin Harriet Winslow, ruinously debili-
tated by a series of strokes:

> You woke wondering why
> you woke in another room,
> you woke close to drowning.
> Effects are without cause;
> your doctors found nothing.
> A month later you were paralyzed
> and never unknotted . . . (*CP* 759; Lowell's ellipses)

The lines link the seizures' elusive physical causes to a grand aporia—
"Effects are without cause"—a rational paralysis reified in the irresolvable
knot of his cousin's paralyzed body. Importantly, however, the lines put
this epistemological failure to emotional ends. Highlighting the close relationship between bafflement and awe, evoking the miracle of Winslow's
survival, they present her thrombosis as a profound emblem of human
frailty. With the anaphora that stages and restages her disoriented waking
("You woke . . . / you woke . . . / you woke"), Lowell implies Winslow's
tenacious will to live, his own recollected relief at her survival, and the
shocking, ambiguous grace of chance, which cripples yet spares her.
Without attempting to resolve or interpret the relationship between these
objective and subjective forces, Lowell leverages the limits of knowledge—
figured in the rhetorical forms of paradox and impasse—to amplify his
poem's emotional impact. He forgoes the churning, impersonal motions
of history for the more modest, empathetic rhythms of his survival "day
by day."[52]

If the putative fact of a mind-body unity, ratified by the revelation of a
de facto chemical cure, contributed to the confident, formally constitutive materialism of *Notebook,* the fact of Lowell's incurability shapes the
premises and formal expression of *Day by Day,* a book committed to
exploring the spiritual and affective possibilities of doubt. "Thanks-
Offering for Recovery" displays this altered perspective and demonstrates
the bearing of this final turn in Lowell's interpretation of his illness upon
the evolution of his style. Lowell's last self-portrait—a likeness, in minia-

ture, of both a mind and the language that issues from it—the poem is the second-to-last of Lowell's authorized oeuvre, followed only by "Epilogue." In it, Lowell contemplates a stirring gift Elizabeth Bishop sent to him during his recovery from the breakdown that would prove to be his last. Presenting the gift—a small wooden head carved from balsa wood—in a letter to her convalescent friend, Bishop describes it as an "ex-voto": an offering "someone cured of a head injury" would present "to his church or the shrine where he'd prayed for recovery."[53] She had sent the votive from Brazil as a souvenir and get-well present, but later worried that Lowell might construe it as a pointed reference to his mental illness. Touched rather than offended, Lowell did in fact see the tragic donnée of his life reflected in the scarred, misshapen head, but in the poem, as Frank Bidart puts it, the object becomes "an emblem of Lowell's prob- lematic specialness, of madness, of the closed-in self-observation and self- recording which apparently grew more unremitting with depression" (272). Lowell's own lost head "mercifully," if temporarily, returned, the "wooden winter shadow" of his illness lifted, his swelling gratitude for the fragile blessings of friendship and health edges the intellect out of the poem altogether, leaving only the pathos of thanksgiving ("I give thanks, thanks— / thanks," he repeats). Inexplicably "delivered," he is the *homme sensuel,* immersed in the sensory pleasures of air and light, indifferent to rational explanations. In this state of receptive sensation, the ques- tions and exclamations that marked his maniacal, philosophical search for understanding wane, and the inclusive, twilit forms of ambiguity and paradox, freighted with spiritual significance, flourish:

> The airy, going house grows small
> tonight, and soft enough to be crumpled up
> like a handkerchief in my hand.
> Here with you by this hotbed of coals,
> I am the *homme sensuel,* free
> to turn my back on the lamp, and work.
> Something has been taken off,
> a wooden winter shadow—
> goodbye nothing. I give thanks, thanks—
> thanks too for this small
> Brazilian *ex voto,* this primitive head

sent me across the Atlantic by my friend . . .
a corkweight thing,
to be offered *Deo gratias* in church
on recovering from head-injury or migraine—
now mercifully delivered in my hands,
though shelved awhile unnoticing and unnoticed.
Free of the unshakable terror that made me write . . .
I pick it up, a head holy and unholy,
tonsured or damaged,
with gross black charcoaled brows and stern eyes
frowning as if they had seen the splendor
times past counting . . . unspoiled,
solemn as a child is serious—
light balsa wood the color of my skin.
It is all childcraft, especially
its shallow, chiseled ears,
crudely healed scars lumped out
to listen to itself, perhaps, not knowing
it was made to be given up.
Goodbye nothing. Blockhead,
I would take you to church,
if any church would take you . . .
This winter, I thought
I was created to be given away. (*CP* 837; Lowell's ellipses and italics)

Lowell's capacity to embrace, rather than resolve, the interpretive uncertainties the head elicits might well be the transitory blessing for which
the poem is most grateful. The head is "holy and unholy," "solemn as a
child is serious," and yet it seems to have seen "splendor / times past
counting." It is "unspoiled" yet lumped with scars. There are signs of
grace in the poem's conjunctions, in the "and"s and "or"s that resist final
explanations and evoke the consolatory principle of true contradiction;
the ambiguous mark on the crown might be a sign of accidental, material
damage, or it might be a tonsure, a mark of meaningful and dignifying
self-sacrifice, or it might, paradoxically, be both. That the head was made
to be offered "*Deo gratias*" only highlights the poem's refusal to identify
how or why or by whom the shadow of illness was "taken off," or what
such anguish could have meant. Having offered up his damaged mind at
a succession of religious and secular shrines—of religious conviction, of

rigorous introspection, and of medical science—Lowell recognizes that his "blockhead" is fit for none. Now, without a shrine at which to offer his thanks, gratitude itself must be enough.

Lowell depicts the offering as a homely reflection of his limits as a person and a poet: "Its shallow, chiseled ears, / . . . lumped out / to listen to itself" evoke his manic egotism and the benign narcissism of the confessional mode alike. But the icon, with its "crudely healed scars," is also an image of Lowell's autobiographical poem itself, which, like the rest of *Day by Day*, externalizes suffering through the knowingly naïve "childcraft" of unpatterned, innocently crude free verse. The salvation the poem describes comes not from anything so ratiocinative as analytical mastery or self-knowledge but from empathetic vigilance (when his head was "shelved" by madness, it was "unnoticing and unnoticed") and from the dislocated self-regard the effigy makes possible, placing private suffering at a distance from which it appears "small" but also "holy." This ecstatic objectivity is a beneficent, corrective answer to the pathological ecstasies of Lowell's illness, for he stands beside himself here in acceptance of his limits, in passionate resignation that is the antithesis of both manic denial and deranged despair. And though no positive definition has emerged to take its place, the speaker's nihilistic definition of the self as mere matter "created to be given away" finally recedes along with the distortions of his winter madness; the poem ends by reasserting the distinction between the inert, wooden artifact that "was made to be given up" and the adaptable human who beholds it, whose humility, in one final paradox, seems to prove his worth.

Dissatisfied near the end of his life even with favorable reviews of his late work, Lowell was once asked what he would prefer his critics say about him. "That I'm heartbreaking," he responded.[54] Over the course of his oeuvre, Lowell interprets the moving target of his illness as a curse, a metaphysical quandary, a physiological symptom, and finally as an emblem of mortal limitation that conducts him, in his last poems, through familiar human zones of hope and despair. Out of an inconclusive farrago of spiritual and medical interpretations of his torment—interpretations that supported the competing, introspective and empirical epistemologies of *Life Studies* and *For the Union Dead*—the initial, remedial promise of lithium emerged to offer not only personal hope but a key that promised to unlock a much larger philosophical puzzle. The drug fostered both the materialist credence and the anomalous, "living" poetics of the *Notebook* experiment, but its subsequent failure reacquainted Lowell with the chastening, ambiguously spiritual and material limits of the will. The causes of Lowell's "high blood" thus prove, in his last poems, to be of much less interest to him than its effects; he comes to regard his own daunting, often "heartbreaking," effort to sustain a unified vision of himself not as an exceptional hardship but as a representative one—as an enterprise his readers, however sound in mind, would be likely to recognize.

CHAPTER 2

Physiological Thinking:
Robert Creeley and A. R. Ammons

WHILE THE EXCEPTIONAL circumstance of Robert Lowell's acute mental illness forced him into conversation with his era's increasingly chemical conception of consciousness, relatively unexceptional circumstances conspired to place A. R. Ammons and Robert Creeley in close dialogue with the biological materialism of their age. Creeley's pivotal circumstance proved to be countercultural; like Lowell's medical treatment with lithium, Creeley's recreational experiments with LSD forced into being a new concept of thought that in turn fostered unforeseeable new experiments in form. For Ammons, the crucial circumstance was nothing more than a scientific temperament; especially drawn, by disposition, to natural beauty and to empirical ways of approaching it, Ammons made a religion of science—an end in itself. "God Is the Sense the World Makes Without God," the title of a late poem, suggests the spiritual possibility Ammons, an avowedly secular poet, finds in natural order and in the "sense" the sciences make of phenomena observable in the physical world.

In his early poem "Hymn," Ammons calls out to nature, acknowledging that if he is to discern its unifying energies, he will "have to stay with the earth"—to train his eye upon the ground of material being.[1] Such scrutiny, he knows, will carry him to the limits of perception, requiring that he use the "thin" (refined, subtle) instruments of science, and of the poem itself, to regard nature's most minute visible forms with devoted precision:

> . . . I know if I find you I will have to stay with the earth
> inspecting with thin tools and ground eyes
> trusting the microvilli sporangia and simplest
>   coelenterates
> and praying for a nerve cell
> with all the soul of my chemical reactions
> and going right on down where the eye sees only traces
>
> You are everywhere partial and entire
> You are on the inside of everything and on the outside

For Ammons, who wrote this poem during the decade he spent managing a laboratory glassware factory, the optics of the microscope were a seamless prosthetic for natural vision; cellular membranes ("microvilli"), minute botanical structures ("sporangia"), and primitive animals ("coelenterates") were easily accessible to his mind's eye and thus to his spiritual imagination.[2] In "Hymn" Ammons effortlessly coordinates the arcane music of his scientific vocabulary with an untutored, folk vocabulary of belief—with the language of trust and prayer, and with the voice of a supplicant. If the soul is an emergent property of chemical reactions, his seamless shifts of register proclaim, then praying is a perfectly appropriate way to approach a nerve cell, and the boundaries between outside and inside—between the "you" of nature and the "me" of the phenomenal self—naturally fall away.

Robert Creeley possessed neither Ammons's consuming interest in nonhuman nature nor his fluency in the biological discourse, and yet Ammons's conception of the soul as a unified extension of "chemical reactions" in "Hymn" is the outcome of an evolution the poets have in common. Ammons and Creeley both reimagined the relationship between physiological being and mental life during the 1960s, and struggled to find, within the infinite possibilities of free verse, rhythms that could capture the continuity of mind and body and impress upon their readers the spiritual implications of that continuity. For both poets, this process set the material particle and the immaterial whole, the local and the universal, the one and the many in dynamic, inextricable interaction, revealing new possibilities for poetry. Each invented, in response, revolutionary forms with which to acknowledge the parallel processes through which voices emerge from impersonal quanta of language and the body. At the close of the decade, Creeley would recall how integrally the grinding friction of flesh and spirit had affected his earliest writing, and just how much his release from that friction subsequently transformed his life and art:

> It honestly, to my mind, isn't until the sixties that people begin to . . . come back into the experience of their own bodies as primary, and to realize that the mind is physiological. It is not some abstract deity that can be apart from the physiological moment of existence. It seems to me that we have moved from that duality that absolutely informs all my thinking when I'm a kid, for example, that "the mind is to discipline the body," or "the body is to relax the mind." . . . The torque that's created by that systematization of experience is just awful. Just incredible. It can *whip*. You know I called a book *The Whip*. And that's why, that's why the title. I don't think I consciously went and said, "What's a word for this particular kind of experience," but . . . I knew that something whipped me constantly in my own experience of things. Something was really, you know, WHAM, WHAM, slashing and cutting me.[3]

The "torque" Creeley identifies with his early, rigidly dualistic philosophy of mind is evident in the syntactic and imagistic torture of early lines that proclaim, for example, "My mind / to me a mangle is."[4] In his poems of the 1950s, Creeley presents the mind as an entity disconnected from the feeling body, an "abstract deity" that represses sensation and subordinates instinct to the artificial impositions of reason and intention. Prompted in part by the use of natural and synthetic psychoactive drugs over the course of the subsequent decade, Creeley would abandon his conception of the mind as a disembodied force whose "disciplin[ing]" exertions upon the body recall the exertions of the superego upon the corporeal id, and he would strive, in poetry that sometimes seems to have no subject at all, to find a place for his altered vision of the mind in language.

The epochal "realiz[ation] that the mind is physiological" proved to be especially profound for both Creeley and Ammons as inheritors of William Carlos Williams's compositional premise that "the poet thinks with his poem."[5] Improvising poems grounded in fugitive gestures of perception and recognition, conceiving of poetry as a fundamentally kinetic activity that is not a trace of experience but a living tool with which to conduct and enhance it, each poet's evolving conception of "mind" necessarily shifts the very premises of his poetics. Born the same year, into devout protestant households in rural North Carolina and Massachusetts, both Ammons and Creeley would reveal themselves to be secular poets who nonetheless harbored, deep in their temperaments and in their poetics alike, religious predispositions. This much is apparent in their early poetry—in the young Ammons's adoption of an Old Testament prophet as a persona, for example, and in the young Creeley's anxious brooding upon moral prohibitions he describes in terms of "sin."[6] As the two matured, however, the mystical apostasy they had in common assumed the more abstract form of a vigilant regard for the presence of irreducible otherness within the self. A scientist by early training and a manufacturer of scientific instruments by early trade, Ammons always recognized that presence in the natural world—in the inanimate, atomic, and cellular parts of animate wholes, and in the energies that course within "the overriding / grand / haul / of the galaxy" (*CP* 206). For Creeley, however, the otherness at work within, but somehow apart from, the personal was embodied first and foremost in language. Creeley would often say that he was "given to write poems," that he was called, that is, to orchestrate the creation and decreation of personhood within an impersonal medium, assembling and disassembling the self with the beloved, small words that were as much real objects to him as Ammons's "microvilli sporangia" and hurtling planets. "I love it," Creeley wrote late in life, that words "have no owner finally to determine them."[7]

Creeley's regard for words in all their objective, unpossessable thingness situated him in a milieu of mid-century poets who deemphasized the referential function of language and exalted what George Oppen called "the concrete materials of the poem."[8] By identifying language with other aspects of physical reality, late modernists such as Oppen and Louis Zukofsky—poets whom Creeley deeply admired—extended a tradition of poetry that rejected the prospect of transcendental meaning and with it "the authority of a reflective, Cartesian ego."[9] Adapting objectivist aesthetics to "concrete renderings" of the mind's movements, as Charles Altieri has proposed, Creeley would extend this tradition and in turn make it available to the generations of poets he influenced (poets as diverse as Rachel Blau DuPlessis, Nathaniel Mackey, and Rae Armantrout).[10] He would also discover, alongside Oppen, the special significance that correspondences between verbal and biological self-making would hold for this poetic heritage, for to conceive of the self in "objective" terms is always to imagine it as plural rather than transparently unitary, as a part and a sum. Atoms of the body politic strung together in arrangements of "rootless speech" and in "beads of the chromosomes" linked "like a rosary," the material selves objectivist poets champion strive to make something of the world of which they are made.[11]

Such aesthetic possibilities remained largely obscure to the young Creeley, however, writing under the pressure of an immense "torque" brought about by a dualistic "systematization of experience" he had not yet presumed to question. With his earliest trade volume—*For Love: Poems 1950–1960* (1962)—he became known for the crippling self-consciousness and aggressiveness he evoked in the sometimes stuttering, sometimes violent ruptures of his line breaks, the short lines with which his speakers hack wildly through thickets of contorted syntax and shyly falter forward, in turns. To Creeley's disappointment, these early poems led Robert Graves, whose children the younger poet tutored, to dub him a "domestic poet"; "my muse therefore a domestic drudge," Creeley smarted, "within that proposedly small world"; "no one who has ever so lived," he proclaimed years later, "would feel it so, that is, a scrunched limit of possibilities."[12] The small poems of *For Love* describe pangs of marital estrangement and crises of masculinity Creeley attributed both to the overwhelmingly female company in which he was raised after his father's early death and to having lost his left eye as a result of a childhood accident.[13] Though the early poems are candid in their representation of relationships and sexuality, they associate the body with sources of shame—lust, vulnerability, and emasculating pain—and identify the mind with torment and containment. It is not only a "mangle"; it is a shroud of darkness, a locked room, a prison of internalized convention.

In "The Mountains in the Desert," Creeley describes a "mind locked" in concentration on its own activity, enslaved by an irrepressible, even compulsive, inclination to reflect on the nature of reflection itself: "Tonight," he pleads, "let me go / at last out of whatever / mind I thought to have, / and all the habits of it."[14] In his frustration and longing to be relieved of the rational "mind," the speaker of "The Mountains in the Desert" recalls the bitterly anguished speaker of "The Kind of Act of," who likewise regards the mind as an entity that the self possesses and that can in turn powerfully and painfully possess the self:

> Giving oneself to the dentist or doctor who is a good one,
> to take the complete
> possession of mind, there is no
>
> giving. The mind
> beside the act of any dispossession is
>
> lecherous. There is no more giving in
> when there is no more sin.

"The Kind of Act of" situates the desire to relinquish the burden of self-consciousness by means of a dentist's or doctor's anesthetic within a moral and religious paradigm, characterizing the longing that occasions the poem as a form of lust.[15] By imagining the mind as a possessed thing, Creeley implies the neoplatonic Christian metaphor of the body as a material veil that shrouds the true, incorporeal noumenon of the self. He thus aligns the ontological dualism of mind and body with the ethical dualism of virtue and vice, demonstrating the emotionally devastating effects of that alignment on its speaker. With the statement "There is no more giving in / when there is no more sin," Creeley acknowledges that his prison is of his own making—that by equating the desire to "dispossess" the mind with spiritual failure ("giving in"), he has subjected himself to an internalized scheme of repressive ideas. (The poem's final couplet, another self-made mechanism of containment, claps shut on the speaker to accentuate his failure.) This recognition does him little good, however; a fracture in the self permeates all aspects of his being, transforming even sensation and perception. In these early poems, Creeley thus makes his glass eye—a figure for the "I" liable to break into brittle fragments—an emblem of various forms of physical and psychic unease; as the visible world fragments before him in "The Window," for example, its speaker declares pitiably, and punningly, "I can feel / my eye breaking."[16] This fragmentation, which accompanies even the most benign mental acts, in turn resembles the refraction of experience through the prism of language—"As soon as / I speak, I / speaks," he writes.[17] Though language intensifies Creeley's dualist anguish, the cascade of dislocations patently begins in an original crisis he evokes with visceral, minimalist concision in "Pieces": "It / hurts / to live / like this," he pronounces, "meat / sliced / walking."[18]

In hindsight, Creeley would pinpoint this fundamental philosophical crisis—which he registers everywhere in his poetry of the 1950s as an urgent crisis of feeling—as the predicament that was "WHAM, WHAM, slashing and cutting" him as he was inventing his earliest forms. This "curious split between the physical fact of a person and that thing they otherwise think with, or about, the so-called mind," a division in his own thinking Creeley attributed to his Protestant upbringing, is the aesthetic and philosophical predicament he would resolve over the course of the subsequent decade in a countercultural milieu enthralled by the "mind-expanding" possibilities of mescaline, LSD, and other hallucinogens.[19] In a conversation with Allen Ginsberg at the Vancouver Poetry Conference in 1963, Creeley observed that "the very premise on which consciousness operates is undergoing modifications that none of us I think are at the moment capable of defining. . . . All the terms of consciousness that I grew up with must disappear, are disappearing momently, daily. The terms of reality are changing."[20] As early as 1960, Creeley's close friends Ginsberg and Charles Olson had been subjects in Timothy Leary's experiments dispensing a synthetic equivalent of hallucinogenic mushrooms. Leary claimed to have proven that "the mind is a tiny fragment of the brain-body complex" and that "the cortex can be cleared" of the myth of the self—"the game of individuality, the ego game."[21] By the time of the Vancouver conference, which brought these poets together in sustained discussion of the relationship between mind, body, and poetry, Olson was retrofitting Leary's findings into his conception of the poem as a projection of "SENSIBILITY WITHIN THE ORGANISM / BY

MOVEMENT OF ITS OWN TISSUES."[22] Olson was one influence who clearly shaped Creeley's evolving "terms of consciousness" and the formal metaphors with which he would strive to evoke them; in his "Working Notes on Charles Olson's Concept of Person," Creeley recalls Olson's enthusiasm for the power of hallucinogenic agents, LSD in particular, to "[put] you on your own autonomic nervous system"—"the autonomic system," Olson lamented, of which "the human race, has been so bereft . . . for so long."[23]

Though often condescended to as a context for his poems of the period, Creeley's own hallucinogenic experiments over the coming months and years framed his reconciliation of the "curious split" that permeated *For Love* and the early sections of *Words*, a reconciliation through which Creeley discovered "the delight of thought as a possibility of forms."[24] Recalling his first experience taking LSD, Creeley describes how his anxiety, his tentativeness, his sense of existential separation—all dimensions of experience that shape the faltering rhythms of his early style—"all that just went."[25] In another account of that first experience, he recalls simply "stepping out" of binary schemes of thought, that "dualism which is 'yes-no,' that binary factor. It was like seeing a vast checkerboard. . . . Then I just, by grace of something, stepped out of it. Just stepped out."[26] What he stepped into was something extraordinary, as he would repeatedly describe it to friends. "Those of you who have had LSD," he explained in 1967, "had the extraordinary experience of finding that you were not separate from quote life unquote . . . that you were constituted like an oil-slick or a swarm of bees, that you were not divisible from all else that was evident in your consciousness . . . that what we experience—place, time, condition, organism—is not divisible, that nothing is more or less in the world, and that it all is in some way literally related."[27] He would summarize the effect of such drugs as a question they put to the user, a question that his poems of the late 1960s embrace with controversially extravagant, minimalist forms: "Can you melt yourself, 'autobiographically' "?[28]

This sudden apprehension of the solubility of the self into "pieces" at once indivisible and discrete collapsed the hierarchy of the physical and mental into a single plane of equivalence, answering Creeley's distinct array of psychic needs. It also notably differed from Allen Ginsberg's framing of such drugs' revelatory effects. For Ginsberg, who longed to recreate the Blakean visionary prophecy that had initially called him to poetry, such chemical engines seemed to "deliver you beyond the universe" and facilitate a "supernatural ecstasy" through which glimpses of a purposive force outside of nature could be perceived.[29] Creeley's experiences, as he described them, delivered him *into* nature—into "place," as he would call it—in what was for him less ecstasis than synthesis, less mystical revelation than information, "extraordinary and deeply *relieving* information," he would specify.[30] It was information that seemed to confirm Alfred North Whitehead's process philosophy and Olson's abstruse theories of the poem as an extension of a living body, but more importantly, it was information that allowed Creeley to feel at home in a universe with which he had always felt misaligned. That embodied experience, per se, could suffice as an authoritative source of knowledge moved him deeply: "Always in my own situation, there was tacit fear some essential information was lacking, that one was dumb, in some crucial sense, left out of the 'larger picture,'" he explains.[31] As a poet averse, early in his career, to a literary tradition he found intimidating and hostile to his aesthetic values of immersive presence and ephemerality, the "information" Creeley derived from chemically altered states of consciousness gave him the right to speak as a part of creation equal to all others. As a painfully insecure person worried always about "keeping himself together" in public, it presented an ontology of the human consistent with his entropic experience of the self, always on the verge of sliding apart to reveal a final absence.[32] With this information, Creeley found a new, perhaps reckless, courage to undertake radical conceptual experiments in which he whittled poetry to its smallest possible units, dissolving the suffering speaker, terrified of coming apart, into innumerable, extravagantly exploded shards of language. Scattering his discrete "pieces" throughout the volumes of the late 1960s and early 1970s, Creeley at once dissolves the self and embeds it here, there, everywhere, in a swarm of minute forms without discernible boundaries, each a partial unit of a series or book, a larger whole.

Poems Creeley composed in the fall and winter of 1963 mark a crucial transition to this more radical formal representation of "the so-called mind" by subjecting the motions of consciousness to ever more emphatic temporal limits. In "I Keep to Myself Such Measures . . ." (1963), Creeley situates thinking in nature by situating it in time.[33] The poem is divided into four 4-line stanzas, "measures" that represent the succession of moments that structure mental experience, but the poem still seems to emerge from a position of unified presence, from an "I" who describes the feeling of thinking, thought by thought:

> I keep to myself such
> measures as I care for,
> daily the rocks
> accumulate position.
>
> There is nothing
> but what thinking makes
> it less tangible. The mind,
> fast as it goes, loses
>
> pace, puts in place of it
> like rocks simple markers,
> for a way only to
> hopefully come back to
>
> where it cannot. All
> forgets. My mind sinks.
> I hold in both hands such weight
> it is my only description.

With the assertion that "The mind, / fast as it goes, loses // pace," Creeley introduces two representational consequences of coming back into the experience of his own body as primary: he characterizes thought not as a force but as a process—as something that "goes fast"—and he frames the limitations of the mind not in terms of containment or repression but in terms of its directional motion in time. Thought is no longer a disembodied force that disciplines the libidinal, emotional aspects of the self but rather an embodied activity that is disconcertingly circumscribed by physical constraints. Poetic "measures" become "rocks" and "markers" carefully positioned in a mnemonic trail behind experience; these are the measures language goes to in order to capture the swift, elusive process of thought, even though the path of consciousness, Creeley insists, cannot really be retraced—the mind cannot "come back to // where it cannot."

As a result of the same drug experiences through which he registered "the shift in *all* terms of human relationship," a shift that "reorganize[s] premises that have existed for thousands of years, concepts of person," Creeley claimed to have "entered upon the seriality of language."[34] (From his own experience, Oliver Sacks describes the tendency to see "a series of static 'snapshots'" instead of continuous motion as a signature effect of hallucinogens.)[35] Having exchanged the violent split between physical and spiritual aspects of being for the relentless, headlong directional flow of the mind in time, Creeley's preoccupations with the seriality and fallibility of embodied cognition in "I Keep Myself to Such Measures . . ." echo throughout the poems that he composes between 1963 and 1966, even before he explodes out of "the bounded lyric" altogether in *Pieces*.[36] In "Distance," Creeley defines the mind bitterly as "nothing / otherwise but / a stumbling / looking after," and in "A Place," he likewise stresses the impossibility of capturing, in retrospect, the vividness of the present, noting that in "memory I fear // the distortion. I do not feel / what it was I was feeling."[37] In "A Birthday," a poem that describes a traditional occasion for reckoning with the imposition of time upon experience, Creeley makes the logical leap from recognizing the mind's incapacity to record the fullness of inner life to recognizing that stasis itself is an impossibility within consciousness, as it is everywhere else in physical reality:

> I had thought
> a moment of stasis
> possible, some
>
> thing fixed—
> days, worlds—
> but what I know
>
> is water, as you
> are water, as you
> taught me water
>
> is wet. Now slowly
> spaces occur, a ground is
> disclosed as dirt.[38]

Creeley defines stasis as an unknowable impossibility; though he had "thought / a moment of stasis possible," all he can *know* is the perpetual flow of his embodied experience in time and space, a flow as tangible and essential as the flow of water. By his own account, the speaker's immersion in process requires that he suppress the impulse to hold abstract concepts at an intellectual remove from material reality: "ground is / disclosed as dirt."

Though Creeley acknowledges his increasingly materialist outlook thematically in "I Keep Myself to Such Measures . . ." and "A Birthday," it is in the stylistically experimental "pieces" Creeley began composing in the mid-1960s, when he had "[grown] inexorably bored with the tidy containment of clusters of words on single pieces of paper called 'poems,'" that his reformed philosophy of mind began to shape his poems formally.[39] These poems—sometimes titled, sometimes not—subordinate the unit of the poem to the unit of the book, "breaking down the walls or frames between poems," Lytle Shaw observes, "that would set them up as instances of self-presence and containment."[40] Of these small poems that melt the autobiographical self into a flow of *pensées* rendered as textual objects, the poem that seems to have garnered emblematic status, if not critical acclaim, is "A Piece":

> One and
> one, two,
> three.[41]

Surprised to discover that "A Piece" was one of the poems most irritating to reviewers, Creeley would defend the poem as "central to all the possibilities of statement."[42]

The "possibility of statement" that "A Piece" at first seems to realize is the possibility of poetry without paraphrasable content. Without contextual cues and identifiable referents, the occasion of the poem and the voice that speaks it remain obscure. This is not to say that the poem has no content, however, for its content in the most literal sense is the purest verbal representation of temporal progression we have: counting. (Here, certainly, the sequence of the musical count—the counting-off of initial beats that might well have been in the background as Creeley, listening to Charlie Parker, Dizzy Gillespie, or Tadd Dameron, composed his poems.)[43] The numbers' discreteness allows Creeley to string them together without finessing them into a significatory message that would distract from the poem's primary aim to make time felt in conscious thought. Emphasizing the status of words and lines as graphical units arranged in an unfolding progression and space, Creeley attunes the reader to the sequential process of comprehending the poem's language, unit by unit, in real time.[44]

This feeling of process likewise constitutes the most significant content of so many of the poems from this period that obsessively stage the evanescence of the linguistic or contemplative moment, dwelling on the page just long enough to specify the ephemerality they enact:[45]

One thing done, the rest follows.	Nothing but comes and goes in a moment.	Where it is was and will be never only here.	Here here here. Here.

These poems describe the words they contain—words that "follow" one another, that come and go from the frame of our attention, that mark the transitory presences of the authorial hand and the readerly eye from here to here to here. Importantly, however, the poems also describe *themselves* as apparently discrete, equivalent units that are nonetheless indivisible, units that compose the larger unities of the sequence and volume, and that exchange the unified voice of the testimonial lyric for something more like the impersonal humming of "a swarm of bees." In this sense, Creeley's poem-pieces endorse a representative model of the self rather than an egotistical one; they affirm that "nothing is more or less in the world," enacting in literary form Creeley's psychedelic revelation that "it all is in some way literally related."

Creeley explores not only the temporal aspect of embodied thinking but also its spatial aspect in these experiments; "here" and "there" recur constantly in *Pieces*, often in the company of rapidly shifting verb tenses that highlight the spatial and temporal ambiguity of the poems' deictics. As an elusive indicator of the embodied speaker's position in space and time, and as a fixed trace of both, "here" becomes a deeply consequential concept in *Pieces*:

The which it
was, form
seen—there
here, re-

peated for/
as/—There
is a "parallel."[46]

"Here" is the present relative to "the which it was" and also the place opposed to "there"; to realize that "There / is a 'parallel'" is to recognize an identity between time and space rather than a gulf of difference, an equivalence grounded in an understanding of each in terms of one's embodied position at any given moment. But "here," situated at the precise center of the very symmetrical poem, shifts fitfully in its reference, delivering the reader to place after place in a relentless process of transport that finally renders all places equivalent. This quality of Creeley's deixis throughout the poems of this period recalls his description of a distinct hallucinogenic effect of LSD: the feeling "that your toe didn't end 'here' . . . that you were not divisible from all else that was evident in your consciousness."[47] It is an impression of being here and there at once that reaches its textual apotheosis for Creeley—perhaps unsurprisingly—in "On Acid," a poem that explicitly connects the mind's drug-induced "sensations" with the shifting meanings of "here" and "there":[48]

And had no actual
hesitancies, always
(flickering) mind's
sensations: here, here, *here**

philo-tro-

bic-port-

a-bil-ity?

End, end, end, end, end, end

Next? Next who/ who/ they we

_____   for she me
*or there?
                    is not we'll

                be . . . . .

The autobiographical signs of presence that appear in the first lines of the poem (the title's identification of a specific circumstance of composition, the residue of personal "hesitancies") disappear as the speaker succumbs to the drug, along with the seams between "they," "we," "she," and "me." Indeed, "she me / is"; there is no boundary between subject and object, nor, for that matter, any future: there is no "we'll / be." The jumbled swirl of syllables drawn from different words coalesce into a legible unity ("port- / a-bil-ity"), while the use of a footnote (of all things!) transports us out of the poem and deeper into it all at once. "[H]ere . . . or there?"—it's all the same; "touch the universe anywhere," as Ammons puts it, "you touch it / everywhere."[49]

The "pieces" of the late 1960s and early 1970s thus represent an especially sustained and coherent aesthetic response to a critical transition in Creeley's philosophy of mind, registering his conception of thinking as physically real and "literally related" to his arrangements of words on the page. To be sure, these experiments willfully decline to evoke the disappointed intimacy and metaphysical agony of his early poems, as well as the anxieties of age that distinguish his later work. Underlying the extravagant eccentricity of his serial style, however, is an exuberance estimable only in terms of the philosophical "nightmare" that preceded it and in light of the possibilities for Creeley's art that changing his mind on the matter of mind represented to him. His sense that the existing terms for understanding consciousness were obsolescing emboldened him and compelled him to ask questions that proved to be not only psychologically necessary but artistically fertile: What, reduced to a disfiguring essence, is a poem, he asked, and what is the poem's relationship to reality?

To the disappointment of some readers and to the relief of others, after this period of intensive chemical and poetic experimentation Creeley's poems once again coalesce into more traditional patterns of lyric unity. Thinking, however, remained Creeley's permanent subject. In 1953, the mind had been a "mangle" to him; by 1969, it had become a mass of liberated pieces of reality best approximated in verbal objects ambiguously distinct from their surroundings. By the final decade of his life, however, the material basis of consciousness had become an "old story" charged with fresh significance, a circumstance to expound upon yet again by adapting his dynamic syntax to evoke the dissolving connections of an aging brain. Though the experiments of the 1960s and 1970s exchanged emotional depth for philosophical ambit, in his late work

Creeley reconciles the findings of his hallucinogenic experiments—
"that the mind and body are one"—with Pound's proposition that "only
emotion endures," a statement he was fond of quoting.[50] In his late poem
"Old Story," Creeley thus imagines the mind's vulnerability to the physical deterioration of advancing age as the vulnerability of a child stranded
on a floating remnant of ice.[51] The poem's unrhymed quatrains form discrete units that float on the snowy field of the page, while the lines' compressed syntax and prominent omissions of articles suggest the erosion
of the ice and the disintegration of the thinking body it represents. As the
poem correlates the erosion of synaptic and syntactic connections, the
deterioration of sense accompanies the physiological decay of "conduits"
and "circuits"; Creeley stresses yet again that sense is ultimately "made"
by reticulations of senseless matter:

> Like kid on float
> of ice block sinking
> in pond the field had made
> from winter's melting snow
>
> so wisdom accumulated
> to disintegrate
> in conduits of brain
> in neural circuits faded
>
> while gloomy muscles shrank
> mind padded the paths
> its thought had wrought
> its habits had created
>
> till like kid afloat
> on ice block broken
> on or inside the thing it stood
> or was forsaken.

Creeley has rewritten the habits of thought that "locked" him in the prison
of the disembodied mind in "The Mountains in the Desert," reinscribing
those habits as neural "paths" reinforced by dynamic natural processes.
The final stanza's jumble of prepositions places the child "on or inside" the
disintegrating emblem of the body, proclaiming that the fate of the self,
whatever its exact relationship to biological substance, depends finally

on the fate of the brain. The predicament of the child on the shifting block of ice is ominously precarious; in the poem's last line, Creeley replaces the possibility that his hard-won wisdom might "stand" with the hopeless prospect that the mind, shrinking like the "gloomy muscles" of the preceding stanza, finally dissolves in death. The mind—the connections it forged, the meaning it made—are inevitably "forsaken," he concludes, for personal knowledge, "accumulated / . . . in conduits of brain," suffers the destiny of the body that gives it being.

As Creeley's poetic forms retreated from conceptual experimentation, the sources of his "information" about the nature of mind took more conventional forms as well, and his conception of the relationship between poetry and mentality acquired an unprecedented scale of perspective.[52] Introducing his *Selected Poems* in 1991, Creeley regards thought embodied in language as his great theme, and commends poetic manifestations of mind for exceeding the possibilities of neurological description:

> Just a few nights ago I heard a friend from college days, talking about artificial intelligence, his authority. He noted the banality, in some respects, of emotions, that is, how, neurologically, they are a familiar spectrum and shift almost crudely from one to another—whereas the intellectual acts which are so sponsored, what we *think* thus funded, are of extreme human interest and consequence. Again Williams: "The poet thinks with his poem, in that lies his thought, and that in itself is the profundity." No doubt it is all a dream, but how language thinks to say it, what it thus makes of its own mind and feeling, is to me forever provocative. "A new world is only a new mind, and the poem and the mind are all apiece."[53]

Creeley and his friend do not respect the same "authority," he suggests, but he also defends the "intellectual acts" his poems describe by citing the empiricist's assertion that thinking, though "funded" by feeling, finally exceeds the emotions at its source. Creeley's situation of the mind in tangibly physical reality awakens in him an alertness to the temporal limitations of embodied thought, but it also precipitates a reckoning with the comparable actions of words and bodies as physical events in the world. The embodied mind thus presents him with a bracing aesthetic challenge he and Ammons shared: to create a poetic language "as real as thinking" while demonstrating, in the particularities of a private idiom and in the shared terms of his zeitgeist, how " 'the poem and the mind are all apiece.' "[54]

Like Creeley's, Ammons's deepening conviction that mind and world are of a single substance forces new poetic forms into being. Creeley becomes ever more attuned to the worldly signature of time upon conscious experience—to the feeling of cognitive motion per se—as he realizes the capacity of serial form to diffuse the autobiographical self into a flow of concrete verbal shapes. For Ammons, however, it is ultimately the feeling of change—of processing and reconstituting the given in a specifically digestive kind of motion—that distinguishes mental life, announcing to him a fundamental continuity between the operations of nature, mind, and language. Creeley's images and formal metaphors present the process of mind on a hurtling, linear trajectory through time, but in Ammons's poems, that line becomes a *limen*: first a static boundary, then a reflective surface, and finally a permeable biological membrane. With this final, physiological model, Ammons expunges the last vestiges of the dualist habits of representing thought through which he, like Creeley, articulates immense psychic pain in his earliest verse. In his later poetry, Ammons goes on to speculate that "When love brushes // through our nerves / and sends / a summary to our brains / perhaps the summary / is sent by / vibrations // really the universe's," signaling a transformed philosophy of consciousness freighted with consolatory potential.[55]

Inventing forms that signal continuity, rather than correspondence, between the synthetic operations of consciousness and poetry itself, Ammons discovers new sources of pleasure and humility in tracking the inextricable dynamics of "processing" experience in natural (somatic) and verbal contexts.[56] *Ommateum, with Doxology* (1955), Ammons's first book, borrows the first part of its title from the scientific name for an insect's compound eye, which aggregates visual information from many slightly different angles. "Ommateum" thus evokes the synoptic perspective of the volume as a whole, which holds an empirical epistemology of the sensory, observable world in unresolved suspension alongside "doxology," an intuitive epistemology of faith.[57] By Ammons's own account, the title "suggest[s] a many-sided view of reality," expressing "a belief that forms of thought, like physical forms, are . . . susceptible to change."[58] Like physical forms but distinct from them, intractable "forms of thought" prove to be an obsession of Ammons's early verse. Though the mind is notably abstract in Ammons's earliest poems, from the first he conceives of the mind as a *formal* thing, identifying consciousness not with freedom but with necessity. In the allegorical landscape of "Turning a moment to say so long," for example, the speaker is contained by "boundaries of mind" that he longs to transcend. The poem begins with an ending, a pivoting farewell to the sensory and communicative offices (seeing, speaking, and hearing) that have placed him under a vague but intolerable social and sensory burden ("I have overheard too much"). As a result, he longs to escape nothing less than "being" itself:

> Turning a moment to say so long
>   to the spoken
>   and seen
>   I stepped into
> the implicit pausing sometimes
> on the way to listen to unsaid things
> At a boundary of mind
>   Oh I said brushing up
>   against the unseen
>   and whirling on my heel
>   said
>   I have overheard too much
> Peeling off my being I plunged into
> the well.[59]

The form of the poem notably reflects not the repressive structure it imagines the mind gives to life but the shifting, unencumbered dynamism of the transcendental spirit Ammons associates with the wind in *Ommateum*, the surging updraft that brushes seductively against the reeling speaker poised to peel one aspect of his being apart from the other.[60] After the speaker's ecstatic leap, however, "Turning a moment to say so long" makes a whirling pivot of its own, turning away from abstract descriptions of reality ("the spoken," "the implicit pausing," "the unseen") and casting itself violently into the concrete. Having "plunged into / the well," the speaker is horrified to discover that he has cast himself not into a symbolic portal in an allegorical landscape but into an actual well, at the bottom of which he finds not transcendence but refuse—"patched inner-tubes beer cans / and black roothairs." In the poem's terrifying conclusion, the speaker recedes into the well's terminal darkness, "night kissing / the last bubbles from my lips."

Ammons fatally punishes the speaker for imagining that he could escape physical reality and retain any meaningful kind of existence—any kind of true "being" in the unseen. Like *Ommateum* as a whole, "Turning a moment to say so long" entertains the fantasy of spiritual deliverance only to frustrate and dismiss it; again and again, poem after poem, Ammons bids "farewell to the earth" (*CP* 4), "[steps] out into the great open" (*CP* 5), "cave[s] in upon eternity" (*CP* 31), and "ris[es] . . . from sifted underwater mud" (*CP* 32), only to find himself back where he started in the next poem, longing for transcendental escape. From the precipitous descent Ammons imagines in "Turning a moment to say so long" to the counterbalance of science and faith poised on the fulcrum of the title's colon, *Ommateum, with Doxology* dissociates the "poles of earth and air" (*CP* 23), seeming to justify Harold Bloom's proposition that Ammons's early theme is "the Emersonian ambition to be possessed fully by the Transcendental Self."[61] As the surprise, undeluded ending of "Turning a moment to say so long" suggests, however, the pole of the transcendental is less credible than convenient for Ammons; it functions not as an actual realm of possibility so much as an expression of psychological resistance to the physical, the sensory, and the mundane. The category of the transcendental proves valuable for constructing an array of binary, agonistic tropes into which the young poet can project diverse currents of emotional unrest.

A more precise picture of Ammons's distinctive spirituality and its relation to the concrete comes into focus in *Expressions of Sea Level* (1964), where the speaker of "Hymn" finds himself not praying for deliverance from material reality but "praying for a nerve cell / with all the soul of [his] chemical reactions"; the Ammons of *Expressions* does not picture "the dissentient ghosts of my spirit" (*CP* 14), as he had in *Ommateum,* but "mind rising from the physical chemistries," as he does in "Mechanism": "mind . . . building and tearing down, / running to link effective chains, / establish molecules of meaning" (78). As the dependence of consciousness on biological actions becomes increasingly emphatic in Ammons's poems of the 1960s, the "boundary of mind" becomes increasingly indistinct, and the enticing symmetries of the mirror—as a metaphor for the mind's reflection of reality and the poem's reflection of mind—emerges as a pervasive formal and thematic presence that blurs the boundaries between world, mind, and poem. In the philosophical idyll "Bridge," Ammons watches couples in a tea garden parading across a footbridge, "rising on the bridge" as their reflections "descend into the pond"; the poet focuses anxiously on the point of convergence "where bridge and mirror-bridge merge // at the bank / returning images to themselves"; he wonders "where ascension / and descension meet / completing the idea of a bridge" (*CP* 84–85). Fretting over the fluid boundary between the real bridge and the ideal one, he enjoins us to "think where the body is"—to consider how the substances of the perceiving body, the reflective water, and the arched structure seem to unify ("merge") the object and its mental reflection. In his celebrated poem "Reflective," Ammons invents a formal metaphor for this mental doubling, using the figure of the mirror to confound the positions of subject and object and to dissolve animal (sentient, conscious) and vegetable (nonsentient, nonconscious) categories of natural being by rendering both "reflective":

> I found a
> weed
> that had a
>
> mirror in it
> and that
> mirror
>
> looked in at
> a mirror
> in
>
> me that
> had a
> weed in it (*CP* 170)

Unlike the pneumatic structure of "Turning a moment to say so long," which took no formal cues from the bounded constraints it ascribed to the mind, the structural symmetries of "Reflective"—its three-line stanzas,

its concentrated repetitions of "mirror" in the central stanzas, and its di-
ametrical repetitions of "weed" in the first and last stanzas—evoke the
acts of reflection and recognition that define mental experience within the
poem. By placing a mirror "in" both himself and the weed, Ammons proposes that an identity of substance may underlie the resemblances he
discerns between mental experience and physical forms, but the image
nonetheless retains the residual, Romantic premise that nature is exter-
nalized mind and mind is internalized nature; indeed, the mirror suggests
that the organic substance of nature and the reflective substance of mind
echo each other across a gulf of ontological difference.[62]

This gulf undermines the symbolic and aesthetic serviceability of the
mirror metaphor for Ammons, as he discovers in an early attempt to investigate the nature of consciousness by transcribing it—by producing a
putatively mimetic "reflection" of the mind in linguistic form. In *Tape for
the Turn of the Year,* Ammons transcribes the flow of his conscious
thoughts in "a long / thin / poem" he composed on a hundred-foot-long
roll of adding-machine tape.[63] The resulting poem, written in daily entries from early December 1963 to early January 1964, proved to be a crucial, ambiguously scientific and poetic experiment for Ammons, if also
an aesthetically unsatisfying one. Greeting the poem with both admiration
and frustration, readers have described it as a "most original and surprising invention," as "a heroic failure," and as a "slightly nutty labor"
that lacks coherence and suffers from "the tedium of indiscriminateness."[64]
Like Lowell's evolving notebook enterprise and Creeley's experimental "pieces," however, Ammons's poem aspires primarily neither to
beauty nor pleasure; the virtue it strives to achieve is accuracy. Much as
Gertrude Stein's experiments in automatic writing sought to disclose
the motions of the unconscious directly, Ammons's experiment aspires
to disclose natural design by "recording" thought.[65] As Ammons explains it, the spontaneous entries of *Tape* answer Emerson's injunction
to himself in "Self-Reliance": "let me record day by day my honest
thought without prospect or retrospect, and, I cannot doubt, it will be
found symmetrical"—symmetrical, that is, to the energetic flow of nature itself; by recording his own shifting perspective in its infinite altera-
tions day by day, Emerson proposes that he will discern the congruence

of "inner" life and "outer" forms ("My book should smell of pines," he proclaims, "and resound with the hum of insects").[66] In Ammons's long, thin poem that ponders the nature of thinking from so many angles—that contemplates how "the nerve / [converts] chemical into electrical energy," that heeds "a little voice / singing / under my brain," that wonders "what's the use of the / vast mental burden / of correspondence?"—the poet updates Emerson's and Stein's "objective" practices of recording thought by inventing a formal trope that emphasizes the physical determinations that shape both consciousness and its expression.[67] The poem's narrow margins bring the restrictive width of the tape continually into view, never allowing the mechanism of the adding machine to recede from the reader's awareness; the obtrusive form of *Tape for the Turn of the Year* constantly reminds us that Ammons has substituted his own mental machinery for the mechanism of the adding machine, which records its activity comprehensively and automatically. Reinforcing the computational concept of mind Ammons implies with this substitution is the resemblance of the adding machine to the tape-bearing Turing machine, a metaphor for the mind favored by philosophers during the early 1960s, and the resemblance of the lines' jagged, typewritten profile to the contour of an EEG—that empirical apparatus promoted at the time as "a mirror for the brain."[68]

Lest his readers forget that *Tape* is meant to suggest a veridical transcription of an operating mind, Ammons signals that his poem, coursing along with the torrent of consciousness, flows in a single direction. The poem is somewhat affectedly unrevised to show, as Creeley puts it in "I Keep to Myself Such Measures . . . ," that the mind cannot "come back to / where it cannot." In the poem's first daily entry, Ammons includes an epic invocation to a sympathetic muse who is herself "caught up in the / serious novelty" of his enterprise, assuaging his worry that he will be unable to bring closure to his process poem; "once started," Ammons frets in the first entry, "can I ever get free / of the thing, get it in and out of typewriter / and mind?"[69] In the poem's second entry, however, Ammons looks back upon the "classical considerations" of the previous day's prologue, recalling with compunction the grand ambitions his epic invocation had disclosed. Advertising his refusal to revise the offending lines, Ammons reveals that for the purposes of his experiment, the accuracy and

authenticity of spontaneous transcription trumps the accuracy and
authenticity of judiciously chosen language—he does not rewrite the lines
that seem "phony & / posed"; he only regrets them:

> *7 Dec:*
>
> today
> I feel a bit different:
> my prolog sounds phony &
> posed:
>   maybe
> I betrayed
> depth
> by oversimplification,
> a smugness,
> unjustified sense of
> security: . . .
> I hadn't meant
> such a long prolog: it
> doesn't seem
> classical to go ahead
> without a plan:[70]

In truth, *Tape*'s (quite classical) pretense of "go[ing] ahead / without a
plan" often does seem "phony & / posed." The poem's central ambition,
after all, is to make itself a mirror of thought, but the mirror is not the most
probing of analytical tools—not least because it attracts distorted postures of self-presentation. The poem's conceit of transcribing consciousness fails not only because it begets the tediousness to which the
poem's readers have objected but because it implies a conception of the
mind as an entity that does not transform its circumstances but passively
reflects them. Offering a rationale for this representational tactic, Ammons uses a geological metaphor to describe the poem's strategy of mimesis; he explains that his poem dwells on the "crusty/ hard-clear surface"
of experience because he can infer from the topography of mind deep, determining stirrings in nature's most elusive quarters, "hot motions / and
intermotions where, / after all, we / do not live." But dwelling on a "crusty,"
"congealed" surface could not ultimately satisfy a poet so obsessed with
life's integral motions. To evoke an underlying identity between "what is

happening in [the] mind and what is happening on the page," as he had hoped to do in *Tape for the Turn of the Year,* Ammons would need to invent a formal metaphor with which to enact in language the mind's active powers of discriminating, assimilating, and transmuting the discoveries of the senses, powers both modeled on and underpinned by the autonomic functions of the body.[71]

First imagistically, then formally, Ammons replaces his model of the poem as a reflection of thought with the model of the poem as an organ that *processes* thought—something more like a pulsating, membranous biological engine than a mirror. This crucial conceptual development enables Ammons to frame the operations of his mind and art not as symmetrical or correlated but as continuous—as integral, concrete mechanisms of synthesis, the process Ammons regards as the ur-principle of life. The poem that charts this transition but gives little indication of the radical formal possibilities it will open for Ammons's late verse is his most famous. The year he was experimenting with the "heroic failure" of *Tape for the Turn of the Year,* Ammons also composed "Corsons Inlet" (*Corsons Inlet,* 1965), another attempt to pin down the relationship between thinking and natural process. A miniature compendium of his early, governing metaphors of cognition, the poem pictures an incremental descent from a transcendental concept of mind to a somatic one.

As many have observed, the poem takes the concept of a walk—a swerving, processual, nonreproducible, embodied excursion—as its central metaphor for thinking.[72] Embedded within the overarching allegory of the walk, however, are successive images that correct and replace one another in a précis of the evolution Ammons's concept of mind undergoes from *Ommateum* to his final volumes *Glare* (1997) and *Bosh and Flapdoodle* (2005). The poem begins by representing thought as an activity framed by "perpendiculars / straight lines, blocks, boxes, binds"—as the kind of static, abstract "being anterior to action" that Ammons had held up as an ideal in *Ommateum.*[73] From this condition the speaker is released into an experience of mind that reflects the dynamism of the living landscape, and which corresponds to the "flowing bends and blends" of nature (*CP* 148). The speaker approaches the sea across the dunes and turns "right along / the surf," setting out on a course that follows the shore and becomes an irregular swerve as he rounds the tip of the headland; just as the "straight lines" of his walk dissolve into congruence with the topography of the landscape, the swerve of his mind ceases to reflect a conceptual order outside nature and comes to correspond to his environment. The liberation the speaker describes entails abandoning a model of consciousness based in "perpendicular" abstraction and adopting instead a model defined by "wandering" and "mirroring"—a model whereby the mind does not categorize and contain but reflects and resembles the motions of the visible world. In fact, Ammons depicts the operations of the mind as the operations of nature (literally) writ small; "the overall wandering of mirroring mind" mirrors in lowercase letters the activity of the "Overall," a system that transcends human comprehension.

As "Corsons Inlet" proceeds, the congruent but discrete motions of the mind, of the walker's body, of the dunes and the sea, and of the poem's dynamic form all come to reflect one another, generating an impression of numinous symmetry. Although there may be, as Ammons himself notes, "no direct contact between words and things," the natural, the mental, and the linguistic powerfully *correspond*.[74] Ammons explains that in "Corsons Inlet" he sought "to insist that somehow . . . the motion of mind and thought corresponded to natural motions"— to insist that mind "meanders, you know, like the winds or streams."[75] As they did in "Bridge" and "Reflective," these correspondences obscure the boundary between the physical and the mental without effacing that boundary, without going so far as to propose contiguity between the mental and the physical. "Corsons Inlet" ultimately does make the leap from a model of correspondence to one of continuity, however, finally repudiating the Emersonian distinction between the *Me* and the *Not Me*.[76] Ammons continues to use the figure of the line to chart this transition from a dualist metaphysics to a materialist one; having implied, ubiquitously, the invisible axis of symmetry across which the processes of mind and nature reflect each other, Ammons proceeds in "Corsons Inlet" to adopt the biological membrane—an active, living line that transforms the substance of its environment and continually reconstitutes itself—as a symbolic form that does not segregate but integrates mental and physical aspects of being.

The conclusion of "Corsons Inlet" first develops the analogy that will thenceforth dominate Ammons's representations of mind: the analogy between the operation of bodily organs and the operation of the poem imagined as a part, rather than a record, of inner life. Having beheld a congregation of tree swallows aloft in the ocean breeze, animals whose mysterious coordination embodies "the possibility of rule as the sum of rulelessness," Ammons turns to the minute, terrestrial orders of which he had always been fond—the humble, accessible forms in which, he believes, the pulsations of universal order can be felt and seen:

> in the smaller view, order tight with shape:
> blue tiny flowers on a leafless weed: carapace of crab:
> snail shell:
>> pulsations of order
>> in the bellies of minnows: orders swallowed,
> broken down, transferred through membranes
> to strengthen larger orders: but in the large view, no
> lines or changeless shapes: the working in and out, together
>> and against, of millions of events: this,
>>> so that I make
>>> no form of
>>> formlessness: (*CP* 150)

The organs of the minnows—the membranes that digest tiny orders of consumed matter "to strengthen larger orders" of the organism, the darting school, the heterogeneous ecosystem—model the mental activity of synthesizing an endless current of sensory "events" without imposing ratiocinative "form" upon the openness of perception. The membranes also model the literary activity of the poet who gives "Corsons Inlet" its distinctive shape and texture, who "make[s] / no form of / formlessness" as he translates natural processes into similarly open, errant, and organic verbal shapes. This process of mental digestion involves, "in the large view," eradicating the distinction between the material and the non-material: drawing "no / lines," relinquishing altogether the notion of ideal, "changeless shapes." In the final movement of the poem, Ammons imagines cresting a dune to find the startled congregation of swallows suddenly taking flight, but he characterizes their synchronized be-havior as an expression of embodied instinct rather than one of ideal order. The mechanism of their coordination is a physical and affective phenomenon—terror—that "pervades but is not arranged" by any intellectual or transcendental design:

> no arranged terror: no forcing of image, plan,
> or thought:
> no propaganda, no humbling of reality to precept:
>
> terror pervades but is not arranged, all possibilities
> of escape open: no route shut, except in
>   the sudden loss of all routes:
>
>   I see narrow orders, limited tightness, but will
> not run to that easy victory:
>   still around the looser, wider forces work:
>   I will try
> to fasten into order enlarging grasps of disorder, widening
> scope, but enjoying the freedom that
> Scope eludes my grasp, that there is no finality of vision,
> that I have perceived nothing completely,
>   that tomorrow a new walk is a new walk. (*CP* 151)

Like the membranes in the minnows' bellies that "strengthen larger orders" through the process of digestion, thinking (and poesis) are acts of "fasten[ing] into order" the humble, the fragmentary, the entropic. Ammons's picture of mental process has become one in which there is "no humbling of reality to precept," and the processing of knowledge depends on and thus shamelessly resembles the processing of food. The speaker proposes that human knowledge, as a product of physiological process, is limited by inexorable, physical constraints (he has exchanged the fantasy of the ommateum's synoptic perspective for a human eye that "perceive[s] nothing completely"); indeed, the speaker finds freedom in those constraints, not least by joyfully surrendering any ambition to transcend them. The poem's concluding tautology ("a new walk is a new walk") suggests the possibility of aesthetic renewal within nature's flow of repetitions, but it also reflects the inevitable circularity of all definitions within a monist paradigm, according to which any phenomenon—thinking, walking, being—must necessarily be defined in terms of itself.

Ever more pervasively after *Corsons Inlet,* Ammons imagines the mind and the poem alike as physical extensions of biological process. The vast paean to "the flow of shapes" that Ammons named *Sphere: The Form of a Motion* (1973) "was the place," he recalls, "where [I] was able to deal with the problem of the One and the Many to [my] own satisfaction," rendering his own thought in a form at once particular and universal, uniquely his own and "representative of what can happen in other minds."[77] A sequence of 155 twelve-line units divided into tercets, *Sphere* enacts the balance of particle and system, diversity and unity, the one and the many. In it, Ammons luxuriates in the imaginative scope that his immersion in the minutiae of physical existence offers ("I figure I'm the exact / poet of the concrete *par excellence,* as Whitman might say"), and experiments with an exultant range of novel somatic metaphors for the mind. The poem was inspired by the early images of the earth sent back from outer space and by the fresh demand their perspective placed on the imagination to conceive of the "sphere" of the planet as a unified system; within that system, Ammons recognized, an unfathomable affluence of systems is contained, even while the earth plays its own parts as a single piece within the ensemble of the solar system, as a particle in the expanse of the galaxy, and as an ephemeral fleck in the expanding universe, all at once. The sphere is also a figure for the poem, the form of which suggests a reticulated matrix of "ideas [that] are human products, / temporal & full of / process," a matrix that registers Ammons's vision of consciousness as both a dynamic sum of minute interactions and a part of reality that is both ephemeral and incomplete.[78] "The head is my sphere," he proclaims soon before writing *Sphere;* "I'll look significant," he schemes, "as I deal with mere wires of light, ghosts of cells, working there" (*CP* 260).

Sphere evokes the unedited flow of consciousness that *Tape of the Turn of the Year* had striven to capture, in part by flouting conventions of lyric propriety—a strategy Ammons takes to audacious extremes in his last volumes. In *Sphere,* Ammons embraces the unseemly and inelegant, refusing to extort moments of unusual beauty or clarity from the brume of cognitive static; he entangles the poetic and the prosaic to give the impression of blundering, spontaneous, "unedited" thought; he spurns the "little rondures" of closed form that both he and Creeley disdained, adopting a textual silhouette that does not simply flow but "gathers and dissolves" in punctuated bursts of integration and dissolution, transforming reality as it is processed into poetry.[79] *Sphere* thus presents a formal picture of consciousness consistent with the mind Ammons describes in the poem as "a little mill that changes / everything, not from its shape, but from change," the motions of which prove that "we are not half-in and / Half-out of the universe but unmendably integral."[80]

Sphere constantly links verbal and somatic acts of integration, in fact. "[T]he human / being is as inscrutable and unformulable as a poem," Ammons proclaims, "or, if / possible, more so," and like the poet dispersing the depths of his experience into a relay of verbal connections, "the gas station attendant has a bottomless / well in him, too—shoots from his brain down his spine, breaks / into incredible ramification, the same as bottomless."[81] Early in his career, from *Expressions of Sea Level* onward, Ammons had replaced the period with the colon in the majority of his poems, a transformation that enabled him to create verbal networks through which no syntactic part is ever made visually subordinate to another. In *Sphere,* however, Ammons's colons suggest more explicitly than ever the reticulated neurological matrices through which "the mind breaks against some configuration and makes off into / netlike effusions."[82] Collapsing his models of mind and poem, Ammons superimposes a graphical, syntactic matrix upon the propulsive flow of thought, using punctuation to process raw experience. This structural matrix is meant to suggest, among other organic connections, the "unformulable" web of the nervous system, the "incredible ramification[s]" of which are felt everywhere in the flow of conscious life. Ammons's colons not only alter the aural texture of the clauses they connect, causing the phrases to end with an anticipatory rise in pitch rather than a conclusive drop, but also transform the poem into a matrix of equivalent textual units—a unified fabric continuous with the world it represents. Ammons describes how colons, unlike the divisive periods and capital letters that frame complete thoughts, unify the substance of the poem: "I hate periods," he explains, "because the gap then suggests that one whole sentence has been separated off from the tissue of the whole poem";

> The world is so interpenetrated that it must be one tissue of size, of letters. . . . So the colon jump should do that, just connect and connect and connect, until you build not just the assertion you're making but this landscape. I've never been interested in single discursive statements as such, as explanation, but I'm interested in clusters of

those, because then they become, they sort of come to be the thing they represent. They're many-sided.[83]

As Ammons uses it, the colon replaces a period or semicolon to form a conjunctive fissure, a caesura that at once connects and disconnects related but independent thoughts. The colon thus atomizes, equalizes, and aggregates those thoughts, allowing the poem to "become" the thinking it represents.

It is clearly one of Ammons's great pleasures in *Sphere* to portray such integral connections between verbal and somatic mechanisms, mechanisms through which we process reality as parts of reality. In one extended conceit, he compares the discriminating intelligence of the critic assembling an anthology, a paradigmatic document of cultural inheritance, to the genetic forces that determine biological inheritance; the critic administers the convergence of "good sayings" ("genes") and "poems" ("chromosomes"), drawing on "gene pool, word hoard" to absorb new poetry within an evolving literary tradition. The scholar's critical exercise involves "hook[ing] in" and "find[ing] . . . attachments" among literary parts, producing from them a "whole body" of cultural knowledge. In a frisson of mixed metaphors, the critic's eye is also the eye of the surgeon who "looks into the body of / the anthology to see if the new thing hooks in," who not only assesses the literary organ's "viability" but facilitates and evaluates the sustaining flow of energy through the osmotic seam—the "attachment"—that unites the part and the whole. The literary apparatus of the anthology, an artificial unity made of poem after discrete poem, is both a repository of inspiration and a source of it—an integral, material force affecting the "becomings of our minds" as much as the "fortunate forwardings" of our DNA.[84]

In *Sphere,* Ammons disavows the mind's illusions of its own transcendental origins, the hubris whereby "the mind studies the soil, wedges / out spudeyes and plants them, attends, devours with its body, / and yet declares itself independent of the soil."[85] As it is for Creeley, the dependence of mind upon the soil of embodied being is, by the end of Ammons's life, an old story, one that emerges in a different timbre under the pressure of advancing age. Ammons's final volumes, *Glare* and *Bosh and Flapdoodle,* emphasize the proximity of an end to life that seems "as close as the next cell of my brain," reframing the concept of embodied consciousness as a felt condition charged with new emotional significance in the face of death. Ammons turned seventy while writing *Glare,* and he alludes on several occasions to a nearly fatal heart attack he had suffered several years before.[86] The poems subject the body to various forms of threatening, medicalized intrusion that prove to be not only physically but existentially uncomfortable (the many pills the aging speaker of *Glare* takes each day, for example, "[make] / me wonder if I'm doing medical emotions or synergetic emotions," he writes).[87] In the late poems, Ammons relatedly fixates on the body's translation of consumed matter into energy and waste, correlating the most unseemly aspects of processing food with the most distinctive aspects of his late style. Enlisting unflinching candor and even brazen vulgarity to reveal the transmutative powers of mind and language, Ammons finally carries his digestive model of mind (and of the poem) to its furthest conceptual extremes in a bracing formal turn to nonsense.

Ammons's late poetry dwells soberly on organs devoted to digestion and excretion—mouth, stomach, intestines, colon, and anus—challenging his readers to assimilate what can appear to be cheap scatological thrills within a broader account of the works' aesthetic ambitions and experimental extravagances. This late poetry extends Ammons's long-standing reverence for the humble organisms whose lives are entirely circumscribed by such processes. In his early poem "Catalyst," the poet had encouraged us to venerate even the most repulsive scavengers:

> Honor the maggot,
>   supreme catalyst:
> he spurs the rate of change:
> (all scavengers are honorable: I love them
> all,
> will scribble hard as I can for them) (*CP* 110)

Such reverence befits a "transformer of bloated, breaking flesh / into colorless netted wing," a larval maggot turned butterfly, whose digestion embodies the poet's transformation of the devastating ruptures of emotional life into the sublime transport of sympathetic recognition. This reverence, rooted in a symbolic association between the activities of scavengers and the activities of literary artists, had gone on to pervade *Garbage* (1993), which is dedicated *"to the bacteria, tumblebugs, scavengers, word-smiths—the transfigurers, restorers,"* and which makes a moldering pile of refuse into an emblem of the mind's nourishing digestion of language itself: "there is a mound, / too, in the poet's mind," Ammons writes, "language is hauled off to and burned down on, the energy held and / shaped into new turns and clusters, the mind strengthened by what it strengthens."[88]

It is in *Glare,* however, that Ammons finds in his own body's trans-mutation of consumed matter a model that unites the mental and semi-otic systems whose morphologies mediate our self-understanding. *Glare* is composed of two parts that were created independently before Ammons chose to join them for publication; the poems are unified, however, by the use of unrhymed couplets and the continuous numbering of the otherwise untitled poems across the two parts. The title of the first part, "Strip," an-nounces Ammons's return to the form of *Tape for the Turn of the Year,* for he composes, yet again, on a strip of adding machine tape that allows a maximum of thirty-six characters per line. The volume thus answers the poet's earlier experiment in recording thought, but here the material constraints of the "skinny" poem charged with digesting meaning are continually shown to reflect the constraints of the body specifically:

> this tape is so skinny: I
> have to crack off the lines and roll
>
> the trimmings back into the next line:
> there is never enough room: the
>
> lines have to digest something, pack
> it down, shove stuff together . . .
>
> I was thinking how this tape cramps
> my style: it breaks down my extended
>
> gestures: it doesn't give your
> asshole time to reconfigure after a
>
> dump: everything happens before its
> time, interrupted, turned back, cracked
>
> up:[89]

In light of such lines, the title "Strip" also suggests the unseemly exposure of the striptease, a style denuded of euphemistic rhetoric and the
stately garb of lyric propriety. While the skinny form evokes the poems'
concrete, scatological referent (the poem presents itself as a "dump" processed and evacuated by the body), Ammons's chatty tone confers upon
the poem a spokenness that enables "Strip" to identify the oral and the
anal as intimate counterparts, affiliating expressive and bodily methods
of processing the given. Embodied knowledge and poesis are not reflections of the world, but by-products that retain traces of the processes that
generate them; just as the rigid limits of his tape determine the representational scope of his poem, the limits of the body impose fundamental,
epistemological limitations on the poem as well. Still, even as the speaker
complains that the medium of the tape "cramps / my style" and leaves little
room for the lines "to digest something," the poem's narrow shape "breaks
down," "interrupt[s,]" and "crack[s] up" the raw matter of his unfolding
ideas.[90]

In the second part of *Glare*, "Scat Scan," Ammons uses a slightly wider
tape that can accommodate forty-five characters per line, allowing him
greater freedom within his chosen limitations. He uses this freedom to
clarify the relationship among three central aspects of his late poetics,
which are condensed in the title "Scat Scan": scatology, nonsense, and
his own enduring interest in the empirical meanings of "mind." "Scat
Scan," of course, contains and rhymes with "CAT scan" and thus evokes,
like "Strip," the exposure of the human body glared upon with ominous intensity. Exchanging the EEG of *Tape for the Turn of the Year* for
the "Scat Scan," the latter part of *Glare* likewise metaphorically "suggests
absolute authenticity," Roger Gilbert observes, "in mapping the ups and
downs, peaks and valleys, and assorted vital signs of its author's inner
life."[91] Unlike *Tape*, however, which figures the reflective, mimetic powers
of mind by transcribing thought "directly," *Glare* registers the invisible
sway of physiological determinations upon the experience of mind by acknowledging the exertions of the poem's form upon its construction of
meaning. By insisting on the obtrusiveness, rather than the transparency,
of somatic and verbal media in making sense, Ammons thus complicates
the very premises of emotional and expressive authenticity. On several occasions Ammons finds, in the medicated contingency of his emotions,

reason to question the reliability of his experience; for example, just as he wonders in "Strip" if he's "doing medical / emotions or synergetic emotions," in "Scat Scan" he wonders whether his feelings are genuinely "lofty" or fraudulently "zolofty":

> so many pills you
>
> can't tell the effects from the side effects:
> and who are you, someone before the medications
>
> or during or after: at least, you are being
> kept, but in another place: are your feelings
>
> lofty or zolofty, red or blue, down or double
> downdown: do you, in this condition, have any
>
> right to speak, for who or what is speaking, is
> it milligrams or anagrams, is it tranquility or
>
> tranquilium: will we psyches be like the
> skies: we'll never again see clouds that may
>
> not be vapor trails: we'll never be clear and
> know our clouds for what they are:[92]

To accept the proposition that emotions are chemical phenomena, Ammons insists, is to realize that who "you" are and "who or what is speaking" in a poem will never again be as clear or stable as they once seemed to be; the emotional exhibitions in the "skies" of our psyches inspire a new kind of skepticism and curiosity about the ambiguously natural and artificial status of their sources. Ammons's zolofty feelings remind him that he is a thinking thing, and that looking to the physical origins of experience generates as many questions about the self as it answers. The CAT scan, it turns out, obscures as much as it discloses.

The "scat scan" is also an investigation of scatological remains, of the evidence of what goes in and what comes out, the traces of interiority that extend in a legible trail behind experience. Knowledge, as a product of cognitive digestion, becomes in these late poems an exalted kind of waste, left over after the given has been processed by the body. One of *Glare's* most striking poems begins with a daunting question innocently posed— "where do poems come from"—that it in turn answers with absolute confidence; poems come, Ammons proclaims, from a swerve of embodied feeling, motion "that is the seed / of form" digested in the process of the poem's creation:

> there's a currency of feeling and it
> flows as unformed, if noticeable, as
>
> a drive, and describes a form of
> itself . . .
>
> motion, going from here to there,
> describes a swerve or arc or salience
>
> and that is form: that is the seed
> of form, born in the very bosom of
>
> its substance, which is motion: next
> to that, tell me what you think of
>
> a sonnet or some fucking cookie-cutter:
> I mustn't become high-handed: I'm
>
> more miserable than most anybody I
> know, so don't take after me: I'm
>
> okay when I'm typing like this, tho:
> I'm in motion and the worm I am
>
> extruding has a long wiggle: it
> seems to me as I look about that I
>
> know some things well: but they are
> about nothing: there is no seedcorn,
>
> there are no potato eyes in my stuff:[93]

To host a process by which a mute sensation "describes" itself into the articulate shape of a poem is a source of consolation for Ammons: "I'm // more miserable than most anybody I / know," he admits, but "I'm // okay when I'm typing like this, tho." He contrasts the "cookie-cutter" (which gives rigid shape to undigested food) to the dynamic "long wiggle" of the poem that issues from the body "in motion" at the typewriter. Indeed, in his poem, *everything* is digested: "there is no seedcorn," Ammons insists; "there are no potato eyes in my stuff." Form itself is a "seed" that is not planted but eaten, that does not grow but breaks down and thus perme-

ates every aspect of the poem's substance, from the contour of its excre-
mental "wiggle" to its integration of aesthetically indigestible parts of
discourse (obscenity, profanity, scatological reference) to its use of punctuation. Punning on the congruent operations of the organic colon and
the syntactic colon, both of which impose peristaltic rhythms on (excre-
mental and semiotic) matter as they process their contents, Ammons
evokes the synthetic motions whereby "mind, too, terribly flows and
stalls, holds and gives way."[94]

In light of *Glare*'s cognitive and scatological interests, then, the title
"Scat Scan" makes sense. That "Scat Scan" is also apparently governed
by a logic of sound, however—that it initially seems to make no sense at
all—is also consistent with Ammons's frequent use of nonsense in his late
verse, yet another practice through which he affiliates the workings of
mind and language by exposing the tacit, formal mechanisms that regulate their operation. Ammons begins his musical poem 105 with a jazzy
"scat" improvisation about a conspicuously familiar writer of "nature
poetry":

> nature poetry, nature poetry
> he's got nature
> poetry up piss ass
>
> nature poetry, nature poetry
> he's got nature
> poetry up piss ass DA de DA
>
> I mean DUM de DUM
>
> music for my opening: overture to my manure
> (you're out on the highway of life when
>
> unfinished you end butt up):
>
> no, I mean UP piss ASS

Exchanging heads for tails ("butt up"), equating the "openings[s]" of the
oral and the anal, interpreting nature's claim on the poetic imagination
as nature's call, Ammons's poem is in many senses "up piss ass." He proceeds to conflate physical and metaphysical forms of inwardness in the
poem, jeopardizing the most sacred, transcendental source of lyric as he
balances his impulse toward self-exposure with our invasive desire to look

inside: "I suppose you would like to / know something about my inner life: well, it // stinks."[95] This chiming "overture" to Ammons's poetic "manure" embraces the musicality of the scat singing that recurs in "Scat Scan" ("bittle de doo doo / daw: de daw daw:"); "DA de DA" and "DUM de DUM" playfully identify the alternating stresses of metrical lines with the musical rhythms of which poetic meter is both a vestige and a signature.[96]

Scat singing is only one permutation of nonsense among many that pervade the final volumes *Glare* and *Bosh and Flapdoodle*; the title of the latter volume, which was published posthumously, suggests the importance to Ammons of both "babble" and "doodle," Northrop Frye's terms for the lyric's essential elements of the heard and the seen.[97] Both volumes contain numerous poems that conclude with provocatively dissonant, unpunctuated words and phrases printed in capitals—tags that are set apart from the bodies of the poems. The relationships of these tags to the poems they follow are in some cases intelligible and in others entirely obscure, but the words and phrases nearly always contain some element of nonsense. In poem 105, the tag's significance is relatively clear: it unifies, with Ammons's familiar, deflationary irreverence, the wind of inspiration that issues from "inner," spiritual life and the wind that issues from anatomically "inner" life:

> anyway, I love you, you know I love you, and I
> want your life inner and outer to be doused
>
> with radiance, even if it is really a
>
> STINKEROO

The final word is syntactically and thematically related to the poem as a whole, which continually dispels forms of transcendence with obscenity, forcing the dignified music of the spirit to mingle with the slangy music of the body.[98] In poem 101 of "Scat Scan," however, the relevance of the tag to the poem that precedes it is much less clear. Ammons contemplates the end of his own life and the end of the world, picturing the convergence of two roads (punningly, "wheys") that come to an undifferentiated terminus in oblivion. The breaking off of the final stanza suggests the

breaking off of the story of the self when "the clabber's all gone"—when
life's possibilities seem to have been consumed entirely:

> if there's any story left
> to tell there'll be no telling what the story
>
> is: differences can be important where it's
> hard to make out a difference: this is so
>
> philosophical! but I better look out: I
> might miss the road (if I don't want to): in
>
> any case, whey leads on to whey and pretty
> soon the clabber's all gone: I think I'll take
>
> a stanza break here. . . .
>
> THE BEE MITES ARE A MIGHTY
> BIG PROBLEM

Led down a relatively neat path of metaphors, the reader finally comes to
an untended plot of chiastic nonsense, a weedy patch of sounds. Whatever else the bee mites might signify, their immediate effect and their primary significance lie in their flirtation with meaning nothing at all. The
final tags of other poems reveal similarly tenuous connections to the lines
that precede them, as they do in poem 71:

> the present drawn forward
>
> and backward into itself, now, just *now*, just
> now:
>
> THERE ARE PLENTY OF SEATS
> UP FRONT

And in poem 108:

> will we be too rare
>
> or too tough or overdone or sauceless: I
> think not: I think we will be acceptable:
>
> anyhow,

LET'S NOT SPOIL THE TRUTH
WITH BEAUTY
HERE, OKAY

And in poem 113:

running through, and

rising, is the constant will that longs for
companionship with an all-keeping indifference

YOU'VE NEVER
SEEN ANYTHING
LIKE IT
OR LIKED
ANYTHING SCENIC[99]

An early reference to the Tower of Babel hints at the ancestry of these unusual, babbling tags. In poem 4, Ammons searches for redemption through "broken sounds," calling out "from the height of / the high place, where speaking is not // necessary to hearing and hearing is / in all languages."[100] During his childhood in rural North Carolina, Ammons regularly witnessed the spectacle of glossolalia in church and recognized early and firsthand the disorienting power of the verbal sign untethered from significance. "I've seen people [speak in tongues] for hours," he explains:

> It's incredible to watch a person whose behavior is absolutely regular as if he were buying ham from a delicatessen speaking to you in totally ununderstandable words. Not done in a frenzy. I remember sitting on a bench in church when a person so possessed would come directly and stand in front of you as if telling you how to bake a cake and would go through this rigamarole and be absolutely unintelligible.[101]

This disconnection that so impresses Ammons—the disconnection between the mien of the speaker who appears not to be in extremis and the "absolutely unintelligible" words with which that speaker pushes language to its furthest limits—is also a model for the operation of the nonsensical poetic tags that appear in Ammons's last volumes. With conventional syntax and allusion ("LET'S NOT SPOIL THE TRUTH / WITH BEAUTY / HERE, OKAY"), chiastic structure and rhythm ("YOU'VE

NEVER / SEEN ANYTHING / LIKE IT / OR LIKED/ ANYTHING SCENIC"), colloquialisms and clichés ("THERE ARE PLENTY OF SEATS / UP FRONT"), and the placement of the tags—in capitals—at the end of his poems (like summary morals printed after children's fables), Ammons makes the tags *behave* as if they make sense and expect to be understood; he places a thoughtful, expressive countenance upon a frenzy of unintelligibility, and generates in us the same expectation of meaning that the "absolutely regular" behavior of the ecstatic Baptist worshippers generated in him as a child.[102] By evacuating rhetorical and syntactic structures of decipherable "content," the tags isolate and expose the tacit operations of form that subliminally digest meaning. Indeed, they wreak an ecstatic separation of the word's spirit—its sense—from its rhetorical (embodied) circumstance in order to reveal their true inextricability. Ammons's spectacle of nonsense makes us feel the coercions of syntax and rhythm and arrangement on the page—the most physical, formal aspects of the language—upon the process of making meaning.

In Ammons's title "Scat Scan," then, excretory, neurological, and verbal forms of "scat" collapse into one another not only punningly but ontologically, for their contiguous forms of digestion reveal that the body, the mind, and language itself are manifold expressions of an integrative kind of motion that unifies human and nonhuman nature. The submission of all phenomena to the entropic forces that govern physical reality coordinates "inner life" with its concrete, somatic, and verbal contexts, Ammons concludes, and thus he finds in the disintegrations of meaning that punctuate his late poems a suitable use for the glossolalic form that had lain fallow as a poetic resource until the final years of his life. In *Tape for the Turn of the Year,* Ammons had entertained a conception of language as a transparent medium, but in the late poems, his ostentatious opacity—his use of nonsense to reveal the "invisible" sway of formal and generic convention on meaning—exposes the surreptitious imprint of material circumstance on the most rarefied mental and linguistic actions. These features invest poetry with the power to digest anything: scientific jargon, vulgarity, cliché, nonsense, the baffling hope and dread of old age, the prospect of dissolving back into insignificant particles of matter.

Ammons and Creeley both long to bring language and mind into the truest possible relation, to make poems of thinking that somehow become what they represent. Their attempts to fulfill these ambitions not only test their sincerity and their conviction but also enliven their inclusive sensibilities, encouraging them to realize mystical potential in the humble forms and local situations to which they are both temperamentally drawn. While Creeley finds himself carrying his humble poetic talk to the vanishing point of voice, Ammons follows the lessons of the deprecated organs and organisms he cherishes to the point in language where sense vanishes into nonsense. "As a non-religious person," Ammons writes, describing a predicament the poets share, "I have no way, / to assuage, relieve, or forgive / myself."[103] But as each grounds the stirrings of consciousness and selfhood in the autotelic legitimacy of the body, he discovers consolatory possibilities for uniting self and circumstance in language—forms of opportunity that James Merrill will cultivate, with characteristic wit and elegance, in the absences that gape in memory.

CHAPTER 3

James Merrill's Embodied Memory

A POET ASSOCIATED with transcendental consolations and spiritualist resurrections of the past, James Merrill has appeared to many to be at odds with his zeitgeist. In *The Changing Light at Sandover,* he famously conjures an epic cast of disembodied spirits at the Ouija board; innovating from within the tradition, he revives ostensibly "dead," superannuated forms (quatrains, couplets, villanelles) in an era of open ones; in his "CHRONICLES OF LOVE & LOSS," luminous mirages of the lived past seem to arise unbidden "from time's trickling sands."[1] But the dualist dream of the Ouija board, the nostalgic yearnings that his inherited forms imply, and especially the persistent manifestations of memory in Merrill's poems all spring from the soil of doubt—from the underlying premises that the soul does not outlast the body, that the meanings of received poetic forms are transformed by their contexts, and that consciousness, as constrained by temporal and physical circumstances as any other bodily phenomenon, forecloses any true revelation of the past. Anything but transcendental, acts of memory in Merrill's poems prove to be embedded in, and inextricable from, their verbal and corporeal sites of production—sites that shape the story of the self through endlessly productive imprecisions and omissions. For all their prominence, the lived and literary pasts—the resources that constitute and define the fragmentary construct of the lyric subject—are ultimately physical, ephemeral, and incomplete.

Merrill died from complications arising from AIDS in 1995, and as the progression of his illness over the preceding decade signaled the encroachment of oblivion upon his historical, biological being, he composed lyrics in which the figurative significance of forgetting becomes increasingly legible. Discerning in Merrill's late self-portraiture the struggle to "find a stylistic equivalent for the quickness of the senses and the spirit even as the deathly dissolution of the body becomes certain," Helen Vendler emphasizes the undiminished wit the poet displays in *A Scattering of Salts* (1995) as he grapples with the wrenching disharmony between his body's enervation and his mind's indefatigable liveliness. "In age and illness (barring dementia) one is as much alive in consciousness as ever," Vendler observes, and in light of his unyielding mental fitness, Merrill's tendency to exaggerate his depictions of mnemonic failure is one sign that his preoccupation with forgetting exceeds that which predictably accompanies advancing age.[2]

Indeed, Merrill is most confident that he is advancing toward the truth of the mind when he is exaggerating failures of memory; throughout his oeuvre, he stresses that the mundane experience of forgetting is an exceptional aspect of mental life, for it allows bodily materiality to bear discernibly upon the operations of consciousness. The images with which Merrill embodies aspects of memory are in some cases conventional (mirror, projector, computer, bank) and in others, novel (postcard, puzzle, hoop-jumping equestrienne), but they have in common the harsh light he casts on them as he illuminates their faults; implicitly and explicitly, he identifies those faults with the biological circuitry that grounds conscious experience. Locked in one another's orbit, the conjoined presences of mortality (the disintegration of the physical self) and forgetting (the disintegration of its conscious record, inscribed within the shifting matter of the body) reveal Merrill's philosophy of consciousness to be consistent with the materialist consensus of his time. But unlike Lowell, Creeley, and Ammons (and like the later Ashbery, as we shall see), Merrill is disinclined to see his neurochemical age as an exception, or to understand its fixation on physical first causes as an unprecedented poetic donnée. Indeed, for Merrill, who is always craning backward for glimpses of human recognition, the most timeless experiential evidence that the mind operates under mortal constraints offers our recent biologization of inner life its most forceful corroboration. Acknowledging his era's empirical vocabulary of mind while holding the long history of poetry's romance with lost versions of the past in view, the poems reflect the integration of late twentieth-century biological materialism within an especially expansive creative consciousness eager to situate mind and memory within ancient currents of Western thought—"Aristotle / And Plato, gristle and dream" (*CP* 604).

Merrill admitted to a dilettantish familiarity with nonspecialist scientific (and pseudoscientific) texts—Isaac Asimov's *Guide to Science,* Lewis Thomas's *Lives of a Cell,* Arthur Young's *Reflexive Universe: Evolution of Consciousness,* Julian Jaynes's *The Origins of Consciousness in the Breakdown of the Bicameral Mind,* to name a few—and his borrowings of their diction and imagery demonstrate the extent to which their content both captures his imagination and supplies, when desired, conceptual frameworks for the translation of spiritual experience into secular, empirical terms. When Merrill writes of Dante that "like Milton or Yeats he had mediumistic powers—a sustaining divinatory intelligence which spoke to him, if only (as Julian Jaynes would have it) from that center of the brain's right hemisphere which corresponds to Weinecke's [*sic*] area on the left," he displays not only his willingness to draw on the culturally ascendant language of brain science to describe subjective experience, but also his canny awareness of the corroborative value of a neuroscientific vocabulary in overcoming readerly skepticism toward his occult literary experiments.[3] Though in his epic poem JM (as Merrill calls himself there) professes to comply only grudgingly when spirits at the Ouija board command him to write "POEMS OF SCIENCE" (*CL* 113) ("Poems of *Science?*," he grumbles, "Ugh. / The very thought" [*CL* 109]), Merrill was in fact a responsive witness to the intensifying disciplinary and conceptual convergence of philosophy of mind and brain science during his lifetime.[4] This much is evident in the early, lapidary poems of *The Black Swan* (1946), where vision is inexorably bound by the "mortal tissue" (*CP* 58) that facilitates it; in the pivotal poems of *Water Street* (1962), where provisional mental representations of personal history, riddled with missing pieces, are drawn into somatic cycles of infirmity and convalescence; and certainly in the *Sandover* books (1976–1980), where God Biology presides over the exertions of embodied and disembodied forms of consciousness alike, and Nature (God B's twin) also bears the aspects of Chaos and Psyche (soul, mind).[5] Such direct intimations of Merrill's conception of the mind in embodied terms, however, are dispersed throughout the poems and prose in the service of shifting rhetorical motives, often revealing little about the ways in which the idea of a mind underpinned by material constraints inflects his interpretation of experience. It is instead in poems that address his most cherished themes—love, loss, memory, poetry— poems that are often unrecognizable as "Poems of Science," that Merrill most fully expresses the affective and imaginative implications of existing in a world where "Mind is Matter" (*CL* 150).

It is in Merrill's last books, *The Inner Room* (1988) and *A Scattering of Salts*, that the embodied mind and the questions it poses for the writing subject come into focus most sharply; as the prospect of his own death hastens into view, the elusive, determining continuity between body and spirit becomes integral to his conception of poetry itself. It is only in "Losing the Marbles," his expansive, dazzling portrayal of mnemonic loss, that the poet draws his materialist philosophies of consciousness and poetry into consummate harmony, but by the time that culminating poem appeared Merrill had become practiced at fusing scientific materialism's concreteness with the abstract, universalizing resonances of myth. "Verse for Urania," from *Divine Comedies* (1976), exemplifies the easy commerce between biological and mythological visions of the mind Merrill cultivates throughout the poems, allowing Lethe and neural circuitry their complementary descriptive claims on mental experience. Situating our faith in science within a long heritage of spiritual dogmas, the poem draws together the material and the imagined, "Warp of physics, woof of whim" (*CP* 346).

The central event of "Verse for Urania" is the baptism of the poet's Greek-American goddaughter, Urania, as she assumes the name borne by Milton's "Heav'nly muse," the Greek muse of astronomy. As the middle-aged poet observes Urania's staggering growth in light of his own putative mental decline, the waters of the baptismal font suggest to him the waters of Lethe, threatening to erase the mental record of his life. Merrill's awkward participation in the religious ritual and good-natured but irritable initiation into the office of godparent are offset by his harmonious intimacy with the child, who is his twin at life's opposite pole; asserting a generational connection "in time embedded," he affirms that "Our bond was sacred, being secular" (*CP* 391). He has in mind the temporal sense of "secular" (Latin *saeculum*, generation, century, age), for the arrival of "the newborn child, whose age begins" ushers in the poet's own child-less middle age, which he prematurely, and somewhat petulantly, names his "second childhood" (*CP* 390); even Urania's celestial name evokes a spray of stars blinking out, for Merrill associates stellar fire with the tran-sient biological fire that courses through neurons—the "Electric cur-rents [that] quicken brain and heart" (*CL* 380). Throughout "Verse for Urania," in fact, Merrill translates the lived experience of mnemonic loss into recognizably physiological terms; addressing his twin at life's oppo-site pole, asserting a generational connection "in time embedded," he finds in time's effects on Urania's growing body an occasion to appraise time's effects on his mind:

> Where has time flown? Since I began [writing this poem]
> You've learned to stand for seconds, balancing,
> And look away at my approach, coyly.
> My braincells continue to snuff out like sparks
> At the average rate of 100,000 a day—
> The intellect suspiciously resembling
> Eddington's universe in headlong flight
> From itself. (*CP* 388)

Merrill draws a facetious but fretful analogy between the expanding void of his aging intellect and the expanding universe, both of which he iden-tifies with innumerable, but ultimately fragile, units of matter in dynamic (chemical or gravitational) interaction. He sets the growing emptiness of the expanding universe, itself projected to pass from a stelliferous heyday to a "degenerate" age of starlessness, against the expanding mental void left by his body's fallible reconstructions of the past.[6]

Merrill's poems often affiliate the brain with the firmament, identifying the biological determinations that structure human experience with the mysterious conscriptions of human fate. But "Verse for Urania" also dem-onstrates Merrill's tendency to regard the limits and losses of memory— aspects of experience he constantly associates with the body—as creative necessities fundamental to his art. He thus overlays, in "Verse for Urania," the mortally flawed, finally material process of remembering the day of the baptism with the faltering process of rendering his memories—the morning's preparations, the hectic drive to the church—in a verbal medium replete with its own material limits (the fertile constraints of pentameter, for example). The process involves translating memory, always inscribed against the dark horizon of impending loss, into a poem that coalesces within the void of the blank page, black on white:

> Finding a moment, I've written: *Rose from bed*
> *Where I'd begun imagining the baptism . . .*
> *To dress for it. Then all of us were racing*
> *The highway to a dozen finishing lines*
> *Every last one unquotable, scored through,*
> *You bubbling milk, your sister in my lap*
> *Touching her rhinestone treble-clef barrette*
> —Made-up touches. Lately I forget
> The actual as it happens (Plato warns us
> Writing undermines the memory—
> So does photography, I should tell your father)
> And have, as now, less memory than a mind
> To rescue last month's Lethe-spattered module
> From inner space—eternal black-on-white
> Pencilings, moondusty palindrome—
> For splashdown in the rainbow. Welcome home. (*CP* 389; ellipses mine)

Racing to the *"finishing lines"* of his poem and of a life that seems to be accelerating toward death, Merrill conceives of his acts of memory in "Verse for Urania" as acts of rescue; he depicts the poet as a cosmonaut navigating the depths of inner space, always retracing—since a palindrome is literally a "stepping backward"—mnemonic imprints as fragile as footprints in lunar dust. But even as he regrets forgetting so much of "the actual as it happens," the poet suggests that memory's erratic, up-to-the-moment self-erasure, in conjunction with the deliberate process of *"scor[ing] through"* unsuitable details, opens a literary space for "made-up touches" that enrich the reality of the past.[7] As the imagination colorfully supplements last month's sketchy, grayscale "pencilings"—Plato's mnemonic images "seen through a glass dimly"—Merrill welcomes the past "home" into the technicolor multiplicity of verse.[8] Indeed, the poem's exaltation of the process whereby "Lethe-spattered" memories, riddled with blanks, are supplemented and enhanced by a poetic touch inspires the poem's unorthodox invocation: "Mother of that hour's muse, Forgetfulness, / Hold me strictly to the might-have-been" (*CP* 390). The goddess Urania's mother, the mother of all the Muses, is Mnemosyne, the goddess of memory; for the purposes of his poem, however, Merrill rewrites his muse's lineage, replacing Memory with Forgetfulness as the ultimate source of his art.[9]

The poet's well of ink and the dark waters of oblivion mingle again in "Dead Center," a metamnemonic villanelle from *The Inner Room*. Like "Verse for Urania," the poem represents memories as unstable perforations of light in darkness, and claims that the fragile cellular circuitry that subtends every act of recollection defines the relationship between memory and poetry. The reflexive rhyme and the permutations of the refrains echo the rippling, liquid surface upon which Merrill stages the convergence of "Now" and "Then" in memory, a surface where the scintillations of a lived past are charged with inscrutable meaning. Burning at the "dead" midpoint of "Dead Center" is a remembered scene of childhood in which the speaker is abandoned at his grandmother's home, his parents' roadster disappearing down a dusty road:

> Upon reflection, as I dip my pen
> Tonight, forth ripple messages in code.
> In Now's black waters burn the stars of Then.
>
> Seen from the embankment, marble men
> Sleep upside down, bat-wise, the sleep bestowed
> Upon reflection. As I dip my pen
>
> Thinking how others, deeper into Zen,
> Blew on immediacy until it glowed,
> In Now's black waters burn the stars of Then.
>
> Or else I'm back at Grandmother's. I'm ten,
> Dust hides my parents' roadster from the road
> Which dips—*into* reflection, with my pen.
>
> Breath after breath, harsh O's of oxygen—
> Never deciphered, what do they forebode?
> In Now's black waters burn the stars. Ah then

> Leap, Memory, supreme equestrienne,
> Through hoops of fire, circuits you overload!
> Beyond reflection, as I dip my pen
> In Now's black waters, burn the stars of Then. (*CP* 540)

Sketched in one tercet, the central memory falls away just as it is brought into being, barely glimpsed before dipping out of sight. Merrill ultimately suggests that the fiery code formed by such glimpses of the past—an answer, in inner space, to the enigmatic code of fate encrypted in the stars—may be fanned "Breath after breath" by poetic inspiration but is "Never deciphered"; "Thinking how others, deeper into Zen, / Blew on immediacy until it glowed," Merrill is left questioning his choice to depict the unreliably mediated reflections of memory in his verse. The closing quatrain's fusion of abstract and embodied ways of imagining memory tentatively reconciles these countervailing aesthetic impulses; figuring memory as a dazzlingly unfettered circus performer and her combusting props as neurological short circuits, Merrill evokes the awe and the exasperation that can arise when memory's flamboyant exhibitions overwhelm the intellect's power to comprehend them. While the "hoops of fire" through which the equestrienne passes recall the flaming, astral "O's" whose light reaches us from the remote past, Merrill also evokes electrochemical circuits in order to represent the limits of his comprehension. Even as he asserts that he will draw on the substance of the immediate moment in his poetry, the poet exults in the audacious performances of his recollection, inviting Memory to leap forth and the fires of reminiscence to burn on beyond the tightly structured villanelle's longing to contain and comprehend them.

Appropriately, this affirmation of aesthetic departure concludes part III of *The Inner Room* and ushers in part IV's "Prose of Departure," a sequence of prose poems that traces, in the up-to-the-moment present tense of a tourist's travelogue, Merrill's geographical and ruminative excursions during a trip to Japan. As a friend at home suffers through the terminal stage of AIDS, Merrill—guilty in his absence and devastated by his own recent HIV diagnosis—imagines himself to be experiencing a "'Hiroshima' of trivial symptoms" (*CP* 557).[10] Following the hybrid *haibun* form adopted in the travelogues of a master far "deeper into Zen" than Merrill himself—Matsuo Bashō—the short sketches frequently contract into crystalline haiku that embody the aesthetics of presence "Dead Center" recommends, and that befit the prospective tenor of a voyage to face the music of mortality. The poetry D. H. Lawrence describes as "the poetry of the immediate present . . . [of] haste, not rest, come-and-go, not fixity, inconclusiveness, immediacy . . . without denouement or close" inevitably holds for Merrill, always inclined to enfold experience into closed forms, the tantalizing appeal of an artistic road not taken; as he observes of his own highly formal verse "in our age of breakthroughs," "Now and then one enjoys a little moonwalk, some little departure from tradition" (*CPr* 123).[11] In "Dead Center," the departure entails crediting the equation between "immediacy" and authenticity embraced by so many of Merrill's American contemporaries in their diverse forms of descent from Williams and Whitman. Though the opposition Merrill proposes in "Dead Center" between a poetics of memory and a poetics of immediacy takes place in the exceptional context of a provisional aesthetic renunciation of remembrance, the opposition points precisely to the mediatory dimension of memory that constitutes the faculty's appeal to him as a poetic subject. For it is through the disruptive traces of memory's exertions—the impression of "forget[ting] / The actual as it happens" or of beholding a fragmentary image that suddenly betrays a missing whole— that he not only feels the mind implicitly intervening and shaping the story of the self, but also senses something *real*, some mechanism that is constrained by the familiar limitations of the physical world, operating behind it.

In "Scrapping the Computer," from *A Scattering of Salts*, Merrill adopts an emphatically fallible machine as his model for that mechanism as he explores how memory's imperfections enrich and complicate the fragmentary chronicle of identity. The poem recounts Merrill's inscription of his memories onto the tabula rasa of a blank hard disk—"*It* had no memories— anyone's would have done"—as he composes a memoir on his new computer. The computer's initial crash deconstructs the memoir-in-progress into an array of indecipherable symbols, but the damage is easily repaired—"The patient left on a gurney, / Returned with a new chip, the following week." A subsequent crash, however, takes place once the memoir has been completed, and proves to be fatal:

> Another year or two, the memoir done
> And in the publishers' hands, the pressure's off.
> But when I next switch it on, whatever Descartes meant
> By the ghost in the machine—oh damn!—gives itself up:
> Experts declare BRAIN DEATH. (The contriver of my program
> Having lately developed a multiple personality,
> My calls for help keep reaching the wrong one.)
>
> Had it caught some "computer virus"? (*CP* 635)

As a model of the mind, the computer's defining characteristic in the poem is its tendency to break, a tendency Merrill emphasizes with the facile joke of the programmer's schizophrenic breakdown. Like the first and last lines of each seven-line stanza, the perfectly consistent rhymes of which frame the interior lines' variable configurations, the computer's monitor frames the shifting projections on its screen, giving the impression that the machine somehow contains (rather than generates) the phenomena it displays. This impression of containment immediately suggests to Merrill—primed by early cognitivism's pervasive computational metaphors of mind—the terms with which Gilbert Ryle famously critiqued Descartes, mocking the dualist "dogma of the ghost in the machine."[12] Following Ryle, the poem embraces a contiguous view of soma and psyche in which material conditions yield phenomenological effects. Merrill's depictions of the malfunctioning computer as a "patient . . . on a gurney," of its crash as the result of a "virus," and of its ruined condition as "BRAIN DEATH" implicitly compare the concrete architecture of the computer, which determines the nature and extent of its memory, to the biological architecture that subtends and shapes the experience of the mind. For the poet, who would succumb to complications of his illness in the year *A Scattering of Salts* was published, the inexorably broken computer becomes a *memento corporis* that yokes the shortcomings of his abortive natural memory with his own incurably fragile, embodied being.

Despite the poem's pervasive losses, "Scrapping the Computer" ultimately recasts the sublime, central cataclysm of losing the self as a renovating gift bestowed by a "selfless" machine:

was the poor thing taking upon itself a doom
Headed my way? Having by now a self of sorts,
Was it capable of a selfless act
As I might just still be, for someone I loved?
Not that a machine is capable of anything *but*
A selfless act . . . We faced each other wordlessly,
Two blank minds, two screens aglow with gloom.

Or perhaps this alter ego'd been under "contract"—*Yep,*
You know too much, wise guy . . . Feet in cement,
A sendoff choreographed by the Mob.
But who the Mob is, will I ever know?
—Short of the trillionfold synaptic flow
Surrounding, making every circumstance
Sparkle like mica with my every step

Into—can that be sunlight? Ah, it shines
On women in furs, or dreadlock heads on knees
(Hand-lettered placards: BROKE. ILL. HELP ME PLEASE),
This prisoner expelled to the Free World,
His dossier shredded. Now for new memories,
New needs. And while we're at it a novice laptop
On which already he's composed these lines. (*CP* 635–636; Merrill's ellipses)

In the sense that nature, cell by mortal cell, conspires against us all—
"women in furs" and dreadlocked vagrants alike—each human is as terminally infirm, as helplessly "BROKE," as the scrapped computer. Still,
it is the very mob of synapses that Merrill imagines bullying his memory
into oblivion that makes "every circumstance / Sparkle like mica," rendering life lustrous by placing it "under 'contract.'" The final stanza's
transition to the third person coincides with the rebirth of an emancipated
self set free through the sacrificial gift of a clean slate, but even as the in-
criminating record of his autobiographical past is "shredded," Merrill remains poised to frame a new history within the confining structure of a
lyric text. Set to begin again, he replaces the euphoria of hypothetical self-
destruction with the euphoria of creation, filling the fresh screen's tabula
rasa with lines that trace their own history even as they anticipate recording "new memories, / New needs."[13]

Technological metaphors emphasizing the somatic fragility of the mind
surround "Scrapping the Computer" in *A Scattering of Salts*. "On the

Block," which immediately precedes "Scrapping," depicts a once-bright idea as a burned-out filament entombed in the light bulb of its annunciation, "Briefly too hot to handle, / Too dim a souvenir"; the bulb that contains "Imagination's debris" suggests the dome of the skull in which real physiological connections continually "give out" (*CP* 633). "A Look Askance," which immediately follows "Scrapping," replaces the exhausted circuit of "On the Block" with an overloaded one, imagining the body as a city and a sudden electrical surge as a lethal event; the surge resembles an incendiary, creative torrent inspired by a supernatural creator and destroyer, who in turn resembles the poet himself ("mad speed-writer plugged into the topmost outlet"). The lines suggest an effluence of the imagination that proves powerful enough to destroy the imaginer:

> Will it be heat of his—our—bright idea
> Makes that whole citywide brainstorm incandesce,
> Sets loop, dot, dash, node, filament
>
> Inside the vast gray-frosted bulb ablaze? (*CP* 637)

As it did in "On the Block," the bulb recalls the brain housed in a skull, assuming here even the color of gray matter as it blows out violently in the combustions of the "brainstorm"; "loop, dot, dash, node, filament" evoke the textual symbols that record the creative rush before death, but they also suggest the contingent and ultimately friable physiological connections that facilitated it.

Long before such explicitly metamnemonic late lyrics, earlier poems that have often been called "Proustian" had begun to reveal that for Merrill, the corruptions, losses, and labors of fallible remembering powerfully affiliate mnemonic acts and literary ones. Since the publication of *Water Street,* critics have discerned traces of Proust's "résurrections du passé" in the subtle spectacles of mnemonic recovery through which Merrill gains his foothold on the void, and have been disposed to regard the novelist as one of Merrill's most self-evident influences.[14] Certainly Merrill and Proust share not only a fascination with the conjugation of the past and the present in consciousness but also a profound skepticism with respect to the mental representations rendered by the work of remembering. As Merrill once put it, "When the muse speaks, Clio, she seems to be saying . . . that things are unknowable and memory plays you false" (*CPr* 131). For Proust, the effortless recrudescences of involuntary memory occasion the quickening of self-knowledge; the work of voluntary or intellectual memory, on the other hand, is "useless" for the purposes of art, for "the pictures which that kind of memory shows us of the past preserve nothing of the past itself."[15] The very instability and waywardness that renders voluntary memory aesthetically dubious for Proust renders it most amenable to Merrill; while Proust invests the extraordinary epiphanies of involuntary memory with the potential to disclose the truth of the past and facilitate a salvific stasis outside of time, Merrill finds in the creativity, the fallibility, and the labor of intellectual memory (whose strict distinction from involuntary memory he is disinclined to recognize) meaningful correspondences to diverse domains of experience, particularly to the process of ushering a poem into being.[16]

Merrill reduces Proust's "edifice immense du souvenir" to rubble in "An Urban Convalescence," for example, which begins at a demolition site.[17] Upon venturing out for a rehabilitative turn around the neighborhood, the poem's speaker, who has been confined to his bed for a week while recovering from an unnamed illness, stumbles upon an unexpected scene of devastation. As he observes a building, possibly a home, in the last stages of demolition, he imagines the mind as an analogous field of destruction, conflating the wreckage on his "block" with the mnemonic wreckage in his head, the debris of a public and a private past made manifest. The vista of churning waste is dismal enough to suggest to Merrill the total cognitive devastation of dementia, emblematized by the personified mechanical crane whose jaws "dribble rubble" as she "Fumble[s] luxuriously in the filth of years"; Merrill embeds one image of senility within another, in fact, as he describes the sinister hysteria of the crane operator, an old man who "laughs and curses in her brain." As the speaker joins the other onlookers who observe this mundane apocalypse "in meek attitudes," Merrill finds in the building's glaring absence an unexpected absence within himself:

> As usual in New York, everything is torn down
> Before you have had time to care for it.
> Head bowed, at the shrine of noise, let me try to recall

What building stood here. Was there a building at all?
I have lived on this same street for a decade.

Wait. Yes. Vaguely a presence rises
Some five floors high, of shabby stone
—Or am I confusing it with another one
In another part of town, or of the world?—
And over its lintel into focus vaguely
Misted with blood (my eyes are shut)
A single garland sways, stone fruit, stone leaves,
Which years of grit had etched until it thrust
Roots down, even into the poor soil of my seeing.
When did the garland become part of me? (*CP* 127)

Behind the poet's gentle censure of relentless urban progress is an implicit condemnation of his own inattention ("I have lived on this same
street for a decade"), a pang of the embarrassment Edward Thomas describes as "shame / That I missed most, even at eye's level."[18] Merrill's
criticism of himself for failing to take the time to see and to care deepens
to a diagnosis of essential, corporeal weakness as he admits the force with
which the etched garland had to thrust itself "into the poor soil of [his]
seeing." The process of recording experience in the first place, the initial
act of memory, is as imperfect as the processes of retrieving and interpreting it. Merrill's organic metaphor associates the faculties of attention
and perception encompassed by "seeing" with corporeal clay, with "poor
soil" that will inevitably bear exiguous mnemonic fruit; he thus locates
the first problems of recollection in the biologically determined conditions of cognitive receptivity. (Indeed, the unidentified illness from
which the speaker is recovering obliquely connects his infirm body with
the toppled remnants of his abortive memory.) It is the self-conscious labor
of voluntary memory that Merrill consecrates as he bows at the chaotic
"shrine of noise," enjoining himself to "try to recall / What building stood
here," conjuring a single, quavering image that seems utterly foreign to him:
"When," he wonders, "did the garland become part of me?" As if to stress
the status of the mnemonic image as a figure constructed rather than discovered, the stone garland that Merrill recollects is itself an etched representation of a perishable artifact, a reiteration of the poem's prevailing
analogy between mental, architectural, and poetic fabrications.

Stephen Yenser singles out as especially "Proustian" the depiction of the etched garland that constitutes the poem's first instance of recollection, but the label applies more obviously, perhaps, to the poem's second mnemonic episode, which follows spontaneously from the first through involuntary association. The decorative architectural detail of the tendril etched in stone reminds Merrill of "a particular cheap engraving of garlands / Bought for a few francs long ago," a print disposable enough to have sheltered a rainy dash toward a Parisian cab; the drawn garlands in turn evoke the hand that had clasped them, which belonged to Merrill's companion in his descent down the Champs-Élysées:

> Also, to clasp them, the small, red-nailed hand
> Of no one I can place. Wait. No. Her name, her features
> Lie toppled underneath that year's fashions.
> The words she must have spoken, setting her face
> To fluttering like a veil, I cannot hear now,
> Let alone understand.
>
> So that I am already on the stair,
> As it were, of where I lived,
> When the whole structure shudders at my tread
> And soundlessly collapses, filling
> The air with motes of stone.
> Onto the still erect building next door
> Are pressed levels and hues—
> Pocked rose, streaked greens, brown whites.
> Who drained the pousse-café?
> Wires and pipes, snapped off at the roots, quiver.
>
> Well, that is what life does. (*CP* 128)

The unfolding complex of remembered images—the engraving, the companion, the arrival home—is "torn down, / Before you have had time to care for it," before being fully realized either visually or connotatively. The significatory implications of the woman's features lie toppled under the trivial, unavailing debris of "that year's fashions"; her diaphanous face, "fluttering like a veil," refuses to assume the solidity of the water lilies on the Vivonne. While "I am already on the stair" verges upon pronouncing the indistinguishability of past and present, "As it were" interrupts as definitively as the etched garland's bloodstained tint; the greater disruption is that of the collapsing, deracinated edifice of memory itself, sprung from "poor soil" and now "snapped off at the roots." The adjacent building, imprinted with rose and green and white strata, is imagined rather than remembered, of course, for the building's collapse is not a memory but a metaphor of forgetting, the visual details of which the speaker imports from the literal demolition before his eyes. Comparing those strata to the variegated layers of syrupy liqueur that coat the drained glass of a pousse-café, Merrill characterizes memory as a kind of feeble residue, a trace of the nourishing but exhausted substance of life lived. While Proust savors a mnemonic banquet as he drains his *tilleul,* Merrill does not even taste his own pousse-café; tantalized by insubstantial impressions of his own history, memory awakens Merrill's appetite for a fuller experience of the past by continually failing to satisfy him.

At the conclusion of "An Urban Convalescence," Merrill arrives, exhausted, at a chastened affirmation of art as an insufficient yet necessary response to mnemonic and historical ruin, identifying the poem's own affective origin in the "dull need to make some kind of house / Out of the life lived, out of the love spent" (*CP* 129). Merrill closes "A Tenancy," another poem of reminiscence in *Water Street,* by equating the roles of poet and host: "If I am host at last / It is of little more than my own past. / May others be at home in it" (*CP* 170). In "An Urban Convalescence," Merrill stresses that the home one builds out of poetry is a temporary one—not an everlasting monument, but a shelter to house the ephemeral conjugations of human empathy. The pervasive analogy between edifice and poem that finally becomes explicit in the concluding verse is expressed formally as the physical contour of the poem, like the speaker, arrives "Indoors at last," moving from irregular verse paragraphs to the symmetrical architecture of embraced quatrains, an architecture that serves to compensate materially, if only modestly, for the poem's various mnemonic demolitions. The stanzas generate the readerly satisfactions that accompany the conformity of sense to the exigencies of musical design, but in their pervasive schematic aberrations—frequent slant rhyme ("air"/"passenger," "his"/"house"), nonrhyme ("prime"/"lasted," "poem"/ "time"), and even an errant alternating (rather than embraced) quatrain—

the stanzas implicitly reiterate the poem's deeply qualified consolations, demonstrating that even the shaping force of received forms cannot tidily square the jagged remnants that are left in the wake of the body's continual reconstructions and demolitions of the past.

It is difficult to imagine a metaphor that could convey the jagged coalescences of memory more evocatively than the puzzle—the sinuously fragmented surface of which presents both an image and the obtrusive evidence of its construction. Like the governing metaphors in many of Merrill's other metamemnemonic poems—the house in "An Urban Convalescence," the reflective waters in "Dead Center," the memoir in "Scrapping the Computer," the manuscript and Parthenon frieze in "Losing the Marbles," to be discussed shortly—the puzzle that forms the central metaphor of "Lost in Translation" produces an unstable picture of the self constructed analogously by body and text alike. In the poem's opening verse paragraph, the speaker recalls his privileged but lonely childhood routine during the summer of 1939, describing his recollection as a "Mirage arisen from time's trickling sands / Or fallen piecemeal into place" (*CP* 362); he thus compares the assemblage of images and episodes that make up autobiographical memory to a puzzle's disjointed assemblage of pieces even before the poem's literal puzzle appears. When the actual puzzle the child desperately anticipates finally arrives from the Manhattan rental shop, it comes "Out of the blue," suggesting the sudden mnemonic arrival whereby "The hour came back" (*CP* 363) to the adult speaker, followed incrementally by aspects of the summer that surrounded it. The involuntary memory arose, Merrill recalls, during an evening's idle reading, as the central image of Valéry's poem "Palme" and a vague recollection of a German translation of it by Rilke reminded him of a blue, palm-shaped jigsaw piece and the multilingual governess who, in the absence of his parents, helped him assemble the puzzle.

Merrill's portrayal of recollection as a constructive process is phenomenologically intuitive, but his choice to adopt a visual model that emphasizes this experiential aspect of memory is exceptional. While many conventional metaphors—tablet, book, storehouse, videotape—imply the status of memories as static wholes recorded and stored in the mind, the puzzle uniquely emphasizes the active and often intentional work of mnemonic construction, the process not of retrieving but of dynamically making and remaking memories anew. Merrill prefers to depict small mnemonic parts that gesture toward, but never fully coalesce into, stable wholes; his memories are made of "Fragments in revolution" that tentatively cohere only to define a succession of shapely absences, each gaping after a missing piece. His representational preferences comport with those of contemporary cognitive theorists of memory, who stress that most perceptual data are not recorded at all; according to such models, discrete units of sensory, emotional, and contextual information are encoded in dynamic neural networks—engrams—that are activated together (though never in precisely the same way twice) and whose ranging complexity accounts for the varying vividness and emotional resonance of mnemonic experiences. Illustrating the nature of memories not as retrieved objects but as novel constructions made afresh with every act of recollection, Daniel Schacter describes the integrative complex of information formed and reformed in memory as "something like a giant jigsaw puzzle."[19]

But "Lost in Translation" proposes that the act of piecing a puzzle together is not only like the act of remembering but also like the act of writing a poem—not least because it is riddled with obstinate but exhilarating forms of limitation. As the boy assembles the puzzle with the help of his governess, the pleasures of working within its various forms of circumscription begin to take shape. Strategically progressing from the edges inward, "Mademoiselle does borders"; just before bed, last-minute discoveries are anchored "to the scene's limits," and even the craftsman's repertoire of carved shapes is "Nice in its limitation" (*CP* 363–364). As soon as the scene depicted in the puzzle comes together, however, it is subjected, like the memory it stands for, "All too soon" to "swift / Dismantling":

> Then Sky alone is left, a hundred blue
> Fragments in revolution, with no clue
> To where a Niche will open. Quite a task
> Putting together Heaven, yet we do.
>
> It's done. Here under the table all along
> Were those missing feet. It's done.
>
>   . . . All too soon the swift
> Dismantling. Lifted by two corners,
> The puzzle hung together—and did not.

Irresistibly a populace
Unstitched of its attachments, rattled down. (*CP* 366)

Proust claims that the only true paradises are lost ones, but in Merrill's poem, it is the iterative and inexhaustible pleasure of poetic and mnemonic craft, of putting experience together in the mind and on the page, that is heavenly. "Lost in Translation" redeems the work of intellectual memory by comparing it to the poem's own synthetic composition. Like "An Urban Convalescence," "Lost in Translation" leaves the seams of mnemonic construction conspicuously apparent as it stitches diverse contexts of experience into meaningful correspondence: the speaker's recollection is riddled with self-doubt ("surely not just in retrospect" [*CP* 363]), with confusion between the imagined and the remembered ("Yet I can't / Just be imagining" [*CP* 367]), and with interpretive self-interruption ("A summer without parents is the puzzle, / Or should be" [*CP* 362]). Though Merrill acknowledges the accident of involuntary association through which Valéry's poem indirectly engenders his own, "Lost in Translation" fundamentally rejects chance as an autonomous principle for disclosing the truth of the past. Merrill's brazenly literary poem—with its intercalation of memory and meditation and its elaborate matrix of allusions to Valéry, Rilke, Proust, Goethe, and many others—flaunts the role of the intellect in making memory meaningfully, if imperfectly and ephemerally, "h[a]ng together."

Before the puzzle was returned to the rental shop, Merrill surmises, "Something tells me that one piece contrived / To stay in the boy's pocket." "How do I know? / I know because so many later puzzles / Had missing pieces." The lines suggest not only that the child was instinctively inclined to withhold his own "bit of truth" from the picture, but that the totality of the past conspires to make itself unknowable. In *The Book of Ephraim*, JM wonders "what vigilance will keep / Me from one emblematic, imminent, / Utterly harmless failure of recall" (*CL* 74). In "Lost in Translation," Merrill attests to the benign inevitability of the missing mnemonic piece, offering the hand-sawn silhouette as an emblem for all aspects of experience lost to time, from "the end of the vogue for collies," and the familiar image of "A house torn down" (366–367) to the spectral Rilke translation of "Palme." Reena Sastri writes that when, in "Lost in Translation,"

"Merrill evokes the Proustian myth that nothing is lost, he does so with his eyes open to its fictional status," knowingly entertaining a consolatory conceit.[20] Proust's conviction that the mind loses nothing implies an implausible transcendence of the limitations of embodied human reality, but the conclusion of "Lost in Translation" suggests that mnemonic permanence can be credibly reconceived in terms compatible with the materiality of the mind.

It is out of an instance of mistrust in memory, as Merrill contemplates the elusive Rilke translation that he "seems to recall" (*CP* 363), that the poem's final lines introduce the embodied terms of this reconception:

> Lost, is it, buried? One more missing piece?
>
> But nothing's lost. Or else: all is translation
> And every bit of us is lost in it
> (Or found—I wander through the ruin of S
> Now and then, wondering at the peacefulness)
> And in that loss a self-effacing tree,
> Color of context, imperceptibly
> Rustling with its angel, turns the waste
> To shade and fiber, milk and memory. (*CP* 367)

Every fragile, mnemonic bit of personal history, like every minute, organic bit of the physical self, loses its identity in the process of being transmuted and reconstituted as something else, blending imperceptibly into its evolving contexts like the "self-effacing" blue palm blending into the puzzle's blue sky. And just as a real palm "turns the waste" of fertile soil into the shade of its fronds and the nourishing milk and fiber of its coconuts, the poem translates private loss, mnemonic and otherwise, into a munificent tissue of signs. For the tree is "self-effacing" in the sense that the translation of experience into art entails, in Eliot's terms, an "extinction of personality," but also in the sense that the reabsorption of the mortal self into the boundless and cyclically permanent organic "memory" of the physical world entails the effacement of the chronicle of selfhood strung together in the mind. Balanced on the fulcrum of its central comma, the last line's four nouns—"shade and fiber, milk and memory"—split neatly into balanced units (A and A, B and B). In such a grouping, "memory" is the abstract final term to which the replenishing qualities of the preceding concrete offerings of the tree—shelter, food, drink—are imputed. The final line's terms can also be read chiastically, however (A and B, B and A), placing "shade" in apposition with "memory" to recognize the spectral dimness of most mnemonic representations, to stress what is lost in their remoteness from the tangible substance—the fiber and the milk—of sensual immediacy. Merrill asserts that in mnemonic ruin—as in the "ruin of S" (his lost love Strato Mouflouzelis, perhaps)—there can be a "peacefulness" that redeems this distance. Evoking the sublime violence of the biblical story of Jacob wrestling with the angel, and recalling that the angel (Greek ἄγγελος, "messenger") is a vehicle for divine acts of "translation," Merrill writes over his pain at what is lost with the gentle swaying of the arching palm, "rustling with its angel" as its carries "every bit of us" from one realm of significance to another.

In his mid-career poems, then, Merrill arrives at "self-knowledge" (*CP* 128) not by studying the disclosures of the past per se but by recognizing in memory the attrition and renovation ubiquitous in the phenomenal world. Conceiving of memory as a fallible process of somatic translation—one that entails making and remaking the past anew in a creative process that necessarily emerges out of loss—Merrill discovers enticing conceptual avenues along which to correlate mnemonic and literary acts. In later poems, physical entropy and imaginative possibility emerge more and more clearly as complementary, interdependent forces, but most striking are the dramatic means Merrill invents to evoke the play of these forces within the substance of lyric form. Adopting concrete, typographic metaphors for mnemonic loss that model the materiality of the poem upon the materiality of mortal consciousness, "Losing the Marbles," Merrill's culminating, seven-part disquisition on poetic monumentality, embodies the erosion of memory in the partial obliteration of a poetic manuscript; engaging in the kind of dreaming "(after the diagnosis)" that Merrill describes in the nearby poem "Investiture at Cecconi's" (*CP* 580), the expansive poem confronts the terrifying void that gapes at the end of life by staging and surviving the intrusion of oblivion upon the emphatically physical substances of text and consciousness.

"Losing the Marbles" is written, Merrill pronounces in its fourth section, from the "highwire between the elegiac and the haywire," a perspective that sets the tragic and the ridiculous in their right orders, and from which rage against the ravages of mortality appears both histrionic and futile. Merrill's affable, familiar tone and propulsive punning create an atmosphere of courageous levity in the face of doom, expressing the magnanimity of one taking his lot in stride; his breezy movement between the intimate and the extravagant, whereby a morning's rummaging around the house gives way to the lofty domains of acrobat, acropolis, and imagined heaven, typifies the poem's effortless dilations of scope. The first part of the poem punningly associates the marbles lost in senility with the Elgin Marbles lost to the British Museum, a correspondence that emphasizes the vulnerability of memories and monuments alike to forms of theft and corrosion. As the poet searches his home for his lost calendar, an emblem of lost time, he introduces many of the poem's stinging forms of belatedness. The noonday feast of life at its peak is palpably over; the guests of the previous day's convivial party had set out to imagine their "heaven[s]," but now the table, swept clean the morning after the festivities, evokes the blankness of the aging speaker's malfunctioning mind. Merrill compares the Parthenon of his own dream to a philosopher in his prime whose unspoiled mind is equipped to pursue his love of wisdom, and the temple's marble friezes are pristine in "early light or noon light"; but when Merrill descends from his reverie, he finds himself in the ominously "gathering dusk," with the twinkling lights of Athens blinking out like forgotten names and addresses:[21]

> Morning spent looking for my calendar—
> Ten whole months mislaid, name and address,
> A groaning board swept clean . . .
> And what were we talking about at lunch? Another
> Marble gone. Those later years, Charmides,
> Will see the mind eroded featureless.
>
> Ah. We'd been imagining our "heaven"'s.
> Mine was to be an acrobat in Athens
> Back when the Parthenon—
> Its looted nymphs and warriors pristine
> By early light or noon light—dwelt
> Upon the city like a philosopher,
> Who now—well, you have seen.

Here in the gathering dusk one could no doubt
"Rage against the dying of the light."
But really—rage? (So like the Athens press,
Breathing fire to get the marbles back.)
These dreamy blinkings-out
Strike me as grace, if I may say so,
Capital punishment,
Yes, but of utmost clemency at work,
Whereby the human stuff, ready or not,
Tumbles, one last drum-roll, into thyme,
Out of time, with just the fossil quirk
At heart to prove—hold on, don't tell me . . . What? (*CP* 572; Merrill's
  ellipses)

Amidst the poem's cascade of forfeitures, the fierce rhetoric with which the Athens press demands the Elgin Marbles' repatriation appears absurd—its "breathing fire" is a part of the carnivalesque unreality evoked by the dreamed-up acrobat and death's ludicrous drum roll. The caricatured futility of the Athenians' demands confirms that the material losses the poem recounts are final; once a marble is lost, it is gone forever.

Such irrevocable losses in "Losing the Marbles" are often compounded by the absence of language sufficient to describe them. Foreshadowed by the silent "groaning board" that no longer sings under the strain of life's banquet, Merrill finds the degradation of the Parthenon unspeakable—the temple once "dwelt / Upon the city" in a magnificent vigil, but now, he evades, "—well, you have seen." Dylan Thomas's declamatory poetic language is deflated by Merrill's earnest doubt about its amplitude ("But really—rage?"), and the final line's attempt to express how a mitigating "fossil quirk" can redeem this process of dispossession trails off into silence. Still, for all the inexpressible mystery they keep in play, the lines retain their conviction that forgetting, as part of the larger process "whereby the human stuff, ready or not, / Tumbles . . . / *Out* of time," is somehow redemptive. Merrill's association of mnemonic loss with both physical erosion and expiation bears out the etymological sense of oblivion as a smoothing over of both glories and mistakes, and his choice to portray his "dreamy blinkings-out" as forms of "grace" and "clemency" recalls the close relationship between amnesia and amnesty, forgetting and forgiving.

This first section of "Losing the Marbles" arrives at an equanimity that clarifies Merrill's choice to address his poem to Charmides, the beautiful young poet who lends his name to Plato's dialogue on the nature of *sophrosyne*, soundness of mind.[22] In the dialogue, Charmides is the young person who best exemplifies sophrosyne among the Athenian youth and who is enticed into conversation by Socrates's promise to cure his chronic headaches. Socrates prescribes both the consumption of an herb and the recitation of a charm—the "fair words" of a lyric that will help to bring about a sound body by restoring a sound mind. In the course of explaining this cure to Charmides, Socrates emphasizes at length the continuity between *psyche* (soul) and *soma* (body) that renders the treatment effective:

> If the head and body are to be well, you must begin by curing the soul; that is the first thing. And the treatment of the soul, my dear youth, has to be effected by the use of certain charms, and these charms are fair words; and by them temperance is implanted in the soul, and where temperance is, there health is speedily imparted, not only to the head, but to the whole body. And he who taught me the cure and the charm at the same time added a special direction: "Let no one," he said, "persuade you to cure the head, until he has first given you his soul to be cured by the charm. For this," he said, "is the great error of our day in the treatment of the human body, that physicians separate the soul from the body."[23]

The "error" perpetrated by the physicians in separating psyche from soma is archetypal; it underlies the mythological expression of psyche as a butterfly, a symbol that draws together the concept's many aspects—soul, mind, spirit, intellectual and moral self—by defining them in opposition to the body, grouping them as what death puts to flight. According to Socrates, the young man's physical suffering must be cured through his psyche, and the young man thus becomes the site of an explicit and corrective merging of material and incorporeal dimensions of selfhood. Merrill alludes to this integration by invoking Charmides in the poem's first stanza; addressing a poem about the infirmity of memory to Charmides, a young man who requires a poem to cure his own affliction of the head, casts the "fair words" of "Losing the Marbles" in the role of a remedy—if not for the "capital" punishments of forgetting and death, then for the anger and intemperance that they can inspire. Merrill restates this conviction about poetry's purview in the austere opening sentences of "Farewell Performance," also from *The Inner Room:* "Art. It cures affliction" (*CP* 581).

The second part of "Losing the Marbles" recounts the obliteration of a poetic manuscript by a rainstorm, its words drowning in "oblivion's ink-blue rivulet." Juxtaposing his disfigured draft with the first section's eroded mind and looted temple, Merrill subjects mind, monument, and text alike to analogous forms of attrition:

> Driving its silver car into the room,
> The storm mapped a new country's dry and wet—
> Oblivion's ink-blue rivulet.
> Mascara running, worksheet to worksheet
> Clings underfoot, exchanging the wrong words.
> The right ones, we can only trust will somehow
> Return to the tongue's tip,
> Weary particular and straying theme,
>
> Invigorated by their dip.
> Invigorated! Gasping, shivering
> Under our rough towels, never did they dream—
> Whom mouth-to-mouth resuscitation by
> Even your *Golden Treasury* won't save,
> They feel their claim
> On *us* expiring: starved to macron, breve,
> Those fleshless ribs, a beggar's frame . . .
> From the brainstorm to this was one far cry.
>
> Long work of knowing and hard play of wit
> Take their toll like any virus.
> Old timers, cured, wade ankle-deep in sky.
>
> Meanwhile, come evening, to sit
> Feverishly restoring the papyrus. (*CP* 573; Merrill's ellipses)

In the face of oblivion, Merrill's words are made flesh; it is precisely the vulnerability of the decimated language that suggests to him the gasping, shivering, starving frailty of human bodies. The lines do not yield much hope for the daunting task of accurately "restoring the papyrus," as the vulnerability of the concrete signifier is matched by the signified's tenuous hold within the speaker's unreliable mind; even Palgrave's *Golden Treasury of English Songs and Lyrics* fails to jog his memory, the mouths of its poets unable to resuscitate his dying words. In light of Merrill's own HIV diagnosis, "virus" lends chilling gravity to the words' dire emaciation and attunement to their own expiring claim on the minds of others. Still, this section of the poem contains the earliest signs that Merrill's reconstructive poetic endeavor holds promise, if not of faithful restoration then of invention. "Driving its silver car into the room," the storm's flamboyant entrance gives the impression of definitive and destructive intrusion, but the storm also shapes the terrain of "a new country" on the page; by introducing the "brainstorm" that generated the poem in the first place, Merrill reminds us that the fructifications of a creative flood can yet recuperate the obliterations of a destructive one. And though the hope that the drowning words might be "invigorated by their dip" is dismissed in the second stanza, in the penultimate section of "Losing the Marbles" we learn that "thanks / To their little adventure," the few surviving words of the original text—"never so / Brimming with jokes and schemes"—are rejuvenated in the youthful company of the rewritten poem's fresh language.

By referring to his sodden worksheets as a "papyrus" and to his words as "starved to macron, breve," Merrill draws an analogy between the recreation of his own text and the academic restoration and interpretation of ancient manuscripts. With his written record compromised, yesterday's intentions seem as elusive as those of a stranger writing millennia ago; his failure to recall gapes on the page like the lacunae in Sappho's fragmentary poems and the lapses in our cultural memory that they betoken. The third part of "Losing the Marbles" sets the reader in Merrill's predicament by reproducing the jagged remnants of the ruined text itself. With the knowledge that—within the narrative world of "Losing the Marbles," at least—a "complete" poem at one time existed, the reader inevitably assumes the role of paleographer, trying to fill in the gaps. But the *disjecta membra* of the original manuscript also form a poem in its own right, one that resembles the graphical open verse of Mallarmé's *Un coup de dés jamais n'abolira le hasard* and that invites the reader to become inter-

preter and critic as well, trying to make sense of the poem as it stands
and to find meaning in the relationship between the text and the empty
field that surrounds it:

> body, favorite
> > gleaned,   at the
> > > vital
> > frenzy—
>
> act and moonshaft, peaks
> > > stiffening
> > Unutter[able]
> > the beloved's
>
> > > > slowly
> > > stained in the deep   fixed
> > > > summer nights
> > or,
>
> > > scornful   Ch[arm]ides,
> > > > decrepitude
> > Now, however, that
> > figures also
>
> > > > body everywhere
> > > > plunders and
> > what we cannot—from the hut's lintel
> > > flawed
>
> > > > > > white as
> > sliced turnip   the field's brow.
> > > our old
> > wanderings
>
> home   palace, temple,
> > having   of those blue foothills
> > > no further   clear
> > > > fancy[.] (*CP* 574)

"Losing the Marbles" would have suffered if Merrill had excluded these
lines, which body forth the absence at the center of the poem by so
dramatically protruding through it. Here Merrill stages a confrontation between the reader and the void that is disarming after the more

traditional free verse that appears in the poem's opening sections, but that also allows the reader unprecedented interpretive freedom. In some cases, the words' arrangement allows a number of nonlinear readings that encourage us to choose our own adventures, and in light of the shaping force of a cataclysmic accident (recollected by the poem's droplet-shaped silhouette), we are freed of the notion of a purely intentional mind at work behind the poem, since its authorship is a putative hybrid of will and chance. With Charmides's reappearance as the ostensible addressee of this poem within the poem, the eroticism of the opening lines ("vital / frenzy—/ act and moonshaft, peaks / stiffening") reminds us that he is a figure handed down by Plato as an exemplum not only of the embodied psyche but also of youthful beauty and sexual interest.[24] It is through this eroticism that Merrill reintroduces the centrality of the body within his poem of memory, setting the vitality of youthful "summer nights" against the "decrepitude / Now, however, that / figures also" within the speaker's senescent point of view. The ramifications of this opposition between youth and age become evident through the experience of memory; the poem concludes with a spatial metaphor wherein ranges of foothills, blue in the distance, are compared to "old / wanderings" that, from the temporal distance of advanced age, can no longer be pictured with the imaginative precision of "clear / fancy." Given Merrill's affinity in "Losing the Marbles" for puns that exploit the conventional metonymic association of the head with the workings of the mind, the description of "the field's brow" as "white as / sliced turnip" associates the fertility of an open field—the agricultural field sprawling beneath the blue foothills, and the white field of the page itself, perhaps—with the phenomenological blankness of forgetting.

Merrill meditates directly on this open field in the next segment of "Losing the Marbles," the pentameter couplets of which seem palpably solid after the reproduced manuscript's diffuse spray of words. Here Merrill offers a critique of the "cloyed / Taste" that his dense lines seem to embody; recasting oblivion's rivulet as the proverbial emblem of irrevocable accident—the white rinse of spilt milk—he considers the virtues of an aesthetic that embraces, rather than laments, the encroachment of absence:

> Yet should milk spilt
> (As when in Rhetoric one's paragraph
> Was passed around and each time cut in half,
> From eighty words to forty, twenty, ten,
> Before imploding in a puff of Zen)
> White out the sense and mutilate the phrase,
> My text is Mind no less than Mallarmé's.
> My illustration? The Cézanne oil sketch
> Whose tracts of raw, uncharted canvas fetch
> As much per square inch as the fruit our cloyed
> Taste prizes for its bearing on the void. (*CP* 575)

The pedagogical exercise of whittling a paragraph to its pith models the poet's calculated invitation—as opposed to the accidental intrusion—of emptiness into poetry. In contrast to the Western association of "void" with the agonizing postreligious emptiness of Beckett or Camus or Kafka, the "puff of Zen" invokes a perspective that values nothingness as a source of enlightenment (*sunyata*) rather than fear. The concentration of matter and energy Merrill suggests with the physical, if facetious, metaphor of implosion brings to mind the condensed aesthetic of the haiku or Zen *kōan*, forms that recognize—like Cézanne's oil sketch, with its estimable negative space—the role of absence in defining the boundaries of luminous being.

Though Merrill has been elaborating the metaphorical assertion that his washed-out "text is Mind" since the introduction of the manuscript plotline, his reference to Mallarmé in this context—in addition to the aforementioned resemblance of the disfigured poem to Mallarmé's late, experimental verse—reminds us that Mallarmé underwent an acute spiritual and intellectual crisis upon confronting the nothingness at the center of a Godless universe. At the depths of his disconsolate meditation on "*le Rien,*" he arrived at the famous epiphany he describes in a letter to his fellow symbolist poet Henri Cazalis in the spring of 1866:

> Yes, I know, we are nothing but vain forms of matter—yet sublime too when you think that we invented God and our own souls. So sublime, my friend! that I want to give myself this spectacle of a matter aware, yes, of what it is, but throwing itself madly into the Dream that it knows it is not, singing the Soul and all those divine impressions

that gather in us from earliest childhood, and proclaiming, before the Nothingness that is the truth, those glorious falsehoods![25]

For Mallarmé, religion's vitiated miracles are redeemed by the miracle of conscious matter, the mind aware of itself and able to populate the void with its own wondrous inventions, *"ces glorieux mensonges."* The poem itself forms a material counterpart to the embodied mind's process of inventing reality, the "surrounding silence" of the page mimetic of a "mental context" in which all experience, including the experience of the poem, takes place.[26] Mallarmé observes with regret that "we write black on white, never like the stars against the dark."[27] Merrill's approval of a poetics that aims to dignify and manifest obscurity while holding sacred its incandescent perforations finds expression in his response to a question about difficult poetry: "My own ideal of the hermetic artist is Mallarmé. Under his difficult surface there's the midnight sky, a skull of stars" (*CPr* 73).

The reader's difficulties piecing together part three of "Losing the Marbles," Merrill's papyrus version of the manuscript, are met with a somewhat ambiguous reward in part five's palimpsest version of the text, where Merrill has rewritten the poem over the remnants of the original, incorporating them into an ode in—what else?—Sapphic stanzas. The two drafts do not appear side by side, as the poem's fourth part intervenes between them; as a result, after struggling to infer the relationships between the papyrus version's fractured parts, we turn the page to find a set of answers that inevitably depart from those to which the fragmentary text directed us. We find, for example, that what had seemed to be a sexual "frenzy" in fact describes an oracular conference with a sibyl, and as the speaker's recollection of an unnamed beloved gives way to reflection on the experience of recollection itself, we see that in the course of filling in the gaps, Merrill has limned yet another picture of forgetting. In the rewritten ode of part five, a beloved and an elite group of poets with whom he associated "begin to slip the mind" of the speaker, who compares his mental image, "plunder[ed]" by the body, to a looted monument. The "flawed image" of the past projected in the mind's eye evokes the reader's initial, inevitably erroneous image of the poem based on the semiobliterated draft; it also suggests the radiant, orphaned images that emerge from Sappho's fragments, divested of context, emerging pendent and solitary in the mind:

> he had joined an elite scornful—as were, Charmides,
> > your first, chiseled verses—of decrepitude
> > > in any form. Now, however, that
> > > > their figures also
>
> begin to slip the mind—while the body everywhere
> > with peasant shrewdness plunders and puts to use
> > > what we cannot—from the hut's lintel
> > > > gleams one flawed image;
>
> another, cast up by frost or earthquake, shines white as
> > sliced turnip from a furrow on the field's brow.
> > > Humbly our old poets knew to make
> > > > wanderings into
>
> homecomings of a sort—harbor, palace, temple, all
> > having been quarried out of those blue foothills
> > > no further off, these last clear autumn
> > > > days, than infancy. (*CP* 577)

The previous draft's concluding suggestion of youth's "old / wanderings" viewed at a hazy distance gives way in the reconstructed ode to the public and poetic accounts of "old poets" like Homer, who facilitate in their archetypal chronicles of wandering heroes the "homecomings" of universal recognition, quarrying sites of epic adventure—"harbor, palace, temple"—out of the common ground of human experience. The speaker's incomplete mental representations of the past and our own incomplete projections of the original poem based on the damaged version are likened to fragments of an ancient frieze, ruins recovered by peasants and placed in the architectural service of "the hut's lintel" or jostled into visibility "from a furrow on the field's brow" by swelling frost or a seismic shudder. That Merrill attributes the fate of the flawed mental image to a body that "plunders" suggests that the poet's own verses may be as "scornful . . . / . . . of decrepitude" as Charmides's own. Still, the resourceful, enterprising body "puts to use" those fragments; Merrill suggests that we salvage these modest, "gleam[ing]" remnants for use in new imaginative dwellings (such as poems).

Perhaps the most striking single revision between the fragmentary draft and the finished ode is the replacement of "fancy" with "infancy," a substitution that evokes the speaker's inevitable "homecoming" into the second childhood of his dotage but that also suggests, through the etymological sense of "infancy," the encroachment of silence where the imagination had once declared itself. This speechlessness recalls the failures of language that permeate the opening section of "Losing the Marbles" and is amplified in the dire neurological terms of the poem's penultimate section. Here, Merrill exaggerates the familiar limitations of the embodied mind through the extreme circumstance of brain damage, finding in aphasia—an impairment of language that can result from a stroke or brain injury—an alternative to the comparably routine, but no less biologically grounded, mnemonic atrophy associated with aging. In three catechistic stanzas of trimeter quatrains, Merrill presents three examples of deductive recovery in the face of material loss: that of the poet (or reader or paleographer) who conjures an ode from the remains of a single metrical foot; that of the steward of a brain-damaged companion, whose patient attention allows him to discern a message in his aphasic friend's torrent of incoherent speech, supplying at last the all-important, misplaced word; and that of the archaeologist who reconstructs a handmaiden's form from an errant finger in the shattered statuary of an ancient pediment:[28]

> Who gazed into the wrack till
> Inspiration glowed,
> Deducing from one dactyl
> The handmaiden, the ode?
>
> Or when aphasia skewered
> The world upon a word
> Who was the friend, the steward,
> Who bent his head, inferred
>
> Then filled the sorry spaces
> With pattern and intent
> A syntax of lit faces
> From the impediment? (*CP* 578)

The persevering gaze, attentive enough to see the ghostly contours of an ancient "pediment" through the "impediment" of millennial decay, draws the fire of inspiration even in the face of ruin. The last of the three stanzas fuses the various circumstances Merrill has superimposed, revealing the conjunction of industry and imagination common to them all: the "sorry spaces" are those left by the handmaiden's missing form, the draft's missing lines, and the impaired man's missing language; the "lit faces" are those of the figures in the sculpted scene, the young poets in the ode, and the struggling aphasiac beaming with the relief of recognition; the "impediment" is in every case the obstacle of incomplete information resulting from vital material limitations. By this point in the poem, the plastic arts of sculpture and architecture, in addition to the verbal art of poetry, are familiar reflections of the mind. Drawing the losses of language associated with aphasia into apposition with signs rinsed from the page and statuary eroded and concealed by time, Merrill emphasizes that the experiences of loss that riddle the phenomenology of thought are likewise symptomatic of concrete, physical conditions that are beyond the administration of human will. In his description of aphasia having "skewered / The world upon a word," Merrill imagines what it is like to suffer from a pathology of expression by amplifying the mundane torment of having a word on the tip of one's tongue, and conjures the shocking feeling of consequential loss that accompanies drawing a blank while all the surrounding structures of intellectual possession remain in play. Merrill's amplification is hyperbolic, hanging the fate of the cosmos on a single, resplendent word, but his hyperbole serves yet another purpose in the context of the surrounding lines' searching questions about the identity of the mysterious and benevolent "steward" who brings order to the chaos of loss. The aphasiac's missing word, through the lines' ambience of cosmic significance, is writ large as Logos itself, the syntax of creation through which divine reason "filled the sorry spaces / With pattern and intent." Like the Word personified, Merrill's personified words undergo a process of fleshly mortification; "starved to macron, breve," their watery sacrifice ultimately proves and glorifies their creator.

That every act of mnemonic re-creation should be exalted for reflecting a more sublime and originary act of design is consistent with Merrill's interest in the countervailing forces of entropy and organization and their bearing on mind and monument alike. "Losing the Marbles" affirms with punning, aphoristic definitiveness that "All stone once dressed asks to be worn," but also asserts that "the will- / To-structural-elaboration"—the human impulse to design, to organize, to interpret—ensures that where recovery may fail, reinvention will inevitably flourish. Merrill imputes this "will- / To-structural-elaboration" to the raw materials of the monuments themselves, suggesting that the will of nature finds expression in the signs that record our public past. By conceiving of monumental artifice not in opposition to nature but as an extension of it, Merrill finds a way to rewrite cultural memory as he has written individual memory—through the rhythms of embodiment:

> Does the will-
> To-structural-elaboration still
> Flute up, from shifting dregs of would-be rock,
> Glints of a future colonnade and frieze?
> Do higher brows unknit within the block,
> And eyes whose Phidias and Pericles
> Are eons hence make out through crystal skeins
> Wind-loosened tresses and the twitch of reins?
> Ah, not for long will marble school the blood
> Against the warbling sirens of the flood.
> All stone once dressed asks to be worn. The foam-
> Pale seaside temple, like a palindrome,
> Had quietly laid its plans for stealing back.
> What are the Seven Wonders now? A pile
> Of wave-washed pebbles. Topless women smile,
> Picking the smoothest, rose-flawed white or black
> Which taste of sunlight on moon-rusted swords,
> To use as men upon their checkerboards. (*CP* 575–576)

Just as Merrill's poem within the poem echoes the fragility of embodied memory by proving to be anything but a *monumentum aere perennius,* his marble monument proves vulnerable to the "warbling sirens" of destruction, finally unable to "school the blood" of poets in their pretensions to immortality. What permanence there is, is a permanence of minute parts: of "wave-washed pebbles" and "shifting dregs of would-be rock"; the monument's permanence proves to be not continuous but cyclical, modeled on the fragility and resilient perpetuity of life, renewed generation by generation. This resemblance between flesh and marble, "rose-flawed white or black," is only visible from the high wire of the imagination or the magnificent perspective of the gods themselves, a height from which humans are merely pawns. The topless women who use the Seven Wonders, now reduced to pebbles, "as men upon their checkerboards" resemble the Muses, daughters of Mnemosyne, and the Fates, too, from whose vantage the markers of cultural memory are shown to reflect, rather than transcend, the mortality of the body.

This organic view of monumentality, in which every end proves to be a beginning, finds a verbal model in the palindrome. Describing the monument that "quietly laid its plans for stealing back" into being, Merrill once again has in mind the palindrome as a literal "running back" along a prescribed path, letter by letter. At the poem's conclusion, Merrill invokes the minute organic parts that form the mechanism of hereditary continuity—the body's chemical plans for stealing into and back out of existence—in the "DNA-like wisps" that twist in the toy marbles that fill a "pregnant" pouch:[29]

> After the endless jokes, this balmy winter
> Around the pool, about the missing marbles,
> What was more natural than for my birthday
> To get—from the friend whose kiss that morning woke me—
> A pregnantly clicking pouch of targets and strikers,
> Aggies and rainbows, the opaque chalk-red ones,
> Clear ones with DNA-like wisps inside,
> Others like polar tempests vitrified . . .
> These I've embedded at random in the deck-slats
> Around the pool. (The pool!—compact, blue, dancing,
> Lit-from-beneath-oubliette.) By night their sparkle
> Repeats the garden lights, or moon- or starlight,
> Tinily underfoot, as though the very
> Here and now were becoming a kind of heaven
> To sit in, talking, largely mindless of
> The risen, cloudy brilliances above. (*CP* 579; Merrill's ellipses)

From the lover's morning kiss and the sparkling poolside chatter to the luminous constellation of targets and strikers, the clement final scene of

"Losing the Marbles" fulfills the poem's earlier claim that "Art furnishes a counterfeit / Heaven" (*CP* 575). In the midst of the human consolations that array his paradisiacal garden party (chief among them the aesthetic consolation of ravishing poetic language), Merrill conceals a sinister emblem of forgetting in plain sight; in a dispassionate metaphorical stroke, the swimming pool—"compact, blue, dancing," and in perfect harmony with the blithe and stylish scene—is transformed into a hidden dungeon, a receptacle for the hopelessly forgotten. The innocuously effete ring of "oubliette" disguises the utter ghastliness of its meaning; accessible only through a hatch in a high ceiling, the oubliette is a terminal prison where one is sent to be, quite literally, forgotten (*oublié*), a chamber designed to foreclose release. Merrill's "Lit-from-beneath-oubliette" thus imagistically, etymologically, and acoustically recalls "Oblivion's ink-blue rivulet," the force of mnemonic destruction that courses throughout the poem's various parts and plotlines. In contrast to the sparkle of the marbles, which "Repeats . . . / The risen, cloudy brilliances above," the pool is illuminated from below, its surface unreflective; in the midst of the deck slats' mimetic firmament, the Lethean swimming pool forms the last in the long line of graphical, verbal, and mnemonic blanks Merrill draws in "Losing the Marbles." It seems appropriate, at the conclusion of the poem, that Merrill should choose to situate the abyss of forgetting at the center of the scintillating fête of life, but he also chooses to neutralize the watery prison's menace through the enticements of its warm glow and gamboling ripples, which seem to invite the heedless pleasure of an "invigorating dip."

The birthday celebration answers the missing calendar of the poem's opening lines by recasting its losses as gifts. Despite its balmy radiance, the celebration takes place in the terminal phase of both the day and the year, not in the "gathering dusk" of the poem's opening section but by a winter's moonlight. Merrill is on the brink of following his own past into oblivion, fulfilling the biological fate prescribed by the deterministic double helix of DNA, that "spiral molecule / Whose sparklings outmaneuver time, space, us" (*CL* 274), and that abides, furtive and inevitable, within the bound-to-be-lost emblems of memory. In "Losing the Marbles," a poem so sensitive to the ways in which the phenomenology of recollection reflects underlying somatic conditions—from the aphasic's brain damage to the speaker's brain cells "blinking out" with age—Merrill proposes that circumstances of embodiment shape the experience of memory as inexorably as the forces of nature and time shape the material legacies of art.

The image of the pool-as-prison that concludes "Losing the Marbles" recurs in "Self-Portrait in Tyvek^(TM) Windbreaker," the penultimate poem of Merrill's last volume. The fragmentary last stanza transcribes an enigmatic "final air" uttered by a dying speaker:

> Love, grief etc. ★★★★ for good reason.
> Now only ★★★★★★★ STOP signs.
> Meanwhile ★★★★★ if you are I've ex-
> ceeded our [?] ★★★ ~~more than time~~ was needed
> To fit a text airless and ★★ as Tyvek
> With breathing spaces and between the lines
> Days brilliantly recurring, as once *we* did,
> To keep the blue wave dancing in its prison. (*CP* 673)

Earlier in "Self-Portrait," Merrill had discovered "lucite coffins / For sapphire waves that crest, break, and recede" among trinkets in a new-age boutique; as the wave of the final line engulfs the poet, its fluid movement suggests not only "the motion of the spirit [contained] in the measure of the poem," but the mind's play within the failing body and the liquid oubliette that both threatens and allures the speaker of "Losing the Marbles."[30] Riddled with omissions, this final stanza resembles the ravaged Sapphic ode that symbolizes Merrill's mind in "Marbles"; the black Tyvek jacket of "Self-Portrait," embroidered with "starry longitudes" in a map of the zodiac, likewise recalls "the risen, cloudy brilliances" that twinkle above the swimming pool and the "rhetoric of starry beasts and gods" the speaker forgets in "Verse for Urania." Just as the snuffed-out stellar sparks and the Athens twilight's "dreamy blinkings-out" evoke mental decay, the astral asterisks at the end of "Self-Portrait" suggest, as Timothy Materer has observed, dying stars.[31] In *The Book of Ephraim*, Merrill compares the cosmic void "peppered" with collapsed stars to the emptiness of the white page, the material universe into which the poem is born and thus also conscripted to fade (with its final ellipses, the poem points assertively to this empty space):

> this net of loose talk tightening to verse,
> And verse once more revolving between poles—
> Gassy expansion and succinct collapse—
> Till Heaven is all peppered with black holes,
> Vanishing points for the superfluous
> Matter elided (just in time perhaps)
> By the conclusion of a passage thus. . . . (*CL* 85–86)

For Merrill, a self-styled chronicler of loss, mental blanks may resemble the void into which all creation ultimately recedes, but they also suggest the promise of a clean page, poised to quarter numinous performances of the imagination. In these late poems, it is not the retention but the erosion of personal histories embodied in textual and somatic forms that attests to a unity between subjective and objective aspects of reality, allowing Merrill to connect horizons of being that the lyric is often said to segregate into internal and external poles. Tracing the uses to which Merrill puts the vocabulary of the embodied mind, we arrive at depictions of mnemonic fallibility that trouble our tendency to associate him with involuntary, epiphanic revelations of the past; we also come to discern how Merrill's depictions of terminal loss allude to and refigure the toll of his terminal "virus," his vision of art's impermanence, and the epistemological instability and aesthetic opportunities he associates with the fragility of textual and biological being alike.

   The speaker's cascade of afflictions in "Losing the Marbles" begins implicitly and intertextually with Charmides's headache and the poetic "charm" that might cure it. The English word "charm" has its origin in the Latin *carmen*—song, incantation, verse—and carries into modernity its superstitious suggestion of a diminutive force that at once excites admiration and dispels, if only temporarily, the threat of mortal danger. Thus, "charm," though often condescended to as an aesthetic attribute of verse, is a form of beauty characterized by a talismanic power to protect its possessor—a power that distinguishes Merrill's voice as he portrays the forms of loss, mnemonic and otherwise, that populate his poetry. The capacity not only to be charmed by mundane aspects of experience but to charm his readers through his resilient felicity of expression enables Merrill to dispel temporarily the anxiety that the irresistible and ubiquitous encroachments of oblivion—upon the self, upon the body, upon history—can generate within us. And yet as aspects of beauty, the self-effacement, poise, and wit that characterize Merrill's charm are also affirmations, ways of asserting the aesthetic freedom that can arise from the powerlessness of the self in the face of forces that constrain it, whether those forces are embodied in flesh, in the enclosures of lyric form, or in the laws of nature.

CHAPTER 4

John Ashbery's Mindlessness

W ITHIN JOHN ASHBERY's lavish poetic output over the last fifteen years, failures to grasp, retain, and produce information are ubiquitous. "I have a friendly disposition but am forgetful, though I tend to forget only important things," *Chinese Whispers* (2002) begins; "Actually I can think of a number of reasons. / Wait—suddenly I can't think of any!" a speaker exclaims in *A Worldly Country* (2007); "We don't deserve our impressions / but are convicted anyway. Most come loose," Ashbery observes in *Quick Question* (2012); "I don't understand," he professes plainly in *Breezeway* (2015).[1] In fact, Ashbery's depictions of mind in the negative extend back sixty years to his earliest poems, where he associates them with the very origins of his art.

Ashbery's prepossessing poem "The Instruction Manual" (*Some Trees*, 1956) contains the first indication of what would become an abiding faith in the aesthetic value of mental lapses and failures, forms of mindlessness that he would come to identify closely with the fate of the soul in the age of the brain. The poem records an extended daydream of Guadalajara— "City I wanted most to see, and most *did not see,* in Mexico!" (*CP* 6, italics mine), its speaker pronounces—a dream he relishes in a moment of distraction from the tedious, instrumental task of writing a manual "on the uses of a new metal" (*CP* 5). Escaping the morose work of veridical description, the young functionary turns away from his banal composition and presents instead a wonderfully strange set of instructions for imagining his invented, unvisited city. As he follows a parade of hypothetical Guadalajaran couples in his mind's eye, his struggle to see and hear objects within his own daydream creates a whimsical reality effect: "I have lost sight of the young fellow with the toothpick. / Wait—there he is," the dreamer reports, spotting the imagined boy in a tryst just out of earshot: "I try to hear what they are saying / But it seems they are just mumbling something—shy words of love, probably" (*CP* 6–7). The poet-dreamer has only limited access to the daydream he has consciously engineered; the young Ashbery has already arrived at his enduring conviction that the fullest, most credible depictions of mental acts are partial ones. Accommodating this paradox with special deftness over the course of his career, Ashbery evokes mental life in its wholeness through constant negation, relishing the possibilities of the incomplete.

Ashbery's unawareness, his forgetfulness, his narrowness of vision, his distractibility, his failures of comprehension, are qualities I condense in the term "mindlessness"—a condition he ascribes to objects and people alike, declining to distinguish between the nonconsciousness of insentient matter and the forms of inattention and non-comprehension that distinguish "the experience of experience," his major theme.[2] While James Merrill attributes to the fragility of memory a special power to evoke the felt presence of the body within the motion of consciousness, Ashbery extravagantly negates all kinds of mental acts, deferring the consolations that Merrill's virtuosic verbal play, telescoping perspectives, and disarming equanimity conspire to offer. From Ashbery's first book, *Some Trees* (1956), to his most recent ones, this mindlessness retains a close association with the resistant surfaces of the object world, but its meanings and forms evolve briskly during the central decades of his career. From the 1970s to the 1990s, his identification of mental failures with physiological necessity waxes and then wanes in explicitness; while "The Skaters," to be discussed shortly, identifies its own expressive obscurities with the brain that projects it into being, Ashbery's subsequent, oeuvre-defining long poems *Three Poems,* "Self-Portrait in a Convex Mirror," "Litany," and *Flow Chart* develop, unravel, reconstitute, and finally exhaust the meanings of any directional, causal relationship in which physiology drives phenomenology. More and more openly, Ashbery attributes the limited resources of "inner" life to its continuity with the world of observable, physical events—from the metaphysical nostalgia of *Three Poems* and "Self-Portrait in a Convex Mirror," in which his mindlessness marks a spiritual vacuum in an era of mechanistic, biological reduction, to the extravagant materialism of "Litany," in which the poet's modeling of mental acts upon intentionless natural processes reaches a formal and discursive crescendo. But unlike Merrill, for whom the shock of his HIV diagnosis seemed to tether consciousness to the body with a new clarity and urgency, Ashbery's sharpening view of death in late middle age, focused by a nearly fatal illness that resulted in physically debilitating neurosurgery, marks a point from which his representation of the mind in neurological terms recedes, its premises wholly assimilated but the charm of its argot apparently exhausted. As Ashbery fashions a poetry of mortality out of a poetry of consciousness, he exchanges "new" terms to describe embodied mentality for timeless ones, and reanimates, with personal rather than philosophical urgency, a fundamental question he entangles with the quandary of mind: "What about your immortal soul?"[3]

Lapses of perception, attention, and memory through which mental limits intrude upon the putatively "free" expression of the imagination thus unite Ashbery's farrago of realist, surrealist, collage-based, narrative, and absurdist poetic modes over the course of his career, even as the meanings of his mindlessness, imprinted in his transformations of style, evolve along a characteristically sinuous course. Early on, the poet is relatively direct in attributing his oblique poetic style to the obtrusively physical medium of mind. Already in "The Skaters," from his 1966 collection *Rivers and Mountains,* Ashbery ascribes the lapses of focus that give "The Instruction Manual" its ingenious, enchanting realism and the verbal obscurity that he had pushed to unforeseen limits in *The Tennis Court Oath* (1962) to inexorable conditions of embodied consciousness. In the poem, Ashbery considers the mental events of an ordinary morning spent in the house among newspapers and letters, while laborers mend the road outside the window. The morning appears pedestrian enough, but "So much has passed through my mind . . . / That I can give you but a dim account of it"; rapidly dissolving into oblivion, the magnitude of even a morning's inwardness makes it impossible for the speaker to say just what he means about it. Ever mindful, like Merrill, of poetic precedent, Ashbery discerns in this impossibility J. Alfred Prufrock's predicament of being unable to say just what he means, and his fantasy of a (poetic) language that, like a "magic lantern," might throw "the nerves in patterns on a screen"—that might project consciousness directly onto the page by bringing the patterned conformities of verbal artifice into perfect congruence with the structure of thought itself. Apparently anything but direct, Ashbery's elliptical account of his morning conceals as it reveals, projecting his experience in an array of "shadows" and partially developed images. The episode alludes cryptically to successive forms of "bad news" that preoccupy the poet, piquing our interest only to deny us his intimacy:

> So much has passed through my mind this morning
> That I can give you but a dim account of it:
> It is already after lunch, the men are returning to their positions around
>   the cement mixer
> And I try to sort out what has happened to me. The bundle of Gerard's
>   letters,
> And that awful bit of news buried on the back page of yesterday's paper.
> Then the news of you this morning, in the snow. Sometimes the
>   interval
> Of bad news is so brisk that . . . And the human brain, with its tray of
>   images
> Seems a sorcerer's magic lantern, projecting black and orange cellophane
>   shadows
> On the distance of my hand . . . The very reaction's puny,
> And when we seek to move around, wondering what our position is now,
>   what the arm of that chair.[4] (Ashbery's ellipses)

While the projections of T. S. Eliot's magic lantern represent a fantasy of translation—the dream of somehow making the mind legible to the world through the inevitably distorting order of language—in Ashbery's rewriting of the image, the lantern corresponds to "the human brain" as it filters reality into consciousness; its projections stand for a process of cognitive distortion that seems to precede language altogether. The brain is the medium that projects experience through a schematic "tray of images," casting shadows of the real in eerie Halloween colors, while Ashbery's images are thrown not on a page-like "screen" but back upon the body itself—on the outstretched writing hand, in fact. Like the chemical reactions whose effects are projected on the magnified scale of human behavior, the "very reaction" of the light and cellophane, though "puny," generates astonishingly amplified effects; among these is existential confusion, for the disorienting shadows leave us unsure of "what our position is" and of the true identities of even the most familiar objects ("the arm of that chair"). Ashbery implies that the many disorienting verbal obscurities of his "dim account"—the ellipses that might be hesitations, omissions, or evasions; the identity of Gerard; the catastrophe buried publicly in the newspaper; the assignations between writer and lover, writer and reader ambiguously heralded by "the news of you this morning, in the snow"— originate in and reflect the shadowy projections of consciousness itself. Indeed, these interpretive uncertainties, integral to the signifying texture of the poem, evoke the epistemological limits Ashbery identifies with the natural conduct of the organ of consciousness—the matter of "the human brain."

The chiaroscuric picture of the mind projecting shadows in "The Skaters"—the mind making meaning through obscurity and negation rather than through illumination—not only remains consistent over the span of Ashbery's oeuvre but also remains associated with the medium of the body. Readers have become used to attributing Ashbery's unorthodox verbal misdirections (his infamous substitutions of pronouns, his fondness for defamiliarized cliché, his interspersals of noise and lucidity) to his view of the nature of language itself—to his conception of the verbal sign not as an index of transcendental meaning but as an unstable coalescence of opaque, shifting material, the limits of which, to paraphrase Wittgenstein, make up the limits of his world.[5] This rationale has obscured the relationship between his concept of mind and the shifting idiosyncrasies of his style, which are widely conscripted to reflect the unstable, shifting, limited material of mind itself. Indeed, Ashbery's mindlessness accrues a conspicuous spiritual significance in his poems that can only be understood in light of his close association of mental failures— especially ones of attention—with the entropic pull of mortal substance against the unity and continuity of the soul.

The physical substance of the brain shapes the phenomenology of mind and the texture of poetic language in "The Skaters," but the quandary of the soul remains beyond its purview. Reimagining the soul within the context of the concrete systems that seem to Ashbery to constitute an integral aspect of its truth, *Three Poems* is the first of Ashbery's books to explore the spiritual significance of the mind's recent collapse into physical substance. The ambition of the vast prose poem is stunning; it sets out to tell the story of, and find a suitable poetic form for, "the new spirit" in a materialist age. As he will do in "Self-Portrait in a Convex Mirror," in *Three Poems* Ashbery charts a transition from a set of concepts that he associates with the past—mystery, illusion, magic, solipsism, intangibility, innocence, and the soul—to a set of concepts he associates with the present—"reality," empiricism, exteriority, tangibility, experience, environment, and embodiment. During the nebulous interval stretching from "then" to "now," the meditative speaker reiterates, credible interpretations of reality have shifted swiftly and drastically; indeed, our conception of psyche proves to be a principal axis along which the poem traces this disorienting transition. "The system was breaking down" (*CP* 280), Ashbery proclaims with exhilarating imprecision, but he goes on to specify that within the intellectual cosmos of *Three Poems,* the notion of the transcendental soul is a defining part of that grandiose, languishing system. What has emerged to replace it is "The only slightly damaged bundle of receptive nerves . . . dispatching dense, precisely worded messages" (*CP* 273), a replacement that seems at times to be an electrifying source of possibility and at times a dismal substitution. In "The New Spirit," the longing to release the "self-propagating wind" of the spirit from the bodily "condition of hardness" that contains it entails dismantling the very idea of the self ("tak[ing] apart the notion of you") and discovering in it a mechanism "like a watch"—a physical system made up of parts that can be "sorted and labeled":

> The wind is now fresh and full, with leaves and other things flying. And to release it from its condition of hardness you will have to take apart the notion of you so as to reconstruct it from an intimate knowledge of its inner workings. How harmless and even helpful the painted wooden components of the Juggernaut look scattered around the yard, patiently waiting to be reassembled! So ends the first lesson:

that the concave being, enfolding like air or spirit, does not dissolve when breathed upon but comes apart neatly, like a watch, and the parts may be stocked or stored, their potential does not leak away through inactivity but remains bright and firm, so that in a sense it is just as much *there* as if it were put back together again and even more so: with everything sorted and labeled you can keep an eye on it a lot better than if it were again free to assume protean shapes and senses, the genie once more let out of the bottle, and who can say where all these vacant premises should end? (*CP* 257–258; Ashbery's italics)

The spirit, a menacing "Juggernaut," was once supernaturally "free to assume protean shapes and senses," but the "first lesson" of "the new spirit" is that these assumptions are "vacant premises." Aside from the potential of the spirit that is always "just as much *there*" in the physical parts, ready to be activated by the orchestrations of nature, the spirit imagined mechanistically is far less numinous, far less imposing, and far less free; it is "harmless," it "comes apart," its "concave being" resembles the humble "hollow" in which the soul will fit in "Self-Portrait," and once it has been deconstructed and demystified, it fits fairly easily within a finite, human point of view—"you can keep an eye on it a lot better."

The old, exalted terms for interiority evoke wistfulness in the occasionally sermonizing speaker of *Three Poems,* but the terms' decline also triggers in him a refractory impulse to root out sources of possibility in such ostensibly debased circumstances. Archaic spirituality and scientific vogue yield equally prejudiced and implausibly myopic descriptions of consciousness, but a compromise between them, Ashbery believes, might recover a subtle, ephemeral, "temporary dignity for the mind" (*CP* 263); he aspires to adopt a credible view of interiority that both acknowledges the mysteries of mental life and ratifies its material constraints. Importantly, the compromise that defines this new, synthetic "spirit" is less a middle ground than a progression through contraries. Intellectually rigorous and yet inclined to subvert his own claims to reason, Ashbery admits the possibility "that knowledge of the whole is impossible or at least so impractical as to be rarely or never feasible" (*CP* 290), but he nonetheless strives to comprehend the nature of mind in its entirety—and in doing so develops the fundamental rationale behind the poem's extravagantly overgrown, digressive prose.

In the next of the three poems, "The System," Ashbery lays out three methods of pursuing knowledge of anything—"reason, sense, or a knowing combination of both," of which "the last seems the least like a winner"; instead, he espouses an "erratic approach" distinctively poised, epistemologically, to "win all" or at least "lose nothing" (*CP* 291). Such a distracted approach involves shifting between contrary perspectives, including Platonic and Lockean philosophies of mind, in which knowledge is imagined to be possessed innately by the immaterial soul (forgotten in infancy and recovered through anamnesis) and to be earned solely through sensory experience, respectively. The perspectives are irreconcilable, but Ashbery will not choose between them. In syntax strained by baroque subordination, in sentences built to tax the attention of his reader, he thus approaches the mind from both transcendental and materialist perspectives at once, situating the experience of inattention at the center of it all:

> For just as we begin our lives as mere babes with the imprint of nothing in our heads, except lingering traces of a previous existence which grow fainter and fainter as we progress until we have forgotten them entirely, only by this time other notions have imposed themselves so that our infant minds are never a complete *tabula rasa,* but there is always something fading out or just coming into focus . . . just, I say, as we begin each day in this state of threatened blankness which is wiped away so soon, but which leaves certain illegible traces, like chalk dust on a blackboard after it has been erased, so we must learn to recognize it as the form—the only one—in which such fragments of the true learning as we are destined to receive will be vouchsafed to us, if at all. The unsatisfactoriness, the frowns and squinting, the itching and scratching as you listen without taking in what is being said to you, or only in part, so that you cannot piece the argument together, should not be dismissed as signs of our chronic all-too-human weakness but welcomed and examined as signs of life in which part of the whole truth lies buried. And as the discourse continues and you think you are not getting anything out of it, as you yawn and rub your eyes and pick your nose or scratch your head, or nudge your neighbor on the hard wooden bench, this knowledge is

getting through to you, and taking just the forms it needs to impress itself upon you, the forms of your inattention and incapacity or un-willingness to understand. (*CP* 298; ellipses mine)

Ashbery's mixed metaphors depict the experience of mind as a process of unrelenting inscription and erasure in which there is "always something fading out or just coming into focus," and even "blankness . . . is wiped away so soon." Acknowledging the extent to which his own sentences aspire to evoke and exaggerate this process—and thus raise such losses above the horizon of conscious awareness—Ashbery sympathetically pictures his reader wriggling uncomfortably on the hard pew of his prose ("you yawn and rub your eyes and pick your nose or scratch your head"). Indeed, Ashbery's syntactic and rhetorical switchbacks, which write over and thus "wipe away" successive propositions, not only enact the negations of mind to which the canonical precedents of Platonic amnesia and the Lockean tabula rasa allude, but also prove to be necessary verbal means of coordinating the minds of writer and reader; mindlessness supplies "the form—the only one—in which such fragments of the true learning" can emerge. *Three Poems* thus takes "just the forms it needs to impress itself upon you," adopting a style that complements the reader's "inattention and incapacity or unwillingness to understand" rather than striving to overcome it.

Three Poems appears to translate the contents of a working mind in real time, setting down the improvised flow of consciousness according to a principle of excessive inclusion that compensates for the constant losses that pervade conscious experience. Ashbery addresses this principle of composition explicitly in the famous opening lines of the first of the three poems, "The New Spirit": "I thought that if I could put it all down, that would be one / way. And next the thought came to me that to leave all out / would be another, and truer, way" (*CP* 247). Having acknowledged that putting in quite a lot of consciousness still leaves out plenty of interiority and external reality, however, and having opted for a compensatory aesthetic strategy of hoarding inclusion rather than a negative, "truer" strategy of subtraction and exclusion, Ashbery faces the challenge of incorporating an urgent sense of epistemological deprivation within *Three Poems'* textual excess—the challenge of absorbing the leaving out *into* the leaving in. Ashbery's strategy for absorbing the omissions of mindlessness into the amplitude of *Three Poems* takes shape on the level of the sentence, where a dense, unrelenting monotone unifies the voice of the book, creating the impression that its dizzying reversals of perspective belong to a single consciousness encountering reality. The intelligibility of that voice, however, varies from sentence to sentence as Ashbery mottles the nearly solid tonal field of *Three Poems* with tracts of clarity and inscrutability that seize and release the reader's own mental hold, in turn.[6]

A vision of consciousness defined by the pervasive effects of inattention thus proves to be the source and justification of *Three Poems'* strategically erratic prose, which presents lapses of attention as effects of physical circumstances—as "signs of life," as small indices of "our chronic all-too-human weakness," and as evidence of "the whole truth" of nature. (Indeed, the premise that prose is a medium capable of translating inwardness more transparently and capaciously than the compressed lyric poem also animates the formal logic of *Three Poems;* explaining the effect of translating unabridged thought "directly" into prose, ostensibly without revision, Ashbery quotes from Max Jacob's *La défense de Tartufe:* "I believe that prose which comes directly from meditation is a prose which has the form of the brain and which it is forbidden to touch.")[7]) If the prose style of *Three Poems,* then, incorporates authorial inattention and induces inattention in the reader, the book's discursive content identifies its style with the somatic determination of conscious life. Critical accounts of *Three Poems* have focused on its style, perhaps because many feel, as Stephen Fredman puts it, that "if one wishes to state what *Three Poems* is 'about' . . . one encounters problems."[8] In support of a nonthematic reading, Fredman goes on to cite Ashbery's own admission that "there are no themes or subjects in the usual sense, except the very broad one of an individual consciousness confronting or confronted by a world of external phenomena."[9] Ashbery's "except" is a significant one, for although evoking the phenomenology of mind is the primary formal ambition of *Three Poems,* the ontology of mind is the volume's central, if still "very broad," subject. The subjective aspects of consciousness Ashbery stresses on the level of the sentence (the mind's autonomous dilations of focus, its waywardness, its obstructions of the given) pose questions about the nature of mind that Ashbery addresses explicitly in the poems, which meditate on the origins of this distinctive texture of awareness, upon his own ambition to produce knowledge with only the very specific means of an imperfect, embodied mind, and upon the question of whether archaic terms for thought or novel ones are truer, ampler, more alive to modern sensibilities.

Ashbery begins "The Recital"—the last, and shortest, of his three poems—with a kind of exhausted admission about the status of the spirit, the problem Ashbery addresses stylistically and thematically in the mindless maneuvers of his grand experiment: "All right. The problem is that there is no new problem" (*CP* 318). Over and over in *Three Poems,* "fragmentary awareness" (*CP* 257) is both the problem and the solution, Ashbery suggests: it is the only way to represent consciousness and the best way; it inhibits empathy but also puts us in touch with the humbling parameters of our being; the "erratic approach" to knowledge is perplexing but it is also unavoidable, and therefore "wins all." At one point in "The System," Ashbery describes an early, failed effort to fulfill the spiritual quest of *Three Poems,* a past attempt to "produce the inner emptiness from which alone understanding can spring up, the tree of contradictions, joyous and living, investing that hollow void with its complicated material self" (*CP* 287).[10] In "The Recital," he wonders why that quest to fill a spiritual vacuum with a slew of contradictions associated with the "complicated material self" had ultimately failed, despite his urgent longing for answers in "the earlier days":

> The point was the synthesis of very simple elements in a new and strong, as opposed to old and weak, relation to one another. Why hadn't this been possible in the earlier days of experimentation, of bleak, barren living that didn't seem to be leading anywhere and it couldn't have mattered less? Probably because not enough of what made it up had taken on that look of worn familiarity, like pebbles polished over and over again by the sea, that made it possible for the old to blend inconspicuously with the new in a union too subtle to cause any comment that would have shattered its purpose forever. But already it was hard to distinguish the new elements from the old, so calculated and easygoing was the fusion, the partnership that was the

only element now, and which was even now fading rapidly from memory, so perfect was its assimilation. (*CP* 325)

This seamless, "easygoing . . . fusion" had been impossible because the new terms to describe the spirit were still too new, because "not enough of what made it up had taken on that look of worn familiarity"; the alluring "new and strong" synthesis of the embodied spirit Ashbery fosters in *Three Poems*—the texture of a whole, natural, weathered thing, like a pebble eroding on a beach—appears only when the idea is "polished over and over again" by the undulating friction of consciousness. This perfectly assimilated, unshatterable unity emerges through the "fragmentary awareness" of the poem itself, but it is also subject to the limits of that awareness; the new spirit begins to recede as soon as it comes into view, "even now fading rapidly from memory." It is a unity that appears only in the past tense, in fact, vanishing as it comes into being; Ashbery elegantly encapsulates this quality of the new spirit in the poem's final image of itself as a finished performance, a fleeting, expressive offering swallowed by silence: "The performance had ended, the audience streamed out; the applause still echoed in the empty hall. But the idea of the spectacle as something to be acted out and absorbed still hung in the air long after the last spectator had gone home to sleep" (*CP* 326). Indeed, Ashbery's enchanted spectacle of uniting the visible and the invisible offers his spectators temporary diversion and consolatory possibility, but most importantly it offers the echoing "idea of the spectacle"—the enduring sense that one has witnessed, in an age when the soul seems stripped of its secrets, the making of a "temporary dignity for the mind" (*CP* 263).

Ashbery thus arrives at the tentative reconciliation of phenomenological and mechanistic aspects of mind in *Three Poems* through a synoptic (that is, distracted) philosophical method—through an erratic, inconsistent kind of reason that complements the mindlessness the poem both evokes and induces. While varieties of cancellation beset all sorts of mental acts in Ashbery's poems—apprehending, knowing, remembering, perceiving, thinking—such cancellations, *Three Poems* demonstrates, are especially dramatic where he depicts interest and attention, the primary cognitive energies that precede and enable all others. Readers have long noticed Ashbery's constant lapses of focus, framing them persuasively as a species of postmodernist revolt against modernist pretentions to imaginative and aesthetic mastery and as a reflection of "changing configurations of capitalism [that] continually push attention and distraction to new limits and thresholds."[11] The impression that Ashbery is a "traveler down the billboard-clotted lanes of modern life" leads Andrew DuBois, for example, to attribute the poet's distractibility to modernity's proliferating claims on our interest.[12] Drawing on Jonathan Crary's premise that "new products, sources of stimulation and streams of information" and a concomitant "crisis of attentiveness" distinguish modernity, DuBois proposes that Ashbery's divided attention is a symptom of a changing world; "among the poets of our era," DuBois writes, "Ashbery is an especially crucial figure for understanding contemporary changes in mental and social life related to shifts in aesthetic reception, the accelerated flow of information, and the general rise in stimuli."[13] Certainly, the commodity fetishism that defines the American cultural landscape pervades Ashbery's poems, which are replete with pop phenomena, from Popeye cartoons to *Antiques Roadshow;* these inclusions amplify the poems' powerful evocation of a sensibility unusually alert to its populous, heterogeneous, dynamic cultural environment. Mutlu Blasing has noticed that this environment influences Ashbery's conception of poetry itself as a cultural commodity; she aligns his critique of the market-driven production of riskless experimental art in "The Invisible Avant-Garde" (1968) with Fredric Jameson's claim that the avant-garde is absorbed into "official culture" in the age of late capitalism, such that "the frantic economic urgency of producing fresh waves of ever more novel-seeming goods . . . now assigns an increasingly essential structural function and position to aesthetic innovation and experimentation."[14] Christopher Nealon sees "the crises born of [capitalism's] victories . . . in the long postwar boom" as a force working not only upon Ashbery's themes but upon his forms— forms in which "a dialectical understanding of style that is always in relation to catastrophe" reflects the fluctuations of faith and fate that typify boom-and-bust economic reality.[15]

Whether the commercially driven torrent of stimuli that makes sources of distraction difficult to avoid in modern life affects Ashbery's fundamental conception of the nature of mind is another question, however. In fact, the spiritual significance of inattention in Ashbery's poems complicates such environmental interpretations of his mindlessness. Distractions themselves tend to play a minimal role in Ashbery's own attempts to explain why his poems lapse into unintelligibility, carrying the reader's attention with them as they swerve in and out of focus. It is not that extrinsic, environmental stimuli intrude relentlessly upon Ashbery's attention, he explains, but rather that spontaneous dilations of focus form an integral dimension of "how," in his words, "experience comes to me":

> It seems to me that my poetry sometimes proceeds as though an argument were suddenly derailed and something that started out clearly suddenly becomes opaque. It's a kind of mimesis of how experience comes to me: as one is listening to someone else—a lecturer, for instance—who's making perfect sense but suddenly slides into something that eludes one. What I am probably trying to do is to illustrate opacity and how it can suddenly descend over us, rather than trying to be willfully obscure.[16]

Ashbery describes the "obscurity" readers often attribute to his poems as mimesis of his own experience of mind, as a method of recruiting the resistant surfaces of language to serve the overwhelmingly conventional ambition of the lyric to evoke how the world presents itself to an unusually responsive array of senses. By his own account, Ashbery's obscurity reflects the endless, rhythmic process of grasping objects of attention and then releasing them and then grasping them again, enacting the sudden "descent of opacity" that can accompany boredom, confusion, and incomprehension alike. Such forms of mindlessness are surely in some cases attributable to a historically specific "sensory glut," but Ashbery tends to historicize them abstractly, as an effect of the conceptual dismantling of the soul itself.[17]

Accordingly, Ashbery's most celebrated depiction of the mind in action, "Self-Portrait in a Convex Mirror," replaces the permanence of immortal spirit with the fallibility of the embodied mind, associating distractibility not with impingements of environmental stimuli but with a specifically embodied ontology of consciousness. The disjunctive force of Ashbery's lapses of attention not only disrupts the continuities of memory and voice in "Self-Portrait" but lends the long, meditative poem its structure; Parmigianino's painting provides a fixed focal point from which the poem's swerves of attention drift away and to which they safely return.[18] The poem begins with all sorts of dualist premises intact, giving such premises pride of place in order to stage their dissolution all the more flamboyantly. Using the painter's body to frame the relationship between the artistic object and the consciousness that generated it, Ashbery first situates Parmigianino's head relative to his hand in the emphatically distorted self-portrait, presenting the relationship between mind and body as a primary philosophical preoccupation of the poem:[19]

> As Parmigianino did it, the right hand
> Bigger than the head, thrust at the viewer
> And swerving easily away, as though to protect
> What it advertises.

Metonymically, Ashbery separates the mind that conceptualizes the portrait from the hand that executes it; the head that recedes from the viewer is so different in scale from the magnified hand thrust into the foreground that the two body parts seem utterly disconnected. Parmigianino's immortally lively face initially appears "intact," and his soul, a "captive" ghost confined in the representational machine of the portrait, is released by Ashbery's "look as it intercepts the picture." Indeed, the soul autonomously "establishes itself" when the immortal essence of the artist and the living spirit of the viewer converge in a moment of transcendental recognition:

> The time of day or the density of the light
> Adhering to the face keeps it
> Lively and intact in a recurring wave
> Of arrival. The soul establishes itself.
> But how far can it swim out through the eyes
> And still return safely to its nest? The surface
> Of the mirror being convex, the distance increases
> Significantly; that is, enough to make the point
> That the soul is a captive, treated humanely, kept
> In suspension, unable to advance much farther
> Than your look as it intercepts the picture. (*CP* 474)

The portrait itself, painted on a convex surface to replicate the perspective of the mirror, in turn mirrors Ashbery's convex eye, establishing a mutual gaze between the painted Parmigianino swelling outward toward the poet and the poet peering forward toward the painting. The portrait gives Ashbery the impression that the distended image—pregnant, after all, with the essence of a person—reaches toward him, decreasing the distance Parmigianino's soul must "swim out" from his painted eyes. But the mixed metaphor replaces the relatively unencumbered motion of the fish, which fails to evoke the classical sense of an immaterial spirit attached to something corporeal, with the flight of a bird bound by instinct to a stationary "nest." The captive soul occupies a dimension of being conceivable only by awkward analogy to the natural elements of air and water, hovering in spectral "suspension" as it reaches out toward us through the surfaces of the bisected wooden globe and the poem itself.

In the fantasy of Ashbery's initial description, then, Parmigianino's artistry facilitates a transcendental rendezvous between the souls of the painter and viewer. The poem proceeds to dispel that fantasy just as soon as it has been constructed, however; just when Ashbery pictures a soul translatable "intact" through the portrait, he recognizes there a reflection of his own familiar "combination / Of tenderness, amusement and regret," the expression with which he is accustomed to greeting the more sobering picture of a demystified psyche, a soul without secrets:

> But there is in that gaze a combination
> Of tenderness, amusement and regret, so powerful
> In its restraint that one cannot look for long.
> The secret is too plain. The pity of it smarts,
> Makes hot tears spurt: that the soul is not a soul,
> Has no secret, is small, and it fits
> Its hollow perfectly: its room, our moment of attention. (*CP* 475)[20]

What is Parmigianino's soul if it is not a soul? The original, immaterial essence resuscitated by Ashbery's intercepting look has been replaced by a small, degraded thing generated by that look. Divested of the dignity of its secrets, that unreal, imagined substitute for the soul fits the tiny chamber of Ashbery's "moment of attention" because it is constrained by the limits of the mind that created it. It is at precisely this moment of deflation, when Ashbery pronounces the soul to be something physically "small" and stripped of its secrets, that the distinction between psyche and soma in *Self-Portrait* begins to break down. Ashbery pictures the convex portrait as "life englobed," symbolically identifying the seductive enclosure of the objet d'art with the skeletally englobed mind, each of which "represents" life according to internal principles; "One would like to stick one's hand / Out of the globe," he writes, "but its dimension, / What carries it, will not allow it" (*CP* 475). "Carries" continues to evoke the dualistic vision the lines ostensibly dismiss, but now that the head and the hand exist in the same material "dimension," nothing can possibly "swim out"; "Everything," Parmigianino's eyes proclaim, "is surface" (*CP* 476).

This flattening means that the demystified "mind" or "soul" or "spirit" is now fundamentally *like* the portrait—it may seem to possess an immaterial depth, but it is merely a sum of parts that converge on a single, material plane. The soul, the speaker remembers regretfully, is as determined by its status as a physical phenomenon as his vision of Parmigianino is determined by the flamboyant, protuberant, emphatically physical features of the self-portrait. It is at this moment of metaphysical collapse that Parmigianino's hand appears to "rov[e] back to the body of which it seems / So unlikely a part" (*CP* 475), and henceforth biological terms emerge to frame mental events and products in *Self-Portrait:* from "memories deposited in irregular / Clumps of crystals" (*CP* 476), to a corporeal experience of recognition that "Mov[es] outward along the capes and peninsulas / Of your nervures" (*CP* 481), to a comparison of the "bubble-chamber" of art (hermetic, autonomous, beautiful) to "Reptile eggs" in which "everything gets 'programmed'" (*CP* 478) genetically— an analogy through which Ashbery situates life at its most primitively slimy and art at its most delicately sublime within a single line of descent from chemical sources. In light of this biological contingency, everything becomes unstable, unhinged; the unity of the subject "englobed" in the mind and in the work of art alike proves to be a precariously fragile illusion, a whole "stable / within instability," a "globe . . . resting / On a pedestal of vacuum, a ping-pong ball / Secure on its jet of water" (*CP* 476).

It is just as Ashbery has deflated his own Romantic vision of the immaterial soul that "the balloon" of attention so very famously "pops," a coincidence that signals the poet's intimate association of the phenomenology of mindlessness with the decline of transcendental descriptions of consciousness. When Ashbery's ekphrastic description of Parmigianino's portrait suddenly breaks off, proving the fugitive transience of "our moment of attention," the interruption reveals Ashbery's mind to be its own obstacle.[21] No external stimulus divides the speaker's focus, shattering his mental image of the portrait into "sawtoothed fragments" like clouds dissipated in a rippling puddle. Nothing intrudes from outside consciousness to pop the balloon of his attention—it simply pops—and its manner of popping proves to be consistent with the overwhelmingly *natural* picture of the mind that emerges as Ashbery goes on to consider, in the lines that follow, the self divested of both cognitive agency and faith in a deity "Whose curved hand" composes reality:

> The balloon pops, the attention
> Turns dully away. Clouds
> In the puddle stir up into sawtoothed fragments.
> I think of the friends
> Who came to see me, of what yesterday
> Was like. A peculiar slant
> Of memory that intrudes on the dreaming model
> In the silence of the studio as he considers
> Lifting the pencil to the self-portrait.
> How many people came and stayed a certain time,
> Uttered light or dark speech that became part of you
> Like light behind windblown fog and sand,
> Filtered and influenced by it, until no part
> Remains that is surely you. Those voices in the dusk
> Have told you all and still the tale goes on
> In the form of memories deposited in irregular
> Clumps of crystals. Whose curved hand controls,
> Francesco, the turning seasons and the thoughts
> That peel off and fly away at breathless speeds
> Like the last stubborn leaves ripped
> From wet branches? I see in this only the chaos

> Of your round mirror which organizes everything
> Around the polestar of your eyes which are empty,
> Know nothing, dream but reveal nothing. (*CP* 477)

As Ashbery's attention turns itself to internal, and apparently idle, subjects—a remembered visit from friends, "what yesterday / Was like"—he wonders if Parmigianino, in the "silence" of his own studio, ever found himself intruded upon by the same kind of internal distraction, by a "peculiar slant / Of memory" of sixteenth-century friends who "came and stayed a certain time." The artist's memory would have conjured the voices of some friends and allowed others to have gone mute, relinquishing them to oblivion; this intimate speech stippled "light or dark" by memory is assimilated into the chiaroscuric "tale" of the self—a tale that "goes on," not an entity but an improvisation. The shadowy filtration of memory obscures the self from itself "until no part / Remains that is surely you," and what is left is a shifting, warped illusion deposited in "irregular / Clumps of crystals," an illusion by which we nonetheless navigate existence; the "polestar" of Parmigianino's world, the eyes that ought to reveal his soul, prove to be empty. In this portrait of consciousness there is no soul, and thoughts, as natural as leaves, are as destined as all other aspects of life to be ripped out of existence; Ashbery suggests that the only "curved hand" is the mindless hand of nature that commands chaos rather than order, whose swerve is contained by a finite cosmos and whose constraints are writ small in all physical phenomena, from clouds and trees to memories.

The epistemological troubles Ashbery describes in "Self-Portrait," then, arise not from environmental chaos but from "the chaos / Of your round mirror"—from the finite, reflective organ of the mind itself. Unlike the adventurous soul that swims out in search of a connection that transcends the death of the artist, the much smaller self Ashbery embeds in nature is one that things happen *to;* it is a self made by others' voices, by extrinsic forces that "filter and influence" self-illumination, and by chemical arrangements in the brain. It is a self—no wonder "hot tears spurt"—that is powerless even to turn its attention as an expression of will. Signs of an irrevocable epistemic transition pervade both *Three Poems* and "Self-Portrait" as they correlate the experience of mindlessness with the dismantling of the immaterial spirit, presenting the poet's and the reader's limited powers of attention as proof that consciousness bears no connection to divinity. In distended sentences that strain readerly focus and in long, canto-like movements that correspond to the erratic motions of authorial inattention, the poems implicate their stylistic innovations in a melancholy process of rending interiority from its putative sources in the infinite, the absolute. But however much these earlier poems use form to ratify the endemic late-twentieth-century conviction that "the soul is not a soul"—to deny consciousness any pretension to ideal sources—they rarely go so far as to assert a direct connection between interiority and nature. Forging these horizontal relationships, after all, is a more decisive act of philosophical commitment than severing the old, vertical ones, already fading into obsolescence.

In "Litany," however, Ashbery's vertical negations of the ideal give way to affirmations of physical authority. Unlike *Three Poems* and "Self-Portrait," which negotiate vertiginous descents into the concrete, "Litany" begins at the bottom and stays there—in the "eiderdown of materialism and space" (*CP* 595), where "it is all, / As you say, horizontal, without / Beginning or end" (*CP* 618). How, Ashbery asks in "Litany," do we survive the uncertainty of viewing the world from this low horizon, whence we can only speculate about *"whatever / Could be happening / Behind tall hedges"* (*CP* 555) of every kind of worldly obstacle—including the obstacle of language itself? A long, epistemological poem outstretched confidently alongside the shorter lyrics of *As We Know* (1979), "Litany" reimagines poetry as we know it even as it wonders whether we know much of anything at all. The most distinctive feature of "Litany," any reader notices, is its silhouette; over a hundred pages long and composed of two narrow pillars of text broken at irregular intervals, "Litany" is printed in roman and italic scripts typeset on facing pages.[22]

	A new alertness changes
	Into the look of things
The windows are open again	*Placed on the railing*
The dust blows through	*Of this terrace:*
A diagram of a room.	*The beheld with all the potential*
This is where it all	*Of the visible, acting*
Had to take place,	*To release itself*

Around a drum of living,   *Into the known*
The motion by which a life   *Dust under*
May be known and recognized,   *The sky.*
A shipwreck seen from the shore,
A puzzling column of figures.   *Hands where it took place*
The dark shirt dragged frequently   *Moving over the nebulous*
Through the bayou.   *Keyboard: the heft*
                                            Now invisible, only fragments
Your luggage   *Of the echo are left*
Is found   *Intruding into the color,*
Upon the plane.   *How we remember them.*

Capturing the "motion by which a life / May be known and recognized" in yet another disarming formal arrangement, "Litany" proves to be a poem not about anything so grandiose as the state of the soul, a subject Ashbery has now forsworn, but rather about the humbler subject of interpretation itself—about the functions of poetry and criticism as modes of thought. Mischievously, perhaps, though at his publisher's request, Ashbery appends a brief author's note to the poem, in which he specifies that "the two columns of 'Litany' are meant to be read as simultaneous but independent monologues" (*CP* 553). The statement clarifies not at all how the perplexed reader ought to go about reading the two texts at once, and indeed in his own comments about "Litany," Ashbery alludes cheerfully to the impossibility of his poem: "I consider the poem as a sort of environment," he explains, "and one is not obliged to take notice of every aspect of one's environment—one can't, in fact."[23] The pleasurable impasse, embodied in the wide gap between the two simultaneous litanies, is both a formal and thematic presence throughout the poem. "*Every collection is as notable for its gaps / As for what's there,*" Ashbery proclaims, characteristically attuned to the equal importance of figure and ground in the composition of a unified whole; "*The wisest among us / Collect gaps, knowing it's the only way to / Realize a more complete collection / Than one's neighbor's*" (*CP* 579). As we have seen, Ashbery integrates mindlessness within the syntax and narrative structure of *Three Poems* and "Self-Portrait," respectively, but inattention emerges here as a poetic raison d'être; the poem is built upon the proposition that "*no one is punished for inattention any more: / It seems, in fact, to further the enjoyable / Side of the world's activities*" (*CP* 623). Indeed, the concrete shape of "Litany" not only forces inattention on its reader but also presents an abstract model for the process of embodied consciousness itself.

An intuition that "Litany" reflects on the origins of mind in material substance has been evident in passing descriptions of the poem's structure: Helen Vendler describes "Litany" as "a somewhat trying imitation of the bicameral mind," for example, and to John Shoptaw, the poem's parts suggest "the two hands or eyes or sides of the brain."[24] The two columns, however, are indistinguishable tonally and thematically; the popularized association of the cranial hemispheres with discrete analytical and intuitive modes of thought (according to left brain–right brain dominance theories) are nowhere to be found in the uniformly erratic voice of Ashbery's divided poem. Indeed, the correspondence between the poem's philosophy of mind and its form lies not in its divided silhouette, per se, but in its conception as a pair of "simultaneous" texts, physically adjacent but temporally overlaid in the process of reading or listening. Among his inspirations for the poem, Ashbery recalls, was an Elliot Carter duo for violin and piano in which "sometimes the instruments would be talking to—or at—each other, and sometimes just to themselves" in a "non-conversational" duet. In other descriptions of the poem in interviews, he emphasizes the aural dissonance and attentional challenge of eavesdropping, at a cocktail party, on two conversations at once—a condition, he concludes, that "should have a poem written about it."[25] In a recorded reading with Ann Lauterbach in 1980, Ashbery demonstrated that the columns of "Litany" could indeed be experienced as "two simultaneous but independent monologues" to marvelous effect. As the poets perform the parallel parts of the poem, the noise of their voices jostling on the verge of intelligibility suddenly resolves into clarity when one reader arrives at a stanza break and the other, for a few moments, speaks alone; the words uttered in that gap, elevated by chance, radiate significance, but as the second reader begins again after only a breath, this amplification of meaning only amplifies its loss.[26]

It is only in this dynamic, experiential superimposition of sonic surfaces in "non-conversation"—in the interaction of discrete but interwoven strains of language that alternately obscure and reveal each other—that the form of "Litany" comes into view as a reflection of the natural mind Ashbery envisions in the poem. The texts remain separate on the page, but by proposing that his texts be read or heard simultaneously, Ashbery weaves his discrete threads of language into a verbal "lattice that is / As narrow as the visible universe" (*CP* 567)—into material that, like the body itself, filters, obstructs, and transforms information on its way into consciousness.[27] Ashbery's many allusions, within "Litany" itself, to the poem's unique form present the columns of text as plies of organic substance overlaid, layer upon layer, to form a single texture; like a bouquet of flowers or the lattice of a bird's nest or a sheaf of leaves (all metaphors he uses for the poem within the poem), "Litany" imagines itself as a bundle of natural material. The organic matter out of which Ashbery bales "Litany" (his "sheaf of selected odes / Bundled on the waters" [*CP* 566]) proves to be thought itself, the raw material overlaid in the poem's signature forms of sonic and textual simultaneity, while the sieve of the mind proves to resemble the *"sheaves / Of nerves"* that somehow both sift through reality and "build it up." Importantly for the poet, this vision of embodied consciousness relegates forms of sublime experience associated with inspiration—the ecstatic, the religious, the transcendental—to the status of mere effects or appearances. The thunderbolt of inspiration, for example, a spiritual *"experience / Unlike any other,"* has become part of the *"lore"* of the past, the speaker proclaims, its sublimity fabricated from within rather than delivered from without, its annunciation "formed" by the perceiving body rather than discovered:

> *That tower of lightning high over*
> *The Sahara Desert could have missed you,*
> *An experience*
> *Unlike any other, leaching*
> *Back into the lore of*
> *The songs and sagas,*
> *The warp of knowledge.*
> *But now it's*
> *Come close*
> *Strict identities form it,*
> *Build it up like sheaves*
> *Of nerves, articulate,*
> *Defiant of itself.* (*CP* 557)

Having descended into the realm of mental fashioning (*"now it's / Come close"*), the visionary moment of heightened awareness is contingent rather than inevitable (it *"could have missed you"*) and is a product of a product, built from the ground up. Generated by the Humean self-bundle—"that connected mass of perceptions, which constitute a thinking being"— the sublime vision is conscripted to material equivalence with the *"sheaves"* of biological matter it only appears to transcend, *"Defiant of itself."*[28]

Ashbery will reserve for volumes that follow *As We Know* some of the perplexities of this fibrous, organic conception of the mind, in which "speculation," for example, is "stacked like leaves / Speckled behind the eyes" (*CP* 568). In *Flow Chart,* for example, he will go on to compare the fabric of mind with the fabric of the painterly canvas (a "compacted mass of fibers that filter truth"), marveling with ambivalent skepticism and credulousness that "I don't see how a bunch of attributes can go walking around with a coatrack labeled 'person' loosely tied to it with apron strings. That blows my mind" (*FC* 183).[29] In the raveling and unraveling strands of "Litany," however, Ashbery cleaves closely to the pragmatic consequences, within the specifically verbal realms of poetry and criticism, of conceiving of the noumenon of the self as a loose "bunch of attributes" subject to entropy and decay. Modeling subjectivity on the fabric of material being, Ashbery finds himself reckoning with the special problems that accrue to a wholly physical picture of consciousness: "The eroding goes on constantly in the brain / Where its music is softest" (*CP* 616), he proposes halfway through "Litany," linking *"That loss of memory / Which is itself a music, / A kind of music"* (*CP* 593) with the poem's contrapuntal form and with its concept of mind *"Rooted in thoughtful soil"* (*CP* 587). To the problem of decay he adds the quandary of pleasure, asking to what kinds of gratification—if not those of permanence or ecstatic vision or any other form of spiritual ascent—his poem ought to aspire, now that we live in an age that demands new forms of reading and writing, a *"Silver Age,"* as he puts it, in which *"no one really pays much attention / To anything at all"* (*CP* 599),

> *Wherein a multitude of glittering, interesting*
> *Things and people attack one*
> *Like a blizzard at every street crossing*
> *Yet remain unseen, unknown, and undeveloped*
> *In the electrical climate of sensitivities that ask*

> *Only for self-gratification.*
> *Not for outside or part-time help*
> *In assimilating and enjoying whatever it is.*
> *Therefore a new school of criticism must be developed. (CP 603)*

The mindless *"electrical"* system of the subject, distinguished only by its worldly desire for *"self-gratification,"* blends in with the chaotic ambience of unrecognized *"things"* that whirl around it. Ashbery seems at first to disparage the corporeal hedonism of the *"climate[s] of sensitivities"* into which the reading and writing selves have dissolved, leaving so much of the violent, *"glittering"* barrage of the real *"unseen, unknown, and undeveloped."* But in the poem's extended, meandering excursus on poetry and criticism in the Silver Age, Ashbery reminds himself that gratification is a legitimate source of value in an earthbound poetics and thus in the *"new school of criticism"* he wants "Litany" to exemplify. Like the heroic grasshopper of Keats's sonnet "On the Grasshopper and Cricket," who "rests at ease beneath some pleasant weed" and affirms that "The poetry of earth is ceasing never," Ashbery is determined to find out just *"how much meaning / Was there languishing at the roots"* (CP 595) and to cultivate that radical, somatic source of significance.[30] Remembering Keats's breezy sonnet—the sprezzatura of its effortless rhyme, the luxurious fluency of its rhythm, its guileless ambition to soothe rather than challenge its reader—he aspires to reproduce, in his own idiom and in his own time, its many varieties of sensuous appeal.

Indeed, Ashbery adopts Keats's sonnet as both a specific aesthetic model and a test case with which to demonstrate his *"new school of criticism"* that sets out *"to dispel / The quaint illusions that have been deluding us"* (CP 603). The subject of criticism preoccupies Ashbery at great length in "Litany"; not only do the poem's columns often seem to function as running commentaries on each other (the italicized right-hand column typographically recalls a marginal biblical gloss), but the distance between the columns suggests the dual position any poet occupies as a writer and a reader. Invoking the title of the collection that contains "Litany" *(As We Know),* Ashbery describes this self-estrangement in the process of reading (and thus criticizing) his own work: "Every once in a while I will pick up a page and it has something, but what is it? It seems so unlike what poetry 'as we know it' is. It's a question of a sudden feeling of unsureness at what I am doing, wondering why I am writing the way I am."[31] The subject of criticism, in fact, seems to have shaped the poem from its very conception. Of its maundering, spoken style, Ashbery explains that "I intended, in "Litany," to write something so utterly discursive that it would be beyond criticism—not because I wanted to punish critics, but because this would somehow exemplify the fullness, or, if you wish, the emptiness, of life, or, at any rate, its dimensionless quality."[32]

A dimensionless flattening of life, art, and criticism is precisely what Ashbery achieves in "Litany" as he collapses the pleasurable effects of Keats's sonnet onto a purely physiological plane. He holds up "On the Grasshopper and Cricket" as a paradigm of the kind of art that comes alive (unlike most "*Creative writing*," which is "*dead / Or was never called to life, and could not be / Anything living*" [CP 605]), and that obviates further commentary by "*talking / Directly into us*":

> *the writing that doesn't offend us*
> *(Keats' "grasshopper" sonnet for example)*
> *Soothes and flatters the easier, less excitable*
> *Parts of our brain in such a way as to set up a*
> *Living, vibrant turntable of events,*
> *A few selected ones, that nonetheless have*
> *Their own veracity and their own way of talking*
> *Directly into us without any effort so*
> *That we can ignore what isn't there—*
> *The death patterns, swirling ideas like*
> *Autumn leaves in the teeth of an insane gale,*
> *And can end up really reminding us*
> *How big and forceful some of our ideas can be—*
> *Not giants or titans, but strong, firm*
> *Human beings with a good sense of humor*
> *And a grasp of a certain level of reality that*
> *Is going to be enough—will have to be.* (CP 605–607)

Importantly for Ashbery's poem, his ideal of poetic sensuousness—of a kind of language that touches the brain in just the right way, setting into motion physical events with unambiguous sensory and emotional effects—suggests a kind of poetic immediacy that renders explanation or interpretation irrelevant. Ashbery thus replicates Keats's *"way of talking / Directly into us"* in his own idiom of "dimensionless" discursiveness and formal simultaneity, serving his own ambition to remind us of the possibilities and limits of consciousness when it is imagined not on the aggrandized, mythological scale of *"giants or titans"* but on a mortal, human, physiological scale that reflects *"a certain level of reality."* Such a poetry, finally, does not really obviate criticism but becomes indistinguishable from it; just as Keats affirms the consolatory power of mimesis by rendering the outdoor and indoor songs of the grasshopper and cricket (the parallel melodies of reality and art) indistinguishable to the sonnet's drowsy speaker, Ashbery affirms the legitimacy of his *"new criticism"* by rendering it indistinguishable from his poem. In terms that resemble Matthew Arnold's definition of poetry as the criticism of life, Ashbery proposes that *"all, / Is by definition subject matter for the new criticism, which is us"* (605). This yearning to describe the whole planar *"field"* of physical reality, to evoke its confinements *"For better or for worse,"* is in fact what unites the acts of writing and reading, "Litany" affirms. Summarizing this realization in a conclusive question and answer (a form appropriate to a litany), Ashbery asks:

> *Who can describe the exact feel*
> *And slant of a field in such a way as to*
> *Make you wish you were in it, or better yet*
> *To make you realize that you actually are in it*
> *For better or for worse, with no*
> *Conceivable way of getting out?*
> *That is what*
> *Great poets of the past have done, and a few*
> *Great critics as well.* (CP 601)

Aiming "to direct the readers' attention to the white space between the columns," Ashbery uses the great, white gap of "Litany" to *"make you realize"* the limits of the field of embodied consciousness, a field from which there is *"no / Conceivable way of getting out."*[33] Reimagining the dialogic structure of the Great Litany as a "non-conversation" that places impossible demands on his reader's attention, Ashbery enlarges the spiritual meanings of mindlessness evident in his earlier work, imputing a "sacred sense" to the limits the body imposes on our access to reality; the poem makes "the chronic inattention / Of our lives" (*CP* 673), as he puts it elsewhere in *As We Know,* a central emblem of the inexorable human frailties for which the sacred Litany scripts the process of repentance.[34] If the words of "Litany," as Ashbery puts it in the poem's conclusion, issue "like arrows / From the taut string of a restrained / Consciousness" (*CP* 654)—a mind modeled on the organic tissue Ashbery associates with the restrictions of a universe bound by physical laws—the blankness those columns frame seems to stand both for a *deus absconditus* and for the forms of "our not-knowing" (*CP* 656) that Ashbery attributes to such a mind, divested of divine illusions.

The impossible form of "Litany," engineered to disallow sustained focus, marks the crescendo of Ashbery's early, meditative poetics and of his sustained, explicit contemplation of the biology of mind in relation to the ontology of it. After *As We Know,* the use of anatomical terms to describe conscious experience—to represent sensation "battering your brain tissues" (*CP* 927), for example, and to designate poetry that "*Soothes and flatters the easier, less excitable / Parts of our brain*" (*CP* 605)—declines in favor of phenomenological descriptions that suture consciousness to the body by tracing the timeless signatures of mortality upon the experience of consciousness. Alongside the emergence of stylistic traits that have come to be associated with the "late Ashbery"—a style more narrative and informal than solemn and contemplative, more populist than philosophical, more absorbed by the verbal textures of demotic English and the familiar rhythms of everyday speech than with "the experience of experience" per se—there arises in Ashbery's poetry of late middle age a thematic transition from a "poetry meant to mirror an idea of mind" to a poetry of urgent mortal awareness, from a poetry of consciousness to a poetry of death. If there had been any consistent theme in the poetry Ashbery wrote in his thirties and forties, he recalls, it could only have been "the movement of my mind as I was writing," but "as I become older I've noticed that indeed there is a theme and it is precisely the theme of getting older, the one thing that nobody anticipates really and nobody expects and it's always a shock. When one is old, one is old for the first time."[35]

Forrest Gander traces this transition from a poetry of the mind tracking itself to a poetry of the body tracking its decline to the poet's nearly fatal illness at the age of fifty-five, when a neurological infection resulted in the sudden onset of full-body paralysis and "ten or eleven hours" of invasive neurosurgery. The surgery saved Ashbery's life but permanently limited his ability to walk.[36] The gradual experience of aging—"always a shock"— seems to have begun in earnest for Ashbery with this particularly shocking episode and with the feeling of premature senescence brought about by what the poet describes as his ongoing "mobility issues."[37] As Gander points out, "the near-death experience, the submersion and surfacing: *darkness, nowhere,* and *pain* (from the poem's very first line) are constant undercurrents" of "'A Wave,' . . . the last great discursive lyric of [Ashbery's] early meditative mode."[38] Written soon after the sudden illness Ashbery described to Mark Ford in 2002 as "the only serious illness I've ever had," the poem's opening lines—"To pass through pain and not know it, / A car door slamming in the night. / To emerge on an invisible terrain" (*CP* 787)—"surely must have been a result of that experience," Ashbery acknowledges, "but I don't remember making that connection at the time. Obviously some other part of my mind—the part that makes these connections—is doing the work for me."[39] The lines, he implies, are all the more authentic for having emerged out of the state of unawareness his poems sanctify; indeed, the muse-like voice that resounds in the avernal landscape of "A Wave" sings "In the black trees: *My mindless, oh my mindless, oh*" (*CP* 788).

If "something started shifting internally" in "A Wave," as Gander suggests, causing the ephemerality of the body to eclipse the motion of consciousness as a primary theme in the sometimes exuberant, sometimes forlorn miscellany of Ashbery's mature verse, the poet fuses these major preoccupations and projects them—sentence by sentence, line by line— into the motion of his long poem *Flow Chart* (1991) and the cascade of shorter lyrics in the volumes that have succeeded it. Having adopted the imprint of mortality on consciousness as the basis of a style, Ashbery's most recent phase of writing attenuates the rational connections between thoughts, accelerating the erratic shifts of attention he identifies with the demystification of the soul in "Self-Portrait in a Convex Mirror" and exhibiting the impossibility of sustained attention that he associates with the "*electrical climate of sensitivities that ask / Only for self-gratification*" in "Litany." This acceleration is so precipitous, in fact, that it appears to

William Logan that Ashbery's recent poems "suffer from a rare neurological disorder, able to recall the sentence just written, but not the one before that"; Logan concludes that the poems nonetheless "live on, almost making sense," and speculates that "readers return for the promise of meaning infinitely delayed."[40] Some readers, however, have been more frustrated than charmed by these stylistic developments. To Andrew DuBois, for example, Ashbery's "rapid, random shifts in language and subject matter" amount to a "performance of senility, which is sometimes obviously a performance ([Ashbery] tells us so) and at other times is more *really* realistic"; in other words, "he seems actually to have lost control."[41]

Much like the ostensible stylistic departure of *The Tennis Court Oath,* which readers perceived as a radical descent into senselessness after the seductive hermeticism of Ashbery's first book, this recent "loss of control" does not depart from existing patterns of experimentation but rather carries them to unprecedented extremes.[42] These capricious, apparently random shifts in register and theme in fact prove to be the primary mechanism through which the later Ashbery "illustrate[s] opacity and how it can suddenly descend over us," asserting that unlikely feats of communication can succeed, unpredictably and occasionally, within that human chaos. It may be that Ashbery's extravagant, experimental negations of mind, stretching back to "The Instruction Manual," were destined to become associated with senility in his old age, but the apparently confused, episodic sentences of the shorter lyrics in *Your Name Here* (2000), *Chinese Whispers* (2002), and *Quick Question* (2012) elaborate principles Ashbery began devising in *Flow Chart*—the poem John Shoptaw describes as "a retrospective ramble, wandering, seemingly without premeditation or embarrassment, from one vaguely defined scene or topic to the next."[43]

The longest of Ashbery's long poems, *Flow Chart* is undoubtedly haunted by death—by the death of the poet's mother, Helen Ashbery, which inspired the writing of the poem, but also by the prospect of the poet's own death dawning suddenly on the horizon. Embarking, after four decades of tireless experimentation, on yet another "over the top" poetic adventure, Ashbery conceived of the poem as a series of daily entries to be concluded on his sixty-first birthday.[44] Diaristic, prosaic, and conversational, written at a stage of life when "the times of mirth / forgotten now" seem to be "recorded in disappearing ink that doesn't outlast winter / and its holidays, its occasions" (*FC* 104), the poem explores the possibilities mindlessness opens for the retrospective genre of the spiritual autobiography. The poem may take place in the winter of life, when "forgetting one's speech isn't such a grand or unique occasion" (*FC* 147), but it nonetheless circumscribes consciousness in terms very consistent with those of Ashbery's earlier poems. Like he did in "Litany," in *Flow Chart* Ashbery connects the "errant circuitry" (*FC* 42) of consciousness with the errancies of his sinuous poem, aspiring to create a cerebral music that reflects "the spongy terrain on which we exist" (*FC* 10); like the speaker of "Self-Portrait," the speaker of *Flow Chart* dwells in "the vacuum of each thought" (*FC* 131), acknowledging that in every act of mind we proceed "with our thoughts / to distract us" (*FC* 28); like the poet of *Three Poems*, the poet of *Flow Chart* perceives the problem of mind to be a semantic one, a problem of terms. The philosophical quandary of conscious matter appears less fresh and urgent to Ashbery in *Flow Chart* than it once did, when the process of fashioning a "new spirit" in a materialist age entailed speaking with "one's mouth full / Of unknown words" (*CP* 464); to this older, wiser, if also curmudgeonly speaker, those "unknown words" now appear to be the all-too-familiar "upstart rephrasing" of an ancient conversation.

One section of *Flow Chart*, for example—which seems, like all the other sections of the book, to pick up transcription of an ongoing internal monologue in medias res—begins in the midst of a lucid, internal debate about the nature of mind. The terms of the debate are so explicit, in fact, and so much less abstract than those of *Three Poems*, that the lines seem to parody philosophical and poetic endeavors to make sense of the mysteries of will and consciousness, including Ashbery's own attempts in his earlier poems ("I know I explained this once but / that was a cold while ago," he recalls):

> But if one's destiny is enclosed in one's brain, or brain pan, how about
>   free will
> and predestination, to say nothing of self-determination? Just how
>   do they
> fit together? I know I explained this once but

> that was a cold while ago and now this upstart rephrasing of it seems
>> to be
> causing a lot of attention, I don't know why. It's only a re-working a
>> scissors-and-paste
> job; the wording is almost identical, and there are some benighted souls
> who follow it, day by day in its lumbering, tumbrel-like progress across
>> edifices,
> burial sites, unnamed and unnamable sumps, for all the world
> to see in its glory, for all the world as though something were emerging
> and they were going to a circus or a party. (*FC* 129)

The speaker takes a long philosophical view from which he regards the proposition that "one's destiny is enclosed in one's brain" as the reframing of the timeless question of "free will" that has always balanced materialist and idealist extremes of perspective ("the wording is almost identical"). The notion that will, "predestination," and "self-determination" now "fit together" more intelligibly than they once did is an illusion cherished by followers of an apparently new, but false, dispensation—by "benighted souls" who tread imperviously over ineffable subtleties of feeling ("unnamed and unnamable sumps") in a vulgar parade, in the "lumbering, tumbrel-like progress" of scientific description. The distinction between the "glory" of explanation and the "circus" of scientific hype is one this speaker is determined to expose, perceiving the putatively demystified immaterialities of will and destiny to be at risk of being "subtracted like the soul we never knew we had and replaced with something / young, and easier, climate of any day and of all the days, postmillenarian" (*FC* 11).

The speaker of *Flow Chart* retreats from this frontal approach to the problem of mind and body, however, not only because he perceives overstated claims for the power of biological description to be the exhausted "re-working" of old news—a "scissors-and-paste / job" that is unduly "causing a lot of attention"—but because this speaker wanders away from *every* subject, unable or unwilling to dwell on anything for very long. There is no fixed point, like Parmigianino's portrait, from which the derailments of *Flow Chart*'s prosy extensions can easily be charted, no sustained thematic traction from which Ashbery's signature distractions mark a release; the poem's rhythms of semantic coalescence and dispersal are so rapid, its motions so episodic, that its structure becomes one of undifferentiated inattention, of drift.[45] Puttering off to another, somewhat less legible topic, apparently losing the plot, the speaker of these lines thus continues:

> . . . going to a circus or a party. Too bad the old people couldn't have
> known about it before it was actually announced. Some of the young
>   too were
> tempted to skip until I stepped down from my soap-box to have a go at
>   lecturing them
> in real earnest, though with a joke or two added as leavening, or gilding the
> pill as you might say. For if they had known first
> they wouldn't have minded not knowing after it had all happened, in vain,
> one supposes, again. It's too bad there aren't more students
> or even a few customers. The weather and the rushes scare tourists away
> and waste sets in. (*FC* 129)

What "was actually announced"? What "students" and "customers"? What "had all happened"? While "the young" may have perpetuated the "upstart rephrasing" the speaker describes in the preceding lines, and his "soap-box" may refer to those lines' antiphilosophical pontificating, by the last sentence, with its weather and waste and tourists, Ashbery has transported us someplace much more indeterminate. If the motion of such sentences resembles senile prattle, the attenuated connections between thoughts that give that impression are also freighted, like all of Ashbery's forms of mindlessness, with spiritual meaning, for the loose semantic synapses across which *Flow Chart* erratically conducts significance simulate the temporary coalescence of the mind—not the aging mind per se but any mind, any subjective unity of the kind that was once described as a soul or spirit—within a world of mindless objects.[46] ("*You* / understand it though, don't you?" the speaker pleads, "I mean how objects, including people, can be one thing / and mean something else, and therefore these two are subtly disconnected?" [*FC* 183].) The "subtly disconnected," rational connections that bind *Flow Chart* together, thought by straying thought, both conjure and question the abstract unity of the grand, poetic diagram, the flow of inner life charted in language; these loose connections resemble the loose sense of metaphysical unity that is ambiguously determined by the physical body, the "regulatory system that organizes us in some semblance of order, binding some of us loosely, / baling others of us together like straw" (*FC* 199).

However loosely bound the system of *Flow Chart* may seem to be, there is "always," its speaker insists, "a connection, albeit sometimes an / extremely loose one like a tendril that brushes against one" (*FC* 199). The tenuousness of the poem's rational connections thus extends Ashbery's oeuvre-defining pattern of inscribing mindlessness in poetic form and of linking that mindlessness with the unruly, opaque determinations of an embodied "system that organizes us in some semblance of order." Just as "The eroding" had "go[ne] on constantly in the brain / Where its music is softest" in "Litany," resulting in a poetic composition that coalesces as "full, static music, / Violent and spongy," the movement of *Flow Chart* reflects "the spongy terrain on which we exist" (*FC* 10)—the shifting ground of a consciousness continuous with the world of which it is a part. That porous terrain is also the ground of Ashbery's "postmillenarian" poetry, which is oblique but insistent in presenting its attenuated logic as an effect of the shifting ground of a material mind. In "Marine Shadow" (*Quick Question*), a compact rewriting of Stevens's "Sea Surface Full of Clouds" ("the most fluid of scenes," A. Walton Litz writes, "where the imagination could be sovereign over physical reality"), Ashbery contemplates how the body winds the "non-fiction" of the given into the intangible substance of experience, that unstable, "stinking phenomenology":[47]

> We're talking
> non-fiction, which pours through at lunch time,
> the whole stinking phenomenology wound into it
> at the base of the stalk. From there it branches
> out into other axioms and metaphors. Like,
> I have a brand in Chicago. You'd better think about it.[48]

Whereas Stevens records a recuperative, resourceful "mind in the act of finding / What will suffice," Ashbery records the operations of a fundamentally privative mind that interferes rather than illuminates.[49] Ashbery upends Stevens's sovereignty of mind over nature, implying through sound as much as sense that the tangled branching of axons and dendrites from a brainstem-like "stalk" is accountable for the recondite connections between "axioms and metaphors" and the poem's "branch[ing]" progression from the comprehensible (the topic of sense-data "pour[ing]" into consciousness) to the inscrutable (the apparent non sequitur "I have a brand in Chicago").

Exhibiting a similar wildness of rational movement, "Heavenly Days" (*Chinese Whispers*, 2002) begins with a dialogue between a speaker whose affinity with the world of objects contravenes the speculative positions of the philosopher:

> The philosopher walked over to me and tapped me on the brow
> with his pencil. Now does *this* remind you of anything?
> Have you ever seen anything like this before?
> Yes, if it's in sync with the marrow of the growing world.
> I can relate to that mattress. I do. I mean I do, sometimes.
> And what day of the week might this be?
> I'll make a wild guess—it's Thursday. You're wrong,
> though it *seems* like a Thursday.[50]

While the philosopher clings to arbitrary taxonomies (the naming of days) and dwells on distinctions between the actual and the experiential ("it *seems* like a Thursday"), the speaker considers the contents of his "brow," quite simply, to be "in sync with the marrow of the growing world"; he regards his mind not as incomparable or extraordinary ("Have you ever seen anything like this before?") but as something unexceptionally real ("I can relate to that mattress"). The late lyrics haven't the attention span for sustained philosophical inquiry and thus disavow it both formally and discursively. "That's why I can never go back to philosophy— / its halls and chambers are a paradigm of emptiness," the speaker of "Heavenly Days" declaims, "for only under stones is the knowledge / of underneath, and my desire is mammoth."[51]

These late lyrics disavow the abstract, specialized terminologies of philosophy and science, declining to leave any demotic, idiomatic, or otherwise earthly stone of poetic material unturned. They are thus at their finest when they hint at the acute delights and sorrows that accompany the choice to dwell, late in life, so insistently in the realm of concrete, recording in "disappearing ink" the transience of every worldly thing.[52] In "Short-Term Memory," from *Your Name Here* (2000), Ashbery subjects the encounter between writer and reader convened in the poem to that irreversible transience, eroding the substance of his legacy by denying that he will be preserved in the minds of his readers. Here, the "broken discoveries" of conscious life dissolve not as a symptom of dementia but as a symptom of merely living—a short-term process that is always, Ashbery insists, covering its tracks:

> It was enough just then to perceive life as a sandbar,
> or a mirage of one, that the tide is frantically
> trying to erase so as to cover its tracks.
>
> Broken discoveries invaded my short-term memory,
> but not so you'd notice. Continuing the polite
> palaver I asked after the health of this one and that one,
> how little Lois was doing in school, what Howie was up to
> in his treehouse. It was as though no one cared.
> Or had seen me. They shuffled aimlessly away
> to come alive later no doubt in some sex sequence,
> while here leaves are browning before the end of summer
> and the groundskeeper waits.
>
> What about your immortal soul?
> I may have lost it, just this once, but other chapters
> will arrive, bright as a child's watercolor,
> and you'd want to be around me.[53]

The leaves are browning, and the ominous groundskeeper, armed with a rake rather than a scythe, ominously waits; all of life seems to this speaker to be like the temporary repository of short-term memory, into which new objects ceaselessly "arrive, bright as a child's watercolor," only to disappear again, unnoticed. Having lost one's immortal soul proves in this poem to be equivalent to having one's "polite / palaver" go unheard, ineffectual and ignored by one generation after another—by an audience of parents in the welter of life at its peak, "shuffl[ing] aimlessly away / to come alive . . . in some sex sequence," and by an absent, future audience of distracted children, already off painting their own scenes.

It is a painful proposition, after a life of writing, for it to seem "as though no one cared. / Or had seen me." Ashbery's, however, has not been a normal life of writing, his literary strangeness having "tak[en] just the forms it needs to impress itself upon you, the forms of your inattention and incapacity or unwillingness to understand" (*CP* 298). Enthralled by the mutual imagining of writer and reader in processes circumscribed by limited resources of attention and interest, Ashbery has always implied that the fate of his immortal soul lies in the mindlessness of his audience. "In you I fall apart, and outwardly am a single fragment, a puzzle to itself," he writes in *Three Poems*, "But we must learn to live in others, no matter how abortive or unfriendly their cold, piecemeal renderings of us: they create us" (*CP* 253). As we will see, the thinness of our "piecemeal renderings" of other souls will haunt Jorie Graham, leading her to devise poetic forms built for the ethical work of straining against our embodied limits of perspective. But Ashbery, who conceives of the soul as a thing made within the matrices of the body and of the poem, seems never to have expected to dwell anywhere but in the margins of our ever-shifting attention. Now that "the very heavens / have lifted off for destinations unknown" (*FC* 205), the embodied artifice of soul making can appear to be meaningless or miraculous in turns, but Ashbery remains certain that "one fits exactly the space of the mind / opposite one," the substance of the self confined to the scale of our passing interest. This revelation may imply a pitiful contraction of human possibility or a great bound forward in human progress, but "As far as I'm concerned it's a draw," Ashbery concludes—"and a decent one at that / if you keep your mind off it" (*FC* 206).

CHAPTER 5

Jorie Graham and the Ethics of the Eye

I N AN EPIGRAPH to *Materialism* (1993), Jorie Graham presents Socrates's image of the sentient psyche dragged down into the physical universe by the pleasures of vision: "the soul," she translates, "when using the body as an instrument of perception . . . is then dragged by the body into the region of the changeable, and wanders, and is confused—the world spins round her—and she is like a drunkard when she touches change."[1] For Graham, our perceptual encounters with the mutable surfaces of the visible are always blundering ones; it is as she traces the eye ranging over the visible world that she becomes most conscious of the physical constraints that furtively shape the character and production of human knowledge. Unlike John Ashbery, whose "eyes proclaim / That everything is surface. . . . / And nothing can exist except what's there," Graham is a poet who craves a wholeness and depth that she associates with the unseen; though both poets conceive of the sensuous manifold as the shifting sum of data filtered through the crude sieve of the body, Graham is haunted by the deprivations wrought by that process, by the impoverished picture of reality available to the senses.[2] Our bungling lapses of attention and perception carry with them dire moral hazards in Graham's poems, since these are the faculties by which we perform acts of vigilance and care as lovers, parents, citizens, and stewards of an endangered planet. And yet while "built-in limits" of the mind and of the eye threaten to restrict our empathetic vision, careful arrangements of poetic language, she insists, are uniquely equipped to jostle us into a more wakeful condition of accountability to one other.[3]

Despite the dualist, Platonic leanings that have been described as her "*donnée* and her demon," Graham's allusions to the sciences of the mind and to cognitive theory—the most direct, informed, and pervasive of any in this book—reveal her sympathies with the diverse disciplinary perspectives that describe conscious life in physiological terms; she has pronounced that the problem of "how to live in the full glare of the knowledge science has given us" frames her writing life.[4] Enthralled by both the maps of consciousness science has drawn in recent decades and by inherited, literary metaphors of mind that remain charged with formidable religious, historical, and artistic freight, Graham enlists both as she sets out to explore questions of spiritual consciousness in a secular age. And though she is committed to forging an empirically conscientious poetics that acknowledges meaningful correlations between the science of the mind and the experience of it, there is nonetheless a threshold at which Graham recoils from scientific revelation summarily; in recent poems, she deploys the very substance of her style to repudiate neurological interpretations of mind that threaten to discredit the reality of the self.

The searching epistemological questions that trouble Graham in her earliest poems—questions about the scope of human perception and the reliability of empirical knowledge—ramify briskly as her poetry evolves, soon extending to encompass the ontological question of how to define the self (and its verbal surrogate, the lyric "I") in terms true to both intuition and science. Disenchanted with cognitive materialists' thin view of the subject as something "virtual" rather than real—a view that has seemed to her to echo the theoretical premises upon which Language poetry launched its own critiques of the unified, poetic voice in the last decades of the twentieth century—Graham develops in her poetry after *Materialism* stylistic features that assert, with new force, the presence of a "real," authorial ghost in the verbal machine. The coalescence of Graham's fluid, evolving, but finally "stable" lyric self is inextricably bound up, these poems reveal, with her philosophies of vision and the mysterious commerce between "mind" and "body"; while Ashbery and his inheritors have found in somatic descriptions of consciousness tools for unraveling the "romantic, unitary, expressive self" and critiquing the "simple-minded model of subjectivity and authority," Graham has found in recent discourses of the embodied mind ethical reasons to defend such putatively outdated notions.[5]

As she comes to reevaluate the obligations and ambit of poetry relative to science and focus ever more intently on what is gained and lost in conceiving of perception and consciousness as aspects of the physical universe, Graham's allusions to the somatic grounds of inner life become increasingly tormented. Deeply conscious of the moral dangers of conceiving of human subjects as empirical objects, she insists with rising urgency that poetry has a special capacity and a special obligation to balance our positivist appetite for proof with the ability to exist "in uncertainties, Mysteries, doubts," an aptitude she associates with both aesthetic success and humane action.[6] Interpreting negative capability not only as a condition of receptive sensation but as an ethical mode, her arguments for the value of poetry thus hinge on its power to facilitate tolerance, to offer practice in abiding contradiction, and to help us inhabit perspectives other than our own. These convictions mean that Graham's conscience is often at odds with her scientific instinct to demystify her own mind—and that she sees in cognitive science a reflection of her own libidinal, occasionally blinding, hunger for truth.[7]

Though her continual returns to sensation have caused her to be known as a poet of the body, Graham's early poems reveal her mistrust of somatic sources of information about reality; like Wordsworth, whose child philosopher "read'st the eternal deep, / Haunted forever by the eternal mind," in her earliest poems she uses spatial metaphors of depth and thickness to express the disparity between the unfathomable wealth of the given and the shallow poverty of the perceived: "For what we want / to take inside of us . . . // there is / no deep enough," she writes in "The Age of Reason," and in "Mist," she longs for "another, thicker, kind of sight."[8] That Graham identifies the eye and the brain with our diminished perception of reality is evident in the ingenious imagery of "Salmon," a poem that implicates the concrete apparatus of the visual system with the process by which, as she puts it in a later poem, depths of reality "[burn] off—without / residue— just by coming into contact with / the verb of human inwardness."[9] In

"Salmon," Graham recounts having watched on television, in a motel room in Nebraska, the muscular convulsions of salmon leaping upstream—"past beauty," she writes, "past the importance of beauty . . . driving deeper and deeper / into less."[10] In one of the disarming juxtapositions characteristic of Graham's early style, she compares the creatures' help-lessness in their genetically programmed resolution toward procreation and death to the act of seeing itself, to the flow of perceptual data "up-stream" from the retina to the brain. In a rugged cascade of free-verse lines, Graham imagines the mind as the receptive "still pool" where con-cepts ("justice"), concrete, visual images ("aspen leaves"), and memories ("mother attempting suicide") spontaneously intermingle in a creative frisson. The spawning of poetry, Graham suggests, like the spawning of salmon, arises from the countervailing necessities of dogged resolve and patient submission to generative forces that transcend conscious will:

> They would not stop, resolution of will
> and helplessness, as the eye
> is helpless
> when the image forms
> itself, upside-down, backward,
> driving up into
> the mind, and the world
> unfastens itself
> from the deep ocean of the given. . . . Justice, aspen
> leaves, mother attempting
> suicide, the white night-flying moth
> the ants dismantled bit by bit and carried in
> right through the crack
> in my wall. . . . How helpless
> the still pool is,
> upstream,
> awaiting the gold blade
> of their hurry. (Graham's ellipses)

Framing vision as a process of reduction, the lines contrast the insubstan-tial mental image with the "deep ocean of the given" from which it is extracted, recalling the salmon's depleting migration from brackish depths to ominously shallow headwaters, "deeper and deeper into less." The "helpless" eye proves to be anything but the Wordsworthian eye that half creates what it perceives; just as the scenery in Graham's "Relativity: A Quartet" "lay[s] itself down frame by frame onto the wide / resistanceless opening of our wet / retina," here, too, the image autonomously "forms / itself," with the eye in a state of total receptivity. Stripped of agency—and thus, Graham will later stress, accountability—the eye is an utterly passive, physical object; it embodies the materialist abrogation of will that Graham will later describe contemptuously as "perfect obedience."[11]

These lines from "Salmon," in which Graham pictures the body's derivation of sense data from "external" reality and its radical, subliminal manipulation of that data in forging mental images, also demonstrate that what Graham knows about vision affects how she experiences it. With her depiction of the salmon projected "upside-down, backward" upon the retina before being inverted again by the brain, Graham suggests that scientific descriptions of visual cognition have confirmed, or perhaps even generated, her intuition that pristine, tantalizing immensities lie untouched by human apprehension.[12] In "Salmon," Graham compares her desire to perceive what lies beyond sensation to erotic desire; in the poem's unfolding triptych, the fish en route to fatal spawning and the helpless eye in the act of perceiving are juxtaposed with a desperate sexual coupling she recalls having witnessed in childhood. The flood of noonday light in which the lovers bathe dispels all shadows but the one that marks them as separate beings, entangled but discrete:

> Once, indoors, a child,
> I watched, at noon, through slatted wooden blinds,
> a man and woman, naked, eyes closed,
> climb onto each other,
> on the terrace floor,
> and ride—two gold currents
> wrapping round and round each other, fastening,
> unfastening. I hardly knew
> what I saw. Whatever shadow there was in that world
> it was the one each cast
> onto the other,
> the thin black seam
> they seemed to be trying to work away

between them. I held my breath.
As far as I could tell, the work they did
with sweat and light
was good.[13]

If vision is Graham's governing metonym for the various forms of sense perception that abet our distorted liaisons with reality, in "Salmon" she stresses that such liaisons depend, like sexual liaisons, on the unyielding boundary between self and other and the desire that forms across it. With the "fastening, / unfastening" of the lovers' bodies, the lines yoke that corporeal seam with the eye as an organ through which the visible world is "unfastened" and transported into the invisible, hermetic realm of consciousness. In this sense, the seam resembles the liminal "wall" drawn alongside "justice" and "aspen / leaves" in the poet's teeming mind; the "white night-flying moth," like the visible world atomized into quanta of light and carried across the physical boundary of the eye, is "dismantled bit by bit and carried in / right through the crack / in my wall."[14]

Though "Salmon" yields the aesthetic consolations of exquisite natural and erotic imagery, it sees the derivation of mental representations from the "outer" world as a terminal migration, and by associating perceptual translation with the gruesome dismantling of the white moth (itself a fragmentary import, perhaps, from Robert Frost's harrowing naturalist sonnet "Design"), "Salmon" betrays Graham's troubled longing for an infinitely capacious, disembodied, and of course purely hypothetical kind of sight. For Graham, the most exasperating limits of mind are visual—she is fascinated by the boundaries of visual perspective, by the wavelengths of light that fall outside the visible spectrum, and by the minute forms the naked eye can't see; in one poem she contemplates "guard cells" and "substomatal chambers," microscopic structures of a leaf she knows to exist but that are invisible to her eye: "I blink," she writes, "I don't *see anything.* / Lord, / I want to see this leaf."[15] Graham articulates this longing to transcend the body's circumscription of inner life by adopting poetic forms that alternately materialize the gap between the knowable and the known and strategically arrange language to compensate for it. In a series of dual self-portraits in *The End of Beauty* (1987), for example—"Self-Portrait as Apollo and Daphne," "Self-Portrait as Hurry and Delay," and "Self-

Portrait as Both Parties," among others—Graham exceeds the limits of embodied perspective by holding two points of view in conjoined suspension; these poems are often split into numbered parts of only a sentence or two each, demonstrating how the poet's transitory glimpses of herself accumulate to form the stitched, distorted wholes of self-portraiture. Graham shares with Ashbery the tendencies to compensate for biological limits of perspective in the structure of her poems and to compare sensory distortions of reality with linguistic ones; just as Ashbery uses his vast prose poems to hoard—in capacious, obsessively inclusive forms— "the gigantic / Bits of pieces of knowledge we have retained," Graham supplements in her synoptic self-portraits "the half-truth that can / be caught" by a single perspective.[16]

In several poems from *The End of Beauty* and her next volume, *Region of Unlikeness* (1991), Graham makes provocative use of underlined blank spaces, mathematical variables, and other formal irregularities to evoke the gaps in perception and comprehension imposed not only by the constraints of the body but by the empirical and intuitive modes of inquiry that a poet might in turn adopt as the basis of a style.[17] These formal irregularities appear, for example, in "To the Reader," a poem in which Graham depicts becoming a poet not as a felicitous awakening or calling but as an experimental process of sampling scientific and artistic methods of investigating reality. Reckoning with the limitations of both methods, the poem anticipates the problems of empirical looking that will escalate in ethical significance as Graham applies her analytical gaze to subjectivity itself, pulling the sentience of living beings apart into physical causes and effects. Assigned as a child to dig up "one square yard of earth" and record her findings in her notebook for a science project—to measure out a hole and "To catalogue and press onto the page *all she could find in it*"— Graham presents the act of carving an abstract form into the ground and naming "the everything" she finds there as her first act as a poet.[18] "Here" in the lines of the poem, Graham suggests, linger the "lines" of that square—the square that captures the small wholes and "the halves of things" that happen to fall inside its arbitrary limits, the square that frames the chaotic accidents of physical existence with a supervening, ordering idea. The chain-link fence that surrounds the science fair's bed of little plots evokes the nested circumscriptions that restrict individual and collective forms of inquiry alike, marking the place where "this"—Graham's poem, and her life as an artist—begins:

> I swear to you this begins with that girl on a day after sudden rain
> and then out of nowhere sun (as if to expose *what* of the hills—
> the white glare of x, the scathing splendor of y,
> the wailing interminable _____?) that girl having run
> down from the house and up over the fence not like an animal
> but like a thinking, link by link, and over
>
> into the allotted earth—for Science Fair—into the *everything* of
> one square yard of earth. Here it begins
> to slip. She took the spade and drew the lines. Right through
> the weedbeds, lichen, moss, keeping the halves of things that landed *in*
> by chance, new leaves, riffraff the wind blew in—
>
> Here is the smell of earth being cut, the smell of the four lines.[19]

As the reappearing sun suddenly illuminates the rain-softened world, the child hurtles—no longer "like an animal / but like a thinking"—toward a rational kind of human knowledge acquired "link by link." Graham undermines the poem's literal and figurative forms of enlightenment, however, with the parenthesis that suddenly exposes the poet's difficulties translating her experience from the past into the present, conveying it "to the reader"; as she searches for a phrase to describe the vista that lay beyond the entrenched plots of perspective, she draws a cognitive and typographic blank. The bigger picture of the landscape—sublime in its effect on the viewer ("the white glare of x, / the scathing splendor of y") and immense in its scope ("the wailing interminable _____?")— never does find its way into the poem, its drawn-in absence concrete and gaping. The abeyance of the vast, totalizing view, replaced by the "one square yard of earth," marks where "it begins / to slip"—where the misalignment between the "interminable _____" Graham longs to know and the dense but partial allotment of what she *can* know becomes suddenly obvious.

By tracing her origins as a poet to a science project, Graham emphasizes affinities between lyric and scientific experiments, but she finally rejects the descriptive and observational methods by which we "[pull] the thriving apart into the true." Cataloging and awkwardly pressing onto the page *"all she could find"* consigns the poet to the realm of surfaces—a dead end in art, Graham believes, if not in science:[20]

> Say we leave her there, squatting down, haunches up,
> pulling the weeds up with tweezers,
> pulling the thriving apart into the true,
> each seedpod each worm on the way down retrieved into a
> plastic bag (shall I compare thee), Say we
>
> leave her there, where else is there to go?[21]

Each item in Shakespeare's catalog of exquisite things—a summer's day, the buds of May, the sun itself—falls short of capturing his subject in language; likewise, Graham's catalog of worms and seedpods merely suffocates (in a plastic bag) and tweezes apart these living wholes, destroying them in the process of describing them. Science's descriptive drive finds a poetic equivalent in the drive to classify, to list, to name—the drive to catalog that Shakespeare exhibits in the plotted turf of his own sonnet—and in a compulsion to scan the surfaces of the visible in what Graham calls, quoting John Ashbery, "a dance of non-discovery."[22] "To the Reader" concludes with the surreal image of a man running with a gaping hole in his chest, a personification of the scientist or poet or philosopher who single-mindedly pursues the truths of the physical universe, covering infinite ground but arriving nowhere. In this tautological nightmare, description begets only more description; the objects visible through the hole grow larger and larger, until finally "a girl with a weed and a notebook appears."

The many holes in "To the Reader"—holes in the ground, in the text, and in the body—suggest the chasm between the objective world "out there" and the subjective world "in here," as well as the limits of the verbal means we use to gauge that incommensurability. The holes also evoke the absences that emerge when we restrict our search for meaning to sensation and the observation of concrete phenomena, blind spots upon which Graham will base a far-reaching critique of scientific looking. Something worth knowing is lost, she insists, when we pull apart "the thriving" of the vital and the whole into empirically "true" parts, but her early poems are replete with signals that this epistemological critique is destined to evolve into an explicitly ethical one. Among these harbingers is the constant presence of nonhuman animal specimens in poems that describe the effects of our limited human perspective on creatures that suffer both in the margins of our view and under the weight of our attention. Graham's animals are sympathetic but also, until her most recent poetry, silent and inscrutable, reminding her speakers that the vast interstices between human points of view are negligible compared to the differences of perspective that gape between species—species whose modes of perception, behavior, and thought reflect specialized purposes. In "The Geese," for example, the early poem in which Graham describes the "bedrock poverty" of embodied knowledge ("your body an arrival / you know is false but can't outrun"), Graham marvels at a flock of birds migrating over her backyard in the form of a "V"—an arrow, a letter, a sign that seems to render the tacit code that orders the animals' life course suddenly visible.[23] The symmetry of their purposeful formation, "tapering with goals," leaves Graham in awe, but the sight also suggests to her how tightly the animals are bound by the rigid geometry of their genetically determined behavior. Even the spiders spinning webs in her yard seem, in their own biological and behavioral idiom, to "imitate the paths the geese won't stray from." Graham's menagerie of animate visual objects—of enthralled geese and suffocated worms and ill-fated salmon, and of butterflies and monkeys and foxes, as we shall see—raise the question of what becomes of the irreducible anima not only when it is reconstituted as a virtual mental representation, but when empirical methods of deriving and organizing knowledge, necessarily dependent on embodied processes of observation and reason, analogously "pull apart" the sentient into the materially "true."

In "Subjectivity" (*Materialism*, 1996), Graham identifies the blind spots of her own empirical gaze when it is directed at living objects by taking the butterfly as her central symbol. With her choice of animal, the poem blossoms into an allegory describing the dangers of treating the mind as an object of science. The poem begins with Graham's discovery of the inert body of the insect, which is at once an archetypal symbol of the disembodied psyche ("my mind hovering . . . / huge, ballooning, fluttering, yellow") and a biological "specimen" objectified by the speaker's analytical gaze ("2 inches of body," Graham notes, "and 5 inches of wing"). The first of the poem's three parts associates the wild incandescence of the monarch's colors with the phenomenal world unprocessed by perception, thought, and linguistic description, those arbitrating systems that Graham likewise associates with the reticulated "black bars" drawn ominously across the "atomic-yellow ground" of the insect's wings. Graham opens the poem with an extended, synesthetic comparison of the butterfly's markings to other disarming impositions of natural and artificial design: to the leaden matrices that steer light through stained-glass windows; to the chimes and flutes that seize and direct supple gusts of air (their tones are imagined as a symphonic spectrum of yellow hues); to the "structure of tenses and persons" used to contain time in language; to the "cries forced through [the] mind's design" in the act of making poetry out of the cry of its occasion; and, finally, to the gauzy sieve of nerves that separates visible and invisible dimensions of reality:

Black bars expanding
    over an atomic-yellow ground—feelers retracted—
the monarch lay flat on the street
    and did not move at all
when I lifted it
    onto my spiral
notebook

    and did not move the whole length of the block
during which I held the purple laminated

cover still as
    possible—
my gaze
    vexing the edges of
the wings, ruffling the surface where it seemed
    light from another century
beat against those black bars—yellow, yellow, gorgeous, in-
                          candescent—

    bells, chimes, flutes, strings—wind seized and blown
open—butter yellow, fever yellow,
    yellow of acid and flax,

lemon and chrome,
   madder, mikado, justic, canary—

yellow the singers exhale that rises, fanged, laughing,
   up through the architraves and out (slow) through the hard
                                          web

the rose-windows press
   onto the rising gaze,
yellow of cries forced through that mind's design,
   like a clean verdict,
like a structure of tenses and persons for the gusting

   heaven-yellow
minutes (so many flecks, spores,
   in the wide still beam
of sun)
   or the gaze's stringy grid of nerves
spreading out onto

   whatever bright new world the eyes would seize upon—
pronged optic animal the incandescent *thing*
   must rise up to and spread into, and almost burn
                      its way

clear through
   to be.[24]

The imagistic torrent that opens the poem lurches back and forth along
the left margin, replicating the restive saccades of Graham's scanning
eye, while the "rose-windows," one of the lines' central metaphors, present
the semipermeable partition as an emblem of embodied vision. Graham
imagines subjectivity as a magnificent interior space defined by its architecture; the fractured light of the vaulted nave signals, however dimly, an
exterior, unmediated realm beyond its walls. It is just as Graham describes the maculate light conducted through the imperfections of the
glass—"so many flecks, spores, / in the wide still beam / of sun"—that she
is reminded of the "stringy grid" of optic nerves that performs a similarly
imperfect kind of filtration and that morphologically resembles the "hard
web" that shapes the light by obstructing it. Importantly, though, the high
windows' obstructions are bidirectional, suggesting the inhibitive determinations of matter and language alike upon self-expression. Not only

does somatic architecture determine the character of what comes in (the color, form, brightness of the light in the cathedral's dim corridors), but the same architecture also sifts and delays what goes out (the voices of the worshippers "that [rise], fanged, laughing, / up through the architraves and out (slow) through the hard / web").

This bidirectional mediation of what enters the self and what issues from the self is also evident in "the gaze's stringy grid of nerves," which Graham has turned inside out and sent protruding from the eye, the "pronged optic animal" with the grasping, appetitive tentacles of a predator. Its winged victim—"feelers retracted"—is stunned and senseless, one *"thing"* about to be consumed by another. The grid of nerves not only spreads out onto the world but is "spread into," like the passive, visual anatomy represented in "Salmon" and "Relativity: A Quartet"—a vehicle for the butterfly's fiery metamorphosis from physical to mental substance. In the second of the poem's parts, Graham imagines what that metamorphosis would feel like if it could be felt—if being an object and being a subject were equally sentient conditions, and one could undergo the process of becoming, rather than forming, a mental image. As a sunbeam, sweeping like a gaze, moves across the room and engulfs her, Graham breaks into "I" and "she," occupying the roles of both subject and object at once. As she dissolves into mental substance, she experiences firsthand the subtraction of being that she has often described from the perspective of the perceiver rather than the perceived:

> my being inside the beam of sun,
>
> and the sensation of how it falls unevenly,
>
> how the wholeness I felt in the shadow is lifted,
> broken, this tip *lit*, this other *dark*—and stratified,
> analysed, chosen-round, formed—[25]

The second of the poem's three parts breaks off here, with the gaze forming a mottled representation that is partially illuminated and partially obscure, fragmenting and dispelling the "wholeness" in the unseen. Exposed to this illuminating beam, Graham submits to a force that possesses properties of both perceptual and intellectual experience; she can feel herself not only being seen but being made sense of ("stratified, / analysed"), dissected into fragments that seem willfully selected ("chosen-round") and indeterminately manipulated ("formed"). In the poem's final section, this alignment of·embodied vision with the intellect's coercive impulse to make meaning becomes explicit, and the forcing of sensation through the "mind's design" reveals itself to be fatally destructive. Graham now feels "thin almost icy beams" emanating from her own eyes, "widening as they sweep down / out of the retina / to take the body in—":

> Home I slid it gently
> into the book,
>   wings towards the center of the
> page,
>   the body denser and harder to press
> flat,
>   my mind hovering over it,
> huge, ballooning, fluttering, yellow,
>   and back and forth,
> and searching for the heaviest book
>   to lay upon
> the specimen,
>   to make it flat—
>
>   as if it were still too plural, too
> shade-giving, where the mind needs it
>   so flat[26]

The exaggerated fragility of those persistently arcing wings and of the small, dense body Graham feels pressing back against her own chilling pressure only exaggerate the brutality of her mind's ambition to flatten them. Accentuating that brutality is the poem's surprise ending, in which a friend alerts Graham, in the nick of time, that the ethereal insect is not dead but merely stunned by the chill of the morning; the poet, we realize, has been unwittingly conspiring not to preserve the revered insect but to kill it. Narrowly escaping the "envelope of glances" that would have smothered it, the butterfly is brought back outdoors and reanimated by the heat of direct sunlight, a salutary, natural foil to her marauding eyes' "almost icy beams." Importantly, Graham proposes that language itself would have been the instrument of this mortal violence against the paralyzed animal; searching for a weight with which to flatten the specimen,

Graham selects, of all things, a dictionary. The noble monarch will be crushed in a mental flattening ("the mind needs it / so flat") and then, as it becomes the subject of the poem, a linguistic one—a violent confinement within "a structure of tenses and persons."

With the image of the "fluttering, yellow" psyche, "Subjectivity" reveals itself to be about the process of "flattening" the concept of mind in order to make it more tractable and empirically accessible. Graham's allegory confronts the blindness built into any science of the mind, whether its investigative labor takes place in the laboratory or in a poem. She attributes this blindness to our consuming instinct to master the unknown, greeting the butterfly's impenetrability and irreducible plurality not with wonder but with a plundering desire to demystify it; importantly, it is in her haste to see the psyche as a *specimen* that she becomes blind to its most important truth—its life. Beginning in the poems of *Materialism,* Graham brings her solicitude to bear not only on the limits of observational, "scientific" modes of investigating animate being but also on the rational conclusions about the nature of consciousness that emerge from such investigation. Though she at first perceives a conflict between acquired and intuitive knowledge—between science and conscience—in the practice of viewing subjective entities as empirical objects, her concern deepens in light of what she sees as a growing tendency to deem the observable, embodied aspects of who we are more "real" than aspects of selfhood and experience that resist physical description. With this deepening concern comes a new challenge: to demonstrate the ethical and aesthetic force of an "expressive" lyricism that can credibly answer the assaults upon the subject that emerge from the quarters of cognitive and poststructuralist theory alike.

Since the last decade of the twentieth century, Graham has reckoned openly with the widespread impression that "what we now know about the mind is radically at odds with the major classical views of what a person is," as George Lakoff and Mark Johnson put it in their extravagantly ambitious collaboration *Philosophy in the Flesh: The Embodied Mind and Its Challenge to Western Thought* (a book Graham quotes directly in her poem "Copy," to be discussed shortly).[27] Indeed, Graham's friendship with Antonio Damasio, her colleague and the chair of the neurology department at the University of Iowa during the 1990s, placed

her poetry in unusually close dialogue with the mind sciences' enterprising assumption of questions that have historically belonged to philosophers and artists. As one of the two epigraphs to his popular book
*The Feeling of What Happens: Body and Emotion in the Making of Con-
sciousness* (1999), Damasio includes lines from one of the five poems in
Materialism (1993) titled "Notes on the Reality of the Self," lines that
begin with the pronouncement: "The question of who I was consumed
me."[28] By invoking Graham, the neuroscientist suggests that his own investigation of consciousness originates in the same consuming curiosity
as the poet's. In a reciprocal endorsement that appears in the opening
pages of Damasio's book, Graham affirms that neuroscientific explanation promises to answer the kinds of introspective questions traditionally associated with the lyric: "There is no simpler way to say this," she
writes, "read this book to learn who you are."[29]

Graham was and is captivated by the biological truths that ground the
self in nature—that connect individual consciousness to the most distant
horizons of human history and to the temperament of our species as a
whole. However, as a poet who is dually committed to truth and good-
ness, to accuracy and usefulness, Graham's cognitivism places her in a
double bind. Concentration on the physiological basis of mental experience sensitizes her to the constraints embodiment imposes on awareness
and agency, cognition and action. But Graham also proposes (in "Subjectivity," for example) that concentration on the intentionless mechanisms that construct and constrain inner life—mechanisms that make us
seem more like helpless creatures than agential persons—can obscure our
responsibilities to one another. In her 2006 collection *Overlord,* published
in the midst of America's torture regime, Graham worries that to imagine
the self as a virtual projection of a body that is not only more substantial
but more *actual* than a soul or mind or conscience—that is "at odds," in
other words, "with the major classical views of what a person is"—places
her on a slippery slope angled precipitously away from the urgent responsibilities of citizenship. The directness with which she posits a speaking
"I" that is recognizably Jorie Graham and a "you" that the reader recognizes to be him or herself are among the stylistic strategies she adopts
in *Overlord*'s "Dawn Day One," "Disenchantment," and "Copy *(Attacks*

on the Cities, 2000–2003)" to gain a foothold on that slope; as her poems become explicit in invoking the impact of brain sciences on the idea of self, they assert an increasingly politicized, coherent, autobiographical lyric subject with a strident, moral point of view.

Revealing her conception of the poem as a form of intercourse in which real selves take part and charting the treacherous "path of reason" that leads from a primarily neurological conception of mind to an unaccountable biological determinism, Graham's meditative poem "Dawn Day One" exemplifies this transformation of voice. The poem begins with the inauspicious ring of two distant gunshots, the second of which awakens Graham; with the inclusion of the symbolic first shot, she acknowledges the iterations of human brutality to which she has not been wakeful, imagining her sudden stirring as a rebirth into ethical vigilance, a fresh start, a "day one." Still, the violently rude awakening anticipates the dire failures of attention to violence and exploitation with which she will find herself complicit. Graham portrays her emergence into consciousness as a washing up into embodied sensation out of the oceanic depths of the unconscious ("The body's weight is / a beaching"); out of the realm of the infinite and irrational, she awakens into the realm of reason and consequence that "puts one back on the walking-path one stepped off of / last night."[30] That Graham rejoins the walking path of reason wearily, even scornfully, becomes evident as her meandering mind traces the inductive routes through which Zeno arrives at his paradoxes—the specious syllogisms that deftly render flying arrows motionless and finite spaces impossible to cross.[31] Having risen and moved across her light-dappled room and having arrived at the bathroom ("Zeno reasoned we would / never get there. Reason in fact never gets there"), she examines her eyes' reflection in the mirror and directly addresses the reader, who peers alongside her. Ever sensitive to the Sartrean "essential poverty" of mental imagery, she compels us to close our eyes and shut out the surfeit of sense data that obstructs the imagining mind; she obliges us to picture with focused intensity a research lab that is remote from the domestic scene but that also resembles the sterile bathroom where her own self-examination is taking place. She describes an experiment related to her by "Tony" (certainly Antonio Damasio), an experiment in which a live subject is used to investigate primate visual cognition; in Graham's hands, the monkey's primary visual cortex, an area at the back of the brain into which visual data is projected from the retina, becomes the "the back / of the cave" depicted in Plato's *Republic,* the surface on which the impoverished shadows of the real are projected:

> Are your eyes shut? I put cream on my lids
> and rub it in. I feel my eyes in there under the skin.
> How impersonal are they, these hardnesses, barely
> attached, in their loosely protected sacks.
> Tony tells me how, in the lab, they cast an image
> —a cross in this case—onto the gaze of a monkey then
>   "sacrifice
> the monkey" and how, when examined, the neurons in the
>   visual cortex
> actually form the imprint of
> the cross. It would have been, the cross (except under very
>   unusual circumstances), erased
> by the next image. Hence the need for
> sacrifice. Of what is it made, I ask. Of cells, of *active*
> cells, he says. It is imprinted, I ask. No. It
> would have disappeared and been replaced except
> the creature was stilled. I like it they
> use the word *stilled.* Then the back
> of the cave in there with its cross of cells.[32]

The lyricism of the opening lines' anapests and internal rhyme ("rub it in" / "under the skin"; "barely attached" / "protected sacks") suits the benign domestic ritual of Graham's toilette, but that lyricism gives way to the agitated and finally ungrammatical effusiveness of the reported conversation with Tony. Her own eyes remind her of the specimen monkey's, and her own manual examination of the organs under her skin reminds her of the scientists' penetrating investigation; she mordantly claims to "like" the suspicious choice of the passive, euphemistic verb "stilled" to describe the extermination of the monkey in the act of perception. Martyred on a cross of active cells, the euthanized animal is "sacrificed" in order to satisfy our desire to hold still what is transient and to understand what is elusive, but also, through the prosthetic gaze of a CT scanner, to satisfy our appetite for an invasive kind of looking *through* matter that supplements and transcends the limitations of embodied, human sight.[33]

Still, the poem's hardness of tone, its detachment, seems closely related to the hardness of those impersonal eyeballs Graham feels under her eyelids, the organs that are "barely / attached" to the subject looking through them. In their total alienness as objectified organs, the eyes become—in a way that makes Graham bristle—stripped of intention and thus of accountability; they are "hardnesses," as she puts it, in both material and moral senses. She associates those hardnesses with the amoral aesthetic and intellectual forms of inquiry that are disposed to treat perception and thought as consequences of nonintentional physical causes and effects; these forms of inquiry, in her view, tend to draw on apparently reasonable premises to justify troubling conclusions about the nature of consciousness. Graham concludes the poem by drawing an implicit analogy between Zeno's pursuit of truth through logic (which, unsupervised by a more practical kind of reason, leads him to useless conclusions) and other aesthetic, empirical, and theoretical modes of pursuing knowledge, which likewise, when unmonitored by practical and moral intuition, lead us nowhere:

> there is an edifice
> you can build level upon level, from first principles,
> using axioms, using logic. Finally you have a house
> which houses you. Now look at you.
> Are you an entire system of logic and truth?
> Are you a pathway with no body ever really on it?
> Are you shatterable if you took your fist now to
> this face that looks at you as you hold to your stare?
> Here. You are at the beginning of something. At the exact
> beginning. Ok. This is awakening
> number two in here, in this poem. Then there are
> these: me: you: you *there*. I'm actually staring up at
> you, you know, right here, right from the pool of this page.
> Don't worry where else I am, I am here. Don't
> worry if I'm still alive, you are.[34]

With the corrective questions she puts to her reader, Graham contests paradigms of selfhood that are derived intellectually rather than intuitively, that conceive of the "I" as theoretical and provisional rather than actual and authentic. As we peer into the poem, which is also Graham's bathroom mirror, the mirror art holds before nature, and the mirrored Narcissan pool where reflections are mistaken for reality (as they are in Plato's cave), we discern not only our own images but an image of Graham herself—the textual reflection through which she manages to be, inasmuch as the text reserves some residue of her *self*, in two places at once ("Don't worry where else I am, I am here"). Intuition guides our invariably negative answers to Graham's rhetorical questions: we can *feel* that we are more than matrices of logic, that we are not senseless paths but embodied nodes of experience and intention that travel along them, that to shatter the bathroom mirror is not to shatter the face reflected there. Graham warns us not to mistake representations of the self—whether those representations are formed out of logic, or light, or language—for something real and alive, an "I" that cannot be contained by such representations. It is thus with a second ethical awakening that "Dawn Day One" concludes, reminding us of the inalienable intuition of agency that we possess through feeling, and that could not accrue to a mere "system of logic and truth" or vacant "pathway with no body ever really on it."

With her barrage of pronouns and deictics in "Dawn Day One" ("I'm actually staring up at / you, you know," she insists, "right here, right from the pool of this page"), Graham objects to cognitive materialism's rational dismantling of the idea of self, a dismantling she perceives to be congruent with poststructuralist assaults on human intention and coherence that have been influencing the formal practices of American poets since the 1980s. "One of the most exciting aspects of moving one's mind along the lines of deconstructive theory," Graham observes, "involves precisely how morally and intellectually impregnable one feels"; she identifies "the sensation of power that comes from that going-underneath, from being able to see through every position" with a "refusal of the limitations and ennobling responsibilities of *choice*."[35] With her poetics of presence in *Overlord*, Graham seems to compensate for what Jennifer Ashton, writing on *Materialism* in 2005, perceives as an eradication of coherent lyric subjectivity under the influence of cognitive science—an eradication that, Ashton argues, affiliates Graham's aesthetic aims with those of Language poets such as Bruce Andrews and Charles Bernstein. In her readings of two poems from *Materialism*—"Notes on the Reality of the Self" and "The Surface"—Ashton claims that Graham, "unlike Damasio . . . portrays the self as something that is at once an *effect* of nonintentional material causes and indistinguishable from them."[36] Thus, Ashton proposes, in Graham's poems, "poetic agency as such becomes . . . one more nonintentional material cause"; no coherent intentionality, in other words, perceives and interprets experience and imparts its perceptions and interpretations to the reader. "[I]f language poetry has been seen— from both within its own circles and without—as an attack on the 'personal, "expressive" lyric,'" Ashton writes, "the subjectivity that emerges in *Materialism* . . . goes at least as far in theorizing the elimination of that 'expressivity' as the claims language poetry makes for the 'open text.'"[37]

And yet the throbbing moral distress of "Dawn Day One," which associates the means and ends of experimental mind science with guilt and recrimination, reveals that the "elimination of . . . 'expressivity'" that Ashton presents Graham "theorizing" and enacting in *Materialism* is precisely the outcome of cognitive materialism that Graham criticizes in *Overlord*. Having embodied the mind in her poetry with unusual (perhaps unprecedented) explicitness and self-awareness, Graham is finally compelled to confront the nihilistic determinism that is the most extreme intellectual consequence of her own fixation on biological necessity. In *Overlord* and beyond, she acknowledges the special descriptive powers of mind science but also charts their limits, answering her own moral charge not to imagine herself as "an *effect* of nonintentional material causes." She worries that a cognitivist poetics that dismantles the self by exposing its origins in contingent, biochemical relationships—like a deconstructionist poetics that dismantles the expressive self by exposing its origins in a contingent array of signs—jeopardizes nothing less than the feeling of accountability that accompanies belief in the self and in an autonomous and intentional, if elaborately constructed, lyric subject.[38]

Graham draws out these theoretical parallels in an NPR interview on the topic of "Emotion, Cognition and Consciousness" (2003), in which she, Antonio Damasio, and Thomas Metzinger, an eliminative materialist philosopher of mind, discuss how the brain "engenders a sense of self in the act of knowing"—how the self, based on Damasio's claims, exists as a virtual representation derived from "a constant barrage of signals that represent the body."[39] The panelists considered Damasio's proposition that what we experience as selfhood emerges from neural signals that register the body's internal states; while Damasio stresses that such signals allow us "to generate a self and . . . to maintain a continuity of self over a lifetime," Metzinger emphasizes the virtuality of the emergent thing he calls a "*phenomenally transparent self-model.*"[40] Metzinger explains to the interviewer, Ira Flatow:

> I would . . . claim that none of your listeners, nor you, Ira, have something or are something like a self. There are just no such things as components of reality. What exists are self models, representations created in brains, which are not any more recognized as representations by brains. But if we look closely, there is no thing, a self thing, that corresponds to these neurorepresentations in the brain, and that is . . . the idea we now have to depart from in this phase of our history.[41]

Metzinger goes on to propose that biological accounts of mental life contradict, and will ultimately invalidate, the illusion of conscious will.[42] Here Graham chimes in, responding to Metzinger by comparing the virtual presence of the lyric voice that emerges from the text to the virtual presence of the self that emerges from the brain, insisting that both possess abiding ethical force, if not ontological credibility:

> I don't think that the constructed voice of any poet or, for that matter, any painter or even composer is naïve in the sense that it doesn't know that it's a construction. But it is concerned with creating a system which will allow a person to feel empathy and to undergo accountability. And, you know, we might not be here really, but we really are killing people. And . . . you could probably prove to me that I'm . . . a total creature of circumstance, but unfortunately, I'm also a creature that has to cast a vote. I'm a person who has to be a mother. I'm a person who's responsible for taking care of somebody wounded in an emergency.[43]

Graham openly subscribes to Damasio's and Metzinger's descriptions of the self as an emergent effect rather than an immanent presence, and yet while she finds the claim that there's no such thing as a "self thing" to be philosophically and empirically credible, she is as troubled by the practical implications of conceiving of the self as merely a cognitive construction as she is by conceiving of the lyric voice as merely a linguistic one. "The solid self is no one's operative illusion," she insists, but "what we're trying to do is figure out . . . what goes into [its] construction, whether it's a poem, a work of art, a work of philosophy or . . . a neurological undertaking that exhibits the characteristics that momentarily coalesce into a self, and then whether that momentary coalescence can last long enough to love or do good or to do harm."[44] Graham may find herself persuaded by Metzinger's thesis that the self is "a virtual agent, perceiving and acting on virtual objects in a virtual world," but she is also inclined to disregard his thesis, adopting a self-conscious naïveté with respect to the objective mechanisms that regulate phenomenal self-experience in order to preserve the free will that cognitivist accounts of subjectivity such as Metzinger's are often inclined to reason away.[45] In the interview, Graham concludes that "maybe we have to have selves and be too simple and naïve, because if we give up on that, there's something horrifying about the degree to which we might slip out from under the mantle of accountability."[46]

Despite Graham's attempts to hold these perspectives in unresolved suspension—to imagine herself as both intentional and biologically determined, as both virtual and autonomous, as an epiphenomenon that emerges as an effect of physical conditions and as an agent that is conscripted to efficacy in the physical world—the poems of *Overlord* warp and buckle formally under the grinding friction between these visions of the self. Riddled with dashes, bracketed self-interruptions, and exclamations, as well as long, breathless, free-verse lines, the second of two poems in *Overlord* suggestively entitled "Disenchantment" evokes the unstable assembly of selfhood by brains and texts alike, drawing the embodied mind into correspondence with language, ideology, and history as one in an array of systems that mediate, below consciousness, all interpretive and expressive acts. The second of the poem's five parts is a passage from Virginia Woolf's *To the Lighthouse,* in which Mrs. Ramsay reflects on her "irrational tenderness" for mute, senseless natural phenomena, considering "how if one was alone, one leant to inanimate things; trees, streams, flowers; felt they expressed one; felt they became one; felt they knew one, in a sense were one."[47] The speaker's oneness with and separateness from the tree, the moon, the road seen through her window, requires her to vacillate between conceptions of "personhood" and their implications for how to live—how to "stand in the disenchantment" of her own skepticism and yet also, somehow, be free. Though Graham will end the poem exhausted and supplicant in the volume's signature posture of prayer, she begins with the sentence "I shift my self," severing with a sure hand the normative possibility "myself"; the "shifting" of the self seems as likely to describe a transcendental mind dragging along a physical body as it is the imperceptible rearrangement of a transient mental representation of the self.[48] Here "I" turns out to be one of an infinite number of possible permutations that form not *the* "me" but *a* "me":

> I shift my self. It's me I shout to the tree out the window
> don't you know it's me, *a* me—I really don't care what we call it,
> this personhood—a hood isn't a bad thing, a place to live, a
>   self-blinding.[49]

The lines suggest Graham's disenchantment not with the idea of self but with the tangled discursive frames surrounding that idea, with the verbal, and of course academic, question of "what we call it." She compares the self to two kinds of "hood," each of which fulfills, if only barely, her modest proposition that "a hood isn't a bad thing": first, she refers to the hood of a doomed prisoner or a captive falcon, which mollifies through perceptual deprivation ("self-blinding" seems to equate personhood with self-deception, admitting the possibility that, whatever we call it, it may be a naïve delusion). Second, Graham invokes the hood that is a home, a provisional "place to live" in space and time, a model of self that recalls Graham's characterization, in "Upon Emergence," of the visible world represented in the mind as "the version of a place / inside a place."[50]

The "you" that Graham addresses in the poem turns out to be a branching, brain-like tree that possesses if not animacy then certainly a unique and living identity. She has used a guidebook to determine the tree's age ("three centuries it is said according to the knowledge"), a book that stands in for the implied textual sources from which Graham has derived her knowledge of the brain as the biological "site" of the mind. To her regret, such sources have encouraged her to imagine the tree as a representation manufactured by physical interactions, as a "cloud" of data, as a "little flash" through which the tree manages to be in two "sites" at once:

> The book tells me I can't see you,
>   it's all frames and lenses and you, you who have been here
>   three centuries it is said according to the knowledge,
>   you are but a little flash, a cloud taking form in my neuron chamber, my
>   brainpan,
>   in your *site* of my manufacturing of you—
>   not to mention all the cultural variables—that I am white, a woman, live in
>   x, earn my means via y—in a
>   city, on a portion of the globe where empire collects its secrets—where I
>   am one of its secrets—prey to the fine dust of its ideology,
>   which slips into my very gaze this dawn,
>   right there into the brain stem along with the feeding-in of
>   your more than seventy-two shifts in the nature of the vertical
>   just in your upward-reaching branch [I counted],
>   which will take, in about 6 minutes, the very first ray of sun coming
>   over the
>   rooftops—[51]

As she looks upon the jointed climbing of a branch in "shifts" toward the sun, she identifies the variable structures of bodily apprehension that shape the "feeding-in" of the visible with "cultural variables" of race, gender, and historical position that likewise determine how a stimulus as mundane as a tree is "manufactur[ed]" as an interpretation of reality.[52] It is through the organizing gaze in familiar collusion with the overzealous intellect ("more than seventy-two shifts in the nature of the vertical / . . . [I counted], / which will take, in about 6 minutes, the very first ray of sun") that Graham absorbs the ideology of empire, her anatomical brain "stem" as receptive as the botanical "upward-reaching branch" that will absorb the sun's energy through its leaves. Here, the forms of "feeding-in" that subliminally define subjective self-experience appear consistent with Lyn Hejinian's proposition that "meanings are nothing but a flow of contexts," a fundamental premise the Language poet claims to underpin the "open text"; in her disenchantment, Graham entertains the possibility that contexts obviate and displace the illusions of authority and voice.[53]

It is Graham's dissatisfaction with such dogmatic premises, however, her skepticism of her own modish skepticism, that rises to prominence as "Disenchantment" proceeds to its conclusion. In the poem's final couplet, Graham entreats her "radical mind" to save her by teaching her to be innocent enough to assume the accountability of the will. The model of mind capable of encouraging such a renovation must be "radical" in dual senses: it must diverge from the poststructuralist dogma that renders the self reducible to its contexts, and it must remain *rooted* in old conceptual ground, in a dualist idea of mind summoned, in historical and intellectual senses, "from afar."[54] Assigning pride of place to the moral aspiration that motivates her willful naïveté, she concludes with a prayer to her "radical mind" that suggests the power of models of mind to shape not only self-perception but conduct: "teach me from scratch how to love. Keep me kind."[55]

Graham presents her commitment to this "radical," naïve mind with unparalleled directness and formal extravagance in a poem that literally writes over sensationally eliminative cognitivist dogma. In "Copy *(Attacks on the Cities, 2000–2003)*," Graham goes so far as to appropriate and willfully distort the language of popular neurophilosophy to articulate her grievances with its reductive antihumanism. Lines in the poem's pivotal fourth section allude to Lakoff and Johnson's *Philosophy in the Flesh* (1999), which aims to undertake "a thorough rethinking of the most popular current approaches [in Western philosophy], namely, Anglo-American analytic philosophy and postmodernist philosophy," in order to advance an "empirically responsible philosophy" consistent with the findings of brain science.[56] In their introduction, the book's authors assert that "the structure of reason itself comes from the details of our embodiment," pointing out the epistemic limitations that necessarily circumscribe our attempts to understand experience from "inside" experience:[57]

> If we are going to ask philosophical questions, we have to remember
> that we are human. As human beings, we have no special access to
> any form of purely objective or transcendent reason. We must neces-

sarily use common human cognitive and neural mechanisms. Because most of our thought is unconscious, a priori philosophizing provides no privileged direct access to knowledge of our own mind and how our experience is constituted.[58]

Though Lakoff and Johnson want to dispense with philosophy of mind that does not refer to empirical investigation outside the self-directed process of a priori reasoning, they admit that in human investigation, there is no true "outside," for the reasoning through which we interpret empirical information is itself structured by the embodied mind that is the object of study.[59] In "Copy," an apocalyptic poem haunted by the horrific violence with which humanity ushered in the current millennium—particularly the terrorist attacks of September 11, 2001, and the retaliatory invasion of Iraq in March 2003—Graham ambivalently redeploys Lakoff and Johnson's language as she asserts the validity of moral intuition irreducible to its biological, social, and linguistic expressions. She redetermines the meanings of Lakoff and Johnson's words (underlined below) by violently wresting them out of context:

> <u>We have to remember that we are human.</u> Something
> said
> that. It is in me, that
> something. But see how I now
> want
> to place it *in you*. Human. As in <u>having no privileged access to</u>
> <u>knowledge of our own mind.</u> Or of the world. Although we
> think otherwise. To place it deep in you. That it *trouble*
> you. You. Yes, it is true, someone is always crying out for you to listen.[60]

In "Copy," the injunction to remember that we are human no longer reminds us, as it does in Lakoff and Johnson's text, that somatic determinations limit our forms of self-understanding; Graham coopts their language to remind us instead that theoretical descriptions of the self as a diaphanously virtual, impotent illusion have jeopardized the experience of selfhood that grounds and guides moral action. Pointedly not a "someone," the "something" that utters the entreaty seems to be conscience itself, an immanent thing "in me" that the poem aspires to awaken "*in you*." From Graham's perspective, our lack of "privileged access to /

knowledge of our own mind" is just another instance of reality's resistance to human understanding (she adds, after all, that this lack of privileged access extends to "the world" at large); this resistance can either provoke a heedless, insatiable yearning to pursue empirical knowledge or confer humility and freedom within limitation. The former—impatient response—is precisely what necessitates the poem's humanist intervention, but the latter entails what can feel like a complacent, if salvific, acceptance of ignorance. Thus, Graham's only explicit motive for inviting us to remember that we are human is to enliven the conscience—to stir it "That it *trouble* / you."

"Copy" is a poem that expresses Graham's desperate desire for the self to survive, to prove its resilience and utility even as artists and scientists and philosophers portray it as fragile and vain; it is also a poem in which Graham attempts to prove that resilience to herself. As the ardent resolve of her ambition to install conscience in her readers gives way to humiliating self-doubt, the real author and the real reader of the poem come to seem so insubstantial that they might disappear at any moment, leaving only "the writing":

> I imagine I can posit
>
> infinitude then it all collapses, poof, and there's just me and you,
>   then of
>
>   course
>   just me, then nothing but the writing. This is a poem about wanting
>   to survive.
>   It must clearly try anything.[61]

It is striking that Graham groups the incomprehensible vastness of "infinitude" and the anonymous, unmet reader who takes up her book—both demanding imaginative constructions by any standard—with "me," the self that she likewise characterizes as something that she can only tentatively, and ultimately ineffectually, "posit." The poem does not end here, however; just as she has made the demoralized admission that her poem is only desperately *trying* to save "the heavy-headed virtuous self" from the forces that threaten to dismantle it, she shrinks from her own doubt, reasserting the viability and validity of the pronoun "you" in a minimal definition of selfhood as the mechanism of moral stewardship: "Something keeps you up at night, though. / Something must. What is it. What is it keeps you up at night. / Let no one persuade you you do not exist."[62] Again and again in the lyrics of *Overlord,* Graham charges herself with this leap of faith in the idea of self and, just as importantly, a *real* reading "you"; the italics that evoke the accents of an actual voice, the brackets and dashes that mark the improvised interjections of an actual mind in process, the exclamations and apostrophes that suggest a spontaneous over-flow of powerful feeling, the titles that couch her poems as a sacred kind of utterance, all amplify the effects of Graham's urgent second-person address. The friction between skepticism and belief forms a backdrop for these formal choices; it is when cognitivists and poststructuralists come closest to "persuading her that she does not exist" that conscience intervenes, persuading her to inhabit "a necessary innocence from which to live and act" and to pursue all available stylistic means to make herself heard.[63]

In *Overlord,* then, the discourses of mind science propel Graham's vacillation between poles of paralysis and activism. In her subsequent collection, *Sea Change* (2008), which was written, she explains, "after a very deep apprenticeship to the facts and issues involved in climate science," Graham reinstates the transcendental "radical mind" she associates with ethical awareness, portraying embodiment as an inexorable thrall: "You / will need to learn / to live in this prison / of blood and breath," she warns in "Undated Lullaby"; "I cannot / go somewhere / else than this body . . . / my cells reach out," she protests in "Embodies."[64] In *P L A C E* (2012), however, Graham comes to imagine poetry itself as a means of inhabiting disenchanted, empirical fact and moral necessity at once, as a place where she can acknowledge the pressures of ecological and neurological realities even as she cultivates the aesthetic responsiveness and personal responsibility those pressures can catastrophically threaten. By couching ecological disaster as a crisis of the imagination—as a predicament that results from and continues to test powers of empathy and vision that may appear more and more finite in the age of the brain—Graham draws ecological crisis into the compass of lyric, a genre she believes to be uniquely equipped to exercise and amplify these powers of mind.

We have seen that throughout her oeuvre Graham identifies the physiological limits of embodied vision—and the blinding hunger that our concentration on such limits can awaken in us—with the limits and failures of human empathy. In turn, the mind, when it is described in pervasive biological metaphors, tends to endanger living beings by diminishing, distorting, and assaulting them in the process of rendering them as mental objects. *P L A C E* extends this pattern of representation by figuring our heedless consumption of the resources of our planet as a failure of foresight and of empathy for future generations who will face radically altered conditions of existence. Fittingly, the volume replaces Graham's earlier metaphors of embodied vision (of subtraction, violent flattening, and solicitous panning from one perspective to another) with the metaphor of looking down a road—a road that connects cause and effect, that connects our lives with lives in the deep future, and that connects the immediacy, depth, and radiance of the present instant with the dim outline of the future that is nearly impossible, but also necessary, for us to imagine. In *P L A C E*, Graham often collocates roads with children and animals, figures that stand for the innocent inheritors of the earth whom we place in harm's way. In "Mother and Child (The Road at the Edge of the Field)," for example, Graham trims the hedgerow outside her home as she stands on a road that conducts her imagination into the future. The poem concludes with the ominous image of seeds from the hedgerow dropping from her child's opened palm onto the unreceptive asphalt, where mother and child see "the ground-breeze drag them / a little distance / to the middle / of the road / then stop."[65] As the question of our accountability to a future reality emerges in the poem, so too does the problem of imaginative limits; Graham looks up into the sky

> to see
> beyond the foaming of
> day's end the place where all in fact
> is, longed-for or over-
> looked altogether by the mind,
> human, which can,
> if it wishes,
> ken them into view
> by imagination[66]

The "mind, / human," always limited in its view, longs to see the future— the place "beyond the foaming of / day's end"—and yet also obliviously "over- / look[s]" it. Importantly, Graham frames that overlooking as both accidental and negligent, for though the mind is constrained by human fallibility, it can also, with concentration, "ken" the future into view.

That the road is an internal representation of the imagined future, and that the embeddedness of the mind in nature imposes a vanishing point upon that road, becomes even more explicit in "Lull," a poem that takes place in the "interglacial lull" of the present, on the eve of environmental catastrophe. As her father dies in the "usual" way, from "natural" causes, Graham solicitously scans her environment for signs of an unnatural ecological apocalypse; "Facts," she writes, "lick their tongue deep / into my ear." The poem centers on an encounter with a hungry fox that Graham, as she guiltily stocks her pantry, observes emerging from the woods in search of food; the animal's hunger signals the cost of our rapacious consumption of resources upon which we are "hooked," doomed by our own appetites. At several intervals, Graham suggests that our distinctly human hunger to contain experience in language represents a similar kind of avarice, and finally she imagines that the fox itself voices this double accusation, attributing our forms of greed to the texture of the nervous system itself, the brain a "rough garment" that catches blindly on whatever it touches. The human mind, the fox suggests, clings to what is accessible and immediate, connecting with little beyond the reach of the individual, physical body and its interests:

>   fox says
>   what a rough garment
>   your brain is
> you wear it all over you, fox says
>   language is a hook you
>   got caught,
> try pulling somewhere on the strings but no
>   they are all through you,
>   had you only looked
> down, fox says, look down to the
>   road and keep your listening
>   up, fox will you not
> move on my heart thinks checking the larder the
>   locks fox
> says your greed is not
>   precise enough.[67]

The "rough garment" of the brain is also a hair shirt, an instrument of conscience; its strings, like nerves, course "all through you." The solicitude Graham identifies with the brain is aimless, however (the fox enjoins her to "look down to the / road and keep [her] listening / up"), and our shortsighted self-interest is "not / precise enough"—our appetites, unchecked by selfless vision, lead us away from long-term survival rather than toward it.

To stand looking down the road, then, is to be in two places at once, taxing the imagination by condensing present and future, possibility and fate. The formal silhouettes of *P L A C E,* like those of *Sea Change,* habituate us to this double consciousness; in short lines that direct the eye from the center of the page to the right margin before forcing it back to the left, Graham exercises the eye relentlessly, propelling the mind forward and back again to enforce upon us jarring, synoptic dislocations of perspective. Unlike film, Graham observes, a genre in which we are accustomed to watching passively as the world is saved over and over just in time, poetry is a genre that has become especially practiced in demanding the kind of rigorous mental exercise that she believes, for both cognitive and ecological reasons, is now more necessary than ever.[68] Citing Richard Louv's argument that the waning of outdoor childhood play in the United States is changing "the formation of the human brain as we know it," Graham explains that "the replacement of open meadows, woods and wetlands by lawns, golf courses, housing developments, provide little opportunity for exploration, but more importantly, for the development of the capacity for imagination"; in this predicament, "we really need," she continues, "to imagine the as-yet-unimaginable racing towards us in order to have a prayer of survival."[69]

From the physiological limits that restrict our apprehension of the world and the conceptual limits that restrict the cognitive sciences' apprehension of the human, Graham thus shifts her attention in her most recent poems to our individual and collective failure to imagine the future, a failure she once again identifies with "built-in" limits of the imagining body. Our failures of vision and empathy—related to our limits as mortal creatures but not, finally, determined by them—are nowhere more evident, insists Graham, than in our ravaged natural environment, which attests to human avarice unchecked by foresight. As she draws the metaphysical and ethical quandaries her cognitivism poses into dialogue with the questions of personal accountability that proliferate under the threat of ecological disaster, Graham attributes environmental catastrophe not only to our limited power but also to our limited willingness to envision "a world moving blindly toward its own annihilation." Now, in the "uneasy lull before an unknowable, potentially drastic change," all human motions seem to propel us irrevocably toward a foreseeably unimaginable life, a life that we and our descendants "shall have no choice but to live."[70]

To take one final example, this predicament finds its most acute metaphorical expression in "Treadmill," a poem in which Graham reconfigures the image of the road to suggest both a future that bears down on the present and a poetics that sets the "as-yet-unimaginable" racing toward us. As Graham runs in place, exercised and exhausted, the treadmill urges her to transcend, or outrun, her "skulled-in mind." "The road keeps accepting us," the poem begins,

> It wants us to learn "nowhere," its shiny
> emptiness, its smile of wide days, so swollen
> with void, it really means it, this is not a vacation, it wants us
> to let our skulled-in mind, its channels and runnels, its
> slimy stalked circuits, connecting wildly, it the road
> wants us
> right now
> to cast it the
> mind
> from its encasement
> forward
> to race up ahead and get a feel for what it is, this always-receding, this
> place in which
> you were to deposit your
> question—the
> destination![71]

The "place" that concerns Graham is one that is always receding from view, both because the "stalked circuits" of the mind are "encased" by physical limits and because we habitually decline to undertake the effort of imagining the deep future, a "nowhere" that is purely conjectural and

yet also, Graham projects, catastrophically barren. Graham's poems in
P L A C E are designed to escort us to that "destination," to train us to
move there imaginatively even after the crutch of the poem falls away. At
the end of "Treadmill," Graham admits her own exhausted desire for a
break from the laborious, simultaneous concentration on the present and
future of the planet that her own poem demands: "O, hasn't enough time /
passed by now, can the moving walkway be shut down for the night," she
begs. She knows all too well, however, that stopping is an impossibility,
both because the mind is locked in physical reality ("the universe / is in
your mind as it / expands," she remembers) and because the fetters of
cause and effect restrict us to the only road there is: our common fate.

Conclusion

Anti-Lyric in the Age of the Brain

IN THEIR MANIFESTO *Notes on Conceptualisms,* Vanessa Place and Robert Fitterman introduce the following obiter dicta amid reflections on the ethics of poetic appropriation, the paradoxes of the poem as a commodity, and the legacies of Duchamp's readymades in conceptual writing:

> Note that in a post-Cartesian world, there is no splitting the baby: minds are bodies, bodies minds. The brain is a piece of body-meat, the body a bit of brain. This thought, once intolerable, is now comforting proof that "I" do not exist.[1]

Place and Fitterman's manifesto divides the world of contemporary poetry in two; there are regressive poets who find the thought of a finally soluble subject "intolerable"—"Let no one persuade you you do not exist," Jorie Graham enjoins us—and progressive poets, like Place and Fitterman themselves, who regard the prospect as not only serviceable but amenable, even "comforting."[2] Isolating "the short lyric of self-definition" as a primary institutional target of conceptual poetry's subversive energies, Place and Fitterman propose that the status of the self as an "imaginary construct" underpins conceptualism's signature compositional practices—plagiarism, appropriation, the use of radical artificial constraints, the implementation of "uncreative" procedures of rewriting and repetition, and the subordination of craft to concept.[3] Place and Fitterman thus not only present resistance to lyric idealism as an animating premise of conceptual writing, they openly anchor its methods in an eliminative materialist philosophy of mind that disintegrates the self altogether.

Indeed, the breezy credence with which Place and Fitterman describe the nonexistence of the self, and their readiness to regard this negation as a long-standing theoretical premise that has lately assumed the status of a "proven" fact, signal the extent to which the biologization of the self has offered twenty-first-century vanguard poets a corroborative vocabulary for describing what they have claimed to know all along; the death of the subject, after all, has been nourishing proliferating species of avant-garde poetry, from Language poetry to flarf, for decades. But durable lyric cannot be so naively essentialist, and durable anti-lyric so naively constructivist, as Place and Fitterman suggest, nor can sensitive, innovative poets writing in the new millennium interpret the varied meanings of embodied mentality in such monolithic terms. As I have sought to demonstrate, the poets who occupy the preceding chapters are not innocently, inflexibly committed to transcendental conceptions of voice and subjecthood, however widely they may be associated with the tradition of "expressive" lyricism.[4] These poets instead chart the incorporation of intentionless, emotionless quanta of anatomical being into their conception of the spirit, approaching the demystification of subjectivity, an ostensibly anti-lyric preoccupation, from the perspective of the private experience of mind, a conventionally lyric point of view. With the possible exception of Graham, who increasingly resists her own enchantment with the empirical terms that have come to define consciousness in the age of the brain, none of these poets find the encroachment of the empirical realm upon the realm of feeling "intolerable"; the zealous formal innovation of Lowell's *Notebook* and the elegiac enthusiasm with which Merrill atomizes himself in "Losing the Marbles," for example, attest to the artistic possibilities these poets find in an antihumanism widely associated with the radical, oppositional side of the entrenched, but ever shifting, boundary separating the canonical tradition from the experimental tradition.[5]

Just as the poets I have addressed in this book, associated to varying degrees with the stigma of "official verse culture," discover great aesthetic potential in the empirical dismantling of subjectivity from within, many poets critical of "the short lyric of self-definition" are now requisitioning the terms and ontological stakes of neurologism in nuanced recuperations of authorial presence, emotional responsiveness, and literary beauty.[6] In these last pages I will therefore turn to just a few suggestive examples of recent poets who bring neurobiological conceptions of inner life to bear on their interpretations of poetic presence and on perennial questions of art's power and its limits. These poets—Tan Lin, Juliana Spahr and David Buuck, Harryette Mullen, and Christian Bök—do not leverage reductive biological materialism to corroborate reductive expressions of linguistic or social materialisms; rather, they incorporate embodied cognition within searching reevaluations of the place of subjectivity within a poetic heritage that has long disavowed what Jack Spicer called "the big lie of the personal," embracing, in the social, textual, and biological senses George Oppen simultaneously conjures, "the meaning / Of being numerous."[7] The poets I have discussed thus far innovate stylistically to evoke the chemical dismantling of selfhood and subjectivity even as they negotiate the unifying pressures of the lyric; conversely, these oppositional poets assert the perseverance of hobgoblin immaterialities (creativity, originality, emotion, voice) while embodying the deconstructive forces of avant-garde and scientific skepticisms alike. At a time when the reputations and communal affiliations of poets tend to determine who reads them and how they are read, these poets attest to the hermeneutic limits of increasingly segregated, self-perpetuating circuits of lyric and anti-lyric reading—and to the obsolescent boundary dividing contemporary poets according to their commitment to the ideal of the unified, sovereign, expressive subject.[8]

Collage, Narrative, and the Uncreative Brain: Tan Lin, Juliana Spahr, and David Buuck

Theoretical opposition to the lyric, predicated on the supposition that retrograde, spiritual pieties are inherent to the mode, has defined the ethos of avant-garde poetry since the advent of Language poetics in the 1980s.[9] Though Language poets' strident, anti-transcendental rhetoric effectively installed the ontology of self as the divisive philosophical issue separating poetic orthodoxy and heterodoxy at the close of the twentieth century, the movement's intense ideological preoccupations, particularly its enchantment with Marxist and Wittgensteinian apparatuses for deconstructing presocial, "natural" subjectivity, appear to have eclipsed the potential influence of biological constructivism on the movement's imaginary.[10] As post-Language and conceptual poetries have emerged at the forefront of the experimental countercanon, however, they have increasingly recognized neurologism's congruent emphasis on the pliable, contingent, made conditions of subjective experience. The embodied mind has thus become an ever more visible presence in various strains of avant-garde poetry since the turn of the millennium. In his mechanistic autobiographical experiment *Fidget,* for example, Kenneth Goldsmith's restless, unraveling attempt to transcribe every movement his body makes over the course of a day dramatizes the impossibility of representing "a body detached from a mind."[11] Craig Dworkin's "Legion," Dan Farrell's "Avail," and Katie Degentesh's *The Anger Scale* all critique empirical instruments of clinical psychology, stressing the ideological coercions of ostensibly disinterested "sciences" of the mind.[12] In her baroque conceptual epic *La Medusa,* Vanessa Place uses the anatomy of the brain to structure modules of content, such that each section of the narrative reflects "particular cerebral constraint[s]": "anger/fear in the amygdala section, aphasia in the Broca/Wernicke's areas," and so on, Place explains.[13] Such thematic signs of the mind sciences' claim on the popular imagination, however, are endemic in twenty-first-century poetry—in the work of poets as aesthetically diverse as Robert Pinsky, Kay Ryan, Fanny Howe, Yusef Komunyakaa, Rachel Zucker, and Tao Lin, to name just a few—and may reveal less about the conceptual diffusions of embodied mentality within recent oppositional poetry per se than its wonted array of experimental stylistic practices.

Among these signature practices is the use of mechanical procedures to perform creative offices traditionally ascribed to the poet's mind. The faithful transcription of found text, for example, becomes the source of defamiliarizing effects once associated with the exertions of individual genius, while Google algorithms are made to perform the esemplastic, recombinatory roles conventionally attributed to inspiration. These appropriative procedures, wielded in original and expressive ways despite conceptualist rhetoric that inveighs "against expression," nonetheless represent the poet as a passive processor of data who executes a narrow array of predictable, predetermined operations. As Craig Dworkin describes it, the citational poetry of "unoriginal genius" (to borrow Marjorie Perloff's phrase) involves "assembling, rearranging and displaying information . . . rather than producing new material from scratch"; the language of such poems, he elaborates, is "more graphic than semantic, more a physically material event than a disembodied or transparent medium for referential communication."[14] The self this poetry thus envisions is not one that creates, drawing on a reservoir of imaginative possibility to render immaterial, mental forms concrete; rather, it is a physical, mechanical self that *recombines* material within a closed system of extant verbal material, producing meaningful differentiation through processes of change rather than addition. Kenneth Goldsmith describes his "uncreative writing" (his transcriptions of the *New York Times* in his successive iterations of *Day*, for example) as a necessary response to technological change over recent decades—to the widespread use of word-processing media that encourage cutting and pasting, plagiarizing, sampling, and so on, and to the invention of digital reading surfaces that present apparently limitless quantities of ready-made text that seem to obviate "new" writing.[15] Underlying and enabling this technologization of subjectivity, however, is the biologization of it; by imagining the poetic mind as one that performs reflexive acts of computation rather than divine acts of creation, and by flaunting the mechanical limits, rather than the possibilities, of human consciousness in a material world, such uncreativity is rooted in a philosophy of mind demonstrably fashioned in the age of the brain.

Among recent conceptualists who use citational practices to refute the long-standing proposition that art should exhibit originality and express authentic truths of personal experience, Tan Lin is unique for many reasons—not least for couching his artistic aims in terms of beauty, pleasure, and consolation, features of literary experience associated with the shamed personal lyric.[16] At a time when we are constantly subjected to the commercial engineering of emotions that encourage us to buy marketed goods and services, and when synthetic and "natural" drugs are used to curate feeling and "help one be oneself," Lin denies, with ambiguous irony, that the expression of selfhood and elicitation of feeling per se are sufficient aims of literary art.[17] "I think that reading that ends in an emotion is lame," Lin proposes, preferring instead to generate "a more generalized overall mood" that is "more reflective of the way we actually spend most of our lives."[18] In his book *Seven Controlled Vocabularies and Obituary 2004: The Joy of Cooking,* for example, he claims to have set out "to create work that would be very very easy and deeply relaxing at . . . [the] synaptic level, and that would be boring in some way—that wouldn't be challenging, that would make you feel good about yourself."[19] The proposition is neither as innocent nor as politically complacent as it sounds. Preferring to use literary style to evoke muted, rather than heightened, forms of feeling, Lin develops a mimetic art that blends in almost perfectly with the familiar patterns of experience that typify an increasingly technologized, consumption-driven reality; with his oblique ironies he creates in his poetry and performances a deliberately imperfect camouflage, a slight misalignment from his surroundings that casts them suddenly into relief. The poet explains to Charles Bernstein that in his absorptive, easy-to-process, often deceptively subtle "ambient" works, he has hoped that all sorts of impressions might "percolate in . . . irritants, relaxants could all be reduced to the same level of material, and at some point the reader would kind of lightly wake himself or herself up and notice something"—would recognize that the pleasures of his art resemble and are implicated in the narcotic amusements of a commodity culture that swiftly absorbs and neutralizes dissent.

Lin's practice of "ambient stylistics" reproduces the aspirations of architecture and ambient music to create "surrounding influence[s]," as Brian Eno puts it—environments that filter tacitly into consciousness and thus enact, as Timothy Morton has written of ambient poetics, "a state of nondual awareness that collapses the subject-object division."[20] By tracing the shallow, seamless flow of information across somatic and technological media, Lin's poetry also explores how material systems of distribution and consumption shape the production of selfhood and knowledge in the digital age. In his poetry and digital artwork (published in the form of blogs, open-source self-publications on Lulu, and text-based PowerPoint performances), Lin avoids the kinds of experiential and analytical depth literary texts—particularly the euphonically, imagistically, and symbolically dense works often labeled as poetry—have traditionally sought to represent and evoke. He aspires instead to produce "shallow space[s] of reading" that are continuous with the digital environments to which reading and writing have migrated since the advent of the Internet, drawing on the aesthetic potential of appropriation, crowdsourcing, misrepresentation, and ephemerality that such environments foster to produce "post-generic" works that he nonetheless categorizes as poetry.[21] Exploiting the Internet's capacity for decentralizing authorship, stressing the dependence of memory and knowledge making on digital prostheses, Lin explores the aesthetic potential of an extended concept of mind in which cognition is distributed across coextensive biological and technological substrates and the process of the self is improvised moment by moment, shifting along with the dynamic media of the imagining body and the virtual (web-based) sites of self-performance.

In his blog *Ambient Fiction Reading System 01,* Lin records the kind of ephemeral, inattentive acts of reading that he expects his audience to apply to his own writing. (As Lin's recent works often do, *Ambient Fiction Reading System 01* has mutated in form as it has migrated across publication media, appearing as an evolving online publication and a physical book: *BIB., REV. ED.*)[22] In his blog, Lin recorded everything he read over the course of several months, noting where his reading took place and for how long. He thereby produced "a stopwatch of various offhand, inefficient, and fragmentary reading practices, really the dated, *after-effects* of reading"; put differently, in *Ambient Fiction Reading System 01* he records a historically specific process of learning that reveals the experience of making knowledge to be contingent on the technologies we use to conduct information into consciousness.[23] Documenting episodes of reading that last less than a minute at a time, that are performed "passim," or that maintain focus for sustained periods (two and a half hours on Wikipedia.com) on "unauthorized" sources ("5:24–9 guardian .co.uk Can You Trust Wikipedia?"), Lin tracks the transient, osmotic processes through which we accumulate knowledge of everything from America's treatment of prisoners of war to Russian fiction to the nature of consciousness itself:

Tuesday, June 6, 2006

10:12–21 Tale of 5 Muslims: Out of Guantanamo and Into Limbo
10:40 HOME OFFICE NYTBR Oracle Bones by Peter Hessler
    Letter from China
11:12 WSJ A Question of Value Zippo Case Sparks Clash: Does
    China's Low Valuation of Fake Goods Coddle Counterfeiters?
11:13–16 Estimates of Copyright Piracy Losses Vary Widely
11:18–19 A Russian Master of the Whodunnit
11:23–1:53 wikipedia.com Richard Dawkins, meme, Susan
    Blackmore, copyleft, open source vs. free software, derived
    works, open source software, collaborative fiction, mythadven-
    tures, tagged, theory of mind,
4:26–5:08 passim Daniel Dennet Consciousness Explained "The
    Third Evolutionary Process: Memes and Cultural Evolution"
    26 pages
5:24–9 guardian.co.uk Can You Trust Wikipedia?

In form, *Ambient Fiction Reading System 01* falls into a subgenre of ency-
clopedic conceptual poems that express aspects of personal experience
through catalogs of texts and objects consumed, from Bernadette Mayer's
record of her education, *Eruditio ex Memoria* (1977), to Alexandra
Nemerov's "First My Motorola" (2007), a sequential record of every
branded object the poet touched over the course of a day.[24] Despite its
deliberate superficiality, Lin's list from June 6, 2006, meaningfully
evokes his sensibility, interests, and aesthetics; it signals his penchant for
the dilutions of authority Internet publication entails, his transgressive
passions for plagiarism and piracy, and the synoptic perspective, as a first-
generation Chinese American, from which he views contemporary Chinese culture and politics (Lin has described his early life in Ohio as a
"Chinese childhood encased inside a Western one").[25] The list also demonstrates Lin's sympathetic regard for the kinds of analogies that Daniel
Dennett, Richard Dawkins, and Susan Blackmore draw between the
packaging of information in genes and in memes, eroding distinctions between biological and technological media.[26] By presenting his reading
list as a poem, Lin frames his sources (Wikipedia, guardian.co.uk, *Wall
Street Journal*) and their subjects (open-source software, the roles of evolution and technological artifice in shaping consciousness and language)
as his muses; indeed, the concrete systems that organize our experience

inspire the forms of constraint that make Lin's works recognizably "poetic." Lin reminds us that poems, computers, and minds are apparatuses defined by their limits, and that "there are no machines of freedom, by definition," as he puts it, invoking Foucault; "reading is a machine, an artificial system. When the mind reads, it is part of this artificial system."[27]

The intrusive role such systems play in parsing and constraining the undifferentiated data flow that makes up experience is one of Lin's greatest themes. Striving to incorporate Ashberian negations of mind into a more capacious theory of beauty, Lin's poetry carries his predecessor's lapses of attention, perception, and memory to extremes commensurate with the ephemeral dynamics of twenty-first-century reading.[28] The systems that interest him in his virtuosic modular collage *Seven Controlled Vocabularies and Obituary 2004: The Joy of Cooking* (*7CV*) range from the reading "system" of the book itself, to the "controlled vocabulary systems" curators and librarians use to standardize their categorization of archived objects, to the distinct lexica that circumscribe genres (poetry, fiction, photography, film, architecture, recipes, obituaries, reality television, restaurant reviews), to the biological systems that structure memory and emotion. Larding the book with misdirections and misplaced category markers, Lin adopts various forms of subversion and disruption to expose these systems' coercive, subliminal roles in making meaning. The acknowledgments that open the book, for example—ostensibly a site for recognizing indebtedness—are lifted directly from an unacknowledged source (Timothy Bewes's *Reification: or The Anxiety of Late Capitalism*, 2002), while the title and author's name appear on the book's back cover; on the recto cover, Lin prints his own, invented Library of Congress Cataloging-in-Publication data, which normally appears in the front matter. Some of the Library of Congress subject headings Lin presents there reflect *7CV*'s patent, metapoetic themes ("Poetry—data processing," "Poetry—therapeutic use," and "Literary criticism and the computer," for example), while others are opaque; the primary heading, "China—poetry," for example, squares neither with Lin's descriptions of his own family's American acculturation in the book's autobiographical vignettes nor with the marginal Chinese phrasal accents that appear only a few times over the course of *7CV*'s 222 pages. By Lin's own account, the "China—poetry" Library of Congress heading functions as a "disappearing first term" that emphasizes the awkwardness of such classifications, inherently limited in their ability to recognize nuances of ethnic identity and experience. "Reading is a coherent, self-contained, mechanical process, Lin observes, ". . . and all visualizations of identity produced within it are illusions of identity."[29]

Such misdirections in *7CV* not only expose the force of generic expectations in shaping interpretation, confirming Lin's proposition that "style is what is statistically likely to induce a reading," but also emphasize the lacunae that constrained, physical systems of comprehension and organization generate.[30] Thus, the chapter "Field Guide to American Painting" contains no images, only numbered plate markers accompanied by blank spaces; facing one of these "erased" paintings is a prose commentary that implicitly compares the technological constraints of the book (traditionally "not very good at reproducing images") to the "hardwired" cognitive processes that determine the scope and duration of syntactic and semantic units in natural language. "7 is generally thought to be the number of things the human brain can readily remember," the pedantic commentator observes; "George Miller did pioneering studies on this and his theory is called Miller's Number Seven."[31] Elsewhere, the "supremely limited" nature of human memory forms a basis for a theory of aesthetics that resembles Lin's own:

> Human memory resources are supremely limited and the most beautiful arrangements of reading material would be as immaterial, diffuse and ambient as the memory attached to them. As anyone who has read a book carelessly can tell you, forgetting a book is the most beautiful thing you can do to it.[32]

In "the era of the short archive"—when digital substrates for recording thought appear to be no more permanent than thought itself—reading is for Lin a process so ephemeral that it resembles forgetting.[33] To ambiguous effect, Lin uses extravagantly mechanistic language to describe all sorts of aesthetic experiences in *7CV*, from reading nineteenth-century novels and watching reality television (both methods, as he puts it, of "emotional information processing") to apprehending color (a process that "triggers biochemical reactions → emotions into moods").[34] On the one hand, Lin is knowingly perverse when he represents "reading as data management" and emotions as units of experience that "can be geometrically crafted to repeat perfectly"; his zombie empiricism parodies comparatively crude scientific descriptions of nuanced sensory experiences.[35] On the other hand, Lin's physical, often explicitly physiological, descriptions of mental actions betray a genuine regard for unsentimental, analytical descriptions of aesthetic experience that flatten hierarchal distinctions between the kinds of feelings we have when we read realist fiction and the kinds of feelings we have when we go shopping or watch television or eat a delicious meal. Lin's scientific patter ratifies the postmodern collapse of such hierarchies, but his excesses and ironies make the mutual reinforcement of anti-literary and empirical perspectives appear both inevitable and suspiciously facile. Amid these tensions, the very concept of the literary hangs in the balance, suspended in a precarious state of limbo.

Reproducing the "fleeting and minor" moods and atmospheres of commodity culture, Lin's collage-based works exemplify one species of poetic response to widespread skepticism of the heightened emotions associated with the lyric—emotions Lin depicts as basic human reflexes ("biochemical reactions") that are predictably stimulated by the languages of marketing, propaganda, and poetry alike. In *An Army of Lovers* (2013), a very different example of genre-bending anti-lyric—a form of collaborative, sometimes appropriative prose indebted to the New Narrative of the 1970s and 1980s—Juliana Spahr and David Buuck express similar suspicions of lyric feeling and dispositional resistance to the binary opposition of mind and environment.[36] Like Lin's collage, their narrative "anti-poetry," as Brian Reed has described it, extends from and dovetails with Language poetry's program of anticapitalist experimental practice.[37] Theirs, however, is not Lin's cool, East Coast ethos of coy, enigmatic irony, elusive tonal play, and uncommitted skepticism. As "card-carrying Bay Area poets," Spahr and Buuck's is an earnest, scrappy, confrontational style of political poetry adapted from mid-century civil rights poetics and the late-modernist Marxism of Louis Zukofsky and Muriel Rukeyser.[38]

Like their avowedly avant-garde peers, Spahr and Buuck recoil from "poetry that tends to portray, in a quiet and overly serious tone, with a studied and crafted attention to line breaks for emphasis and a moving epiphany or denouement at the end, the deep thoughts held by individuals in a consumerist society."[39] Their distaste for the meditative complacencies and emotive egotism of "bourgeois individualist lyricism" places them in a bind, however, for they also aspire to express and incite the potent emotions—particularly rage and love—that motivate social consciousness and activism.[40] They thus arrive, in their attempt "to figure out some possible new configurations for political art" in the twenty-first century, at an impasse that to them represents a crisis in American poetry at large.[41] This impasse manifests itself symbolically in *An Army of Lovers* in an array of neurological afflictions that impair seditious artists—figures whose political agitations imply a neatly dualist distinction between the subversive consciousness of the creative individual and the coercive, putatively external environments from which the self can be dislocated or excepted. By stressing the vulnerability of subjectivity itself to forms of infection and chemical manipulation, Spahr and Buuck identify the material continuity that enmeshes consciousness and environment with forms of complicity that jeopardize the force of political art; effacing even physical distinctions between self and society, their monism undoes binaries upon which any subversive poetics depends. Overcome with intense, utopian emotion, yet divested of the pretense of expressive autonomy that imbues acts of authorship with authority, Spahr and Buuck emphasize the paralyzing effects of their own materialist convictions on the idealist practice of political creativity.

In the self-referential yet often surreal and even phantasmagoric frame narrative of *An Army of Lovers,* Demented Panda and Koki, fictionalized versions of the collaborating poets, meet to take long walks together and discuss the subject of "poetry and its particular lostness." An early description of that "lostness" attributes it, at least in part, to the resemblances between the slick, celebratory, easy-to-absorb aesthetics of instruments of mass psychology and the lyric's sensuous packaging and dissemination of bourgeois values:

> It is important to realize that in the time of Demented Panda and Koki
> poetry was an art form that had lost most, if not all, of its reasons for
> being. It was no longer considered, because of its ties to song, the su-

perior way for a culture to remember something about itself. And at the same time, it was no longer considered the superior way for a nation to inspire patriotism and proclaim, with elaborate rhyme and rhythm, that its values were great and universal values. This was especially true in the nation that claimed Demented Panda and Koki among its citizens. This nation had long ago realized that the best way to inspire patriotism and convince other nations that its values were great and universal was to offer a series of tax breaks and incentives that encouraged the international distribution of colorful moving pictures and songs that celebrated soldiers, government agents, and upwardly mobile consumers as heroes.[42]

What is especially striking about *An Army of Lovers* is how immediately and privately physical this abstract aesthetic predicament, this "lostness" that Spahr and Buuck associate so closely with the vast, impervious atmosphere of late capitalism, becomes. The social and discursive channels by which apparently benign expressive acts (putatively apolitical lyric poems, for example) become implicated in corrosive processes of cultural imperialism prove to be continuous with the physiological channels through which mind, body, and environment mutually interpenetrate, causing the poets to register artistic and political quandaries as physical symptoms—as the "felt-sense of impasse and contagion."[43] The two-part story of Demented Panda and Koki's frustrated attempts to collaborate in the writing of their poem bookends the ABCBA structure of *An Army of Lovers;* embedded within the outer narrative are parallel episodes, both of which are titled "The Side Effect," that use neurological symptoms to represent stalled expressive enterprises and the complicity of American art in violent, consumption-driven, ecologically devastating global politics. In these episodes, the nervous system emerges as the neuromolecular threshold where self and world meet and mutually constitute each other—a biological limen that resembles the "foyer" of the lyric itself, as Bonnie Costello has described it, where "the world enter[s] into the life of the individual."[44]

The permeability of the biological self and the political environment forms a crucial backdrop for these echoing vignettes. In one, a performance artist (a version of the Buuck/Demented Panda figure) suffers from what he calls "an inward focus of the brain-place," a lack of feeling combined with anger and futility, for which he seeks chemical treatments to "modulate pre-synaptic transmitter releases of excitatory amino acids such as glutamate and aspartate."[45] Despite these treatments, the artist— "ill with late capitalism," he quips—watches in horror as the somatic boundary separating self and world becomes porous to the point of liquescence. In a disturbing allegorical turn, his face begins to leak from "the space between the dermis and the epidermis," reminding him that "something . . . had entered his body and reshaped him."[46] In the parallel iteration of "The Side Effect," a version of the Spahr/Koki poet figure is assembling a sonic collage that depicts acts of torture in military prisons when she is bitten by a tick that infects her with *Mycoplasma fermentans incognitus*, a coinfection of lyme disease originally engineered, her Internet searches tell her, by the U.S. government as a biological weapon. The composer imagines the organism mutating in the hostile environment of her enraged body, altering the substance of her mind: "Not only am I not in control of my thoughts," she explains to the homeopathic healer she visits, "they're not even my thoughts."[47] The healer advises her to reconcile herself to the irrevocable, finally incurable presence of what she imagines as the reprehensible, infectious "other" within her *self*: "What is there inside you will still come," the healer warns; "it's growing inside you, it's the you that's not you that's coming."[48]

Like the disintegrating boundary between the dissident self and its benighted, institutional milieu, the dilution of experience into information—information that flows freely, mindlessly, and instantaneously across somatic and technological media—is a source of deep ambivalence for Buuck and Spahr in *An Army of Lovers*. The composer clearly identifies this flow of information with transparency and accessibility, with the circulation of knowledge that might ostensibly facilitate justice. But sitting at her laptop, fussing over her composition, and wondering how it could possibly "capture all that she [is] now seeing, thinking, feeling . . . her desire for some right action in the world outside her computer," the artist also worries that the precise arrangement of her sonic collage "will be reduced to . . . vague signals and sensations on her screen and in her brain, in her bloodstream and her guts," its meaning diffused as her body resolves it, like a computer assimilating data, into an impassive flow of information.[49] Like the unreliable official denials and the conspiracy theories surrounding the engineering of *Mycoplasma fermentans incognitus* offered up by Google, the information the conceptual artist assembles by "surfing and watching and clicking and thinking and collecting and downloading and storing" is likewise too intangibly, spectrally digital, too estranged from firsthand experience, to count as credible evidence of the atrocities she wants to describe.[50] The composer thus associates processes by which information is "abstracted" and "reduced . . . on her screen and in her brain" with the unmooring of fact from origins and thus from the touchstones of veracity and authenticity that legitimize an art of witness.[51] The disjunctive and appropriative methods of her composition, she recognizes, may be better suited to reproducing this surfeit of data and this flattening of its significance than to capturing and inciting the political emotions of "hot anger, shame and frustration" that the composer most urgently aspires to communicate and evoke.[52]

Spahr and Buuck thus prove to be full of self-doubt in their ambitious, faltering attempt to "bend the sound of poems and anti-poems beyond the fenced horizon."[53] Out of the quandary of "poetry and its particular lostness" they make a long narrative in prose, suggesting that theirs has been a defeated recourse to fiction; likewise, they depict the book's frustrated, infected conceptual artists as versions of themselves. And yet *An Army of Lovers* offers glimpses of possibility in an unlikely source that Spahr and Buuck soberly, begrudgingly, ambivalently, characterize as "lyric." In a self-mocking parody of their own avant-garde coterie's political sanctimony, at the center of the book Buuck and Spahr present a dialogue among disillusioned poets and academics that culminates in a taboo confession of admiration for Romantic lyricism and its ultimately ineffectual but beautiful annunciations within experimental modernism. "If I had it to do all over again, I'd be a lyric poet, you know?" the vignette's protagonist, a gin-soaked poetry professor, bitterly admits. Upon hearing Wordsworth's "Daffodils" read aloud, the performance artist with the leaky face returns home and composes a work called "The Remedy," which crescendos in a soaring affirmation: "Through all of this I will continue to contribute, to bend and to leak, to adapt and mutate, adding yet more ingredients that we do not own to things that are beautiful, revolutionary, and irretrievable." And to remedy the composer's artistic impasse, Spahr and Buuck offer a surprising prescription in the voice of the homeopathic healer, who remonstrates against the sound artist's perception of herself as a passive body intruded upon by a corrupt, extrinsic world outside.[54] "Listen to your meat," the healer declares, no longer describing the sound artist's work as a depersonalized "composition" or a "jumble of noise" but as a "song"; "mov[e] through the world with a tenfold increase in interest in it, because everything that happens to you and by you, here in your body and out there in the world, all that everything is in you now, and all that everything should be in your song."[55]

Like so many other recent works by ambitious avant-garde poets, *An Army of Lovers* and *7CV* ask how to make dissolved selves—selves that aggregate convictions and moods and experiences but lack recognizable ideological or even material boundaries—*speak*. Spahr and Buuck's collaboration proposes that what is lost with the dilution of the authority and political efficacy of the unified, individual voice might be recuperated by the creative possibilities of a boundless one, theoretically infinite in its political and expressive compass; if "everything is in you," to survey internal life is always to survey the foreign, to regard and reconstitute an inexhaustible breadth of "ingredients that we do not own." It is no coincidence that the works of Lin and that of Spahr and Buuck exhibit ambiguities of form that test the limits of poetry as a genre; through collaborative composition and particularly through the widespread use of prose, they eschew the formal compression and musicality that have traditionally made poems recognizable as poems.[56] By opening the category of genre—like the categories of mind, self, and environment—to new forms of indeterminacy, such experimentalism reflects the fluid boundaries of the twenty-first-century subject on the level of form.

Radical Limits of the Avant-Garde Mind:
Harryette Mullen and Christian Bök

Adopting extravagantly exacting formal constraints rather than amorphous, intergenre structures, Harryette Mullen and Christian Bök nonetheless share with Lin and Spahr and Buuck a concept of mind defined by material—embodied and environmental—limitation; at the extreme formalist pole of the experimental spectrum, Mullen and Bök evoke somatic determinations of mental experience in flagrantly coercive forms, marveling at the emergence of voice and will out of capricious, non-intentional arrangements of linguistic and biological matter. Inspired by the poetics of the Oulipo (*l'Ouvroir de litterature potentielle*)—the international literary group that has generated poems according to apparently arbitrary but systematic textual rules since the 1960s—Mullen and Bök are among recent "noulipian" poets who have added phenomenological and physiological resonances to the critique of bourgeois subjectivity that the Oulipo's arduous impediments to expressive presence originally implied.[57] Through the anagrammatic reorganization of letters, the lipogrammatic exclusion of letters, and the procedural game S+7 (in which every noun in a text is replaced by the noun that appears seven entries later in the dictionary), for example, these ecstatic formalists substitute the generative force of linguistic limitation for the generative force of transcendental inspiration, insisting that the tacit limits of verbal and embodied media always determine the insubstantial idea; "nothing we apprehend is immaterial," as Johanna Drucker puts it in *The noulipian Analects,* and "we only get 'ideas' through their material expressions—language, image, text, sound signals, and pulses." Setting out to define the "cultural project" of such experimentalism, Drucker argues "for immanence, against wish-dreams of transcendence, for the ludic over the orthodox, for the non-aligned over the licensed."[58]

Among recent hyperformalists who resist their own "wish-dreams of transcendence," Mullen and Bök strike a noteworthy balance between conveying their most cherished values and expunging the narcissism and naïveté of "self-expression" from their poems. With their rigorous forms, they also widely allude to the constraints embodiment imposes on consciousness, putting their self-imposed rules to very different representational ends. In her abecedarian volume *Sleeping with the Dictionary,* Mullen identifies in noulipian formalism and cultural neurologism alike possibilities for effacing the authorial ego, but uneasily assumes the demystificatory *ethoi* of both. As a poet determined to voice her objection to the repressive forces women writers and writers of color face, and as an experimentalist influenced by earlier generations of Language poets, her poems exhibit countervailing political and theoretical impulses toward voicing marginalized subjectivity and dismantling it.[59] In the playfully subversive "Wipe That Simile Off Your Aphasia," for example, Mullen presents a deconstructive critique of analogy—the verbal tool for translating nuances of putatively prelinguistic, abstract feeling into accessible, concrete forms.[60] A litany of similes, the poem seems to court comparison with metaphysical lyrics from Marvell to Eliot, which carry the defamiliarizing effects of analogy to ingenious lengths, and with the traditional lyric blazon, whose (female) subject seems to exist to be described in terms that flaunt the (male) poet's imaginative powers. Mullen's poem, however, finally contains no meaningful comparisons, and leaves it to the reader to diagnose the exact symptoms, and causes, of the "aphasic" replacements that generate the poem's elliptical structure:

> as horses as for
> as purple as we go
> as heartbeat as if
> as silverware as it were
> as onion as I can
> as cherries as feared
> as combustion as want
> as dog collar as expected
> as oboes as anyone
> as umbrella as catch can
> as penmanship as it gets
> as narcosis as could be
> as hit parade as all that
> as icebox as far as I know
> as fax machine as one can imagine
> as cycles as hoped
> as dictionary as you like
> as shadow as promised
> as drinking fountain as well
> as grassfire as myself
> as mirror as is
> as never as this

Forestalling conventional lyric expressiveness with her erratic diction, Mullen makes the poem's formal procedures themselves her primary expressive medium. Grafting the analogical "as" onto each in a litany of phrases that use the word in nonanalogical senses (*"as for* me," "we'll figure it out *as we go*," "he looked *as if* he hadn't slept"), Mullen's rigid, anaphoric column of conjunctions represses her array of nonconforming "as" idioms, forcing them out of colloquial, demotic usage into vertical, analogical, conventionally "poetic" roles. Mullen's procedure of replacing the adjectives her syntax anticipates with concrete nouns ("silverware," "oboes," "grassfire"), however, renders the ostensibly clarifying mechanism of the simile impenetrable—the analogy becomes a concrete wall rather than a window into the poet's consciousness. It is the final simile, however, triumphant in its deviation from the established pattern, that draws the poem to a defiant, expressive conclusion; having thwarted the domineering poetic analogy with her whimsical nouns and intractable idioms, Mullen suddenly interjects the sole adverb "never," attributing the resistance the word connotes—now clearly directed at the simile per se—to the grand sum of grammatical transgressions that constitute "this" (the poem itself).

"Wipe That Simile Off Your Aphasia" describes its procedures of "wiping" away context and discursive content as neurological symptoms of a specifically verbal cognitive disorder ("aphasia" literally means "speechlessness"). By presenting the poem's method in such terms, Mullen naturalizes her heterodox poetics as an outcome of her eccentric, exceptional brain, even as she acknowledges that the voluntary, apparently anti-expressive uses of language to which she commits herself in *Sleeping with the Dictionary* will appear rebarbative if not pathological to some readers. By effacing the cryptophrase "wipe that smile off your face" with her punning title, Mullen identifies the expressive smile with the accustomed poetic simile, and uses "aphasia," her metonym for the deliberately encumbered lyric voice, to displace "face," the site where the signals of interiority are made manifest. Such aphasic replacements, through which the title both cracks a joke and scolds us for smiling, prove to be neither facetious nor incidental in Mullen's poems; *Sleeping with the Dictionary* begins, in fact, with a similar array of implications in the prose poem "All She Wrote," which takes the form of a torrent of excuses for not writing. The poem's increasingly strained deferrals—"Now I'm unable to process words. I suffer from aphasia. . . . What can I tell you? I forgot what I was going to say," the speaker rambles—imply the crippling imperatives to be original, and above all expressive, to which Mullen's Oulipian formalism openly responds, thereby framing the unorthodox style of the book as a whole ("all she wrote") as the result of the poet's *inability* to express herself "normally."[61]

What might be most striking about Mullen's choice of aphasia as a model for her poetics is that it is a symptom of brain trauma, suggesting that her dislocations of language arise from unchosen circumstances that impose themselves violently on her experience. The "aesthetic apartheid" that separates African-American and avant-garde poetics and effectively suppresses black literary experimentalism certainly constitutes such a donnée for Mullen. Drawing influence from politically committed poetry of social protest in the lyric tradition and from radical vanguard poetries from Gertrude Stein to the Language school and beyond, she resists both traditional, lyric conceptions of presence and avant-garde poetry's tendency to blot out the meanings of racial and sexual difference by suppressing biographical and affective signatures of voice.[62] Mullen insists that African-American poets whose work falls outside the normative array of aesthetic schemes associated with "representative blackness"—those of protest, solidarity, and other forms of racialized self-fashioning— unsettle the dominant, agonistic critical narratives that readers and poets alike use to teach and market poetry; as a result, "formally innovative minority poets" are excluded from both the mainstream and avant-garde canons. Without critical recognition, the "erasure of the anomalous black writer abets the construction of a continuous, internally consistent tradition," Mullen writes, "and it deprives the idiosyncratic minority artist of a history. . . . She is unanticipated and often unacknowledged because of the imposed obscurity of her aesthetic antecedents."[63]

Perhaps unsurprisingly, Mullen figures this "imposed obscurity" in neurological terms as well, applying ludic practices of productive constraint to the very serious work of describing and redressing processes of cultural erasure. In the backdrop of her poem "Fancy Cortex," for example, is the reification of such processes in the autocorrect function of her "ethnocentric word processing program," which replaces the surname of the eminent Black Arts poet Jayne Cortez with the familiar word "cortex."[64] This attempted suppression of Mullen's literary forebear by an authoritative verbal technology (an electronic dictionary) inspires Mullen to compose a response in the form of an extravagantly anatomical encomium to Cortez's genius. "I'm using my plain brain to imagine her fancy cortex," the self-effacing poem begins; in what Mullen speculates "may be the first blazon that praises a woman's brain," she goes on to imagine the "exalted . . . mantle" of Cortez's "pontifex pallium," the delicate mesh of her "synaptic network of condensed neural convolutions," and "the *terra incognita* of her undiscovered hemispheres."[65] The poem's extended conceit and intricate sonic patterning reveal the speaker's transcendence of whatever imaginative limits she attributes to the "gray matter" of her "dim bulb," much as Mullen acknowledges the representational constraints of inherited language and the repressive constraints of race as a social category by rendering them aesthetically productive. The attitude with which she greets the impositions of the embodied mind and the ethnocentric dictionary thus exhibit the spirit of opportunity with which she frames her own position as a black experimentalist (quoting Margo Jefferson): " 'race is not just a series of obstacles,' " Mullen affirms, " 'but also a set of possibilities.' "[66]

Mullen's send-up of the lyric contraption of the analogy in "Wipe That Simile Off Your Aphasia" and her attempt to remediate the exclusion and replacement of a marginalized experimental voice in "Fancy Cortex" display her harmonious commitments to anti-lyric iconoclasm and to the circumstantial and emotional specificity of her experience in *Sleeping with the Dictionary* as a whole. While Mullen transcends her self-imposed limits by refusing to cede creative control to language at crucial turns (in the deviating final line of "Aphasia," for example), Christian Bök transcends his invented procedures through a more radical, masochistic obedience to his own rules. Bök's acclaimed book *Eunoia* exemplifies his faith in the occult meanings inherent within apparently arbitrary forms of textual and biological matter—meanings that become manifest, he demonstrates, only through an exacting, almost mystical, surrender to form. A prelude to his unprecedented biopoetic experiment *The Xenotext, Eunoia* anticipates Bök's translation of his antiexpressive principles into a somatic context, where a microbial genome itself becomes the primary determinant of poetic consciousness. The book's title, *Eunoia,* literally means "beautiful thinking," and is also the shortest word in English that contains all five vowels. Bök divides the book into five sequences, each of which contains only one vowel; he limits himself further by requiring himself to avoid repetition, to abide by a number of thematic rules, and to use at least 98 percent of the repertoire of univocal words in English.[67] As each vowel comes to express a distinct personality—an effect Bök and his readers have widely observed ("A is courtly, E is elegiac, I is lyrical, O is jocular, U is obscene," according to the book jacket's précis)—each letter assumes a life, and a mind, of its own; since Bök requires himself to use nearly all of the available words containing only one vowel, these "personalities" appear to be inherent rather than imposed. Bök's thinking language, which seems to exert its own will on the formation of the poem, thus appears to possess not only an immanent "consciousness" but, through assonance and internal rhyme, an immanent and distinctive voice.

And yet as visually concrete and thick with sound as *Eunoia* is, its language remains transparent enough to disclose the persistent specter of its author. The protagonist of the "I" sequence, for example, is both the letter "I" and an expressive speaker, crafted by intentional design, who emerges in silhouette behind the poem's densely woven integument of assonance:

> Writing is inhibiting. Sighing, I sit, scribbling in ink
> this pidgin script. I sing with nihilistic witticism,
> disciplining signs with trifling gimmicks—impish
> hijinks which highlight stick sigils. Isn't it glib?
> Isn't it chic? I fit childish insights within rigid limits,
> writing shtick which might instill priggish misgiv-
> ings in critics blind with hindsight. I dismiss nit-
> picking criticism which flirts with philistinism. I
> bitch; I kibitz—griping whilst criticizing dimwits,
> sniping whilst indicting nitwits, dismissing simplis-
> tic thinking, in which philippic wit is still illicit.[68]

Even as Bök's "rigid limits" dragoon and impersonalize his meaning, a recognizably irritable, defensive, pompous, impotent, witty, perverse, *presence* persists and shapes the poem across its lipogrammatic chapters. Like the generations of Language poets that preceded him, Bök threatens, with his own brand of "nihilistic witticism," to cede the production of meaning to the will of his medium. His retreat from such absolute negativity is definitive, however; as his title suggests, aesthetic experience is another primary effect of the exertions of semiotic limits on consciousness, and the "beautiful thinking" Bök captures in *Eunoia* emerges from the friction between his own will that precedes the text and "the hidden wish of words," as James Merrill put it.[69] "[*Eunoia*] makes a Sisyphean spectacle of its labour," Bök writes in the book's postscript, "willfully crippling its language in order to show that, even under such improbable conditions of duress, language can still express an uncanny, if not sublime, thought."[70]

It is in his unfinished, conceptual poem *The Xenotext* that Bök renders *Eunoia*'s implied analogy between the embodied and textual limits of thought explicit, adopting the chemistry of life itself as a form of verbal constraint. While in *Eunoia* language is the denaturalized, alien force against which authorial consciousness contends, *The Xenotext* (*xenos*, "stranger" + *text*, "woven") is biologically alien—it is a chemical poem built to be implanted in the DNA of a host organism, where it will not only reproduce itself but produce new "poems" in the form of proteins. The organism Bök has chosen to host *The Xenotext* is *Deinococcus radiodurans*, an extremophile bacterium that can survive, with its exceptionally damage-resistant DNA intact, even in the vacuum of outer space, indefinitely protecting the information embedded in its genome. Able to withstand the intense gamma radiation emitted in a nuclear holocaust, "the dire seed," as Bök has referred to it, could conceivably preserve his poem after the extinction of our species and even our planet.[71] Bök frames the *The Xenotext* as a means of archiving human consciousness within a biological medium for hundreds of millions of years, redressing the otherwise exclusively "unhappy" legacies of our civilization that will persist after any superficial evidence of human civilization on earth has disappeared (the background radiation emitted by our nuclear waste, Bök points out, and the fossil evidence of the mass extinctions humanity has already wrought). In the backdrop of this apocalyptic conceptual poem, to be sure, lies the threat of ecological disaster. Driving it, however, is a sense of the precious unlikeliness of animate matter, let alone *conscious* matter, within a cosmic context, and the need to preserve human interiority in some permanent, verbal form given the physical fragility of human bodies and conventional poetic substrates as repositories of meaning. By dismantling an expressive object (a poem) and "returning" it, in a sense, to biochemical form, and by inventing a kind of ventriloquism with which to make apparently unconscious matter "speak," Bök stresses in *The Xenotext* that all creativity takes place in and through the unlikely, inhibitory, and eminently delicate environment of embodied being.

Engineering the microbe in order to make it "not only a durable archive for storing a poem, but also a useable machine for writing a poem," Bök composes his apocalyptic text so that once it is assimilated into the genome of *D. radiodurans*, the organism will "read" the lines and respond by expressing a protein whose chemical structure encrypts a second poem.[72] That *D. radiodurans* brings the protein poem into being independently has suggested to some commentators that the bacterium "coauthors" *The Xenotext,* but of course Bök scripts the primary genetic poem and the complementary protein poem in advance; the microbe's role in the construction of the poem's meaning lies in the astronomically limiting constraints its chemical complexity imposes on its diction and syntax. The process through which Bök applies these constraints to the conception and execution of his poem—and reminds his readers, through exaggerated artifice, that consciousness and expression arise only as emergent effects of natural mechanisms—is extravagantly intricate. In order to encrypt his own words into the DNA of *D. radiodurans*, Bök assigns the letters of the English alphabet to twenty-six codons, the triplets of nucleotides that make up genes. During the process of RNA transcription, which allows the instructions in the gene to be translated into amino acids and thence proteins, each of the nucleotides is translated into its biochemical complement (thymine [T] translates to adenine [A]; guanine [G] to cytosine [C]; cytosine to guanine, and adenine to uracil, which replaces thymine). Thus, in order for the RNA sequence to make a second poem that is "beautiful and makes sense," Bök had to find, within the 7,905,853,580,625 ways of pairing the alphabet's letters, a cipher that would allow him to write two codependent poems at once, neither of which, when translated into codons, would mutate or impair the host organism. Bök devised a computer program to help him find a suitably versatile cipher and found himself with an unexpectedly narrow range of words in each case. "I actually have to generate these texts in response entirely to [the bacterium's] own constraints," Bök explains. "I'm not telling it what to do. Its biological rules are in fact telling me what to do."[73] Allowing his poem to be circumscribed by the chemical vocabulary of *D. radiodurans*, Bök subjects his imagination to "improbable conditions of duress" prescribed by nature. In 2011, Bök settled on a cipher (ANY-THE 112), which he has used to compose and implant *The Xenotext* into the test bacterium *E. coli*, where it has successfully undergone transcription and translation.

The Xenotext clearly features many traditional hallmarks of avant-garde literary experimentation. It strains existing definitions of what poetry is, rendering a transparent idea suddenly opaque (Can a "protein" be a poem? Can a poem live?). It uses extravagant formalism to call the poet's authority over the text into question (Is the poem, in any meaningful sense, composed by *D. radiodurans*? Without will, can an entity—a machine or a bacterium—be an author?) and it "foregrounds its . . . inscription technology," as N. Katherine Hayles puts it, using its materiality "as connective tissue . . . joining the physical and mental."[74] In the final, expressed protein (not the genetic code itself but the macromolecule it scripts), Bök fashions a physical object resistant to "reading" in the conventional sense, undermining the distinction between surface and depth implicit in hermeneutic practice. *The Xenotext* likewise bears out Sol LeWitt's proposition that "when an artist uses a conceptual form of art . . . the execution is a perfunctory affair," for Bök's partially realized idea has nonetheless become a target of enthusiastic analysis among poets, critics, media theorists, and the popular press.[75] Most significantly, by extending poetry beyond the formal limits of the page and the screen, and by inventing an apparently unprecedented poetic form (a pair of poems that mutually encipher each other), Bök's experiment is built to satisfy the vanguard imperative to "make it new." Observing that "postmodern life has utterly recoded the avant-garde demand for radical newness," Bök frames his project in opposition to a narrowly expressive lyric tradition. "The future of poetry," he explains, "may no longer reside in the standard lyricism of emotional anecdotes, but in other exploratory procedures, some of which may seem entirely unpoetic, because they work, not by expressing subjective thoughts, but by exploiting unthinking machines, by colonizing unfamiliar lexicons, or by simulating unliterary art forms."[76]

And yet in light of Bök's description of his procedural experiment as the kind of poem that resists lyric emotion and voice and that exploits the "unthinking," "unliterary" biological apparatus of his host germ, the style of *The Xenotext* itself is surprising. Bök nicknames the original poem to be assimilated directly into the DNA of *D. radiodurans*—the poem which makes a treacherous descent from visible, textual form into an invisible, encrypted molecular structure—*Orpheus,* and names the derived poem, guided by *Orpheus*'s chemical music from a state of obscure, enciphered possibility into macromolecular expression, *Eurydice.* Letter by letter, in a pair of fourteen-line poems that allude to the erotic tensions of the sonnet, the poems are interlocked in a formal duet, singing to each other in complementary (and distinctly masculine and feminine) voices.[77]

ALPHABET: a b c d e f g h i j k l m n o p q r s t u v w x y z
XENOCODE: t v u k y s p n o x d r w h i g z l f a c b m j e q

POET (DNA ENCODED TEXT)	GERM (RNA ENCODED TEXT)
any style of life	the faery is rosy
is prim	of glow
oh stay	in fate
my lyre	we rely
with wily ploys	moan more grief
moan the riff	with any loss
the riff	any loss
of any tune aloud	is the achy trick
moan now my fate	with him we stay
in fate	oh stay
we rely	my lyre
my myth	we wean
now is the word	him of any milk
the word of life	any milk is rosy

The speaker of the first poem—a conflation of its Orphic, human engineer and the poem itself—is preoccupied by the generative constraints that underpin nature; having adopted the "wily ploy" of appearing in a living strain of DNA, the singer proposes that any "style" of life, whether instantiated in the evolved form of a species or in the exacting design of Bök's poem, is "prim" in its expression of an immanent, natural order. The singer thus enjoins his lyre, a metonym for its counterpart technology, *D. radiodurans,* to impede ("stay") the flow of his song, ensuring its biological and aesthetic permanence through its submission to inherited, chemical rules. Drawing a punning link between the expressive, improvised "riff" of artistic will and the restraining force of formal "fate," the speaker, humble at first, longs to "moan . . . any tune aloud"—to produce a poem *allowed* by the germ's genetic constraints that is also intelligible enough to be heard by audiences in the present and the deep future. The poem's self-effacing tone soon shifts, however, in recognition of its author's extravagantly ambitious enterprise; *Orpheus* demands that the organism sing "now," and that it intone not just any permissible "riff" but a legible account of poetry's past, present, and future—what the poem, standing in for its genre, calls "my fate." As the word is made flesh and the ur-myth of Western lyric ("my myth," *Orpheus* boasts) is translated into the language of life itself, nature ("the word of life") emerges as the central myth that has "now," at the moment of the poem's writing, supplanted divinity as a final object of reverence, having come to underpin the fate of poetry as both a constraining muse and a substrate for inscription.

Appropriately, *Eurydice,* the poem composed "autonomously" by the alien germ itself, "speaks" in a more cryptic idiom than the enciphered "human" poem to which it ambivalently responds. Invisibly tiny, immortally resilient (if not supernatural), *Eurydice* imagines herself as a "faery"—a tutelary spirit charged, since Bök imagines the poem as a permanent molecular archive, with the destiny of human expression. Archived in the felicitous word "faery" itself, which descends from *fatum* (that which has been spoken), is the numinous, ultimately verbal force personified in the Celtic faeries' classical precursors, the Fates. *Eurydice* recognizes that her own fate, letter by letter, is tied inexorably to this indulgent, anthropocentric poetry of human loss ("with him we stay" she helplessly vows), and discerns the apocalyptic, melancholy origins of Bök's genetic gimmick, which she mournfully describes as an "achy trick." Emerging from oblivion in a "rosy / . . . glow," *Eurydice* alludes to the nostalgic ambience surrounding her conception and to the poem's concrete means of innovative, molecular genesis. On the one hand, that rosy glow evokes the twilight of human civilization that *The Xenotext* perceives itself to occupy and, within a specifically literary heritage, the mythic resurrections with which the Celtic Twilight, full of its own Yeatsian faeries and wistful archaisms, responded to a benighted modern milieu. On the other hand, the "rosy / . . . glow" that surrounds *Eurydice* alludes to the red fluorescent protein that the geneticists conducting *The Xenotext* experiment use to signal the successful expression of the *Eurydice* gene as a protein. The climactic final lines of the poem thus refer to the Romantic glow of this annunciatory flare, even as *Eurydice* rises to her threatening assertion that she—and the cascade of identical protein poems that will follow her—may not preserve the subjectivity of their hubristic human maker but rather "wean" *The Xenotext* of the "milk" of its human origins.

For all his mistrust of "standard lyricism" and subversive regard for the "unliterary," Bök does not surrender morbidly to biological rules in *The Xenotext* but choreographs an extravagant, elegiac performance within them—one that expresses his ecological solicitude and the amplitude of his speculative imagination as it ranges over vast panoramas of time and space, adopting a perspective from which human consciousness and its cultural manifestations appear as unfathomably unlikely as the earth appears from outer space, a luminous, fragile exception in an ominous void. The emergence of mind out of the mindless processes of nature forms a backdrop for Bök's fetishization of the material process of poetic composition, both to instill skepticism toward the transcendental sources of art and to inspire wonder at the emergence of voice from the meaningless silence of matter. Indeed, with its elaborate verbal engineering in the medium of life, Bök's poem reanimates Romantic analogies between divine creation and poesis (in its most capacious sense of "making"). By adopting cells as durable substrates for writing and reading, Bök reminds us that the semiotic activities of enciphering and decoding underpin creation. Conceiving of genomes as codes, assigning letters to

nucleotides, describing chemical processes as "transcription," "translation," and "expression," we have grown accustomed to imagining our cells
(and, by extension, our selves) as machines made out of language, as William Carlos Williams imagined poems to be—and to conceiving of our
poems as reflections of the natural mechanisms whence they issue.[78]

Beyond the Fenced Horizon:
Lyric and Anti-Lyric Reading

The wary vanguardisms of Lin, Spahr and Buuck, Mullen, and Bök thus
suggest the diverse sources of inspiration and anxiety twenty-first-century
poets now find in the dissolving boundary between mind and world that
brain science, genetics, and the digital revolution have pictured for us in
recent decades. The atomization of complex sums of human experience
into bits of information processed by biological and technological media
holds obvious appeal for poets committed to the dogmas of the avant-garde
tradition, to its soluble subject and zealous epistemology of the concrete.
But poetic projects like the ones I have addressed in these last pages—
works that aspire to "bend the sound of poems and anti-poems beyond the
fenced horizon," as Spahr and Buuck put it—have been among the most
artistically exciting and insightful in surveying the implications of cultural neurologism for theoretical questions that urgently preoccupy contemporary poetry and its readers.[79] Recruiting cognitive materialism not
to expunge lyric values *tout court* but to diffuse and redistribute those
values in novel arrangements, these poets express aesthetic and political
conviction, flaunt imaginative ingenuity, and voice nuances of inarticulate
feeling even as they go to radical formal lengths to dispel illusions of
authorial autonomy and inviolable expressive authenticity.

Driven by earnest political and philosophical conviction to stress the impersonal forces through which culture tacitly supervenes upon individual
experience, these poets present themselves with a worthwhile challenge
when they incorporate the phenomenological realities of personal will and
emotion within their work. In a summary of the searching questions that
motivate the most shrewd and insightful conceptualists, Caroline Bergvall
implies the stakes of such questions for our very conception of the literary:

> If literature is perceived as a mediating apparatus, a symbolic repre-
> sentation that highlights features of social engineering as much as of
> individual motivation, how does one create textual works where the
> authorial hold over the text is somehow distanced, perhaps neutral-
> ized, yet where the structural impact of experience, of living, of loving,
> of knowing, of reading are in fact recognized. . . . How does one make
> conceptually-led work that does not do away, ignore, silence or mute
> some of the messy complications of socio-cultural belonging, but
> rather collects from the structure itself?[80]

The primary points of contention in contemporary poetics to which
Bergvall's précis alludes—the status of the (engineered or essential, de-
centered or unified) subject and the status of affect and sensuousness as
autotelic sources of value in literary art—are cruxes that are by now all
too familiar to readers of recent poetry. As I suggested at the beginning
of this book, these are also precisely the axes along which the practice of
poetry criticism has become polarized in recent years, as readers of
poetry have gravitated, since the advent of cultural criticism, toward
opposing methodological positions that represent countervailing conceptions of selfhood and authorship. At one pole, the poet remains an
autonomous maker of original meaning; the hermeneutic style Virginia
Jackson has named "lyric reading" entails projecting a congeries of idealist values (voice, presence, coherence, authorized meaning) onto *all*
poems, even ones originally produced and circulated without reference
to, or in opposition to, the historical category of "lyric."[81] At the other
pole, the poet is a passive, permeable construct whose imagination reflects
cultural circumstance; this conception of authorship tends to characterize
sociological criticism that mines poetic texts for indices of contingent,
shared contexts and, in doing so, risks, as Rachel Blau DuPlessis observes,
"reduc[ing] a text to a message."[82] The special challenges that poetry's
concentrated verbal patterning, diversity of forms, and affective dimensions have presented for symptomatic reading have exacerbated this critical division, as some readers have made a fetish of the individual poetic
imagination while others have declined to recognize it.

But as the " 'expressive lyric' " has become, in Gillian White's words,
"the chief abjection of a powerful and increasingly canonical avant-garde
anti-lyricism now forty years in the making," entrenched fissures in the

landscape of contemporary poetry itself have reinforced and perpetuated the methodological opposition between putatively canonical, New Critical, lyric readerships and progressive, culturally oriented, anti-lyric ones.[83] Like Maria Damon and Ira Livingston, critics who, in their introduction to *Poetry and Cultural Studies: A Reader* (2009), prefer to regard poetry as one piece of the big picture of "expressive culture," Craig Dworkin, in his introduction to *Against Expression: An Anthology of Conceptual Writing,* calls for "a theoretically based art that is independent of genre, so that a particular poem might have more in common with a particular musical score, or film, or sculpture than with another lyric."[84] Vanessa Place and Robert Fitterman go so far as to propose that conceptualism "might best be defined, not by the strategies used but by the expectations of the readership or *thinkership,*" suggesting that an anti-institutional, oppositional, materialist ethos of reception does not merely characterize the audience for conceptual writing but in effect constitutes that writing.[85] Much as "the reading of the lyric," according to Jackson, "produces a theory of the lyric that then produces a reading of the lyric" in a self-perpetuating hermeneutic circle, mutually reinforcing assemblages of values, it seems, have engendered anti-lyric modes of reading and writing that complement and promote one another.[86]

Unsurprisingly, these insular circuits of lyric and anti-lyric composition and interpretation have proven ill equipped to recognize the philosophical eccentricity within contemporary poetry's putatively idealist "mainstream" and putatively materialist "avant-garde." It has therefore been among the methodological ambitions of this book to propose that the coercive biases of idealist and materialist reading are most valuable when they are applied perversely—to reveal lyric superstition abiding in poems that militate "against expression" and to reveal irrepressible doubt abiding in apparently naïve forms of lyric speakership. The surfaces and depths of psychoanalytic reading and the interlocked binaries of deconstructive reading might legitimately justify such critical perversity, but so too does the simple conviction that durable art, however impassioned, is not doctrinaire—that we make poetry, to paraphrase Yeats, out of the quarrel with ourselves, including the internalizations of institutional power the self condenses. Echo chambers of solidarity among writers and readers risk muting, rather than revealing and amplifying, poems' nuances of internal dissent, and threaten to drown out the quarrels that make poetry—"the clear expression of mixed feelings," in Auden's words—something different from mere argumentation. Better for readers, I should think, to balance the pleasure of discovering our own values reflected in poems with the pleasure of having our values challenged by them, and to greet the sociological and aesthetic terms artists use to frame their endeavors with respectful skepticism. By demonstrating how a "social element" pervasive within poems, to borrow from Adorno, can "lead not away from the work of art but deeper into it," I have therefore pursued here a method that inverts the priority of context over text in the practice of cultural poetics, asking not what kind of cultural work poems perform but what kind of insight into individual poems and oeuvres we can gain by tracking a lineament of culture through the ambitious, imaginative distortions of unique creative minds. Such a method is well positioned to read poetries of the soi-disant "mainstream" and "avant-garde" for countercurrents that attest to the heuristic limits of this belabored opposition—particularly when it is seen to hinge on antithetical conceptions of the seat of consciousness, the self, the lyric "I."[87]

For while the binary of tradition and experiment carries enduring intellectual and emotional significance for oppositional poets and readers alike, this binary conceals more than it clarifies the flexibly materialist picture of consciousness upon which poets of both affiliations have lately converged—a picture of emergent rather than transcendental, constrained rather than capacious subjectivity, underwritten by a fundamentally somatic conception of mental life. If, for the "experimentalist" Tan Lin, twenty-first-century consciousness reflects the mechanisms of body and computer such that reading resolves into "information linked to other information" and "the web appears to do one's thinking (or writing/reading) for one," so too does the embodied mind seem to administrate the "mainstream" laureate Kay Ryan's experience, as she imagines persons as "scant information / timed to supplant / the same scant / information" and attributes to the brain "this built-in autonomic faith" that "apparently keeps all the bits animated"; if Juliana Spahr and David Buuck imagine forms of political repression and frustration as neurological disorders in their antipoetic, conceptual prose, so too does Cathy Park Hong, a poet of "high lyricism" by her own account, in *Dance Dance*

Revolution, a dystopian allegory "textured through and through by neurological symptoms"; if Christian Bök imagines human consciousness, encrypted in DNA, adrift in the vacuum of outer space, so too does Jane Hirshfield's lyric speaker at her kitchen table, imagining "Desire inside A C A G G A T / Forgiveness in G T A C T T" as she affirms that "In a world of space and time, arrangement matters."[88] For each of these poets, forms of friction and limitation familiar from somatic experience permeate the experience of thinking, and the discourses of the embodied mind offer enticing opportunities to unravel the transcendental pieties that are woven into the history of poetry. But as such opportunities have proliferated to a surfeit, the challenge of credibly reconstituting lyric ideals has become for these poets newly enticing as well. Straining against outdated lyric and anti-lyric chauvinisms grounded in absolute, idealist and materialist conceptions of the self, they acknowledge sources of value in the expressive powers of a redefined lyric mode—one that has proven to be less naïve and more adaptable than we have yet been prepared to acknowledge.

Notes

Introduction

1. A. R. Ammons, "Mechanism," in *Expressions of Sea Level* (Columbus: Ohio State University Press, 1963), 34–35.
2. For a recent cultural history of the rise of brain science and its effects on our understanding of human behavior over the latter half of the twentieth century—decades during which the neurobiological premise that "mind is what brain does" (3) evolved from a progressive, scientific stance to a tacit pillar of our self-understanding—see Nikolas S. Rose and Joelle M. Abi-Rached, *Neuro: The New Brain Sciences and the Management of the Mind* (Princeton, NJ: Princeton University Press, 2013).
3. James Merrill, *The Changing Light at Sandover: With the Stage Adaptation Voices from Sandover,* ed. J. D. McClatchy and Stephen Yenser (New York: Alfred A. Knopf, 2006), 110; Jorie Graham, *Erosion* (Princeton, NJ: Princeton University Press, 1983), 40.
4. See J. A. Fodor, *The Modularity of Mind* (Cambridge, MA: MIT Press, 1983), and *The Mind Doesn't Work That Way* (Cambridge, MA: MIT Press, 2000); Daniel Dennett, *Elbow Room: The Varieties of Free Will Worth Wanting* (Cambridge, MA: MIT Press, 1984), and *Freedom Evolves* (London: Penguin Books, 2003); Paul Churchland, *Plato's Camera: How the Physical Brain Captures a Landscape of Abstract Universals* (Cambridge, MA: MIT Press, 2012); Patricia Smith Churchland, *Braintrust: What Neuroscience Tells Us about Morality* (Princeton, NJ: Princeton University Press, 2011); John Searle, *Mind, Language and Society: Philosophy in the Real World* (New York, NY: Basic Books, 1999).
5. See, for example, Steven Pinker, *How the Mind Works* (New York: W. W. Norton, 1999), and *The Blank Slate: The Modern Denial of Human Nature* (New York: Penguin, 2003); Antonio Damasio, *Descartes' Error: Emotion, Reason, and the Human Brain* (New

York: G.P. Putnam, 1994), *The Feeling of What Happens: Body and Emotion In the Making of Consciousness* (New York: Harcourt, 2000), and *Self Comes to Mind: Constructing the Conscious Brain* (New York: Pantheon Books, 2010).

6. Paul and Patricia Churchland have made a particular target of "the prescientific, commonsense conceptual framework" they call "folk psychology," claiming that terms such as "belief, desire, pain, pleasure, love, hate, joy, fear, suspicion, memory, recognition, anger, sympathy, intention, and so forth" ought to be eliminated in favor of a neuroscientific terminology they deem more philosophically precise (see Churchland and Churchland, *On the Contrary: Critical Essays, 1987–1997* [Cambridge, MA: MIT Press, 1998], 3). Neuroscientists and cognitive scientists have been among the most visible recent critics of organized religion on rational and empirical grounds, particularly Daniel Dennett (*Breaking the Spell: Religion as a Natural Phenomenon* [London: Penguin Books, 2007]) and Sam Harris (*The Moral Landscape: How Science Can Determine Human Values* [New York: Free Press, 2010]).

7. John Ashbery, *Flow Chart* (New York: Knopf, 1991), 129.

8. Adrian Desmond and James Moore quote Darwin's "bon mot" in *Darwin* (New York, NY: W. W. Norton, 1994), 251.

9. Charles Darwin, *The Descent of Man, and Selection in Relation to Sex,* vol. 1 (New York: D. Appleton, 1872), 35.

10. Charles Darwin, *On Evolution: The Development of the Theory of Natural Selection,* ed. Thomas F. Glick and David Kohn (Indianapolis, IN: Hackett, 1996), 77; Charles Darwin and Paul H. Barrett, *Charles Darwin's Notebooks, 1836–1844: Geology, Transmutation of Species, Metaphysical Enquiries* (London: British Museum of Natural History, 1987), 300.

11. George John Romanes, *Mental Evolution in Man: Origin of Human Faculty* (New York: D. Appleton, 1888), 2.

12. For a thorough timeline of pivotal developments in neurology, psychology, and the commerce between Western mind science and modernist literature, see Mark S. Micale, *The Mind of Modernism: Medicine, Psychology, and the Cultural Arts in Europe and America, 1880–1940* (Stanford, CA: Stanford University Press, 2004). On literary and cultural representations of genetically inherited memory and unconscious cerebration, see Laura Otis, *Organic Memory: History and the Body in the Late Nineteenth and Early Twentieth Centuries* (Lincoln: University of Nebraska Press, 1994).

13. Raymond Williams, *Problems in Materialism and Culture: Selected Essays* (London: Verso, 1980), 40.

14. Simon Jarvis, "Adorno, Marx, Materialism," in *The Cambridge Companion to Adorno,* ed. Thomas Huhn (Cambridge: Cambridge University Press, 2004), 79.

15. See Thomas Nagel, "What Is It Like to Be a Bat?" in *Mortal Questions* (London: Cambridge University Press, 1991), 165–180.

16. Raymond Tallis, "What Neuroscience Cannot Tell Us about Ourselves," *New Atlantis* 29 (Fall 2010): 3–26, http://www.thenewatlantis.com/publications/what-neuroscience-cannot-tell-us-about-ourselves.

17. David Chalmers, "Facing Up to the Problem of Consciousness," *Journal of Consciousness Studies* 2, no. 3 (1995): 200–201.

18. Philip Fried, "'A Place You Can Live': An Interview with A. R. Ammons," in *Critical Essays on A. R. Ammons,* ed. Robert Kirschten (New York: G. K. Hall, 1997), 105.

19. A. R. Ammons, *Sumerian Vistas: Poems* (New York: Norton, 1987), 7.

20. Ammons, "Mechanism," 35. Describing her own habit of initially improvising and then rigorously repeating stanzas, Marianne Moore draws a similar comparison: "Words cluster like chromosomes," she explains, "determining the procedure" (*A Marianne Moore Reader* [New York: Viking Press, 1961, 263]).

21. Graham, *Erosion,* 27 (Graham's italics).

22. Matthew Arnold, "Preface to First Edition of Poems [1853]," in *The Complete Prose Works of Matthew Arnold,* vol. 1, *On the Classical Tradition,* ed. R. H. Super (Ann Arbor, MI: University of Michigan Press, 1960), 1.

23. It is worth acknowledging that there is no universally accepted definition of the lyric. In her critique of the "lyricization" of poetry in the twentieth century—the tendency to ascribe expressive voices to all kinds of poetic texts that may have circulated without intentionally participating in this idealized practice of "lyric" self-expression—Virginia Jackson strenuously objects to the widespread projection of personal presence into poetic texts, a phenomenon she attributes to the popularization of New Critical reading practices. In his recent *Theory of the Lyric,* however, Jonathan Culler valuably emphasizes that the influential, Hegelian definition of the lyric to which the poets in this book are heirs does not require that a lyric meditate explicitly upon the flow of inward impressions, or be naively self-expressive, or even obviously *voiced;* rather, Hegel specifies that the "linkage" that unifies the diverse features of the lyric poem "consists solely in the fact that one and the same self carries them" (G. W. F. Hegel, *Aesthetics* [Oxford: Oxford University Press, 1973], 1133). "Thus, despite the centrality of subjectivity to [Hegel's] account of the essential nature of the lyric," Culler observes, "subjectivity functions as a principle of unity rather than a principle of individuation: what is essential in this theory is not that the formulations of a lyric reflect the particular experience of an individual but that they be attributed to a subject, which brings them together" (95). It is in this much more capacious sense, I think, that the lyric continues to be understood profitably as the genre of inner life, or of subjective self-experience; the writerly and readerly expectation that the poem emanates from a single consciousness manifesting its energies in (harmonious or discordant, organized or entropic) sonic and visual patterns strikes me as a perfectly plausible and productive understanding of lyric as a generic category. Indeed, for my purposes in this book—the central chapters of which are addressed to poets who may or may not write poems of personal experience in the first person but for whom the boundaries and sources of selfhood and consciousness are primary philosophical and aesthetic concerns—no narrower, formal, or content-driven subgenre of poetry (sonnet, elegy, ode, dramatic monologue, verse epistle, epic) would suffice. As Culler observes, "the romantic model of the lyric . . . has remained very much on the horizon for poets in the twentieth century—if only as a model to be resisted or rejected" (85); as a result of the endemic "lyricization" of poetry Jackson laments, lyric has remained, up to the present, the dominant paradigm in relation to which late twentieth-century poetry asks to be read.

24. I resist the temporal terms "avant-garde" and "vanguard" to describe poets who are critical of aesthetic norms and bourgeois values, for the great innovation of the

"historical avant-gardes," as Peter Bürger has argued, was to transform "the historical succession of techniques and styles" into a simultaneity in which "no movement . . . can legitimately claim to be historically more advanced *as art* than any other" (*Theory of the Avant-Garde* [Manchester: Manchester University Press, 1984], 63). Such terms, however, remain necessary, both for their abiding significance to the many poets who do credit narratives of advancement and because "avant-garde" effectively signifies the ethos of aesthetic and ideological opposition that gives meaningful coherence to distinct lines of descent within the history of American poetry. I therefore accept and deploy these terms with the understanding that the mainstream/vanguard divide is a crude, overfamiliar "sorting engine" (Oren Izenberg, *Being Numerous: Poetry and the Ground of Social Life* [Princeton, NJ: Princeton University Press, 2011], 8) with which to describe recent poetry; that the experimental tradition, for all its forms of freshness, is replete with its own orthodoxies fostered in institutional harbors; and that the pejorative label "mainstream" represents a false unity that this binary constructs and promotes. What I question here (and what readings attuned to the concept of mind implicit in much recent poetry are well positioned to contest) is the proposition that idealist and materialist conceptions of the self are condensed in this binary—that the ontological coherence of the expressive self, in other words, continues to be a meaningful axis along which to distinguish poetic kinds in the twenty-first century. For sensitive arguments in favor of and against the continuing use of the term "avant-garde" in the context of contemporary poetry, see Marjorie Perloff, *Radical Artifice: Writing Poetry in the Age of Media* (Chicago: University of Chicago Press, 1991), and Izenberg, *Being Numerous*, respectively.

25. It is a testament to these diverse poets that readers will immediately recognize the limits of these categorizations. Ashbery and Graham have been claimed at times by both readerships, and A. R. Ammons's reception history has placed him in an idealist lineage my own readings challenge, emphasizing experimental features that affiliate him more closely with William Carlos Williams and Robert Creeley than with Ralph Waldo Emerson and Wallace Stevens. The proposition that materialist and idealist modes of reading have exaggerated philosophical oppositions between these groups of poets is precisely the point to which I will turn at the end of this introduction and in the conclusion. The quoted phrase is Cole Swensen's; see her introduction to *American Hybrid: A Norton Anthology of New Poetry*, ed. Cole Swensen and David St. John (New York: W. W. Norton, 2009), xviii, for a representative description of "the fundamental division" of American poetry along these philosophical lines.

26. Ezra Pound, *Cantos of Ezra Pound* (New York: New Directions, 1993), 538.

27. Robert Lowell and Frederick Seidel, "Robert Lowell: The Art of Poetry No. 3," *Paris Review* 25 (Winter–Spring 1961), http://www.theparisreview.org/interviews/4664/the-art-of-poetry-no-3-robert-lowell.

28. See James Longenbach, *Modern Poetry after Modernism* (Oxford: Oxford University Press, 1997), 7; Marjorie Perloff, *21st-Century Modernism: The "New" Poetics* (Malden, MA: Blackwell, 2002), 5; Jennifer Ashton, *From Modernism to Postmodernism: American Poetry and Theory in the Twentieth Century* (Cambridge: Cambridge University Press, 2005); Christopher Ricks, *True Friendship: Geoffrey Hill, Anthony Hecht, and*

Robert Lowell under the Sign of Eliot and Pound (New Haven, CT: Yale University Press, 2010).

29. See Altieri's "From Symbolist Thought to Immanence: The Ground of Postmodern American Poetics," *boundary 2* 1, no. 3 (1973): 605–642. In his argument that postmodernist poetry exhibits "renewed attention to the biological" and "the necessary as opposed to the creative" (613), Altieri has confessional poets particularly in mind. He writes of Robert Lowell, for example, that "along with [Lowell's 'habit of conceiving human problems along the metaphorical lines of biological process'] goes an increasing passivity, a surrender of a faith in man's creative processes in favor of at least the appearance of becoming merely a vehicle for experience" (615–616).

30. The importance of biological "environments" to contemporary poets raises the question of why those of us who are interested in literature written since the cognitive revolution have largely neglected contemporary literature's ambitious and self-conscious representations of the embodied mind. Predictably, perhaps, the influence of the philosophy and science of the mind upon contemporary literature has been recognized primarily within the study of science fiction; see Nikki Skillman, "James Merrill's Embodied Memory," *Twentieth Century Literature* 59, no. 4 (Winter 2013), for references to recent criticism by N. Katherine Hayles, Joseph Tabbi, Robert Chodat, and others who have addressed themselves to mind science in recent fiction.

31. Jack Spicer, *The House That Jack Built: The Collected Lectures of Jack Spicer,* ed. Peter Gizzi (Middletown, CT: Wesleyan University Press, 1998), 5.

32. On the materialist poetics and philosophy of mind that preceded this idealist continuum, see Jonathan Kramnick, *Action and Objects from Hobbes to Richardson* (Stanford, CA: Stanford University Press, 2010).

33. See especially M. H. Abrams, *The Mirror and the Lamp: Romantic Theory and the Critical Tradition* (Oxford: Oxford University Press, 1971). Long-standing recognition that philosophy of mind profoundly informs the phenomenology and aesthetics of Romantic poetry has encouraged literary critics to explore the commerce between mind science and literary representations of cognition during the Romantic period (see, for example, Alan Richardson's *British Romanticism and the Science of the Mind* [Cambridge: Cambridge University Press, 2001] and Noel Jackson's *Science and Sensation in Romantic Poetry* [Cambridge, UK: Cambridge University Press, 2008]). Likewise, there has been vast contextual inquiry into modernism's formative absorption of psychoanalytic theory, neurology, and the philosophy of mind. Observing how the cultural transformations of modernism "occurred precisely when the distinctively modern disciplines of psychology, psychiatry, and psychoanalysis began to establish their 'scientific' foundations," Micale assembles in *The Mind of Modernism* an impressive variety of essays addressing the intellectual commerce between literary and scientific discourses during this period.

34. William Wordsworth, *The Prelude; or, Growth of a Poet's Mind: An Autobiographical Poem* (London: E. Moxon 1850), 48; William Wordsworth, *The Poems of William Wordsworth,* ed. Samuel Weiselberg (London: E. Moxon, 1847), 144.

35. Ralph Waldo Emerson, Alfred Riggs Ferguson, and Jean Ferguson Carr, *The Essays of Ralph Waldo Emerson,* vol. 1 (Cambridge, MA: Harvard University Press, 1987), 38.

36. *Brooklyn Daily Eagle,* November 16, 1846. Nathaniel Mackey traces the documentation of Whitman's interest in phrenology to this year, when the poet also clipped an article about phrenology from an issue of *American Review.* Mackey's essay "Phrenological Whitman," in *Paracritical Hinge: Essays, Talks, Notes, Interviews* (Madison: University of Wisconsin Press, 2005), 21–39, situates Whitman's various writings on and references to phrenology within the contexts of a rising commercial self-help industry, social reform movements, racist evolutionism, and American expansionism. See also Arthur Wrobel, "Whitman and the Phrenologists: The Divine Body and the Sensuous Soul," *PMLA* 89 no. 1 (1974): 17–23, and Madeleine Betting Stern, *Heads and Headlines: The Phrenological Fowlers* (Norman: University of Oklahoma Press, 1971).

37. Quoted in Mackey, "Phrenological Whitman," 23; Ralph Waldo Emerson, Alfred Riggs Ferguson, and Jean Ferguson Carr, *The Essays of Ralph Waldo Emerson,* vol. 3 (Cambridge, MA: Harvard University Press, 1987), 5.

38. Walt Whitman and David S. Reynolds. *Leaves of Grass* (New York: Oxford University Press, 2005), v, 112, ix.

39. Charlotte Fowler Wells, "Sketches of Phrenological Biography," *Phrenological Journal and Science of Health,* vol. 2 (New York: Fowler & Wells, 1895), 318.

40. Orson Squire Fowler and Lorenzo Niles Fowler, "The American Phrenological Journal for 1849: Its Prospects and Course," *American Phrenological Journal and Miscellany,* vol. 11 (Philadelphia: A. Waldie, 1849), 10.

41. Walt Whitman, *Complete Poetry and Collected Prose* (New York: Literary Classics of the United States, 1982), 569.

42. Ibid., 1.

43. Emily Dickinson, Thomas Herbert Johnson, Cid Corman, and Mary Ellen Solt, *The Complete Poems of Emily Dickinson* (Boston: Little, Brown, 1960), 493.

44. Ibid., 439, 162, 478, 128.

45. Ibid., 312.

46. Thomas Henry Huxley, "Science," in *The Reign of Queen Victoria: A Survey of Fifty Years of Progress,* ed. Thomas Humphrey, vol. 2 (London: Smith, Elder, 1887), 322; William Wordsworth and Samuel Taylor Coleridge, *Lyrical Ballads: 1798 and 1800,* ed. Michael Gamer and Dalia Porter (Toronto: Broadview, 2008), 288.

47. John Brenkman, "Freud the Modernist," in Micale, *Mind of Modernism,* 172.

48. D. H. Lawrence, "Preface to the American Edition of *New Poems,*" in *Poetics of the New American Poetry,* ed. Donald Merriam Allen and Warren Tallman (New York: Random House, 1974), 195.

49. James Joyce and Theodore Spencer, *Stephen Hero* (New York: New Directions, 1955), 190.

50. T. E. Hulme, "Romanticism and Classicism," in *The Collected Writings of T. E. Hulme,* ed. Karen Csengeri (Oxford: Clarendon Press, 1994), 62.

51. Albert Gelpi, *A Coherent Splendor: The American Poetic Renaissance, 1910–1950* (Cambridge: Cambridge University Press, 1987), 10. With characteristic critical emphasis on the reductive threats of economic (rather than biological) materialism, Charles Altieri further defends high modernists against the charge of Romantic naïveté by arguing that "they flirted with idealism largely because that thinking provided the best practical means to oppose an increasingly dominant and reductive empiricism that was commodi-

fying everything in its path." Altieri, "The Sensuous Dimension of Literary Experience: An Alternative to Materialist Theory," *New Literary History* 38, no. 1 (Winter 2007): 79.

52. In *Irresistible Dictation: Gertrude Stein and the Correlations of Writing and Science* (Stanford, CA: Stanford University Press, 2001), Steven Meyer traces the deep influence of William James's radical empiricism—and physiological psychology more generally—on Stein's philosophy of mind and aesthetics; Meyer proposes "that the neuron doctrine played a crucial, and among major writers unique, role in the development of Stein's compositional practices" (xx).

53. Gertrude Stein, *The Autobiography of Alice B. Toklas* (New York: Vintage Books, 1960), 99.

54. William James, *The Principles of Psychology* (Cambridge, MA: Harvard University Press, 1981), 185 (James's italics).

55. Lewellys F. Barker, *The Nervous System and Its Constituent Neurones: Designed for the Use of Practitioners of Medicine and of Students of Medicine and Psychology* (New York: D. Appleton, 1899), 60. Former peers in the scientific community, as if in caricature, would attribute Stein's strange literary forms to undiagnosed neurological and psychological pathologies. A *Newsweek* article covering Stein's 1934 lecture tour, for example, reports that Dr. Morris Fishbein, editor of the *Journal of the American Medical Association,* concluded after hearing Stein read that "she might be suffering from palilalia . . . a frequent hangover from encephalitis"; see Meyer, *Irresistible Dictation,* 52–54.

56. During her undergraduate years at Radcliffe, Stein published two articles in the *Psychological Review* that investigate the phenomenon of automatic writing. The first, entitled "Normal Motor Automatism" (1896), was largely the work of her coauthor Leon Solomons; two years later, during her final year, she authored "Cultivated Motor Automatism; a Study of Character in Its Relation to Attention" (1898), which extended the first study by increasing the number of subjects. In response to B. F. Skinner's accusation that her poetic experimentation was the result of automatic writing practices she had honed in James's lab, Stein later claimed never to have credited the phenomenon of automatic writing. For a full account of Stein's repudiation of automatic writing, see Meyer's chapter "Writing Psychology Over: Toward a More Radical Empiricism" in *Irresistible Dictation,* 214–240.

57. Gertrude Stein, *Everybody's Autobiography* (New York: Random House, 1937), 249–250.

58. Meyer, *Irresistible Dictation,* 3. Throughout *Irresistible Dictation,* Meyer presents close readings that correlate Stein's stylistic experiments with her evolving philosophy of mind during this period. Given his ample discussion of the subject and the constraints of space here, it would be redundant to present further readings. See especially "Part One: The Neurophysiological Imagination" (1–51 passim).

59. Gertrude Stein, *Selected Writings* (New York: Knopf Doubleday, 2012), 256.

60. Gertrude Stein, *Writings, 1932–1946: Stanzas in Meditation, Lectures in America, The Geographical History of America, Ida, Brewsie and Willie, Other Works* (New York: Library of America, 1998), 331.

61. Gertrude Stein and Thornton Wilder, *Narration: Four Lectures* (Chicago: University of Chicago Press, 1935), 56.

62. See Manju Jain's *T. S. Eliot and American Philosophy: The Harvard Years* (Cambridge: Cambridge University Press, 1992), especially the chapters that consider Eliot's reading and writing for Josiah Royce's seminar on philosophical methodology and his extensive graduate research into "the 'varieties' of psychological and mystical experience" (pp. 112–204).

63. T. S. Eliot, *Knowledge and Experience in the Philosophy of F. H. Bradley* (London: Faber and Faber, 1964), 113.

64. Ibid., 205–206.

65. Ibid., 153–154.

66. Despite his disapproval of the increasingly positivist bent of Harvard psychology among William James's successors, Eliot appears to have borrowed the famous scientific metaphor with which he pictures this impersonal poetic mind—that of a catalytic "shred of platinum" that transmutes disparate substances into new compounds—from the behaviorist psychologist Edwin Holt, a student and successor of James and Münsterberg who envisioned the mind as an expression of integrated reflexes. See Jain, *T. S. Eliot and American Philosophy*, 165.

67. T. S. Eliot, *The Waste Land and Other Writings* (New York: Modern Library, 2001), 106. See my note below on Eliot's theory of poetic impersonality and "the substantial unity of the soul" in "Tradition and the Individual Talent."

68. Eliot, *Waste Land*, 5–7.

69. "The Post-Georgians," *Athenaeum* 4641 (April 11, 1919): 171; Eliot, *Waste Land*, 134.

70. In his theory of poetic impersonality, Eliot followed Remy de Gourmont, a practitioner of cognitive literary criticism *avant la lettre* whom the young poet honors in his essay "The Perfect Critic" and who proclaims, for example, that "one does not give himself his style; its form is determined by the structure of his brain" (Remy de Gourmont and Glenn S. Burne, *Selected Writings* [Ann Arbor: University of Michigan Press, 1966], 122). Gourmont influenced Eliot deeply as he was formulating his early, now canonical statements of aesthetics; like Gourmont, who proposes that the artist ought to slough off the contingencies of the personal in pursuit of the universal ("The proper end of man's activity," he writes, "is to scour his personality"), Eliot prescribes "a continual extinction of personality" through which "art may be said to approach the condition of science" (Eliot, *Waste Land*, 103). As Eliot strives to make his impersonal theory of poetry comprehensible to his readers, he admits toward the end of "Tradition and the Individual Talent":

    > The point of view which I am struggling to attack is perhaps related to the metaphysical theory of the substantial unity of the soul: for my meaning is, that the poet has, not a "personality" to express, but a particular medium, which is only a medium and not a personality, in which impressions and experiences combine in peculiar and unexpected ways. (Eliot, *Waste Land*, 106)

    Poetry does not express inwardness, Eliot proposes; poetry projects into language the embodied, material "medium" of the poet that is the visible core, the concrete instantiation, of his transcendental soul.

71. Charlotte Eliot and T. S. Eliot, *Savonarola: A Dramatic Poem* (London: R. Cobden-Sanderson, 1926), xi–xii.

72. William Carlos Williams, *The Embodiment of Knowledge* (New York: New Directions, 1977), 51.

73. W. H. Auden and Edward Mendelson, *Selected Poems* (New York: Vintage International, 2007), 102.

74. Ibid., 309.

75. Langston Hughes, Arnold Rampersad, Dolan Hubbard, and Leslie Catherine Sanders, *The Collected Works of Langston Hughes*, vol. 9 (Columbia: University of Missouri Press, 2001), 408.

76. Wallace Stevens, *Collected Poetry and Prose* (New York: Library of America, 1997), 665.

77. William Carlos Williams, A. Walton Litz, and Christopher J. MacGowan, *The Collected Poems of William Carlos Williams* (New York: New Directions, 1986), 178. Pound alludes to the "rose in the steel dust" in Canto 74. See Pound's appraisal of the poetic mind in "Psychology and Troubadours," in *The Spirit of Romance: An Attempt to Define Somewhat the Charm of the Pre-Renaissance Literature of Latin Europe* (London: J. M. Dent & Sons, 1910), which is stark in its dissociation of consciousness from the materiality of the body.

78. Marianne Moore, *Collected Poems* (New York: Macmillan, 1961), 134.

79. Helen Vendler, "A. R. Ammons's Last," *Yale Review* 90, no. 1 (2002): 174.

80. Maria Damon and Ira Livingston, *Poetry and Cultural Studies: A Reader* (University of Illinois Press, 2009), 2.

81. See Stephen Greenblatt's introduction to *Renaissance Self-Fashioning: From More to Shakespeare* (Chicago: University of Chicago Press, 1980), in which Greenblatt proposes that literary criticism "must be conscious of its own status as interpretation and intent upon understanding literature as a part of the system of signs that constitutes a given culture. . . . Its central concerns prevent it from permanently sealing off one type of discourse from another or decisively separating works of art from the minds and lives of their creators and their audiences" (4–5).

82. Michael Davidson, *On the Outskirts of Form: Practicing Cultural Poetics* (Middletown, CT: Wesleyan University Press, 2011), 13. For Davidson's positioning of cultural poetics against symptomatic reading strategies, see his afterword, "Impossible Poetries"; there he writes, "One reason why poetry has fallen off the cultural studies map—if it was ever there in the first place—has been a tendency on the part of cultural critics to treat poetry as a symptom rather than a practice, cultural capital rather than cultural production" (281).

83. Barrett Watten, *The Constructivist Moment: From Material Text to Cultural Poetics* (Middletown, CT: Wesleyan University Press, 2003), xxv.

84. Rachel Blau DuPlessis, "Social Texts and Poetic Texts: Poetry and Cultural Studies," in *The Oxford Handbook of Modern and Contemporary American Poetry,* ed. Cary Nelson (New York: Oxford University Press, 2012), 60–61.

85. In *The Constructivist Moment*, Watten contextualizes the formal procedures of Soviet constructivism, American objectivism, the Language school, and other avant-garde movements to describe how radical art instantiates cultural opposition by devising forms that lay bare the devices of their construction and "disrupt communicative ideals" (xxviii). He stresses the politically progressive, utopian dimensions

of poetic forms that emphasize their own materiality in the process of cultural critique, arguing that articulations of social negativity in concrete aesthetic forms work "both to disclose the nature of the system and to develop an imagined alternative" (xxii). Davidson likewise stresses the dynamic contexts in which aesthetic postures acquire meaning by addressing poetry that lies "on the outskirts of form"; "it is only when poetry refuses to *con*-form to expectations," he writes, "that its function is revealed as provisional and contingent" (*On the Outskirts,* 19). Social and linguistic cataclysm emerge as distinct preoccupations of practitioners of cultural poetics; while Davidson argues, in *On the Outskirts of Form,* that objectivists and New American poets use verbal texture to articulate "a crisis of representability brought about by the globalization of exchange and the corporate destruction of local agency" (15), Christopher Nealon describes how poets responding to the civilizational crisis of advanced capitalism resist "the reduction of the poetic to the lyrical" by "struggl[ing] to develop a kind of poetry that references its textual character as a defense against capitalist spectacle" (*The Matter of Capital: Poetry and Crisis in the American Century* [Cambridge, MA: Harvard University Press, 2011], 34).

86. Within the regrettably small subset of critics attempting to theorize how we ought to relate poetic texts and contexts, Rachel Blau DuPlessis diverges from her peers in considering a diverse range of modernist poets less concentrated at the fringes of formal experimentation. As she proposes a "post-formalist, yet formally articulate cultural analysis of poetry" in *Genders, Races, and Religious Cultures in Modern American Poetry, 1908–1934* (Cambridge: Cambridge University Press, 2001), 6–7, DuPlessis takes as her subject the subtle textual construction of social identities through classic literary phenomena—syntax, rhyme, lineation, imagery, metaphor, and so on. By demonstrating how these formal dimensions of texts facilitate and complicate identity construction, DuPlessis performs exacting, imminent analysis that repositions New Critical strategies "in the service of social identifications, social entitlements, and possibly ideological critique." She calls this the practice of "social philology"— linguistic analysis that sets out to identify how texts perform "cultural work" (11).

87. Helen Vendler, *The Music of What Happens: Poems, Poets, Critics* (Cambridge, MA: Harvard University Press, 1988), 2, Vendler's italics. Vendler inherits her critical emphases on the uniqueness and pleasure of literary experience from Walter Pater, who offered a similar definition of aesthetic criticism as the genre dedicated to disclosing the properties through which works of art "[affect] one with a special, a unique, impression of pleasure" (*The Renaissance* [London: Macmillan, 1900], xi).

88. Altieri, "Sensuous Dimension," 80–81.

89. See, for example, Walter Kalaidjian, "Marketing Modern Poetry and the Southern Public Sphere," in *Marketing Modernisms: Self-Promotion, Canonization, Rereading,* ed. Kevin J. H. Dettmar and Stephen Watt (Ann Arbor: University of Michigan Press, 1996), 297–319; Cary Nelson, *Repression and Recovery: Modern American Poetry and the Politics of Cultural Memory, 1910–1945* (Madison: University of Wisconsin Press, 1989). Nealon criticizes Perloff and Altieri in *The Matter of Capital* for "[giving] us a powerfully depoliticizing language for poetry in the 1980s and 1990s" (11).

90. Susan J. Wolfson, "'Romantic Ideology' and the Values of Aesthetic Form," in George Lewis Levine, *Aesthetics and Ideology* (New Brunswick, NJ: Rutgers University Press,

1994), 212; quoted in DuPlessis, *Genders, Races,* 10. In addition to the critics I've already mentioned (especially Michael Davidson, who stresses "the social and culturally coded meanings attached to formal features" that he calls "ideologies of form" (*Ghostlier Demarcations: Modern Poetry and the Material Word* [Berkeley: University of California Press, 1997], 25), Charles Bernstein is an articulate exponent of historicizing form in the critical process of what he calls "social formalism"; see, for example, "Comedy and the Poetics of Political Form" in *A Poetics* (Cambridge, MA: Harvard University Press, 1992).

91. Marjorie Perloff, "Presidential Address: It Must Change," *PMLA* 122, no. 3 (May 2007): 654. For objections to Perloff's arguments in this address by practitioners of the materialist "New Lyric Studies," see Brent Hayes Edwards's, Stathis Gourgouris's, and Yopie Prins's articles in *PMLA* 123, no. 1 (Jan 2008).

92. Vendler, *Music,* 2.

93. Observing that "the artist uses ideas . . . as functional parts (rather than as ideological determinants) of the work" (*Music,* 4), Vendler's definition of aesthetic criticism acknowledges this structural function of ideological components.

94. George H. W. Bush, Presidential Proclamation 6158, July 17, 1990, http://www.loc.gov /loc/brain/proclaim.html.

95. Fredric Jameson, *Marxism and Form: Twentieth-Century Dialectical Theories of Literature* (Princeton, NJ: Princeton University Press, 1974), 34.

96. There are signs that both extremes are already migrating toward middle ground. The various instantiations of cultural poetics that I have already mentioned obviously recoil from materialist reduction. Reciprocally, historical consciousness is waxing among aesthetic critics. See, for example, Bonnie Costello's *Planets on Tables: Poetry, Still Life, and the Turning World* (Ithaca, NY: Cornell University Press, 2008), a thematic study of one of the most apparently decorative subgenres in fine art—the still life. For Costello, poetic still lifes rendered by Wallace Stevens, William Carlos Williams, Elizabeth Bishop, and Richard Wilbur reveal the function of the twentieth-century lyric as a "foyer," or threshold, "where the individual welcomes the world into his domain and into his 'unofficial view of being'" (xv); maintaining focus on the public realm but reorienting the dominant perspective of the novel, "the lyric concerns itself not so much with the individual going out into the world as with the world entering into the life of the individual" (ix).

97. Though Virginia Jackson condemns "lyric reading" (a concept she adapts from Paul de Man's description of "lyrical reading" in "Anthropomorphism and Trope in the Lyric"), I am inclined to see reading for voice, interiority, expressive individuality, and aesthetic autonomy as one valuable critical orientation among many—one that is especially useful for reading against the grain of poetries that claim to forsake these features. (My readings of "anti-lyric" poets in the conclusion aim to demonstrate this important function of idealist reading.)

98. William Empson, *Seven Types of Ambiguity* (London: Chatto and Windus, 1930), 7.

1. Robert Lowell and the Chemistry of Character

1. Robert Lowell, *The Letters of Robert Lowell,* ed. Saskia Hamilton (New York: Farrar, Straus and Giroux, 2005), 151. Subsequent page references to this volume will be given parenthetically in the text of this chapter as *L.*

2. Esther Brooks, "Remembering Cal," in *Robert Lowell, Interviews and Memoirs,* ed. Jeffrey Meyers (Ann Arbor: University of Michigan Press, 1988), 285. In 1965, Randall Jarrell was hospitalized for a nervous breakdown after being prescribed Elavil, an antidepressant that led him to become manic. A consolatory letter to Jarrell, who would die later that year in what Lowell and many others believed to be a suicide, attests to the fundamental questions of selfhood—of "you" and "not you"—that these breakdowns compelled Lowell to consider in hindsight: "I have been through this sort of thing so often myself that I suppose there's little in your experience that I haven't had over and over," Lowell writes. "What looks as though it were simply you, and therefore would never pass does turn out to be not you and will pass" (*L* 458).

3. Norman Mailer, *The Armies of the Night: History as a Novel, the Novel as History* (New York: New American Library, 1968), 83.

4. Stanley Kunitz, "Talk with Robert Lowell," in Meyers, *Interviews and Memoirs,* 89.

5. Robert Lowell, *Collected Poems,* ed. Frank Bidart and David Gewanter (New York: Farrar, Straus and Giroux, 2003), 114. Subsequent page references to this volume will be given parenthetically in the text of this chapter as *CP.*

6. Saskia Hamilton, in her introduction to *The Letters of Robert Lowell,* notes that "having to integrate his different experiences of self was a pressing and unsolvable problem for Lowell throughout his life, both as he interpreted it and was encouraged to interpret it through the psychiatric and psychotherapeutic treatments he received" (xiv).

7. David Healy, *Mania: A Short History of Bipolar Disorder* (Baltimore: Johns Hopkins University Press, 2008), xviii.

8. See Dan Chiasson, *One Kind of Everything: Poem and Person in Contemporary America* (Chicago: University of Chicago Press, 2007), 25–26.

9. On December 15, 1947, Bishop wrote to Lowell: "I must confess . . . that I am green with envy of your kind of assurance. I feel that I could write in as much detail about my uncle Artie, say—but what would be the significance? Nothing at all. . . . Whereas all you have to do is put down the names! And the fact that it seems significant, illustrative, American, etc., gives you, I think, the confidence you display about tackling any idea or theme, *seriously,* in both writing and conversation. In some ways you are the luckiest poet I know!—in some ways not so lucky, either, of course" (Elizabeth Bishop and Robert Lowell, *Words in Air: The Complete Correspondence between Elizabeth Bishop and Robert Lowell,* ed. Thomas J. Travisano and Saskia Hamilton [New York: Farrar, Straus and Giroux, 2008], 247). Critics such as Maria Damon, for example, have stressed Lowell's "luck" in less admiring terms than Bishop's: "I hope to emphasize [Lowell's] poetry and personal conduct *as social practice*—privileged white male poet(ry) in crisis" Damon writes. "Supremely privileged, preeminently public, and insistent on self-disclosure, Lowell serves as a powerful case study of the pathos of failed liberalism." Maria Damon, *The Dark End of the Street: Margins in American Vanguard Poetry* (Minneapolis: University of Minnesota Press, 1993), 122–123.

10. Chiasson, *One Kind of Everything,* 28.

11. Ibid., 29.

12. In "Soft Wood," for example, Lowell offers his dying cousin Harriet Winslow the sympathy of recognition, "knowing / each drug that numbs alerts another nerve to pain" (*CP* 371); he likewise discerns a kindred spirit in Nathaniel Hawthorne, who "felt those flashes / that char the discharged cells of the brain" (*CP* 351).

13. Lowell, *Collected Poems,* 358 (Lowell's ellipses).

14. Rudolph Allers, *The Psychology of Character* (London: Sheed & Ward, 1931), ix.

15. In a 1945 review of *The Psychology of Character,* Helen Sargent observes that "Allers's neglect of constitutional temperamental factors" reaches a "somewhat startling" extreme in his statement about cerebral legions (Book Reviews, *Journal of Criminal Law and Criminology* 259 [1944–1945]: 251). Lowell recommended *The Psychology of Character* in an undated letter to Peter Taylor, which Saskia Hamilton tentatively dates at 1942. Allers's translator, E. B. Strauss, describes him as a "Catholic Adlerian" (vii), who fuses Catholic thought with Adlerian individual psychology. Allers maintains that "problems arising out of purely practical psychology and characterology immediately open up universal problems insoluble except in terms of metaphysics"; "these problems," he goes on, "lead us still further into the realm of revealed religion" (375). Recommending a book per category under the headings of "History," "Psychology," "History of Philosophy," "Polemic," and "Autobiography" (*L* 34), Lowell selects Allers's *Psychology of Character* as the indispensable book under the "Psychology" category.

16. Robert Lowell, *Collected Prose,* ed. Robert Giroux (New York: Farrar, Straus, Giroux, 1987), 354.

17. For a discussion of his various treatments, including electroshock therapy, sedatives, and psychotherapy, see Lowell's letters, Saskia Hamilton's introduction to the *Collected Letters,* and two biographies of Lowell: Ian Hamilton's *Robert Lowell: A Biography* (New York: Random House, 1982), and Paul Mariani's *Lost Puritan: A Life of Robert Lowell* (New York: W. W. Norton, 1994). The imprint of psychoanalysis upon Lowell's confessionalism is obvious and has been noted widely. Substantiating the proposition that "psychodynamic models of the causes of [Lowell's] disorder were highly influential not only in American psychiatry . . . but also in American culture, affecting the way he and his society understood his manic behavior" (xv–xvi), Saskia Hamilton cites letters from Elizabeth Hardwick to Elizabeth Bishop in 1958 and 1959, years when Lowell was institutionalized at McLean Hospital after acute breakdowns. Hardwick writes, for example, "Cal is now in the hands of a first-rate Freudian analyst. . . . There is no doubt in my mind that Cal needs depth analysis—and it is in any case a last resort, like an amputation, since everything else has been tried" (Hardwick to Bishop, January 20, 1958, Vassar College Libraries, cited in *L* xvi). "Gulping Freud" in 1953, Lowell had announced himself to be "a confused and slavish convert" (*L* 200) to psychoanalytic thinking.

18. In his afterword to the *Collected Poems,* Frank Bidart claims that "Skunk Hour" "dramatizes, perhaps for the first time in the history of lyric, the moment when the mind sees, acknowledges its insanity" (*CP* 998). It seems likely that Lowell himself would have attributed that invention to Baudelaire, whose introspective, embodied images

of insanity Lowell redrew in the heightened corporeal language of his *Imitations* (1961)—in translated images of "gangs of demons . . . boozing in our brain" (*CP* 233) and of a fire that "burns our brain tissue" (*CP* 255) in "To the Reader" and "The Voyage," for example.

19. In his review of *Life Studies,* M. L. Rosenthal defines "confessional" practice for subsequent generations of critics by identifying confessional poetry with the psychoanalytic talking cure, observing that "Robert Lowell seems to regard [publication] as the soul's therapy." "Poetry as Confession," in M. L. Rosenthal, *Our Life in Poetry: Selected Essays and Reviews* (New York: Persea Books, 1991), 109.

20. Fittingly, two of the primary tropes of *Life Studies* and particularly of "Memories of West Street and Lepke"—clothing and animals—condense this opposition between the exertions of culture and embodiment upon the expression of identity.

21. The draft version of the poem, titled "My Season in Hell (West Street Jail, 1943)," Houghton Library ms, bMS Am 1905 220, is reprinted in *Collected Poems,* 1042–1043.

22. Vereen Bell, *Robert Lowell, Nihilist as Hero* (Cambridge MA: Harvard University Press, 1983), 144.

23. Michael Davidson describes his aspiration to read James Schuyler's *The Crystal Lithium* "as the first chronicle of what we might call a post-therapeutic poetics, one that eschews the confessionalist Freudian framework that dominated the poetry of the 1950s, for a more medicalized . . . experience of cognitive disability" (177), only to find that no evidence suggests that Schuyler ever took the drug (*On the Outskirts of Form: Practicing Cultural Poetics* [Middletown, CT: Wesleyan University Press, 2011]). Lowell's *Notebook* experiments, I argue, exemplify just such a "post-therapeutic poetics."

24. Robert Giroux, introduction to *Collected Prose,* xiii–xiv. When Lowell was discharged from McLean's following his annual breakdown in February 1967, he had recently been placed on lithium, as his letter to Bishop describes (see also Mariani, *Lost Puritan,* 347). The breakdown was, by my count, his ninth in ten years. His letter to Peter Taylor of June 4, 1967 (his daughter's half birthday, which he commemorates in "Harriet," the philosophical first poem of *Notebook 1967–68*), demonstrates his cautious but finally uncontainable hope in the drug: "I'm in terrific shape! I even have pills that are supposed to prevent manic attacks, something (probably a sugar pill unnoticed when taken or after but which supplies some salt lack in some obscure part of the brain and now for the rest of my life, I can drink and be a valetudinarian and pontificate nonsense" (Hamilton, *Robert Lowell,* 359).

25. The letter, which demonstrates just how dramatically Lowell felt his life to have changed and exemplifies his tendency to pivot between the subjects of lithium and his evolving notebook enterprise (the two major developments in his life during this year), is worth quoting at greater length. Lowell writes to Bishop in January 1968, the month of the visit to Cuernavaca he describes in "Mexico":

> Yes, I'm well. The pills I am taking really seem to prevent mania. Two or three years will be necessary, but already critical months have passed. Ordinarily I would certainly have been in a hospital by now. The great thing is that even my well life is much changed, as tho I'd once been in danger of falling with every step I took. All the psychiatry and therapy I've had, almost 19 years, was as irrelevant as it would have been for a broken leg. Well, some of it was interesting, tho most was jargon.

> My long poem is now over a thousand lines, and will probably go on another 500,
> will go on till June when it began. Then I'll polish through the summer. I am writing
> as if it were my last work. Someone asked me if [I] expected to die when I finished
> it—no, but trying to write with such openness and not holding back. (*L* 494)

The previous month, the night before he left for Cuernavaca, Richard Stern had
recorded in his diary the following account of Lowell during this period of fe-
verish composition:

> He is sitting in bed in socks, a blue pocket-buttoned shirt, loose tie. Poems, the new
> "fourteen-liners" are spread and piled on the red quilt. Cal reads ten or twelve of them
> aloud. . . . Since June, he's written seventy-four of them. It was after he'd started the
> lithium treatments. . . . He showed me the bottle of lithium capsules. Another medical
> gift from Copenhagen. Had I heard what his trouble was? "Salt deficiency." (Richard
> Stern, "Extracts from a Journal," *TriQuarterly* 50 [1981]: 270–271.)

26. The *OED* traces the first iteration of the expression "miracle drug" to the sociologist
    Read Bain's statement in 1944 that "we seem to be entering a period of 'miracle'
    drugs" ("Man Is the Measure," *Sociometry* 7, no. 4 [November 1944]: 454); for a nu-
    anced discussion of lithium's circuitous path to celebrity status in the 1960s, see
    Healy, *Mania.*

27. Robert Lowell, *Notebook 1967–68* (New York: Farrar, Straus and Giroux, 1969), 27.
    Subsequent page references to this volume will be given parenthetically in the text of
    this chapter as *N;* references to the revised *Notebook* (London: Faber & Faber, 1970)
    are specified in footnotes. Citations from *History* and *For Lizzie and Harriet,* the last
    iterations of the notebook experiment, appear in Lowell's *Collected Poems* and are
    drawn from that volume.

28. Ian Hamilton, "A Conversation with Robert Lowell," in Meyers, *Interviews and Mem-
    oirs,* 157.

29. Lowell, *Notebook,* 264.

30. Hamilton, "A Conversation," 157.

31. Bell, *Robert Lowell,* 7.

32. What we know of Thales of Miletus's cosmology derives from *Metaphysics* 1.3.983b–
    984a, in which Aristotle describes Thales's hypothesis that "the only cause is of the
    kind called 'material'" (Aristotle, *Metaphysics,* vol. 1, trans. Hugh Tredennick [Cam-
    bridge: Harvard University Press], 1933), 1.3.984a. "Most of the earliest philosophers,"
    Aristotle writes, "conceived only of material principles as underlying all things. That
    of which all things consist, from which they first come and into which on their destruc-
    tion they are ultimately resolved, of which the essence persists although modified by
    its affections—this, they say, is an element and principle of existing things. Hence
    they believe that nothing is either generated or destroyed, since this kind of primary
    entity always persists. . . . Thales, the founder of the school of philosophy, says the
    permanent entity is water" (1.3.983b).

33. Aesop presents one version of the story of Thales's demise in his parable of "The As-
    tronomer Who Fell in a Well." See Plato's *Theaetetus,* 174a, for Socrates's version of
    the story.

34. Jonathan Raban notes this echo of *Prometheus Bound* in "Harriet"; see *Robert Low-
    ell's Poems: A Selection* (London: Faber, 1974), 182.

35. Aeschylus, *Prometheus Bound,* trans. Robert Lowell (New York: Farrar, Straus & Giroux, 1969), v–vi.

36. Ibid., 52–53. In draft versions of "Do You Believe in God?," Lowell's language echoes these lines from *Prometheus Bound* even more faithfully: the revelation of the final line appears, in the first draft of June 1967, as "a face still friendly to chaos" (mss., the Robert Lowell Papers, Houghton Library, Harvard University, reprinted in Alex Calder, "Notebook 1967–68: Writing the Process Poem," in *Robert Lowell: Essays on the Poetry,* ed. Steven Gould Axelrod and Helen Deese [Cambridge: Cambridge University Press, 1986], 122). The first several drafts retain "chaos" as the poem's final word.

37. The line "In sickness, the mind and body make a marriage" (29) appears in the poem "In Sickness," in the sequence titled "Autumn in the Abstract," in *Notebook 1967–1968.* A version of the line reappears with a slight but significant change, however, in *The Dolphin.* In "Sick," from "Leaving America for England," Lowell writes: "It might have been redemptive not to have lived—/ in sickness, mind and body might make a marriage / if by depression I might find perspective—" (*CP* 698). As I will argue, the conditional framing of the assertion is consistent with the metaphysical doubt that emerges in the latter volume.

38. Juvenal's famous description of a sound mind in a sound body, *"mens sana in corpore sano,"* appears in the *Satires,* 4.10.356.

39. Hardwick to Tate, June 1, 1959, quoted in Mariani, *Lost Puritan,* 277.

40. Hamilton, *Robert Lowell,* 373.

41. Joseph Epstein, "Mistah Lowell—He Dead," *Hudson Review* 49, no. 2 (Summer 1996): 198–199.

42. Donald Hall, "The State of Poetry—a Symposium," *Review* 29–30 (Spring–Summer 1972): 40. The insult ringing in his ears, Lowell invokes Donald Hall's assessment of *Notebook*'s "seedy grandiloquence" in "Last Night" (*CP* 601).

43. David Bromwich, "Reading Robert Lowell," *Commentary,* August 1, 1971, http://www .commentarymagazine.com/article/reading-robert-lowell/.

44. This internal chaos is evident in Lowell's habit of revising individual lines in successive versions of the poems of *Notebook* by adding or excising negative particles to reverse their meaning in a single stroke. The exposure of such apparently arbitrary revisions in the successive iterations of *Notebook* contributes to the interplay of chaos and order in the poem, which Vereen Bell attributes to the perennial philosophical problem of "mind and nature" (*Nihilist,* 186). He sees Lowell's perplexity in the face of the problem reflected in the poem's fractured, atomized form.

45. Lowell, *Notebook,* 211.

46. As an alternative to history, Alex Calder posits Foucauldian genealogy—the "critical examination of patterns of descent and emergence" in which "there can be no separating out of identities" (*Notebook 1967–68,* 134–135)—as a model for the book's mapping of time. Drawing the book into closer philosophical correspondence with the embodied materialism of *Notebook* as I have described it, Frank Bidart expands on Calder's reading to find in Foucault's description of Nietzschean genealogy a précis of Lowell's ordering principles in *History,* observing that for the genealogist, "The body is the inscribed surface of events (traced by language and dissolved by ideas), the locus of a dissociated self (adopting the illusion of a substantial unity), and a volume in per-

petual disintegration" (quoted in *CP* 1074). Bidart's entropic interpretation of Lowell's genealogy of the self in *History* suggests tacit but profound continuities between the materialisms of *Notebook* and its later, apparently "ordered," counterpart.

47. Lowell's doubts about the drug contradicted his doctors' "universal faith" in it. Lowell writes to Blair Clark in March 1976 that "the air is full [of] rumors against lithium, hard to check on because it is almost a universal faith with English doctors. It's the preventative effectiveness that shakes me, I can't really function against two manic attacks in one year" (*L* 645). He concludes the letter with a postscript: "P.S. Tell if you come across anything more detailed on lithium. I am trying to find a substitute" (*L* 646).

48. On Lowell's uses of the terms "real" and "unreal," see Barbara Estrin, *The American Love Lyric after Auschwitz and Hiroshima* (New York: Palgrave, 2001).

49. Having changed and softened the use of quotations in *The Dolphin* per Bishop's "objection they were part fiction offered as truth," Lowell explained to Stanley Kunitz: "Most of the letter poems . . . can go back to your old plan, a mixture of my voice, and another voice in my head, part me, part Lizzie [Elizabeth Hardwick], italicized, paraphrased, imperfectly, obsessively heard" (Kunitz, "The Sense of a Life," in Meyers, *Interviews and Memoirs*, 233).

50. Bishop and Lowell, *Words in Air,* 707–708 (Bishop's italics).

51. Kunitz, "The Sense of a Life," 233. Lowell's letter to Kunitz does not appear in the *Collected Letters*. In a letter of the same month (April 1972), Lowell writes to Frank Bidart of the revisions to *Notebook*: "Now the book must still be painful to Lizzie [Hardwick] and won't satisfy Elizabeth [Bishop]. As Caroline says, it can't be otherwise with the book's donnée" (*L* 593).

52. By suggesting that Lowell's formal jaggedness in *Day by Day* reflects not only psychological and physical exhaustion but philosophical disintegration, my reading complements and expands on Rebecca Warren's observation that *Day by Day* "makes an offering of its brokenness" ("On Robert Lowell," *Salmagundi* 141/142 [Winter–Spring 2004]: 160) and Reena Sastri's claim that the book's frayed conversationalism, fuzzy intersubjectivity, and eschewal of facile polarities contribute to a form of aesthetic collapse that "does not revisit an earlier poetic but breaks new ground." "Intimacy and Agency in Robert Lowell's *Day by Day*," *Contemporary Literature* 50 no. 3 (2009): 496.

53. Bishop and Lowell, *Words in Air,* 787.

54. Helen Vendler, "Robert Lowell's Last Days and Last Poems," collected in Meyers, *Interviews and Memoirs*, 298–311.

2. Physiological Thinking: Robert Creeley and A. R. Ammons

1. A. R. Ammons, *Collected Poems, 1951–1971* (New York: Norton, 1972), 39. Subsequent page references to this volume will be given parenthetically in the text of this chapter as *CP*.

2. On Ammons's effortlessly "natural" use of scientific terms in his poetry as a result of his education and his efforts to stay "pretty much aware of what was taking place as of late in science," see Ammons's interview with Jim Stahl, "The Unassimilable Fact Leads

Us On . . . ," in *Set in Motion: Essays, Interviews, and Dialogues,* ed. Zofia Burr (Ann Arbor: University of Michigan Press, 1996), 49. The most sustained study of the "expansive influence of science on Ammons's poetry" (194) is Steven P. Schneider's *A. R. Ammons and the Poetics of Widening Scope* (Rutherford, NJ: Fairleigh Dickinson University Press, 1994). Other sources that address Ammons's thematic uses of science include Roger Gilbert, "Science in Contemporary American Poetry: Ammons and Others," in *The Cambridge History of American Poetry* (Cambridge: Cambridge University Press, 2015), 913–936; Alan Holder, *A. R. Ammons* (Boston: Twayne, 1978); Miriam Marty Clark, "The Gene, the Computer, and Information Processing in A. R. Ammons," *Twentieth Century Literature* 38, no. 1 (1990): 1–9, which addresses Ammons's depictions of biological information processing; and Willard Spiegelman, "Myths of Concretion, Myths of Abstraction: The Case of A. R. Ammons," in *The Didactic Muse: Scenes of Instruction in Contemporary American Poetry* (Princeton, NJ: Princeton University Press, 1989), 110–146.

3. Robert Creeley, interview by Lewis MacAdams, *Contexts of Poetry: Interviews, 1961–1971,* ed. Donald Allen (Bolinas, CA: Four Seasons Foundation, 1973), 166–167.

4. "Chasing the Bird," in *The Collected Poems of Robert Creeley, 1945–1975* (Berkeley: University of California Press, 1982), 60.

5. Creeley was fond of quoting this adage of Williams's, that "the poet thinks with his poem, in that lies his thought, and in that itself is the profundity" (see Williams's author's note to *Paterson* [New York: New Directions, 1963]). Though the poets rarely appear in print together, readers have long acknowledged that for Creeley and Ammons, the poem is an enactment of a mind in action rather than a composed reordering of reality—that Creeley "sings the very process of thinking" (Robert Creeley, *Selected Poems, 1945–2005,* ed. Benjamin Friedlander [Berkeley: University of California Press, 2008], 16), and that Ammons is "more concerned with rendering the *experience* of reflection, its rhythms and contours, than with delivering completed thoughts" (Roger Gilbert, *Walks in the World: Representation and Experience in Modern American Poetry* [Princeton, NJ: Princeton University Press, 1991], 209). On Ammons's critical estrangement, despite important stylistic affinities, from Williams and the Olson-Creeley circle during the "countercanonizing" of the so-called other tradition in the 1990s, see Marjorie Perloff, "Whose New American Poetry? Anthologizing in the Nineties," *Diacritics* 26, nos. 3–4 (1996): 104–123. Perloff attributes the exclusion of Ammons from this "avant-garde consensus" (104) to his association with Harold Bloom at Cornell, whose criticism obscured the influence of Pound and Williams on Ammons's poetry by situating him in the Romantic, idealist tradition of Emerson, Whitman, and Stevens.

6. Creeley, *Collected Poems, 1945–1975,* 122.

7. See Creeley's introduction to *George Oppen: Selected Poems,* ed. Robert Creeley (New York: New Directions Books, 2003), xxi.

8. George Oppen, "The Mind's Own Place," in *Selected Prose, Daybooks, and Papers,* ed. Stephen Cope (Berkeley: University of California Press, 2007), 32.

9. Michael Davidson, introduction to *New Collected Poems,* by George Oppen, ed. Michael Davidson and Eliot Weinberger (New York: New Directions, 2008), xxxviii. See also Steve Shoemaker, ed., *Thinking Poetics: Essays on George Oppen* (Tuscaloosa: Univer-

sity of Alabama Press, 2009), for a range of essays that consider Oppen's "poetics of thought" (4), drawing out relevant precedents and analogues to Creeley's strategies for representing mind. In his essay *"Discrete Series* and the Posthuman City" (62–90), Shoemaker proposes that Oppen's *Discrete Series* "map[s] an early moment in our evolution toward the posthuman condition," and anticipates Katherine Hayles's definition of that new order as one in which "informational pattern" is privileged "over material instantiation" (63). I propose the opposite in Creeley's case—that his poetry of the late 1960s and early 1970s does not anticipate the dualist crisis of posthumanism but rather signals an integral monism that many forms of process poetics (including Ammons's and Lowell's experiments of the 1960s) embody.

10. Charles Altieri, "Placing Creeley's Recent Work: A Poetics of Conjecture," *boundary* 2 6, no. 3 (Spring–Fall 1978): 523. Nathaniel Mackey summarizes the influence of Creeley's early poetry on his own work by describing precisely its dissolution of the "I" in the context of lyric: "for all the obvious first-person insistence one finds in Creeley, the 'I' is neither unified nor self-evident. . . . And there had been Williams earlier still, in 'The Desert Music': 'I am that he whose brains / are scattered / aimlessly'," Mackey explains. See Jeanne Heuving, "An Interview with Nathaniel Mackey," *Contemporary Literature* 53, no. 2 (2012): 214–215. (Creeley was fond of quoting the same lines from "Desert Music"; see, for example, Robert Creeley, *The Collected Essays of Robert Creeley* (Berkeley: University of California Press, 1989), 42, 495, 545.

11. Oppen, *New Collected Poems,* 169, 92. The lines "Tell the beads of the chromosomes like a rosary, / Love in the genes, if it fails // We will produce no sane man again" appear in *Of Being Numerous,* the title poem of which negotiates the thinking of the embodied individual and the consciousness of the collective. On the "almost audible click in the brain" Oppen identifies with that negotiation and around which " 'Of Being Numerous' is constructed," see *The Selected Letters of George Oppen,* ed. Rachel Blau DuPlessis (Durham, NC: Duke University Press, 1990), 402. (DuPlessis suggestively identifies an early, abortive attempt at technical avant-gardism in Oppen's uncollected experiment "Brain" [*New Collected Poems,* 292–293], first published by Ezra Pound in 1933 ["Uncannily in the Open: In Light of Oppen," in Shoemaker, *Thinking Poetics,* 212]). I also paraphrase here the concluding line of Oppen's stunning poem "Sara in Her Father's Arms," from *The Materials,* which suggests just how closely and consciously he associated the materials of biological and linguistic form (see Oppen, *New Collected Poems,* 51). In his poetry of the 1960s, Oppen frequently compares inert, intentionless, verbal, and somatic materials of self-making, elements of what he called, hesitantly, "the real"; see, for example, Oppen, "The Mind's Own Place," 32. Oppen's embodied "objectism" resounds in Charles Olson's proposition that "a man is himself an object, whatever he may take to be his advantages." "Projective Verse," in *Collected Prose,* ed. Donald Allen and Benjamin Friedlander (Berkeley: University of California Press, 1997), 247.

12. Creeley, introduction to *Oppen: Selected Poems,* xx.

13. Rachel Blau DuPlessis has recently compared the countercultural "hysterical masculinities" through which Creeley, Ginsberg, and Olson critiqued and consolidated conventional manhood; see *Purple Passages: Pound, Eliot, Zukofsky, Olson, Creeley, and the Ends of Patriarchal Poetry* (Iowa City: University of Iowa Press, 2012): 89–197.

14. Creeley, *Collected Poems, 1945–1975,* 269. All composition dates included parenthetically after poem titles are available in Mary Novik, *Robert Creeley: An Inventory, 1945–1970* (Kent: Ohio Kent State University Press, 1973).

15. Creeley, *Collected Poems, 1945–1975,* 122.

16. Ibid., 284. As he looks through his window, the speaker attempts to comprehend the arrangement of objects in the visual field by pairing them off—a water tank and a church, a man and his car—fragmenting the visual scene the eye perceives in accordance with the dualistic organization of reality projected by the riven, speaking "I." For a compelling reading of this poem among Creeley's dozens of other poems entitled "Windows," see Marjorie Perloff, "Robert Creeley's Windows," *Bridge* 2, no. 1 (2002): 187–194.

17. Creeley, *Collected Poems, 1945–1975,* 294.

18. Ibid., 342.

19. Robert Creeley, *Autobiography* (Madras: Hanuman Books, 1990), 122.

20. Creeley, *Collected Essays,* 532.

21. See Leary's "How to Change Behavior," a paper he presented at the International Congress of Applied Psychology in Copenhagen in August 1961, reprinted in *Timothy Leary: The Harvard Years,* ed. James Penner (Rochester, VT: Park Street Press, 2014), 18–37. As Leary's paper demonstrates, little was known in the early 1960s about how psychoactive drugs worked; most research—by Leary at Harvard and later, in the 1970s, by L. Jolyon West and Ronald Siegel—focused on hallucinogenic experiences rather than the biological mechanisms that induced them. On the origins and cultural history of LSD through the 1970s, including Olson's and Ginsberg's participation in Leary's psilocybin experiments, see Jay Stevens's *Storming Heaven: LSD and the American Dream* (New York: Perennial Library, 1988).

22. See Olson, *Collected Prose,* 181. Olson defines the "objectism" of Pound, Williams, and their late modernist inheritors as "the getting rid of the lyrical interference of the individual as ego, of the "subject" and his soul. . . . For man is himself an object" (247). Creeley often invokes Olson in his assertions that apparently incorporeal and corporeal aspects of the "soul" or "self" are integral, that "the mind and the body are one" (Creeley, *Contexts of Poetry,* 167). Creeley laments of the word "soul," for example, that "the *OED*'s first listing of this word's definition, 'The principle of life in man or animals; animate existence,' is noted as obsolete, while the second definition not only survives but defines our problem entirely: 'The principle of thought and action in man, commonly regarded as an entity distinct from the body.'" For Creeley's reading of Olson's definition of the soul as "proprioceptive" and inexorably linked to the "movement of its own tissues," see Creeley, *Collected Essays,* 137–138. On the role of Alfred North Whitehead's process philosophy as a mediating discourse from which "the avant-garde," including Olson and Creeley, "culled their ideas of the human and social implications of the new physics" (121), see Daniel Belgrad's chapters "Subjectivity in the Energy Field: The Influence of Alfred North Whitehead" and "The Beats" in *The Culture of Spontaneity: Improvisation and the Arts in Postwar America* (Chicago: University of Chicago Press), 1998.

23. Creeley, *Collected Essays* 137. Reiterating the intellectual "usefulness" of hallucinogens, Creeley recalls in 1969: "What becomes—to my own mind deeply useful—so explicit

with either mescalin [*sic*], or acid, is the *finite* system of the *form* of human-body life, i.e., that [it] is of no permanent order whatsoever, in the single instance, however much the species' form is continued genetically, etc. . . . That the I can accept its impermanent form and yet realize . . . it is one of many, also *one*." Robert Creeley, *The Collected Prose of Robert Creeley* (Berkeley: University of California Press, 1988), 312–313.

24. Creeley, *Contexts of Poetry*, 169. On this period of experimentation in the mid-1960s, during which Creeley "began writing in different states of consciousness," see Ekbert Fass, *Robert Creeley: A Biography* (Hanover, NH: University Press of New England, 2001), 291–298. Discussions of Creeley's poetry of the 1960s and early 1970s often make obligatory reference to his drug use as a context for his writing, usually with embarrassment or disdain that suggests the need for a fuller picture of the imaginative and philosophical significance of these experiments. In a footnote to his "Revisiting Seriality in Creeley's Poetry"—in which he observes the significance of *Pieces* as an experiment in which Creeley uses serial form to invite a "non-biographical (or perhaps abiographical) reading of his work" (51), Alan Golding notes that "another context for Creeley's dispersal of subjectivity in serial form . . . is that of 1960s drug experimentation. With specific reference to the writing of *Pieces*, Creeley explains, 'There also was that extraordinary experience of acid for the first time, and that had a large impact on ego-structures.'" "Revisiting Seriality in Creeley's Poetry," in *Form, Power, and Person in Robert Creeley's Life and Work*, ed. Stephen Fredman and Steve McCaffery (Iowa City: University of Iowa Press, 2010), 64.

25. "Robert Creeley, The Art of Poetry No. 10," interview by Lewis MacAdams and Linda Wagner-Martin, *Paris Review* 44 (Fall 1968), http://www.theparisreview.org/interviews/4241/the-art-of-poetry-no-10-robert-creeley.

26. Ibid.

27. Creeley, *Contexts of Poetry*, 131–132.

28. Creeley, *Collected Essays*, 560.

29. Allen Ginsberg, *Howl: Original Draft Facsimile, Transcript and Variant Versions, Fully Annotated by Author, with Contemporaneous Correspondence, Account of First Public Reading, Legal Skirmishes, Precursor Texts and Bibliography*, ed. Barry Miles and Carl Solomon (New York: HarperCollins, 1995), 4. On Ginsberg's "supernatural formalism"—his attempt to "turn poetry into a spiritual practice that would parallel, and in his personal life take the place of, the exploration and transformation of consciousness that he had long sought through the use of visionary drugs" (28), see Amy Hungerford's *Postmodern Belief* (Princeton, NJ: Princeton University Press, 2010). Of Ginsberg's famous return to the body—and to a conception of the relationship between poetry and physiology more consistent with Creeley's—after his transformative travel in India, see Ginsberg's interview with Thomas Clark: "Allen Ginsberg, the Art of Poetry No. 8," *Paris Review* 37 (Spring 1966), http://www.theparisreview.org/interviews/4389/the-art-of-poetry-no-8-allen-ginsberg. Ginsberg had returned for the Vancouver Poetry Conference to which Creeley had invited him; Ginsberg recalls that "when I got to Vancouver, Olson was saying 'I am one with my skin.' It seemed to me at the time when I got back to Vancouver that everybody had been precipitated back into their bodies at the same time. It seemed that's what Creeley had been talking about all along. The place—the terminology he used, the place we are. Meaning this place,

here . . . / Because I'd always thought that that meant that he was cutting off from divine imagination."

30. Creeley observes that the poets of his generation were converging on a common resolution to "the dilemma" of consciousness by various routes that reflected their own "particularity of thinking," including the route of LSD experimentation that allowed users "to get beyond the thinking that was the bad trip all the time." Creeley, *Contexts of Poetry*, 168.

31. Creeley, *Collected Essays*, 143.

32. Ibid., 533.

33. Creeley, *Collected Poems, 1945–1975*, 297.

34. Creeley, *Collected Essays*, 532, 168.

35. Oliver Sacks, *Hallucinations* (New York: Vintage Books, 2013), 103. In his chapter on "Altered States" (90–121), Sacks describes his own experiences as a medical student, neurology resident, and recreational user of the "classical hallucinogens" investigating "how the brain embodies consciousness and self." He describes this period during which Creeley was undertaking his own experiments as the burgeoning of a new, "neurochemical age" (104).

36. Golding, "Revisiting Seriality," 51.

37. Creeley, *Collected Poems, 1945–1975*, 371, 325.

38. Ibid., 371.

39. Lytle Shaw, *Fieldworks: From Place to Site in Postwar Poetics* (Tuscaloosa: University of Alabama Press, 2013), 132. Shaw examines Creeley's poetry of seriality and place in the context of the hippie community of Bolinas, California, where Creeley lived in the late 1960s and early 1970s. Shaw proposes that "Bolinas might be considered, within poetry history, a kind of synecdoche for the utopian 1960s, the 1960s of hippies, communes, consciousness—a set of aspirations that often seem to disqualify themselves, to fall into caricature, before they open up for analysis" (116–117). I share Shaw's interest in taking Creeley's "hippie phenomenology" (118) seriously as a site of philosophical inquiry.

40. Shaw, *Fieldworks*, 132.

41. Creeley, *Collected Poems, 1945–1975*, 352.

42. Creeley, *Contexts of Poetry*, 41–42.

43. Creeley's conception of the poem as an extension of its material contexts includes both the embodied mind and the embodied process of composition. As Michael Davidson observes, Creeley and Ginsberg's recorded conversations in Vancouver (transcriptions of which appear in Creeley's *Contexts of Poetry*) notably emphasize "the most banal aspects of writing—the use of pens or typewriters, the kinds of paper they preferred, whether or not they like to have music in the background." Davidson, *Ghostlier Demarcations: Modern Poetry and the Material Word* (Berkeley: University of California Press, 1997), xi. Stephen Burt writes of *Pieces*, "Often those pages explore not what we mean and how we feel but what it is to expel sound from the larynx, to have a body, to stand in a room." Burt, "A. R. Ammons," 261.

44. In reference to the poetry of Oppen and Robin Blaser, Rachel Blau DuPlessis proposes that "the interest in making a serial poem is in establishing what kinds of links can be presented between any two units, and among all units"; she stresses that the serial poem

is an "image of sociality (community)." The connections Creeley creates through the seriality of *Pieces* represent inner life in terms of such connections between reticulated units. See DuPlessis, "The Blazes of Poetry: Remarks on Segmentivity and Seriality with Special Reference to Blaser and Oppen," in *The Recovery of the Public World: Essays on Poetics in Honour of Robin Blaser,* ed. Charles Watts and Edward Byrne (Burnaby, BC: Talonbooks, 1999), 287–299.

45. Creeley, *Collected Poems, 1945–1975,* 382, 388, 391. These poems were published originally in *Pieces* (1969); they were written in 1968 and 1969, though their specific composition dates are difficult to determine because they are untitled "serial" poems.

46. Creeley, *Collected Poems 1945–1975,* 423.

47. Asked by his interviewer, "How do you regard the reality of that perception?" Creeley responded, "I believe in it." Creeley, *Contexts,* 131–132.

48. Creeley, *Collected Poems, 1945–1975,* 508.

49. Ammons, *Sphere: The Form of a Motion* (New York: W. W. Norton, 1974), 72.

50. Creeley, *Contexts of Poetry,* 167.

51. Creeley, *The Collected Poems of Robert Creeley, 1975–2005* (Berkeley: University of California Press, 2006), 489.

52. These sources include wide, inquisitive reading, traces of which appear in Creeley's later prose; he cites, for example, the *Brain/Mind Bulletin* and W. Grey Walter's *The Living Brain* (New York: W. W. Norton, 1963), an enthusiastic history of electroencephalography written for a popular audience by the neurophysiologist, in a 1980 review of Arakawa and Madeline Gins's *The Mechanism of Meaning,* a collaborative exhibition the ambition of which was to map visually "what is emitted point-blank at a moment of thought," as the artists put it (quoted in Creeley, *Collected Essays,* 421). In light of Walter's account of "the 'mechanical' construct of the brain," Creeley identifies the representational demand Arakawa and Gins face in their exhibition as one of capturing thoughts as they speed along in real time, as a matter of "rate" (422).

53. Creeley, *Selected Poems* (Berkeley: University of California Press, 1991), xix–xx.

54. Creeley, *Collected Poems, 1945–1975,* 379.

55. Ammons, *Sumerian Vistas: Poems* (New York: W. W. Norton, 1987), 52.

56. On the trajectory of Ammons's representation of the natural landscape in relation to consciousness, see Bonnie Costello, *Shifting Ground: Reinventing Landscape in Modern American Poetry* (Cambridge, MA: Harvard University Press, 2003). Costello identifies three successive stages in Ammons's poetic development marked by the subject positions his speakers occupy—that of the "pilgrim," the "sage," and the "ordinary man." In terms consistent with my own here, Costello observes of the last phase of Ammons's writing that it "answers the Over-Soul's call to theory with the compelling, tangible struggles of the ordinary man to put himself on the side of motion and flow" (171). Though she does not focus on *Glare* and *Bosh and Flapdoodle,* as I do here, Costello observes of the former poem, quite consistently with my own reading, that it is "a record of the embodied mind" (167).

57. "Doxology" is also the title of a three-part sequence that is longer than the other poems in the volume; it is a religious hymn framed by ironic negations (the subtitle of the poem's first part, for example, is "Heterodoxy with Ennui").

58. Ammons, *Ommateum, with Doxology* (New York: W. W. Norton, 2006), 23.

59. Ammons, *Collected Poems, 1951–1971* (New York: W. W. Norton, 1972), 10.

60. See also the very similar repertoire of images—the bounded area, the transcendental wind—in poem 26 of *Ommateum*: "In the wind my rescue is . . ." (69).

61. Harold Bloom, "When You Consider the Radiance," reprinted in *Considering the Radiance,* ed. David Burak and Roger Gilbert (New York: W. W. Norton, 2005), 48.

62. Harold Bloom's Emersonian readings of Ammons in the Romantic tradition have shaped his reception by generations of readers. See the preceding footnote, in addition to Bloom's "Emerson and Ammons: A Coda," *Diacritics* 3 (Winter 1973): 45–47, and "The New Transcendentalism: The Visionary Strain in Merwin, Ashbery, and Ammons," *Chicago Review* 24 (Winter 1973): 25–43.

63. A. R. Ammons, *Tape for the Turn of the Year* (Ithaca, NY: Cornell University Press, 1965), 1.

64. Harold Bloom, *Critical Essays: A. R. Ammons* (New York: Chelsea House, 1986), 23; Alan Holder, *A. R. Ammons* (Boston: Twayne, 1978), 116; Willard Spiegelman, *The Didactic Muse: Scenes of Instruction in Contemporary American Poetry* (Princeton, NJ: Princeton University Press, 1989), 344.

65. See my introduction, including references there to Steven Meyer, *Irresistible Dictation: Gertrude Stein and the Correlations of Writing and Science* (Stanford, CA: Stanford University Press, 2001).

66. Ralph Waldo Emerson, *Essays and Lectures* (New York: Library of America, 1983), 256. Explaining his practice of "recording" experience in an interview with Steven Schneider, Ammons mistakenly attributes the lines to "Nature," paraphrasing the statement: "Let me record from day to day my honest thought without prospect or retrospect. . . . I have no doubt it will be found to have been symmetrical." Ammons explains that the statement "affected me more deeply than anything [Emerson] ever said." Schneider, *Complexities,* 335–336.

67. Ammons, *Tape,* 148, 50, 14.

68. See *The Oxford Handbook of the Philosophy of Mind* (2009), which describes the Turing machine as a primitive computer "consisting of a tape, on which is written some pattern of distinguishable symbols . . . and a writer/scanner that can move right or left along the tape" (614). W. Grey Walter describes the EEG as "a mirror for the brain." *The Living Brain,* 20.

69. Ammons, *Tape,* 3.

70. Ibid., 5–7.

71. Ibid., 6. Philip Fried, "'A Place You Can Live': An Interview with A. R. Ammons," in *Critical Essays on A. R. Ammons,* ed. Robert Kirschten (New York: G. K. Hall, 1997), 101.

72. See, most significantly, Roger Gilbert's *Walks in the World: Representation and Experience in Modern American Poetry* (Princeton, NJ: Princeton University Press, 1991).

73. Ammons, foreword to *Ommateum, with Doxology* (Philadelphia: Dorrance, 1955), 4.

74. Fried, "Interview," 106.

75. Ibid., 107.

76. See Emerson, *Nature: Addresses and Lectures* (Boston and Cambridge: James Munroe, 1848), 2–3.

77. Ammons, *Set in Motion,* 65.

78. A. R. Ammons, *Sphere: The Form of a Motion* (New York: Norton, 1974), 65; Ammons, *Tape,* 32.

79. Ammons, *Sphere,* 72; 18.

80. Ibid., 42–43.

81. Ibid., 58–59.

82. A. R. Ammons, *Glare* (New York: W. W. Norton, 1997), 240.

83. Fried, "Interview," 105.

84. Ammons, *Sphere,* 11.

85. Ibid., 61.

86. Ammons, *Glare,* 208.

87. Ibid., 59.

88. Ammons, *Garbage* (New York: W. W. Norton, 1993), 20.

89. Ammons, *Glare,* 135, 175.

90. Ammons likens the cognitive cramping of "trying to remember a memory" (175) to digestive cramping in poem 64 of *Glare* as well. Roger Gilbert has observed that "the strongly somatic language Ammons uses to describe the tape's effects [in "Strip"]— cramps, cracked shoulder blades, etc.— . . . suggests that his textual and corporeal bodies have become intimately connected, and that the limitations of the former reflect the attrition of the latter" (Roger Gilbert, "Mobius Meets Satchmo: Mixed Metaphor as Form and Vision in Glare," *Complexities of Motion: New Essays on A. R. Ammons's Long Poems,* ed. Steven P. Schneider [London: Associated University Press, 1999], 192).

91. Gilbert, "Mobius," 207.

92. Ammons, *Glare,* 283.

93. Ibid., 51–52 (ellipses mine).

94. Ammons, *Sumerian Vistas,* 7.

95. Ammons, *Glare,* 267.

96. Ibid., 203. The comparison between musical improvisation and the flow of cognitive interiority appears elsewhere in *Glare;* in poem 91, Ammons compares the electrochemical "effusions" that underpin mental acts to "improvisational melodies" (240). Roger Gilbert also observes the relationship between the poem's musical nonsense and jazz improvisation in "Mobius," 208–209.

97. Northrop Frye, *Anatomy of Criticism: Four Essays* (Toronto: University of Toronto Press), 2006.

98. *Glare,* 269.

99. Ibid., 261 (Ammon's ellipses), 197, 276, 285.

100. Ibid., 13.

101. Fried, "Interview," 104.

102. The most committed readers of Ammons to have addressed these tags are Roger Gilbert and Helen Vendler, both of whom see in them a novel manifestation of Ammons's perennial resistance to closure. Roger Gilbert sees in these tags "deferred titles"; he writes that "by refusing to position them conventionally at the beginning of the text, Ammons illustrates the way his themes emerge out of his process rather than preceding and dictating it" ("Mobius," 209). Helen Vendler writes that "in *Glare,* true nonclosure is dared, often with an irrelevant capitalized phrase at the end of an individual

poem, a gesture toward a new start." "A. R. Ammons's Last," *Yale Review* 90, no. 1 (2002): 168.

103. *Glare,* 13.

3. James Merrill's Embodied Memory

1. James Merrill, *The Changing Light at Sandover: With the Stage Adaptation Voices from Sandover,* ed. J. D. McClatchy and Stephen Yenser (New York: Alfred A. Knopf, 2006), 176. Subsequent page references to this volume will be given parenthetically in the text of this chapter as *CL;* James Merrill, *Collected Poems,* ed. J. D. McClatchy and Stephen Yenser (New York: Alfred A. Knopf, 2001), 362. Subsequent page references to this volume will be given parenthetically in the text of this chapter as *CP.*

2. Helen Vendler, *Last Looks, Last Books* (Princeton, NJ: Princeton University Press, 2010), 117.

3. *James Merrill, Collected Prose,* 184. Julian Jaynes (1920–1997) was a Princeton biology professor two years Merrill's senior. He proposed that early "bicameral" humans had not evolved the metaconscious awareness that characterizes modern humans' experience of consciousness, and that before roughly 1200 BCE, neural activity in the left hemisphere of the brain was modulated by the right temporal cortex, which projected auditory verbal hallucinations that were interpreted as the voices of the gods. (For consideration of the possible relationship between Jaynes's conception of the bicameral mind and the bats of the *Sandover* cosmos, see Stephen Yenser's *The Consuming Myth,* 263–264). Wernicke's area is located in the left temporal lobe and refers to a region of the brain associated with the production and comprehension of language. Wernicke's aphasia affects several aspects of verbal processing, impairing the ability to form comprehensible utterances and causing speech to become riddled with "semantic substitutions as well as the production of nonwords (neologisms)" (Eleanor M. Saffran, "Wernicke's Area," *Encyclopedia of the Human Brain,* ed. V. S. Ramachandran [New York: Academic Press, 2002], 805–818).

4. During the 1950s, when Merrill was publishing his first books, the increasingly evident limitations of behaviorist descriptions of mental states, A. J. Ayers's defenses of phenomenalism, Gilbert Ryle's critiques of Descartes, and developments in biochemistry and physiological psychology converged to augment the plausibility of materialist perspectives and transform Anglo-American philosophical thinking about mindedness. These years saw a surge of interest in the philosophical defense of identity theory—a species of materialism that holds that states and processes of the mind are identical to states and processes of the brain. This surge was succeeded by the ascendancy of functionalist materialism, which proposes that any system that possesses mental states is wholly physical and produces those states by means of its causal organization. The bat-minion of God Biology in *Mirabell's Books of Number,* 176, speaks the divine "truth" of identity materialism when he explains that "THE LIFE FORCE IS / A RATIO WE ARRIVE AT OF ELECTRONIC CHARGES / THOUGHT-PROCESSES THE BURNING OF CERTAIN FUELS" (144); when Merrill identifies his computer with a brain in "Scrapping the Computer," he adopts the model of mind favored by functionalists from Hilary Putnam to Jerry Fodor.

5. Stephen Yenser, Reena Sastri, Phoebe Pettingell, and C. A. Buckley, among others, have focused on Merrill's use of evolutionary biology and nuclear physics in drafting the grandiose armature of the *Sandover* cosmos, and Claudia Ingram has demonstrated that within the unique time-scape (and fabulously inclusive language-scape) of the Ouija board sessions, "culturally authoritative but unassimilated and therefore 'futuristic' information from the [physical] sciences may be set in metaphoric relation to angels," that is, to imaginative inventions that are charged with symbolic freight and that are ostensibly remote from nature. Though Ingram notes that "the trilogy is less preoccupied with assimilating news from the biology lab," Yenser, tracing the poet's shifting commitments to monism and dualism, emphasizes that it is the biologist who "SEEKS THE FRUITFUL UNION" (*CL* 115) of mind and nature in *Mirabell's Books of Number*. See Stephen Yenser, *The Consuming Myth: The Work of James Merrill* (Cambridge, MA: Harvard University Press, 1987), 273; Reena Sastri, *James Merrill: Knowing Innocence* (New York: Routledge, 2007); Phoebe Pettingell, "Voices from the Atom," in *A Readers Guide to James Merrill's "The Changing Light at Sandover,"* ed. Robert Polito (Ann Arbor: University of Michigan University Press, 1994), 158–161; Claudia Ingram, "'Fission and Fusion Both Liberate Energy': James Merrill, Jorie Graham, and the Metaphoric Imagination," *Twentieth-Century Literature* 51, no. 2 (2005): 149–150.

6. Sir Arthur Stanley Eddington's claim that "the whole material universe of stars and galaxies of stars is dispersing, the galaxies scattering apart so as to occupy an ever-increasing volume," appears in *The Expanding Universe* (Cambridge: Macmillan, 1933), v.

7. Urania's *"treble-clef barrette,"* for example, anticipates the recording of "The Blessed Virgin's Expostulation," which will play in the smoldering dusk of the poem's conclusion; Purcell's piece heralds the advent of yet another infant whose birth marks the dawning of a new age in the life of man.

8. Plato, *The Dialogues of Plato,* trans. Benjamin Jowett (London: Oxford University Press, 1924), 456. Merrill's reference to Plato in the quoted lines are from the *Phaedrus*, where Socrates asserts that writing "will create forgetfulness in [writers'] souls, because they will not use their memories; they will trust to the external written characters and not remember of themselves" (Jowett 1:484).

9. Merrill's awareness of the Muses' traditional mythological lineage is evident in his foreword to Daniel Hall's *Hermit with Landscape:* "If Memory is the mother of the Muses, concision is their mentor. Faced even with the vast canvases of Dante and Proust, we appreciate how much is foreshortened or left out." James Merrill, *Collected Prose,* ed. J. D. McClatchy and Stephen Yenser (New York: Alfred A. Knopf, 2004), 316. Subsequent page references to this volume will be given parenthetically in the text of this chapter as *CPr*.

10. Langdon Hammer dates Merrill's HIV diagnosis to 1986; Hammer chronicles the impact of the AIDS epidemic on Merrill as he saw friends and loved ones suffer and die from the disease before and after he knew conclusively that he was infected. See especially Hammer's chapter "Art and Affliction: 1986–1989" in *James Merrill: Life and Art* (New York: Knopf, 2015), 692–739.

11. D. H. Lawrence, "Preface to the American Edition of *New Poems,*" in *Poetics of the New American Poetry,* ed. Donald Merriam Allen and Warren Tallman (New York: Random

House, 1974), 71. When asked about his choice to compose formal poetry "in a period when that sort of thing is not particularly valued," Merrill responded, "I don't think I have very much choice. It's simply the way that I know how to write. Even when I sort of slyly thought of changing to irregular line lengths I always found some way to justify them by secret scanning and rhyme" (*CPr* 96).

12. Gilbert Ryle, *The Concept of Mind* (New York: Barnes & Noble, 1949), 17.

13. My readings here universally emphasize Merrill's creative redemption of the act of forgetting and are thus consistent with a growing understanding of Merrill not as a backward-looking formalist but as an innovator whose models for the writing of poetry stress invention over recovery; see Mutlu Konuk Blasing, *Politics and Form in Postmodern Poetry: O'Hara, Bishop, Ashbery, and Merrill* (Cambridge: Cambridge University Press, 2009); Siobhan Phillips, *The Poetics of the Everyday: Creative Repetition in Modern American Verse* (New York: Columbia University Press, 2010); Stephen Yenser, *The Consuming Myth;* and Reena Sastri, *James Merrill: Knowing Innocence.*

14. Since the publication of *Water Street* (1962), critics have characterized Merrill as a poet of memory, particularly by association with Proust. Encouraged by Merrill himself, who counted Proust, along with Elizabeth Bishop and W. H. Auden, as a "surrogate parent" (*CPr* 8), readers have been disposed to discern traces of Proust's "*résurrections du passé*" in Merrill's intricate reconstructions of personal history. Harold Bloom writes that like Proust, his "truest precursor . . . Merrill too is always in search of lost time" (*James Merrill* [New York: Chelsea House, 1985], 2–3); in *The Consuming Myth,* Stephen Yenser traces Proust's imprint on some of Merrill's most celebrated lyrics; John Hollander has said that Merrill continually reengages "those Proustian themes of the retrieval of lost childhood, the operations of involuntary memory and of an imaginative memory even more mysterious" ("Memorial Tribute to James Merrill," *Proceedings of the American Academy and Institute of Arts and Letters,* 2nd ser., 46 [1995]: 81); Christopher Coffman notes that Proust's involuntary memories "provid[e] a pleasurable glimpse into . . . 'the essence of things . . . outside time,'" and that "Merrill's characters experience revelations of a similar sort" ("'Swann's Way:' Basic Training': Interpretation in James Merrill's Late Collections and *À la recherche du temps perdu*," *Comparative Literature* 61, no. 4 [2009]: 403).

15. Marcel Proust, *Remembrance of Things Past,* trans. C. K. Scott Moncrieff and Terence Kilmartin (New York: Vintage Books, 1981), 1:47. Proust, possibly influenced by Henri Bergson, draws the famous distinction between voluntary memory, which is accessed through conscious will, and involuntary memory, which is often triggered by sensory or emotional stimuli, and which is extremely rare in the vividly intense, epiphanic form that is depicted on several occasions in the *Recherche.* For Proust, this typology of memory entails a hierarchy of aesthetic value. Proust's assessment of the relative veracity of voluntary and involuntary memory is perhaps overstated but also empirically sound, for episodic memories that remain available for conscious retrieval tend to integrate novel information and emotional valences from the successive contexts in which they are retrieved, rendering them less and less faithful the more frequently they are recollected. (See Daniel Schacter, *The Seven Sins of Memory: How the Mind Forgets*

and Remembers [Boston : Houghton Mifflin, 2002].) From the comparative accuracy of long lost memories, Proust extrapolates the supposition that memory is permanent, that no experience is ever lost since "each past day has remained deposited in us, as in a vast library where, even of the oldest books, there is a copy" (*RTP* 3:554). This idealist principle Proust shares with Freud, who takes the view "that in mental life nothing which has once been formed can perish—that everything is somehow preserved and that in suitable circumstances . . . it can once more be brought to light" (Sigmund Freud, *Civilization and its Discontents,* eds. James Strachey and Peter Gay [New York: W. W. Norton, 1989], 16–17). Richard Terdiman describes the "suspicion which for Proust attaches to any recollected thought or emotion, any proffered interpretation—to any memory save the epiphanic upon which he rests responsibility for the redemption of the world" (*Present Past: Modernity and the Memory Crisis* [Ithaca, NY: Cornell University Press, 1993], 201); see his chapters on Proust in *Present Past* for an extended discussion of the historical and epistemological context of Proust's mistrust of conscious thought and faith in the authenticity of involuntary cognitive experience.

16. In the spirit of homage, Merrill's tribute poem "For Proust" reveals this contrast pointedly. The behind-the-scenes poem exposes and glorifies Proust's alchemical transformation of memory into art; the poem concludes with an account of the past "becoming literature," but it begins by representing Proust in the weary stage of laborious mnemonic recovery that precedes that final apotheosis—and that could hardly look any less like the spontaneous, revelatory *memoire involuntaire* Proust distinguishes as the type of memory most condign to immortalization in art. It is a striking representational choice on Merrill's part, when so much detail clearly did remain available to Proust's capacious memory, to portray him under the humbling strain of frustrated recollection; Merrill's choice to represent Proust in this way clearly arises, however, from a panegyric impulse to give him credit for the extraordinary mnemonic and artistic labor that was necessary to usher his great work into being. Put differently, "For Proust" demonstrates two ways of directing the impulse towards realism in literary representations of memory: while Proust occupies himself with constructing a Barthesian "referential illusion" (Roland Barthes, *The Rustle of Language* [Oxford, UK: Blackwell, 1986], 148) of the past—a process of supplementing memory with abundant details to signify verisimilitude—Merrill devotes himself to "realistically" exposing the contingent, fallible, constructive act of remembering, replete with distortions and absences. When Merrill observes that "Proust is subtle enough to persuade us that the real feat has been one not of style but of memory, and therefore within even the common man's power to duplicate" (*CPr* 124), he acknowledges that the *Recherche* perpetrates a benign deception; he recognizes that Proust's feat of recollection originates not in the veridical translation of prodigious acts of memory, but in subtleties of literary effect. Merrill relishes "the rips and ripples that make the reader know there is a fabric of illusion" (*CPr* 95), and finding no loose threads to tug in the pristine mnemonic tapestries of Combray or Venice, he instead exposes Proust's illusion by portraying him in the act of assiduously piecing it together.

17. Marcel Proust, *À la recherche du temps perdu,* ed. Jean-Yves Tadié (Paris: Gallimard, 1989), 1:46.

18. Edward Thomas, *The Poems of Edward Thomas* (New York: Handsel Books, 2003), 20.

19. Daniel Schacter, *Searching for Memory: The Brain, the Mind, and the Past* (New York: Basic Books, 1996), 87. The puzzle's most glaring limitation as a model for memory is, of course, that the image it displays when assembled is always identical—it is reassembled rather than truly re-created.

20. Sastri, *Knowing Innocence,* 45.

21. For an exemplary reading that addresses the correspondence of literary and cultural monuments in "Losing the Marbles" and "Bronze" (*Late Settings,* 1985), see Guy Rotella's *Castings: Monuments and Monumentality in Poems by Elizabeth Bishop, Robert Lowell, James Merrill, Derek Walcott, and Seamus Heaney* (Nashville: Vanderbilt University Press, 2004).

22. On Charmides's identity and significance in "Losing the Marbles" as the addressee of both the poem and the poem within the poem, criticism has been very scant. In the only accounts of Charmides's presence that I have been able to discover, Evans Lansing Smith observes that the reconstructed ode (discussed later) "is addressed to Charmides, a poet and lover whose name alludes to the title of the Platonic dialogue devoted to the concept of 'sophrosyne' (nothing in excess)" (*James Merrill: Postmodern Magus: Myth and Poetics* [Iowa City: University of Iowa Press, 2008], 109–110), while Christopher Coffman writes that "Merrill's Charmides character is developed only slightly, serving as he does as an audience rather than interlocutor. His presence, like the Charmides of Oscar Wilde, is not used to invoke temperance, the topic of the Socratic dialogue that bears his name; rather, the name gestures toward Charmides's youthful beauty and the juxtaposition of naïveté and wisdom in the dialogue" ("*Swann's Way:* Basic Training," 407). In the context of *Charmides,* "sophrosyne" (σωφροσύνη) is often translated as "temperance," "rightmindedness," "rationality," or "modesty," but as W. R. M. Lamb points out, "its most basic meaning is 'wholeness or health of the faculty of thought (φρονεῖν)'" (W. R. M. Lamb, trans., *Plato* [Cambridge: Harvard University Press, 1937], 3). Liddell and Scott give "soundness of mind" as the primary definition (Henry George Liddell, Robert Scott, Henry Stuart Jones, and Roderick McKenzie, *A Greek-English Lexicon* [Oxford: Clarendon Press, 1940]); Jowett notes that the term "may be described as '*mens sana in corpora sano,*' the harmony or due proportion of the higher and lower elements of human nature which 'makes a man his own master,' according to the definition of the *Republic*" (Plato, *Dialogues,* 1:3). Incidentally, and perhaps significantly, the father of the sculptor Phidias (mentioned in part 4 of "Losing the Marbles") bears the name Charmides as well.

23. Plato, *Dialogues,* 1:13.

24. Plato unmistakably emphasizes Charmides's erotic appeal in the dialogue; before he has begun the interview, Socrates admits that upon being told "that it was I who knew the cure [for his headache], [Charmides] gave me such a look with his eyes as passes description, and [I] was just about to plunge into a question . . . when I saw inside his cloak and caught fire, and could possess myself no longer" (Lamb, *Plato,* 17).

25. See Mallarmé's letter to Henri Cazalis, April 1866, in Stéphane Mallarmé, *Correspondance*, ed. Henri Mondor and Lloyd James Austin (Paris: Gallimard, 1959), 207–208. Roberto Calasso, whose translation I borrow here, writes of this sentence: "The threads that interweave in this sentence would go on spinning out until Mallarme's death. And likewise the ambiguities: above all in that verb *s'élançant* ('throwing itself') in which converge both the subject who wants to give himself 'this spectacle of a matter,' etc., and the matter itself observing its own behavior" (translation and quote 111).

26. Merrill writes of *Un coup de dés jamais n'abolira le hasard* that "the idea is more interesting than the execution" (*CPr* 69). In the "Comment," with which he prefaced the initial 1897 publication of *Un coup de dés,* Mallarmé summarizes "the idea" in his own words: "The 'blank spaces,' " he explains, "in reality, assume the importance and catch the eye at once; versification has always demanded them, as a surrounding silence. . . . The paper intervenes every time an image ends or withdraws of its own accord. . . . At the moment when [regular sound patterns or lines] appear and as long as they last, in some precise mental context, the result is that the text establishes itself in varying positions, near or far from the implicit leading train of thought, for reasons of verisimilitude." See *Collected Poems and Other Verse,* ed. H. Blackmore and A. M. Blackmore (Oxford: Oxford University Press, 2006), 262–263.

27. "On n'écrit past, lumineusement, sur champs obscur, l'alphabet des astres . . . ; l'homme poursuit noir sur blanc." Stéphane Mallarmé, *Œuvres Complètes,* ed. Henri Mondor and G. Jean-Aubry (Paris: Gallimard, 1945), 370.

28. I am indebted to Stephen Burt for observing that Merrill likely has in mind his friend and correspondent William Meredith, whose stroke in 1983 resulted in an expressive aphasia. Only after years of intensive therapy was Meredith, a former Poet Laureate Consultant in Poetry to the Library of Congress, able to write poetry again.

29. As Reena Sastri observes, the DNA double helix lends its form to the silhouette of Merrill's "An Upward Look," in which caesuras splice the narrow, descending strip of text in two (see Sastri, *Knowing Innocence,* 194); in the poem, Merrill depicts the motion of human consciousness as the result of genetic expression and mockingly suggests that the vacillation of thought might be causally, rather than coincidentally, related to the physical composition of the doubled chemical strains, "halves of a clue"

> In bright alternation minutely mirrored
> within the thinking   of each and every
>
> mortal creature (*CP* 674)

30. Vendler, *Last Looks,* 134.

31. Timothy Materer, "James Merrill's Late Poetry: AIDS and the Stripping Process," *Arizona Quarterly* 64, no. 2 (Summer 2008): 136.

4. John Ashbery's Mindlessness

1. John Ashbery, *Chinese Whispers: Poems* (New York: Farrar, Straus and Giroux, 2002), 3; *A Worldly Country: New Poems* (New York: Ecco, 2007), 41; *Quick Question: New Poems* (New York: Ecco, 2012), 36; *Breezeway: New Poems* (New York: Ecco, 2015), 50.

2. John Ashbery and A. Poulin Jr., "The Experience of Experience: A Conversation with John Ashbery," *Michigan Quarterly Review* 20, no. 3 (1981): 245.

3. John Ashbery, *Your Name Here: Poems* (New York: Farrar, Straus, and Giroux, 2000), 105.

4. John Ashbery, *Collected Poems, 1956–1987,* ed. Mark Ford (New York: Library of America, 2008), 149–150. Subsequent references to this volume in this chapter will appear parenthetically as *CP.*

5. These readers include not only critics but generations of Language poets who have found crucial poetic models in Ashbery's most extreme experiments; see, for example, Bruce Andrews, "Misrepresentation (A text for *The Tennis Court Oath of John Ashbery*)," in *In the American Tree,* ed. Ron Silliman (Orono, ME: National Poetry Foundation, 1986), 520–529; Barrett Watten, *Total Syntax* (Carbondale: Southern Illinois University Press, 1984), 89–91; Peter Nicholls, "John Ashbery and Language Poetry," in *Poetry and the Sense of Panic: Critical Essays on Elizabeth Bishop and John Ashbery* (Amsterdam: Rodopi, 2000), 155–168. As Jerome McGann notes, "[Ashbery's] unmistakable style has been read as the poetic equivalent of a deconstructive mode" by such literary inheritors (see McGann, *Social Values and Poetic Acts: A Historical Judgment of Literary Work* [Cambridge, MA: Harvard University Press, 1988], 200), and certainly by Harold Bloom, who uses "Self-Portrait in a Convex Mirror" as his deconstructive "proof-text" (22) in "The Breaking of Form" (*Deconstruction and Criticism,* ed. Harold Bloom, Paul De Man, Jacques Derrida, Geoffrey Hartman, and J. Hillis Miller [New York: Seabury Press, 1979], 1–38). In Richard Jackson's 1981 interview of Ashbery, Jackson finds in the poet's style resonances of poststructuralist philosophers such as Derrida, Foucault, and Lacan. Ashbery corrects him by attributing any such resemblances not to influence ("I am not very familiar with these authors") but to shared interests "that tend to happen simultaneously in history from certain causes." See John Ashbery and Richard Jackson, "The Imminence of a Revelation: An Interview with John Ashbery," in *Acts of Mind: Conversations with Contemporary Poets,* ed. Richard Jackson, Michael Panori, and Carol Rosenberg (Tuscaloosa: University of Alabama Press, 1983), 71.

6. Ashbery praises Gertrude Stein's *Stanzas in Meditation* for its comparable strategy of demanding perseverance through obscurity, inducing the helpless confusion and the rare bursts of clarity that characterize "'real-life' situations, the aesthetic problem being a microcosm of all human problems." Just as he does in the prose of *Three Poems,* shading in impenetrabilities to evoke the primary encounter with reality, in *Stanzas,* Ashbery contends, Stein uses language not to represent the world but to *evoke* the experience of experience, in which obscurity and clarity constantly alternate and structure subjectivity through this essential contrast. See John Ashbery and Eugene Richie, *Selected Prose* (Ann Arbor: University of Michigan Press, 2004), 13–14.

7. "John Ashbery, the Art of Poetry No. 33," interview by John Ashbery and Peter Stitt, *Paris Review* 90 (Winter 1983), http://www.theparisreview.org/interviews/3014/the-art-of-poetry-no-33-john-ashbery.

8. Fredman, *Poet's Prose,* 104. In the appendix to his chapter on *Three Poems,* Fredman lists for the benefit of "the reader anxious for some heuristic device" forty-nine "descriptive titles" summarizing the volume's successive themes (178–180).

9. James Vinson, *Contemporary Poets* (London: St. James Press, 1975), 36.

10. See Ashbery's use of the tree as an image of conscious matter in "The New Spirit": "Can it be identified with some area in someone's mind? The answer is yes, if it is experienced, and it has only to be expected to be lived, suspended in the air all around us. As I was going to say, this outward-hanging ledge over the pitfalls of mankind, proves that it is something you know; not just as the tree is aware of its bark, but as something left with you on consignment" (*CP* 251).

11. Jonathan Crary, *Suspensions of Perception: Attention, Spectacle, and Modern Culture* (Cambridge, MA: MIT Press, 2001), 14.

12. Andrew DuBois, *Ashbery's Forms of Attention* (Tuscaloosa: University of Alabama Press, 2006), xiv.

13. Crary, *Suspensions,* 13–14; DuBois, Ashbery's *Forms of Attention,* xiv.

14. Fredric Jameson, *Postmodernism; or, The Cultural Logic of Late Capitalism* (Durham, NC: Duke University Press, 1991), 4–5. See Mutlu Konuk Blasing, *Politics and Form in Postmodern Poetry: O'Hara, Bishop, Ashbery, and Merrill* (Cambridge: Cambridge University Press, 1995), 110–155.

15. Christopher Nealon, *The Matter of Capital: Poetry and Crisis in the American Century* (Cambridge, MA: Harvard University Press, 2011), 73.

16. Louis A. Osti, "The Craft of John Ashbery," *Confrontation* 9 (1974): 87. That distraction informs how experience comes to Ashbery is apparently evident to his interlocutors as well; in a preface to his interview with Ashbery, Louis Osti writes, "Speaking in a distinct, full-bodied voice, he answered my questions after making short pauses to frame his response. Often he abandoned a sentence mid-way, and began anew; his thoughts seemed to interrupt one another" (84). Peter Stitt observes of Ashbery in the preface to his own interview that "Ashbery's answers to my questions required little editing. He did, however, throughout the conversation give the impression of distraction, as though he wasn't quite sure just what was going on or what his role in the proceedings might be." The extent to which Ashbery sees his own experience of mind as representative is difficult to determine. When asked about his reputation for "obscurity," about "the way the details of a poem will be so clear, but the context, the surrounding situation, unclear," Ashbery explains, "This is the way that life appears to me, the way that experience happens. . . . I often wonder if I am suffering from some mental dysfunction because of how weird and baffling my poetry seems to so many people and sometimes to me too" ("John Ashbery, the Art of Poetry No. 33").

17. DuBois, *Ashbery's Forms of Attention,* xv.

18. The six segments of *Self-Portrait* are determined by five distinct ruptures of mental focus, beginning with "the balloon pops"; the next breach in the flow of text appears with the intervention of "thoughts of tomorrow" (*CP* 477), much like the earlier thoughts of "what yesterday / Was like"; the fourth segment begins with a shift of attention occasioned by a failure of memory ("As I start to forget it" [*CP* 479]); the urgent intrusion of a mental picture of marauders dazzled by the "inventions" they found in Parmigianino's studio during the sack of Rome sets off the fifth section; and in the final section, the artist's face reappears, conjured by "A breeze like the turning of a page" (*CP* 481).

19. Countless readings of "Self-Portrait" have stressed "the mutual influence of thing and perceiver," as R. Bendikter and J. Hilber have recently put it (see "The Post-Modern

Mind: A Reconsideration of John Ashbery's 'Self-Portrait in a Convex Mirror' from the Viewpoint of an Interdisciplinary History of Ideas," *Open Journal of Philosophy* 2 [2012]: 65). The poem's sensitive questioning of the dualism of subject and object, however, is framed by and embedded within its melancholic deconstruction of the dualism of mind and body, a project that likewise contributes to the epochal resonance of Ashbery's most famous poem.

20. Ironically, it is a flash of recognition of Parmigianino's soul—his "combination / Of tenderness, amusement and regret"—that leads Ashbery to deny that he can discern any aspect of Parmigianino's soul in the painting; the moment of sympathy in fact embodies precisely the imaginative connection between the painter and viewer Parmigianino is likely to have aspired to foster in his art. In *On Painting* (1435), Leon Battista Alberti prescribes that "the *istoria* will move the soul of the beholder when each man painted there clearly shows the movement of his own soul" (Alberti, *On Painting*, trans. John Spencer [New Haven, CT: Yale University Press, 1966], 77).

21. Ashbery's poem asks how the long tradition of describing visual art in verbal art is transformed and complicated by our heightened sensitivity to cognitive deficits of all kinds, particularly deficits of attention. Much critical treatment of "Self-Portrait" has focused on its participation in the tradition of poetic ekphrasis (see especially James A. W. Heffernan, *Museum of Words: The Poetics of Ekphrasis from Homer to Ashbery* [Chicago: University of Chicago Press, 1993]; Willard Spiegelman, *How Poets See the World: The Art of Description in Contemporary Poetry* [New York: Oxford University Press, 2005]; Barbara K. Fischer, *Museum Mediations: Reframing Ekphrasis in Contemporary American Poetry* [New York: Routledge, 2006]; Michael Davidson, *On the Outskirts of Form: Practicing Cultural Poetics* [Middletown, CT: Wesleyan University Press, 2011]) without acknowledging that ekphrasis in any period expresses historically and culturally specific assumptions about the nature of mind. As Ruth Webb notes in her study of classical ekphrases, *Ekphrasis, Imagination and Persuasion in Ancient Rhetorical Theory and Practice* (Farnham, UK: Ashgate, 2009), her study of ekphrasis is necessarily "almost as much a study of ancient psychology as of rhetoric" (5). Ashbery's ekphrasis is, at least in part, so striking a development within the mode because of the epochal philosophy of mind it reflects on the level of style, adopting exaggerated mindlessness as a formal principle.

22. John Ashbery, *Collected Poems*, 558–559.

23. "John Ashbery, the Art of Poetry No. 33."

24. Helen Vendler, *The Music of What Happens: Poems, Poets, Critics* (Cambridge, MA: Harvard University Press, 1988), 232; John Shoptaw, *On the Outside Looking Out: John Ashbery's Poetry* (Cambridge, MA: Harvard University Press, 1994), 226.

25. John Ashbery and Mark Ford, *John Ashbery in Conversation with Mark Ford* (London: Between the Lines, 2003), 60.

26. For Ashbery's description of this effect, see Ashbery and Ford, *John Ashbery in Conversation*, 61. Lauterbach's 1980 recording with Ashbery is available online at http://writing.upenn.edu/pennsound/x/Ashbery.php. For Lauterbach's account of performing "the second voice," see "What We Know as We Know It: Reading 'Litany with JA,'" *Conjunctions* 49 (Fall 2007).

27. Ashbery uses the metaphor of filtration to describe the metacognitive "experience of experience" he tries to capture in lieu of paraphrasable content: "Most of my poems

are about the experience of experience . . . the particular occasion is of lesser interest to me than the way a happening or experience filters through me. . . . I'm trying to set down a generalized transcript of what's really going on in our minds all day long." Poulin, "The Experience of Experience: A Conversation with John Ashbery," 245.

28. David Hume, *A Treatise of Human Nature,* ed. L. A Selby-Bigge, rev. ed. P. H. Nidditch (Oxford: Clarendon Press, 1987), 207. John Koethe offers a contrasting picture of Ashbery's philosophy of mind in "The Metaphysical Subject of John Ashbery's Poetry" (in *Beyond Amazement: New Essays on John Ashbery,* ed. David Lehman [Ithaca, NY: Cornell University Press, 1980], 87–100), where he argues that "the conception of the self underlying Ashbery's poetry is . . . that of the transcendental or metaphysical subject" (96).

29. John Ashbery, *Flow Chart* (New York: Alfred A. Knopf, 1991), 128. Subsequent page references to this volume will be given parenthetically in the text of this chapter as *FC.*

30. John Keats, *Complete Poems and Selected Letters of John Keats* (New York: Modern Library, 2001), 45.

31. "John Ashbery, the Art of Poetry No. 33." In "The Moment Unravels: Reading John Ashbery's "Litany," *Twentieth Century Literature* 38, no. 2 (1992): 125–151, John Keeling presents "the intimacy and distance that grow out of 'our fertile misunderstanding[s]'" (125) as the central crux of "Litany," citing Ashbery's acknowledgment that "any art, once it leaves the studio, is going to be misinterpreted for better or worse"; "'misprision,'" Ashbery explains, "is the term used by Harold Bloom for our fertile misunderstanding of the poet's aims. It often seems that the artist's role is precisely to make himself misunderstood, that misunderstanding and appreciation are much the same." John Ashbery and David Bergman, *Reported Sightings: Art Chronicles, 1957–1987* (New York: Knopf, 1989), 258–259, cited in Keeling, 125.

32. "John Ashbery, the Art of Poetry No. 33." In the same interview, Ashbery frames the ambition of "Litany" to obviate criticism in terms that suggest a rivalry between poetry and criticism in the age of theory; John Shoptaw surmises that the poem may have had its origins in Ashbery's "jealousy" of the booming art of criticism at the time (*On the Outside,* 234–235). Whatever defensiveness of poetry per se may have framed its inception, "Litany" emphasizes the shared aims of "the best" poetry and criticism to facilitate pleasure and revelation, collapsing distinctions between them by emphasizing their readerly effects.

33. "John Ashbery, the Art of Poetry No. 33."

34. "I was going to church a lot at the time," Ashbery recalls of the poem's conception. "I was thinking about the great litany. . . . And of course 'Litany' is one of those words that mean many different things—it can be a list of complaints, a droning on and on, but it has a sacred sense too" (Ashbery and Ford, *John Ashbery in Conversation,* 61).

35. Forrest Gander, "In Search of John Ashbery," *Boston Review,* July 1, 2007, http://www .bostonreview.net/gander-in-search-of-john-ashbery; John Ashbery, interview by Vasilis Papageorgiou, *Chromata,* April 15, 1989, http://chromatachromata.com/interview-with -john-ashbery/.

36. Roger Gilbert proposes that "a growing awareness of mortality," which he, like Gander, traces to Ashbery's "near-fatal spinal infection" of 1982, "seem[s] to have accelerated

his rate of [poetic] production" in the 1990s and 2000s (Roger Gilbert, "Ludic Eloquence: On John Ashbery's Recent Poetry," *Contemporary Literature* 48 [2007]: 197). Describing the dramatic medical event in some detail to Mark Ford in 2003, Ashbery draws a clear picture of his acute symptoms and the inept medical care that permitted their escalation:

> I had an excruciating pain in my neck, which started in my class at Brooklyn College. . . . It kept getting worse and worse over a period of several days. My doctor just kept giving me pain killers, which didn't work. My legs started to get paralysed and I was taken by ambulance to New York Hospital, where nobody could figure out what I had. My doctor offered David his condolences on my impending death, and left. They left me on a gurney in a deserted area far from the emergency room. David stayed with me, and when I was paralyzed up to the neck and having difficulty breathing, he raised hell at the hospital and called everybody we knew, until finally the doctor of friends of ours came in and ordered an immediate operation. It lasted ten or eleven hours, at which point the surgeon told David and other friends who were waiting that I'd survived but would remain a vegetable, i.e., quadriplegic. I had an epidural abscess with a staph infection of the spinal fluid. . . . I had such a terror of going to the hospital—if I had gone earlier, when it first started, I might not have had to have such a severe operation, which has had a number of residual side effects. It's affected my walking and hip. (Ashbery and Ford, *John Ashbery in Conversation*, 62–63)

37. Quoted in Forrest Gander, "In Search of John Ashbery."
38. Ibid.
39. Ashbery and Ford, *John Ashbery in Conversation*, 63.
40. William Logan, "Collateral Damage," *New Criterion* 31 (June 2013): 61.
41. DuBois, *Ashbery's Forms of Attention*, 114 (DuBois's emphasis).
42. It has been widely noted that there have emerged, in the history of the poet's reception, two Ashberys: the Ashbery that derives from Stevens and the Ashbery that derives from Gertrude Stein, the Ashbery cherished by critics attracted to the symbolist tradition (Harold Bloom and Helen Vendler, for example) and the Ashbery cherished by oppositional critics and poets committed to tracking the history of the "other tradition" (Bruce Andrews and Barrett Watten, to name just two). Vernon Shetley observes that "the binaristic thinking of critics like [Andrew] Ross and McGann," who favor the experimentalism of *The Tennis Court Oath* because it seems to them to be more rife with political potential than later poems' putatively complacent lyricism, "compels them to see John Ashbery as having taken a wrong turn in his career—as being, ultimately, a failure or a sellout" (*After the Death of Poetry: Poet and Audience in Contemporary America* [Durham, NC: Duke University Press, 1993], 145). This divided picture of Ashbery reflects divisions in critical taste, not any tormented division in Ashbery's work per se; see my conclusion, "Anti-Lyric in the Age of the Brain," for discussion of the interpretive blind spots that have emerged as a result of this restrictive critical opposition between lyric and anti-lyric modes of reading.
43. Shoptaw, *On the Outside Looking Out*, 302.
44. Gander, "In Search of John Ashbery."
45. These gyrations of coalescing and disintegrating sense are matched by the contractions and relaxations of form that punctuate *Flow Chart*. The most famous of these con-

tractions is the double sestina that Angus Fletcher reads as an attempt "to control the poem's meander," an attempt through which there "emerges a notion of the poet as philosopher, the poet as world-definer, whose forms control the flowing picture of conscious life, yet without seeking to crush variety" (*A New Theory for American Poetry: Democracy, the Environment, and the Future of Imagination* [Cambridge, MA: Harvard University Press, 2004], 221, 223). Without making substantial reference to the "content" of the sestina, which borrows its end words from Charles Algernon Swinburne's "Complaint of Lisa," and without attempting to track its "lugubrious excess of internal reference" (223), Fletcher's reading is based on the mere presence of such a rigorous form in the midst of the chaos of *Flow Chart*, a form that "anchors or gives shape to an otherwise exceedingly elusive poem" (224). While the appearance of the double sestina may present "the poet as world-definer, whose forms control the flowing picture of conscious life," as Fletcher puts it, the obscurity of the sestina itself renders the outcome of that attempt ambiguous at best. John Shoptaw tracks the sestina's "excess of internal reference" in *On the Outside Looking Out*, noting Ashbery's willful (or mindless?) disregard of Swinburne's source text in the double sestina: "Ashbery, the postmodern poet of latent destiny," Shoptaw writes, "did not consult the Boccaccio tale (*Decameron*, 10.7) on which Swinburne's "Complaint" is based (imagine Joyce or Eliot not investigating the story of Tristan and Isolde). By choosing to know only the transmuted form of Lisa's complaint, he transcribes the double sestina into a twelve-tone serial composition through which undertones of the original pass unrecognized and changed" (316–317). Such unawareness complements the sestina's erratic rational movements and forms of semantic indeterminacy, qualities that presumably exemplify the "variety" Fletcher claims that the sestina contains but does not "crush." It is noteworthy, however, that such forms of "variety" pointedly subvert the sestina's philosophical, "world-defin[ing]" formal ambition. John Emil Vincent, objecting to Fletcher's reading, proposes that "the sestina functions . . . to suggest that the veering of *Flow Chart* has so completely trained Ashbery's readers to expect veering that even the extremely showy veerings that are necessary to work within the form of a double sestina are less strange or obvious than the veerings" (66–67) of the rest of the poem. Indeed, Vincent goes so far as to propose that "the poet finds the double sestina project purposeless." *John Ashbery and You: His Later Books* (Athens: University of Georgia Press, 2007), 68.

46. Fletcher categorizes Ashbery as a maker of "environment poems" that aim not to describe but to create environments that "enable the reader, for a moment, to live inside a poem" (196). Like Walt Whitman and John Clare, Fletcher argues, Ashbery "remain[s] sharply conscious of the extended real world, whose materiality tempers the Romantic surmise"; for such poets, he writes, "horizon is a guide to natural constraints, necessary to any critical reading of the surrounding natural environment" (7). Stressing the poetic methods through which Ashbery reorients us to our chaotic environmental surround, emulating and ordering that surround in language, Fletcher exchanges vertical, hierarchal, symbolist dualisms for the horizontal, democratic, metonymic dualism of self and environment. I share Fletcher's emphasis on Ashbery's horizontal, materialist aesthetics, but want to stress here the extent to which Ashbery diffuses the

self across the environmental "horizon" by framing consciousness itself as a material phenomenon contiguous with "outer" environmental reality.

47. A. Walton Litz, *Introspective Voyager: The Poetic Development of Wallace Stevens* (New York: Oxford University Press, 1972), 151.

48. Ashbery, *Quick Question*, 83.

49. Wallace Stevens, *The Collected Poems of Wallace Stevens* (New York: Vintage Books, 1990), 239.

50. Ibid., 93.

51. Ashbery, *Chinese Whispers*, 96.

52. Ashbery, *Flow Chart*, 104.

53. Ashbery, *Your Name Here*, 105.

5. Jorie Graham and the Ethics of the Eye

1. Jorie Graham, *Materialism* (New York: Ecco Press, 1993), ix–x.

2. John Ashbery, *Collected Poems, 1956–1987*, ed. Mark Ford (New York: Library of America, 2008), 476.

3. The phrase "built-in limits" appears in Graham's "To a Friend Going Blind," in *Erosion* (Princeton, NJ: Princeton University Press, 1983), 27, an early poem I discuss in the introduction to this book.

4. Helen Vendler, *The Given and the Made: Strategies of Poetic Redefinition* (Cambridge, MA: Harvard University Press, 1995), 92; Jorie Graham and Sharon Blackie, "An Interview with Jorie Graham," *EarthLines* 1, no. 2 (August 2012): 39, http://www.earthlines.org.uk/JorieGrahamInterview#.

5. Lyn Hejinian, *The Language of Inquiry* (Berkeley: University of California Press, 2000), 329.

6. John Keats, *Complete Poems and Selected Letters of John Keats* (New York: Modern Library, 2001), 492.

7. James Longenbach usefully describes Graham's modernist zeal for asking "ambitious questions of spiritual and cultural redemption" (*Modern Poetry after Modernism* [Oxford: Oxford University Press, 1997], 160) as an expression of *hunger;* he quotes Graham in an interview with Thomas Gardner: "I think many poets writing today realize we need to recover a high level of ambition, a rage, if you will—the big hunger." Thomas Gardner, *Regions of Unlikeness: Explaining Contemporary Poetry* (Lincoln: University of Nebraska Press, 1999), 81, quoted in Longenbach, 160.

8. Graham, *Erosion*, 20, 5.

9. Graham, *Overlord* (New York: Ecco, 2005), 21–22.

10. Graham, *Erosion*, 40.

11. Graham, *Materialism* (New York: Ecco, 1993), 36; Graham, *Overlord*, 19.

12. It is noteworthy that the visually striking migration in "Salmon" is projected on a television screen in a process that resembles the projection of the image onto the retina; in the succession of optical media through which the quanta of sensory information must pass—camera, television, eye—the intervention of the television is yet another instance of the transformative bearing of "mechanical necessity" (*Overlord*, 19).

13. Graham, *Erosion*, 40–41.

14. The architectural metaphor for the eye's restrictive mediation of sensory information recalls the metaphor of the medieval walls of the Italian town in "To a Friend Going Blind."

15. Graham, *Materialism,* 38. In the same poem, "Relativity: A Quartet," Graham elaborately compares the eye's scanning of the landscape to a camera's recording of visual information "frame by frame"; as she contemplates the "mounted, scanning, videocam" and its bounded range of surveillance, she reveals an ethical concern about the moral transgressions that take place beyond our range of apprehension: *"Where is,* I think, / watching again, / *the blind spot in its turn?"* (*Materialism,* 35).

16. Ashbery, *Collected,* 466; Graham, *Overlord,* 54.

17. For sustained, insightful analysis of the function of these spaces through which "nothingness acquires a feeling of solidity" (239), see Thomas J. Otten's "Jorie Graham's _____s," *PMLA* 118, no. 2 (2003): 239–253.

18. Graham, *The End of Beauty* (New York: Ecco Press, 1987), 24.

19. Ibid., 23–24 (Graham's italics).

20. Ibid., 23.

21. Ibid., 24.

22. Graham describes watching a river "lapped-at all day in / this dance of non-discovery" (3) in "Notes on the Reality of the Self," the opening poem of *Materialism;* see Ashbery's "Clepsydra," *Collected Poems,* 144.

23. Graham, *Erosion,* 38–39.

24. Graham, *Materialism,* 25–26 (Graham's italics).

25. Ibid., 29.

26. Ibid., 29–30.

27. George Lakoff and Mark Johnson, *Philosophy in the Flesh: The Embodied Mind and Its Challenge to Western Thought* (New York: Basic Books, 1999), 5.

28. Antonio R. Damasio, *The Feeling of What Happens: Body and Emotion in the Making of Consciousness* (New York: Harcourt Brace, 1999), ix.

29. Ibid., iii.

30. Graham, *Overlord,* 4.

31. The famous dichotomy paradox is one example. "That which is in locomotion," Zeno proposes, "must arrive at the half-way stage before it arrives at the goal" (Aristotle, *Physics,* trans. Philip Henry Wicksteed and Francis Macdonald Cornford [Cambridge, Mass.: London: Harvard University Press, 1957], 6.9.239b); thus, in order to arrive at the goal, one must complete an infinite number of intervening tasks, which he claims is an impossibility. The second problem that the paradox poses is that the trip cannot begin—it is impossible to cover the first segment of distance, since any possible first distance could be divided in half and thus would not be first after all. Zeno's conclusion is that no travel over any finite distance can ever be completed or begun, and that therefore motion must be an illusion.

32. Graham, *Overlord,* 4–5.

33. The figure below is from Roger B. H. Tootell, Martin S. Silverman, Eugene Switkes, and Russell L. De Valois, "Deoxyglucose Analysis of Retinotopic Organization in Primate Striate Cortex," *Science, New Series,* 218, no. 4575 (November 26, 1982): 902–904, Figure 1(A), p. 902. The study generated a result of the kind Graham describes

in "Dawn Day One." The left image is the visual stimulus perceived by the macaque monkey; the right image is a tissue section from the monkey's brain.

(This figure is reproduced by kind permission of the authors and the American Association for the Advancement of Science.)

34. Graham, *Overlord,* 6–7.

35. Jorie Graham, "Friendly Fire: A Presidential Lecture" (lecture, Iowa Writers' Workshop, Iowa City, February 3, 1991), http://sdrc.lib.uiowa.edu/preslectures/graham91/index.html.

36. Jennifer Ashton, *From Modernism to Postmodernism: American Poetry and Theory in the Twentieth Century* (Cambridge: Cambridge University Press, 2005), 161–162.

37. Ibid., 161–162. Ashton argues that the autonomy of the poem and the determinacy of its meaning (associated with modernism and the New Criticism) gives way over the course of the twentieth century to the poetics of indeterminacy that Marjorie Perloff has described—to the "open text" that refuses to assert an intentional lyric voice and that demands readerly participation for the construction of meaning. Ashton concludes her book by drawing Jorie Graham into this trajectory.

38. Insightfully comparing Language poets to nineteenth-century antecedents she deeply admires, Graham notes in 1986: "I often think the Language poets—who interest me more than any other 'group' writing at present—are simply replacing nature with language—(it is after all a vast self-possessed field indifferent to our single instances and efforts). And that they are repeating the Transcendentalist/Romantic venture with it as the *other*" (Ann Snodgrass, "Interview: Jorie Graham," *Quarterly West* 23 [1986]: 155–156). By the time of her presidential lecture at the Iowa Writers' Workshop in 1991, however, Graham sees fit to clarify her philosophical divergence from the Language poets, and from many fundamental premises of poststructuralism, by outlining her own philosophy of language:

> What we are experiencing in our critical procedures sometimes resembles a great adolescent crisis in relation to reality. Reality as parent; the human mind as furious child, hovering upstairs above the problem of Life, refusing to come down, in a state of fury self-flatteringly referred to as "aporia"—the mystical overtones of that notion masking its deeply adolescent all-options-open refusal of the limitations and ennobling responsibilities of *choice*. Especially the kind of choice the belief in a stable terminology, in the possibility of stable reference, involves. After all, just because words are indefinite doesn't mean they're indeterminate. Just because things don't have provable, objective, forensic meanings, doesn't mean they have *no* meaning. As human beings, haven't we always had to count on things we can't prove? Maybe we could just think of this as the *greater* dizziness—the enabling, *ennobling*, metaphysical dizziness—this understanding and acceptance of the true fluidity of

words, and this choice to believe their *relative* meaning sufficient to hold us. (Graham, "Friendly Fire")

39. Ira Flatow, with guests Antonio Damasio, Jorie Graham, and Thomas Metzinger, "Emotion, Cognition and Consciousness," *Talk of the Nation/Science Friday,* National Public Radio, October 10, 2003, 4.

40. Ibid.; Thomas Metzinger, *Being No One: The Self-Model Theory of Subjectivity* (Cambridge, MA: MIT Press, 2003), 331.

41. Flatow et al., "Emotion, Cognition and Consciousness," 6.

42. The popular science of consciousness has recently been especially preoccupied with the question of what neuroscience can contribute to our understanding of human will (or to our recognition of the *illusion* of human will, in many cases). See, for example, John Searle, *Freedom and Neurobiology: Reflections on Free Will, Language, and Political Power* (New York: Columbia University Press), 2007; Thomas Metzinger, *The Ego Tunnel: The Science of the Mind and the Myth of the Self* (New York: Basic Books, 2009); Bruce Hood, *The Self Illusion: How the Social Brain Creates Identity* (Oxford: Oxford University Press, 2012); Michael Gazzaniga, *Who's in Charge? Free Will and the Science of the Brain* (New York: HarperCollins, 2011); and Sam Harris, *Free Press* (New York: Free Press, 2012).

43. Flatow et al., "Emotion, Cognition and Consciousness," 8.

44. Ibid., 12.

45. Thomas Metzinger, *Being No One: The Self-Model Theory of Subjectivity* (Cambridge, MA: MIT Press, 2003), 416. Metzinger argues in *Being No One* that "what in scientific or folk-psychological contexts frequently is simply referred to as 'the self'" (331) does not exist in reality, that there are only "phenomenal selves" that are aspects of conscious experience. These phenomenal selves are not things but processes, and can therefore be interrupted, suspended, and dynamically reconstituted. In *The Ego Tunnel: The Science of the Mind and the Myth of the Self* (New York: Basic Books, 2009), he reframes the intricate, empirically grounded theory for a general audience, concisely addressing the implications of his theory for the notion of free will, projecting that "from a scientific, third-person perspective, our inner experience of strong autonomy may look increasingly like what it has been all along: an appearance only" (127–129). See also Slavoj Žižek, "The Solar Parallax: The Unbearable Lightness of Being No One," part 2 of *The Parallax View* (Cambridge, MA: MIT Press, 2006), in which Žižek traces many of the undeniable impasses of recent cognitive philosophy and the "'freedom versus brain sciences' debate" (203).

46. Flatow et al., "Emotion, Cognition, and Consciousness," 8. Graham's position bears out Metzinger's speculation in *The Ego Tunnel:* "Now that the neurosciences have irrevocably dissolved the Judeo-Christian image of a human being as containing an immortal spark of the divine, we are beginning to realize that they have not substituted anything that could hold society together and provide a common ground for shared moral intuitions and values. An anthropological and ethical vacuum may well follow on the heels of neuroscientific findings" (213).

47. Graham, *Overlord,* 62.

48. *Overlord* in fact contains five poems with the title "Praying," each dated and subtitled an "attempt," a desperate repetition that suggests the value of the action despite the hopelessness of its outcome. The volume's moral anguish declares itself through the concrete details of man-made destruction that seem to prove human prayers unheard, from the gruesome carnage of Operation Overlord, particularly the allied invasion of Normandy ("bullets up through our feet, explosion of Jack's face, more sudden openings / in backs, shoulders, one in a neck" [37]), to bodies falling from the twin towers ("Headfirst some of the people, others not" [75]) to the catastrophic effects of global climate change ("grasses gone at / the root, the birds in drifts at the feet of the trees" [79]). Graham quotes Yehuda Amichai in one of the collection's three epigraphs: "The gods keep changing, but the prayers stay the same" (*O*, xiii).

49. Graham, *Overlord*, 61.

50. Ibid., 20.

51. Ibid., 61.

52. It is noteworthy that in her poetic reckoning with cognitivist philosophy of mind, Graham concentrates on the extreme naturalization of agency posed by philosophers such as Metzinger, despite the prominence of more moderate cognitivist perspectives. Daniel Dennett, for example, shares the view that "there is no central Headquarters, no Cartesian Theatre where 'it all comes together'" (*Consciousness Explained* [Boston: Little, Brown, 1991], 253), but he also entertains and defends the existence of autonomous will (see *Freedom Evolves* [New York: Viking, 2003]). Graham chooses to respond to the most extreme assaults on selfhood and freedom that cognitivist philosophers are prepared to propose, the assaults that are especially congruent with the most radical dispersals of agency social constructionists have proposed.

53. Hejinian, *The Language of Inquiry*, 43. In *What Should We Do with Our Brain?* (New York: Fordham University Press, 2008), Catherine Malabou echoes Graham's correlation of the transparent determinations of the embodied mind with the transparent determinations of ideology: "Playing on the title of a well-known work by Daniel Dennett, we are not seeking to explain or explicate consciousness, but to *implicate* it. To implicate consciousness, to ask what we should do with our brain, means, starting from these clarifications, to attempt to develop a critique of what we will call *neuronal ideology*. . . . [The question *What should we do with our brain?*] should allow us to understand why, given that the brain is plastic, free, we are still always and everywhere 'in chains' . . . and why, given that it is clear that there can no longer be any philosophical, political, or scientific approach to history that does not pass through a close analysis of the neuronal phenomenon, we nonetheless have the feeling that we lack a future, and we ask ourselves *What good is having a brain, indeed, what should we do with it?*" (*What Should We Do with Our Brain?* [New York: Fordham University Press, 2008], 11).

54. Ibid.

55. *Overlord*, 64.

56. Lakoff and Johnson, *Philosophy in the Flesh*, 3.

57. Ibid., 4.

58. Ibid., 7.

59. In *Being No One,* Metzinger describes this lack of "privileged direct access to knowledge of our own mind" as "autoepistemic closure," claiming that "conscious experience severely limits the possibilities we have to gain knowledge about ourselves" (175); "the pre-reflexive, preattentive experience of *being someone* results directly from the contents of the currently active self-model being transparent" (337). This aspect of experience—that of transparently *being someone*—is one that he explains in evolutionary terms, arguing that awareness that the self is a mere representation would inhibit goal-directed action: "the phenomenon of *transparent* self-modeling developed as an evolutionary [*sic*] viable strategy because it constituted a reliable way of making system-related information available without entangling the system in endless internal loops of higher-order self-modeling" (338). This obsessive self-modeling— suppressed, according to Metzinger, by evolution but also enacted in his philosophy— resembles the introspective entanglement that Graham identifies with moral negligence.

60. Graham, *Overlord,* 76–77, underlining mine. Graham cites her use of Lakoff and Johnson's language in "Copy" in the appended notes to *Overlord,* 93.

61. Ibid., 78.

62. Ibid.

63. Graham and Blackie, "An Interview," 39.

64. Ibid., 39; Jorie Graham, *Sea Change* (New York: Ecco, 2008), 52, 6.

65. Jorie Graham, *P L A C E* (New York: Ecco, 2012), 12.

66. Ibid., 9–10.

67. Ibid., 58.

68. See Graham and Blackie, "An Interview," 38. She refers to Richard Louv's *Last Child in the Woods: Saving Our Children from Nature-deficit Disorder* (Chapel Hill, NC: Algonquin Books of Chapel Hill), 2005.

69. Ibid., 36.

70. Graham, *P L A C E,* 81.

71. Ibid., 34.

Conclusion

1. Vanessa Place and Robert Fitterman, *Notes on Conceptualisms* (New York: Ugly Duckling Presse, 2009), 38.

2. Jorie Graham, *Overlord* (New York: Ecco, 2005), 78. Place and Fitterman's valuable *Notes on Conceptualisms* exemplifies the oppositional rhetoric that characterizes avant-gardism in the field of contemporary poetry. On my hesitant use of the terms "mainstream," "avant-garde," and "vanguard," see my notes to the introduction.

3. Place and Fitterman, *Conceptualisms,* 51, 19. In a list of "things to be considered in institutionalism," Place and Fitterman include alongside "'the short lyric of self-definition'" aspects of expressive culture ("the reading" and "the reading series"), academic culture and literary canons ("the course materials," "the Conference"), publication practice ("the blurb," "the introduction / afterword"), and "the transparency of language" (50–51). For an introduction to conceptualist writing and its inheritances from the tradition of conceptual art, see Kenneth Goldsmith's "Why Conceptual Writing? Why Now?" and Craig Dworkin's "The Fate of Echo,"

introductory essays to their co-edited anthology *Against Expression: An Anthology of Conceptual Writing* (Evanston, IL: Northwestern University Press, 2011), and Laynie Browne's and Caroline Bergvall's essays in Caroline Bergvall, Laynie Browne, Teresa Carmody, and Vanessa Place, *I'll Drown My Book: Conceptual Writing by Women* (Los Angeles: Les Figues Press, 2012). In *Unoriginal Genius: Poetry by Other Means in the New Century* (Chicago: University of Chicago Press, 2010), Marjorie Perloff contextualizes the conceptualist tenet of "unoriginality" by tracking the history of appropriative or "citational" and concrete, constraint-driven poetries from Walter Benjamin's *Arcades Project* through Language poetry to the present. Brian M. Reed's *Nobody's Business: Twenty-First Century Avant-Garde Poetics* (Ithaca, NY: Cornell University Press, 2013) contains insightful and informative essays on these subjects as well.

4. Despite conceptualists' remonstrations against "expression"—a notion tainted by association with the naïve conception of a unified lyric ego whence expression or voice is said to issue—conceptualist texts express all kinds of feelings and perspectives, as my readings acknowledge. For a thoughtful review addressing such inconsistencies in conceptualist theory and practice, see Stephen Burt, "Must Poets Write?" *London Review of Books* 34 no. 9 (2012): 33–34, available at http://www.lrb.co.uk/v34/n09 /stephen-burt/must-poets-write. For influential descriptions of the expressivist/experimentalist binary, see Marjorie Perloff's account of the "expressivist paradigm" in *21st-Century Modernism: The "New" Poetics* (Malden, MA: Blackwell, 2002); Hank Lazar's *Opposing Poetries*, vol. 1, *Issues and Institutions* (Evanston, IL: Northwestern University Press, 1996); and Ron Silliman's casting of the binary between the traditionalist "School of Quietude" and "post-avant" poetics on *Silliman's Blog* (http:// ronsilliman.blogspot.com). For a succinct and relatively evenhanded retrospective account of the opposition, see also Cole Swensen's introduction to *American Hybrid: A Norton Anthology of New Poetry,* ed. Cole Swensen and David St. John (New York: W. W. Norton, 2009).

5. The legacy of Language poetry, to rehearse a familiar story, has shaped the rhetoric of this naturalized opposition. At the close of the twentieth century, the rift between mainstream and oppositional poetic kinds was associated closely with the antithesis of closure and openness, with formal procedures that might facilitate and resist readerly "absorption," to borrow Charles Bernstein's term (see "Artifice of Absorption," in *A Poetics* [Cambridge, MA: Harvard University Press, 1992], 9–89). Susan Howe's techniques of historicist collage, for example, which emphasize the material and phonetic dimensions of language, and Ron Silliman's "new sentence," a species of antinarrative prose built to resist the "will to integration" projected by paragraphs, plots, and other conventional structures, exemplify the formal means by which Language poets have manifested ardent materialist commitments. In his two epigraphs to "Disappearance of the Word, Appearance of the World" (1977), Silliman pinpoints the movement's philosophical roots in nineteenth- and twentieth-century epistemological transitions within linguistic and social theory, to Edward Sapir's summary conclusion that "the fact of the matter is that the 'real world' is to a large extent unconsciously built up on the language habits of the group," and to Karl Marx's proposition that "it is not the consciousness of men . . . that determines their being, but on the contrary,

their social being that determines their consciousness" (quoted in *New Sentence* [New York, NY: Roof, 1987], 7). Thus, from the beginning, linguistic and social determinations of subjectivity underpinned the disjunctive forms Language poetry adopted as it devoted itself to the self-reflexive exposure of the cultural and semiotic forces through which selves are made. Observing the basis of the "two-camp model" (xvii) in what are widely seen to be countervailing interpretations of "the stability and sovereignty of the individual," Cole Swensen proposes that "the split is more than a stylistic one; it marks two concepts of meaning: one as transcendent, the other as immanent" (*American Hybrid*, xviii).

6. Charles Bernstein's phrase "official verse culture" appears throughout his essays collected in *A Poetics;* see especially his explanatory footnote, pp. 93–94.

7. Jack Spicer, Peter Gizzi, and Kevin Killian, *My Vocabulary Did This to Me: The Collected Poetry of Jack Spicer* (Middletown, CT: Wesleyan University Press, 2008), 150; George Oppen, Michael Davidson, and Eliot Weinberger, *New Collected Poems* (New York: New Directions, 2008), 166.

8. Observing that the "two camps" model has dominated critical conceptions of contemporary poetry since the 1950s, Cole Swensen's anthology reflects the conviction that "the contemporary moment is dominated by rich writings that cannot be categorized and that hybridize core attributes of previous 'camps' in diverse and unprecedented ways" (*American Hybrid*, xvii). Promoting the notion that "the long-acknowledged 'fundamental division' between experimental and traditional is disappearing in American poetry in favor of hybrid approaches that blend trends from accessible lyricism to linguistic exploration" (jacket copy), Swensen and St. John's 2009 anthology harmonizes with perspectives articulated by Stephen Burt in his review of Susan Wheeler's *Smokes* (*Boston Review* 23, no. 3 [Summer 1998], http://www .bostonreview.net/ poetry/stephen-burt-review-smokes) and Juliana Spahr and Claudia Rankine (*American Women Poets in the 21st Century: Where Lyric Meets Language* [Middletown, CT: Wesleyan University Press, 2002]) at the turn of the millennium. This convergence suggests the obsolescence of the binary model as the values of traditional lyric and Language poetry merged into what Brian M. Reed has described pejoratively as a formally and politically tepid "new consensus"—a spate of "learned, complex 'hybrid' poetries, which make use of disjunctive and other formally disruptive techniques toward traditionally literary ends" (xv). The ascent of conceptual poetics, not represented in Swensen and St. John's anthology and exalted by Reed for reinventing avant-garde poetics after the institutionalization and domestication of Language poetry, has revitalized this opposition and reanimated the anti-lyric rhetoric of Language poetry's earlier waves.

9. The materialist enthusiasm of Language poetry installed the interpretation of self at the center of oppositional poetics' self-conception in the 1980s and 1990s, and as the avant-garde frontier has shifted, the status of the self has continued to shape the oppositional rhetoric and formal practices of conceptual poetries as they have emerged at the putative vanguard. Tracing the familiar trajectory of "a paradoxical 'avant-garde tradition'" that descends from Pound, Stein, and Williams through the "objectivist" poetics of George Oppen and Louis Zukofsky's circle to poets included in Donald Allen's anthology *The New American Poetry, 1945–1960* (New York: Grove Press, 1960),

and finally to the Language poets, Oren Izenberg observes the complex ethos of failure and possibility these diverse movements cultivate out of a fundamentally anti-idealist constructivism: "This 'alternative' tradition," he writes, "pits a thoroughgoing skepticism about the representational powers of language and the coherence of selves against a theoretical optimism about the constructive possibilities of language and its capacity to remake selves or to release them from conceptual fetters" (6). Though "hybrid" or "new consensus" poets of the early 2000s, by borrowing "freely and unapologetically from both sides of the longstanding experimental / mainstream divide" (Swensen 29), may have threatened to dissipate these subversive, radically materialist energies, "today's formally adventurous utopian poets" (28), Brian M. Reed observes, have upheld the unique combination of "incapacity" (42) and activism that Izenberg traces to historical and contemporary avant-gardes' fundamentally constructivist conception of the self.

10. Among the exceptions to this generalization, Rae Armantrout is especially noteworthy. The eclectic influences on her dissolution, distancing, and reconstitution of the lyric voice very clearly include biological discourses of mind. "As we know from physics, and from neuroscience," she explains, "any single object we will ever see is, in fact, a buzzing multiplicity which we have found it practical to identify as a single entity. We ourselves are colonies of cooperating (*knock wood*) cells" (Rae Armantrout, interview by Ben Lerner, *Bomb* 114 [Winter 2011], http://bombmagazine.org/article/4720/rae -armantrout). See *Money Shot* (Middletown, CT: Wesleyan University Press, 2011), particularly "Working Models," "Measure," "Eyes," "Outage," and "The Vesicle"; and *Just Saying* (Middletown, CT: Wesleyan University Press, 2013), especially "Suggestion," "At Least," "Things," and "Meant."

11. See Perloff, "'Vocable Scriptsigns': Differential Poetics in Kenneth Goldsmith's *Fidget*," reprinted in *Fidget*, 91. Perloff quotes Goldsmith's account of his ambitions in the poem in a letter to her on October 9, 1998.

12. Craig Dworkin's "Legion" appears in *Strand* (New York: Roof Books, 2005); Dan Farrell's "Avail" appears in *Last Instance* (San Francisco: Krupskaya, 1999). Katie Degentesh's *The Anger Scale* (Cumberland, RI: Combo Books, 2006) may be the most acclaimed example of flarf poetics.

13. Vanessa Place, "Massive People (10): Interview with Blake Butler," *htmlgiant.com,* April 23, 2009, http://htmlgiant.com/massive-people/massive-people-10-vanessa -place/.

14. Perloff, *Unoriginal Genius;* Craig Dworkin, "The Fate of Echo," in Dworkin and Kenneth Goldsmith, *Against Expression: An Anthology of Conceptual Writing* (Evanston, IL: Northwestern University Press), 2011, xlii–xliii.

15. Kenneth Goldsmith, *Day* (Great Barrington, MA: Figures, 2003).

16. See Gillian White, *Lyric Shame: The "Lyric" Subject of Contemporary American Poetry* (Cambridge, MA: Harvard University Press, 2014).

17. Tan Lin, *Seven Controlled Vocabularies and Obituary 2004: The Joy of Cooking [Airport Novel Musical Poem Painting Film Photo Hallucination Landscape]* (Middletown, CT: Wesleyan University Press, 2010), 92.

18. Tan Lin and Angela Genusa, "A Book Is Technology: An Interview with Tan Lin," *Rhizome,* Oct. 24, 2012, http://rhizome.org/editorial/2012/oct/24/interview-tan-lin/.

19. Tan Lin in conversation with Charles Bernstein, *Close Listening WPS1.org,* May 23, 2005, http://writing.upenn.edu/pennsound/x/Lin.php.

20. Timothy Morton, "Why Ambient Poetics?," *Wordsworth Circle* 33, no.1 (Winter 2002): 52. In the liner notes to *Music for Airports/Ambient 1,* Brian Eno defines an ambience as "an atmosphere, or a surrounding influence: a tint. My intention," he goes on, "is to produce original pieces ostensibly (but not exclusively) for particular times and situations with a view to building up a small but versatile catalogue of environmental music suited to a wide variety of moods and atmospheres." Lin widely alludes to the influence of Brian Eno's ambient music on his poetry. I am indebted here to Jennifer Scappetone, who links Timothy Morton's formulation of ambient poetics to Lin's ambient stylistics in her article "Versus Seamlessness: Architectonics of Pseudocomplicity in Tan Lin's Ambient Poetics," *boundary 2* 36, no. 3 (2009): 63–76.

21. Published as a book of poetry by Wesleyan University Press, *7CV* courts resistance to its being labeled, both by its press and by its author in its concocted Library of Congress data, as poetry. This readerly resistance is integral to the work's production of meaning. "What is peripheral in or to reading?" Lin asks. "A bar code? Chinese characters? The Wesleyan Poetry series? *7CV* focuses on elements that codify reading in specific, rigid, and/or standardized ways. These processes are tied as much to publishing, marketing, distribution, layout, inclusion on syllabi, etc. as they are to writing or composing, which I think are relatively weak forms of 'authorship' or text production" (Christopher W. Alexander, Kristen Gallagher, Danny Snelson, and Gordon Tapper, "Writing as Metadata Container: An interview with Tan Lin," *Jacket 2,* January 20, 2012, http://jacket2.org/interviews/writing-metadata -container).

22. The unfinished experiment "Ambient Fiction Reading System 01: A List of Things I Read Didn't Read and Hardly Read for Exactly One Year," which runs to October 16, 2007, appears online at http://ambientreading.blogspot.com/. After its initial online publication, it appeared, running to October 31, 2007, as *BIB.* in the UbuWeb series "Publishing the Unpublishable," ed. Danny Snelson, Brian Kim Stefans, and Kenneth Goldsmith. It was then published in book form as *BIB., REV. ED.* by Westphalie Verlag in 2011: "The third version of this ongoing text," the book's product description notes, runs to July 21, 2008.

23. Tan Lin, preface to "Ambient Fiction Reading System 01," January 12, 2006, http:// ambientreading.blogspot.com/2006_01_12_archive.html.

24. Bernadette Mayer, *Eruditio Ex Memoria* (Lenox, MA, and New York: Angel Hair Books, 1977). Alexandra Nemerov's "First My Motorola," previously unpublished, appears in Dworkin and Goldsmith's *Against Expression,* 457–462.

25. Tan Lin, "The Patio and the Index," *Triple Canopy* 14 (October 25, 2011), http://www .canopycanopycanopy.com/contents/the_patio_and_the_index.

26. See Daniel Dennett, *Darwin's Dangerous Idea: Evolution and the Meanings of Life* (New York: Simon & Schuster, 1995); Richard Dawkins, *The Selfish Gene* (Oxford: Oxford University Press, 1999); Susan Blackmore, *The Meme Machine* (Oxford: Oxford University Press, 1999).

27. Tan Lin, interview by Katherine Elaine Sanders, *Bombmagazine.com,* March 2010, http://bombmagazine.org/article/3467/.

28. In one of the apparently autobiographical vignettes in *7CV,* Lin describes a period of limited means during his early years in New York that signals some of his literary influences: "The only other book I kept in that apartment at that time [besides *James Beard's Theory and Practice of Good Cooking*] was a copy of *Self-Portrait of a Convex Mirror* by John Ashbery, which I had stolen from Viking Penguin when I had interned there the summer before" (112).

29. Christopher W. Alexander et al., "Writing as Metadata Container."

30. Tan Lin, interview by Katherine Elaine Sanders.

31. Ibid.; Lin, *7CV,* 24.

32. Lin, *7CV,* 143.

33. Christopher W. Alexander et al., "Writing as Metadata Container."

34. Lin, *7CV,* 125, 138.

35. Lin and Genusa, "A Book Is Technology"; Lin, *7CV,* 132.

36. The book borrows its title from Rosa von Praunheim's *Army of Lovers or The Revolt of the Perverts,* the 1979 documentary chronicling the gay rights movement in San Francisco after the Stonewall riots.

37. Reed, *Nobody's Business,* xii.

38. Juliana Spahr and David Buuck, *An Army of Lovers* (San Francisco: City Lights Books, 2013), 125.

39. Ibid., 11.

40. Ibid., 128.

41. Ibid., 13.

42. Ibid., 9–10.

43. Ibid., 56.

44. Bonnie Costello, *Planets on Tables: Poetry, Still Life, and the Turning World* (Ithaca, NY: Cornell University Press, 2008), xv, ix.

45. Spahr and Buuck, *Army of Lovers,* 91–92. In this iteration of "The Side Effect," the second of the two, the performance artist holds the poses of torturers and tortured figures for painfully extended periods of time, allowing the violent gestures "to shape his body" (112) in an empty room with no witnesses. When he sets out to report the meaning of his performance in textual form, however—to communicate "his attempt to think of his life as part of a series of complex, passionate, antagonistic, and necessary relations to others who act and are acted upon" (112)—he finds himself unable to use language to translate his private acts into public expression. His impasse mirrors that of the frustrated composer in the first vignette and is ambiguously resolved in his composition of "The Remedy," discussed later.

46. Ibid., 100–101.

47. Ibid., 56.

48. Ibid., 66.

49. Ibid., 47, 56.

50. Ibid., 46.

51. Ibid., 55.

52. Ibid., 51. Spahr and Buuck choose to represent the sound artist's emerging work, which eschews the shapeliness and processability of melody, in terms that resemble the kind of disjunctive, appropriative poetry that the authors prefer ("the sort that uses open

forms and cross-cultural content, the sort that appropriates images from popular culture and the media and refashions them" [11–12]).

53. Ibid., 129.

54. Ibid., 82, 122. The dialogue among disillusioned poets and critics appears in "What We Talk about When We Talk about Poetry," the central chapter of the book, which appropriates its style and title from Raymond Carver's "What We Talk about When We Talk about Love"; in this chapter, a disaffected group of poets and academics who affiliate themselves with recent, politically progressive incarnations of the poetic avant-garde uncomfortably trace their roots (through Pound) to fascism.

55. Ibid., 63, 66.

56. Indeed, just as Spahr and Buuck describe a "fenced horizon" of "poems and anti-poems" (129), Brian M. Reed describes generically ambiguous texts—such as Lin's and Spahr and Buuck's—as "post-9/11 anti-poetry" (*Nobody's Business*, xii).

57. See Stephen Burt's influential essay "Sestina! or, The Fate of the Idea of Form," *Modern Philology* 105, no. 1 (2007): 218–241, on the widespread use of rigorous, closed forms in the work of twenty-first century poets of diverse affiliations. Linking noulipian formalism to the resurgence of the sestina and other inherited forms, Burt reads the rampant deployment of binding formal constraints as an indication of aesthetic crisis—of an impasse that conspicuously resembles the one Spahr and Buuck describe in *An Army of Lovers*, in fact. As I demonstrate in my readings here, in theme and form twenty-first-century poets are also signaling the extent to which technological developments in genetics, mind science, and new media, dovetailing with and reinforcing poststructuralist premises, have contributed to the negation of the expressive, authentic self and other ideals historically integral to poetry's self-conception. And yet while Burt observes that the "constrained but nonrhyming forms" of conceptual hyperformalists such as Bök exhibit "kinds of sad play that reveal writers' sense of helplessness, their failure to find stable grounds for value in poems" (233), I am less inclined to read the ludic performances of Mullen and Bök as nihilistic play than as productive recuperations and reimaginings of lyric ideals within their materialist milieux.

58. See Drucker's entry "Materiality!" in *The noulipian Analects*, ed. Christine Wertheim and Matias Viegener (Los Angeles: Les Figues Press, 2007), 122–123. Alluding to the anti-transcendental concretism of Oulipian extravagances, Harryette Mullen writes, "The most liberating aspect of Oulipo for me was their demystification of 'inspiration' in favor of 'potential literature' (*The Cracks between What We Are and What We Are Supposed to Be: Essays and Interviews* [Tuscaloosa: University of Alabama Press, 2012], 45).

59. For Mullen's framing of these tensions, see her essays "Poetry and Identity" and "Theme for the Oulipians" in *Essays and Interviews.*

60. Harryette Mullen, *Sleeping with the Dictionary* (Berkeley: University of California Press, 2002), 80.

61. Ibid., 3.

62. Mullen, *Essays and Interviews,* 12. There has been much debate, especially among feminist writers and critics, regarding the relative value of expressive and experimental poetics in subverting cultural hegemonies; for influential perspectives, see Alicia

Ostriker, *Stealing the Language: The Emergence of Women's Poetry in America* (London: Women's Press, 1987); Nancy Miller, *Subject to Change: Reading Feminist Writing* (New York: Columbia University Press, 1988); Rachel Blau DuPlessis, *The Pink Guitar: Writing as Feminist Practice* (New York: Routledge, 1990); and Juliana Spahr, "Resignifying Autobiography: Lyn Hejinian's *My Life*," *American Literature* 68, no. 1 (1996): 139–159. Against the proposition that only the expressive (lyric) voice of political protest can be truly subversive, experimental feminists such as Lyn Hejinian ("The Rejection of Closure," in *The Language of Inquiry* [Berkeley: University of California Press, 2000], 40–58) and Rae Armantrout ("Feminist Poetics and the Meaning of Clarity," in *Collected Prose* [San Diego: Singing Horse Press, 2007]) have claimed that the critique of representation itself is the only way to subvert patriarchy. For recent perspectives on the subject of race and avant-garde poetics since the advent of Language poetry, see Cathy Park Hong, "Delusions of Whiteness in the Avant-Garde," *Lana Turner* 7 (November 2014), http://www.lanaturnerjournal .com/7/delusions; Evie Shockley, *Renegade Poetics: Black Aesthetics and Formal Innovation in African American Poetry* (Iowa City: University of Iowa Press, 2011); and Timothy Yu, *Race and the Avant-Garde: Experimental and Asian American Poetry since 1965* (Stanford, CA: Stanford University Press, 2009).

63. Mullen, *Essays and Interviews*, 10.

64. Mullen, quoted in Tony Reaves, "Harryette Mullen Speaks to UMaine," *Maine Campus*, October 20, 2005, http://mainecampus.com/2005/10/20/harryette-mullen -speaks-to-umaine/.

65. Harryette Mullen, quoted in Malin Pereira, *Into a Light Both Brilliant and Unseen: Conversations with Contemporary Black Poets* (Athens: University of Georgia Press, 2010), 117; Mullen, *Sleeping with the Dictionary*, 28.

66. Mullen quotes Jefferson in *Essays and Interviews*, 207.

67. There are even more limits; see Bök's postscript to *Eunoia* (Toronto: Coach House Books, 2009), 112.

68. Bök, *Eunoia*, 50.

69. James Merrill, *Collected Prose*, ed. J. D. McClatchy and Stephen Yenser (New York: Alfred A. Knopf, 2004), 210.

70. Ibid., 111.

71. See J. R. Battista. "Against All Odds: The Survival Strategies of *Deinococcus radiodurans*," *Annual Review of Microbiology* 51 (1997): 203–224.

72. Christian Bök, "The Xenotext Experiment," https://www.yumpu.com/en/document /view/6511784/abstracts-voice-and-vision-conference-university-of-manitoba/3. The final version of *The Xenotext* has yet to appear in print. Bök has recently published *The Xenotext: Book I* (Toronto: Coach House Books, 2015), which presents the scientific framework for the experiment and poems based on atomic and molecular models. For the most in-depth critical account of *The Xenotext* experiment up to 2012, see Darren Wershler, "The Xenotext Experiment, So Far," *Canadian Journal of Communication* 37 (2012): 43–61. For other descriptions, see Alexander Kim, "The Xenotext Experiment," *Triple Helix Online: A Global Forum for Science and Society,* January 8, 2014, http://triplehelixblog.com/2014/01/the-xenotext-experiment/; and Stephen Voyce,

"The Xenotext Experiment: An Interview with Christian Bök," 2005, http://pmc.iath .virginia.edu/text-only/issue.107/17.2voyce.txt.

73. Kim, "The Xenotext Experiment."

74. N. Katherine Hayles, "Print Is Flat, Code Is Deep: The Importance of Media-Specific Analysis," *Poetics Today* 25, no. 1 (2004): 72.

75. Sol LeWitt, "Paragraphs on Conceptual Art," *Artforum* 5, no. 10 (Summer 1967).

76. Voyce, "Interview," n.p.

77. Christian Bök, presentation of *The Xenotext* at "North of Invention: A Canadian Poetry Festival," the Kelly Writers House, Philadelphia, January 20, 2011, http://writing .upenn.edu/pennsound/x/North-Of-Invention.php.

78. In his application for the government funding necessary to implement *The Xenotext* experiment, Bök acknowledges that his ambition to infect the passive microbe with his own words echoes Christopher Dewdney's conception of language itself as a living anomaly that inhabits and shapes human consciousness—as " 'a psychic parasite which has genetically earmarked a section of the cortex for its own accommodation' " (Proposal, 6).

79. Spahr and Buuck, *Army of Lovers,* 129.

80. Bergvall et al., *I'll Drown My Book,* 21.

81. Jackson includes "the critical fiction of a speaker, the assumption of a voice, the intersubjective confirmation of a self," among "the orthodoxies of modern lyric reading" in *The Lyric Theory Reader: A Critical Anthology* (Baltimore: Johns Hopkins University Press, 2014), 90.

82. Rachel Blau DuPlessis, "Social Texts and Poetic Texts: Poetry and Cultural Studies," in Cary Nelson's *The Oxford Handbook of Modern and Contemporary American Poetry* (New York: Oxford University Press, 2012), 60.

83. White, *Lyric Shame,* 4.

84. Damon and Livingston, *Poetry and Cultural Studies,* 2; Dworkin, "Fate of Echo," xxii.

85. Place and Fitterman, *Notes on Conceptualisms,* 10.

86. Virginia Jackson, *Dickinson's Misery,* 10. To observe that readerships have aligned with factions of poetic production along the "two camps" divide is to state the obvious to readers of recent poetry and criticism. It seems appropriate to note in this context, however, that idealist and materialist readers alike have appealed to neurological "facts" to authorize and justify their aesthetic preferences. Opening a passionate debate in the *Boston Review* with his diatribe "Against Conceptualism: Defending the Poetry of Affect," the idealist critic Calvin Bedient proposes that the *real* emotions we want to see in poetry are the heighted affects we associate with lyric, characterized by "distinctive patterns of chemical and neural responses" of the sort that Antonio Damasio refers to in the subtitle of his book *Looking for Spinoza* (2003), namely "Joy, Sorrow, and the *Feeling* Brain" (Bedient's emphasis). Responding to Bedient in "Flarf Is Life: The Poetry of Affect," Drew Gardner defends "the cerebral avant-gardes," as Bedient calls them, by deconstructing the distinction between emotion and thought, invoking his own neurological authority (the workings of the amygdala) to deliver his coup de grâce: conceptual poetry cannot ever truly jettison emotion because processes of thinking and feeling, "widely distributed through different brain regions," are physiologically

intertwined. See Calvin Bedient, "Against Conceptualism: Defending the Poetry of Affect," *Boston Review,* July 24, 2013, http://bostonreview.net/poetry/against-conceptualism; Drew Gardner, "Flarf Is Life: The Poetry of Affect," *Boston Review,* February 11, 2014, http://www.bostonreview.net/poetry/drew-gardner-flarf-life-poetry-affect); and Rachel Galvin's response to Bedient, "Lyric Backlash," *Boston Review,* February 11, 2014, http://www.bostonreview.net/poetry/rachel-galvin-lyric-backlash.

87. Theodor W. Adorno and Rolf Tiedemann, "On Lyric Poetry and Society," in *Notes to Literature* (New York: Columbia University Press, 1991), 38.

88. Chris Alexander et al., "Writing as Metadata Container"; Angela Genusa, "A Book Is Technology: An Interview with Tan Lin," *Rhizome,* October 24, 2012, http://rhizome.org/editorial/2012/oct/24/interview-tan-lin/; Kay Ryan, *The Best of It: New and Selected Poems* (New York: Grove Press, 2010), 6; "Marin County, Sort Of," *Poetry,* November 2009, http://www.poetryfoundation.org/poetrymagazine/article/238044; Cathy Park Hong and Robyn Creswell, "Cathy Park Hong on 'Engine Empire,'" *The Daily* (blog), *Paris Review,* August 23, 2011, http://www.theparisreview.org/blog/2011/08/23/cathy-park-hong-on-engine-empire/; Cathy Park Hong, *Dance Dance Revolution: Poems* (New York: W. W. Norton, 2007); Seo-Young Chu, "From Desertitis to Jamais Vu: Symptoms of the Future of the Korean DMZ in *Dance Dance Revolution*" (paper presented at the annual conference of the Modern Language Association, Chicago, Illinois, January 5, 2014); Jane Hirshfield, "How Rarely I Have Stopped to Thank the Steady Effort," Tax Break, *New York Times,* April 14, 2012, http://www.nytimes.com/2012/04/15/opinion/sunday/at-tax-time-no-accounting-for-poetry.html.

Acknowledgments

I am fortunate to have several mentors to whom I am eager to extend my heart-felt gratitude in print. My deepest thanks are to Helen Vendler, under whose direction I began this work and whose example as a scholar and teacher has been a consummate gift. The failings here are all my own, but any distinctions these pages can claim were fostered by her erudition, open mind, and constant support. I hope that this book and future ones will bear the visible trace of her influence. Stephen Burt offered intellectual and practical guidance that substantively shaped the manuscript, attending to its rhetorical and structural dimensions with special intensity and to its great benefit; it has been a privilege to have him as a thorough reader and an unforgettable model in his teaching of poetry. Elaine Scarry's insights expanded the horizons of this book, especially at its earliest stages; I am in her debt for the lucid criticism and encouragement she issued in a steady stream of generosities over several years. Her passionate interest in the nature of mental experience amplified my own interest in poetic accounts of it, and I am grateful to her for demonstrating that the endeavor to draw scientific and artistic voices into conversation is enriched and ennobled by its challenges.

Two other scholars offered especially sustaining encouragement and rigorous feedback at later points in the evolution of this project. Amanda Claybaugh, an inspiring model in all respects, echoed my ideas back to me in ways that made them seem strange and new, enlivened by her literary intelligence. Patricia Meyer Spacks, whose insights and enthusiasm came at a particularly crucial time, helped me redefine the fundamental ambitions of this book. Her acquaintance was just one of the boons the American Academy of Arts and Sciences extended to me; I will always be grateful for the residential fellowship that afforded me indispensable writing time and introduced me to lasting friends—Hillary Chute, Matthew Karp, Peter Wirzbicki, and Melinda Baldwin—all of whom inspired me with their own scholarship and fostered an exhilarating atmosphere of interdisciplinary conversation.

I am very grateful to be in the company of my stellar colleagues in the English department at Indiana University, who have supported me in countless ways as I have brought this project to its completion. Their generosity allowed me to finish it sooner than I would have been able to otherwise. Nicholas Williams, Samrat Upadhyay, and Paul Aarstad were kind enough to review parts of the manuscript, and Scott Herring offered especially precise and beneficial feedback; I look forward to repaying their time and energy in years to come. Ed Comentale, Jonathan Elmer, Jennifer Fleissner, Susan Gubar, Paul Gutjahr, Patricia Ingham, Walton Muyumba, and Alberto Varon have offered especially valuable encouragement and advice at various stages throughout the writing process. Librarians at Harvard and Indiana—Laura Farwell Blake, Christina Davis, and Nazareth Pantaloni III—offered their invaluable expertise, increasing this project's scholarly breadth and depth through their accessibility and interest.

Roger Tootell and Eugene Switkes generously granted me permission to reproduce an image from their article "Deoxyglucose Analysis of Retinotopic Organization in Primate Striate Cortex" in the notes to Chapter 5. A similar version of Chapter 3 was first published as "James Merrill's Embodied Memory" in *Twentieth-Century Literature* 59, no. 4 (Winter 2013), 539–574, and is reproduced by kind permission of Duke University Press.

I wish to thank the readers for Harvard University Press for their insightful and considered responses to my manuscript. My editor, John Kulka, offered crucial guidance and decisive opinions when I needed them, making the process of publishing my first book a pleasure. I am also very grateful to Brian Ostrander, Jamie Thaman, and Stephanie Vyce, always solicitous and attentive to detail, who worked efficiently to usher the book through the production process; it was reassuring to know that the manuscript was in such good hands.

I owe the most to my friends and family. By filling my life with pleasure and purpose, they have made thinking and writing possible. There is no way to thank Chris Barrett for her example and for her dearest friendship over the years that saw this project from its conception to its completion. Only my parents know how much they are present in my work, and how much their support—in so many concrete ways and so many intangible ones—enabled me to undertake this endeavor. This book is for them. And here, where I must thank Jonathan Schlesinger, words fail. I had thought that a life in the company of great poems had equipped me with a sense of wonder, but I was not prepared for the serendipity of finding you. Thank you for your love.

Index

Adorno, Theodor, 45, 270

Aesthetic criticism, 41–46, 282n87. *See also* Idealist reading; Lyric reading

Against Expression (Dworkin and Goldsmith), 269

Agency: transference of to physiological causes, 21, 22; eye's lack of, 209; dispersals of, 314n52

Aging, Ashbery on, 195–196. *See also* Mortality; Senility

AIDS, 130, 136, 299n10

Allers, Rudolf, 55, 285n15

Altieri, Charles, 42–43, 91, 277n29, 278–279n51, 282n89

Ambient poetry, 244, 260, 319n20

Ammons, A. R., 1–3, 5; "Mechanism," 1–3, 11–13, 106; *Expressions of Sea Level,* 11–12, 106; use of colon, 11–12, 116–117; "Corsons Inlet," 12–13, 111–114; biological materialism of, 13; and membrane metaphor, 19, 104, 112–114; "God Is the Sense the World Makes Without God," 87; attraction to science, 87, 90; secularism of, 87; "Hymn," 87–88, 106; interest of, in nonhuman nature, 87–88; scientific vocabulary of, 88, 298n2; and relationship between physiological being and mental life, 88–90; forms of, 89, 104, 105, 115, 119; and otherness within self, 90; and religion, 90; philosophy of consciousness, 104; rejection of dualism by, 104; *Ommateum, with Doxology,* 104–106, 111; conception of consciousness, 105; early work of, 105; "Turning a moment to say so long," 105–106, 107; longing for transcendental escape in poetry of, 106; spirituality of, 106; Bloom's reading of, 106, 190n5, 296n62; consciousness's dependence upon biological actions in poetry of, 106–107; "Bridge," 107, 112; mirror metaphor of, 107–108; "Reflective," 107–108, 112; experimental work of, 108; *Tape for the Turn of the Year,* 108–111, 119, 127; transcription of consciousness by, 108–111; on thinking, 109; *Bosh and Flapdoodle,* 111, 117, 124, 295n56; *Glare,* 111, 117, 118, 119–127, 295n56, 297nn90,96,102; late work of, 111, 117–118; models of poem, 111; concept of mind, 111–114, 116; transition from dualism to materialism, 112; representations of mind by, 112–115; picture of mental processes, 114; flouting